BIOGRAPHICAL DICTIONARY OF ENSLAVED BLACK PEOPLE IN THE MARITIMES

STUDIES IN ATLANTIC CANADA HISTORY

Editors: John G. Reid and Peter L. Twohig

This monograph series focuses on the history of Atlantic Canada, interpreting the scope of this field in a way that is deliberately inclusive and accommodating. As well as studies that deal wholly with any aspect of the history of the Atlantic region (or part thereof), the series extends to neighbouring geographical areas that are considered in conjunction with or in parallel with a portion of Atlantic Canada. Atlantic Canada's oceanic or global relationships are also included, and studies from any thematic or historiographical perspective are welcome.

For a list of books in this series, see page 237.

Biographical Dictionary of Enslaved Black People in the Maritimes

HARVEY AMANI WHITFIELD

UNIVERSITY OF TORONTO PRESS
Toronto Buffalo London
and
ACADIENSIS PRESS
Fredericton

© University of Toronto Press 2022
Toronto Buffalo London
utorontopress.com

ISBN 978-1-4875-4381-5 (cloth)   ISBN 978-1-4875-4383-9 (EPUB)
ISBN 978-1-4875-4382-2 (paper)   ISBN 978-1-4875-4384-6 (PDF)

Studies in Atlantic Canada History

Library and Archives Canada Cataloguing in Publication

Title: Biographical dictionary of enslaved Black people in the Maritimes / Harvey Amani Whitfield.
Names: Whitfield, Harvey Amani, 1974–, author.
Series: Studies in Atlantic Canada history.
Description: Series statement: Studies in Atlantic Canada history.
Identifiers: Canadiana (print) 2021034119X | Canadiana (ebook) 20210341211 |
    ISBN 9781487543815 (hardcover) | ISBN 9781487543822 (softcover) |
    ISBN 9781487543839 (EPUB) | ISBN 9781487543846 (PDF)
Subjects: LCSH: Slaves – Maritime Provinces – Biography – Dictionaries. |
    LCSH: Slavery – Maritime Provinces.
Classification: LCC HT1052.M37 W45 2022 | DDC 306.3/620922715 – dc23

Cover illustrations: Engraving: Nova Scotia Archives, "Leonard Parkinson, a captain of the Maroons," by Abraham Raimbach. From B. Edwards, *The Proceedings of the Governor and Assembly of Jamaica, in Regard to the Maroon Negroes ... to which is prefixed an Introductory Account ... of the Maroons ...* (London, 1796) (F210/Ed9) negative number: N-6202. Document: Nova Scotia Archives, "Halifax List: Return of American Refugee Negroes who have been received into the Province of Nova Scotia from the United States of America between 27 April 1815 and 24 October 1818." Department of State records relating to United States claims against Great Britain under the Treaty of Ghent and the Conventions of 1818, 1822, and 1826. National Archives and Records Administration (Washington DC) RG 76 Entry 185 GB 1814 number 51 G.B. 6 (microfilm 13577).

We wish to acknowledge the land on which the University of Toronto Press operates. This land is the traditional territory of the Wendat, the Anishnaabeg, the Haudenosaunee, the Métis, and the Mississaugas of the Credit First Nation.

University of Toronto Press acknowledges the financial support of the Government of Canada, the Canada Council for the Arts, and the Ontario Arts Council, an agency of the Government of Ontario, for its publishing activities.

Canada Council **Conseil des Arts**
for the Arts **du Canada**

ONTARIO ARTS COUNCIL
CONSEIL DES ARTS DE L'ONTARIO
an Ontario government agency
un organisme du gouvernement de l'Ontario

Funded by the   Financé par le
Government   gouvernement
of Canada   du Canada

Contents

Acknowledgments

I am deeply indebted to the University of Calgary for providing funds for the publication of this book – specifically the Dean of the Faculty of Arts. The Department of History at the University of Calgary, especially Jewel Spangler, provided intellectual support for the book, but the friendships and positive atmosphere my colleagues offered contributed so much in terms of the project. At the University of New Brunswick, Donald Wright and Elizabeth Mancke cajoled, criticized, and demanded I write a better book and were always there to read through the introduction or various entries. Stephen Dutcher has been a friend and mentor to me for nearly 20 years. My former graduate student Sarah Chute, now a doctoral student at the University of Toronto, has served as a patient and outstanding research assistant. I am also very thankful to Len Husband and the staff at the University of Toronto Press for their wonderful help. Acadiensis Press also helped this project to completion in many ways. This book would not be possible without the staff of the following institutions: Nova Scotia Archives, the Provincial Archives of New Brunswick, the Public Archives and Records Office of Prince Edward Island, the New Brunswick Museum, the Loyalist Collection at the University of New Brunswick, and the Guysborough Historical Society.

I presented parts of this book as the MacNutt Lecturer at the University of New Brunswick, the Riley Lecturer at the University of Winnipeg, and the Creighton Lecturer at the University of Toronto. I am thankful to the faculty and students at these institutions for their critiques of my work. T.H. Breen and Ruma Chopra provided thoughtful comments about the trajectory of this book and where it fit into my overall career. Significantly, I am indebted to my friends and colleagues in the field of slavery studies in Canada, including Afua Cooper, Karolyn Smardz Frost, and David States. I am also thankful for the opportunity to work with Charmaine Nelson and the Institute for the Study of Canadian Slavery. My dear friends, Krista Kesselring and Sean Field, encouraged me to complete this project over the last several years. Most of all, I would like to thank my wife, Natalie, and daughter, Hope, for their support.

Foreword: Harvey Amani Whitfield, Slavery, and the Decentring of Canadian History

When whiteness is decentred – when it's not taken for granted – the past looks very different. Certainly, it's more complicated, making it difficult for historians to offer general observations and large conclusions. But the historian's obligation is to the truth, not convenience. After all, the past is never neat and tidy, something Harvey Amani Whitfield (Amani) understands. Across the length and breadth of his career, in books, articles, and public lectures, he has revealed a history of slavery in Canada that is as long and painful as it is difficult and messy. Stretching over 200 years, from 1629 (when the first enslaved African, a six- or seven-year-old boy from either Madagascar or Guinea, was brought to New France) to 1833 (when Britain abolished slavery throughout the British Empire) slavery existed both in fact and in law in New France and British North America. Of course, Whitfield is not the first historian to document slavery or its impacts. But he has pushed our understanding in new and sophisticated ways and, in the process, has decentred some of our cherished myths about Canada – that slavery, for example, was "an American thing." But if Canadian slavery wasn't American slavery, it was still slavery.

This biographical dictionary, a co-publication between the University of Toronto Press and Acadiensis Press, continues an intellectual journey that began when a young Amani Whitfield graduated from Edmund Burke High School in Washington, DC, in 1993.

I never intended to become a historian of the African diaspora in Atlantic Canada.
                                                            – Harvey Amani Whitfield, 2017

By his own admission, Whitfield was an indifferent student in high school. Although both of his parents were academics – his father was a professor at the University of Michigan Medical School before joining the National Institutes of Health in Bethesda, Maryland, and his mother was also a professor at the University of Michigan before joining the Department of Biochemistry and

Molecular Biology at Howard University in Washington, DC – he didn't see himself following in their footsteps, certainly not in the sciences. Insofar as he was interested in school, he leaned toward history and English because he liked reading. Yet he pretty much hated his freshman year at Antioch College, a small liberal arts college in Yellow Springs, Ohio.

Actually, not many people liked Antioch's Department of History in 1993–94. Accused of racism and denied tenure, Ralph Luker, a white southern professor of African American history and a collaborator on the Martin Luther King, Jr. Papers Project, went on a six-week hunger strike, vowing to attend commencement on a stretcher, if necessary, and prompting a debate on race and racism.[1] Accusations were made. Petitions were circulated. Flyers were printed. Sides were taken. And a career was ruined. Meanwhile, local newspapers weighed in – Antioch has sided with "political correctness" over "intellectual freedom," the *Dayton Daily News* said[2] – and colleagues wrote generous letters of support, including Eugene Genovese, author of *Roll, Jordan, Roll: The World the Slaves Made,* Michael O'Brien, an award-winning historian of the American South, and the great John Hope Franklin, author of *From Slavery to Freedom,* a classic text that defined the field of African American history.[3]

Although just 19 years old, Whitfield understood that, untethered from facts, campus debates can take on a life of their own, leaving victims in their wake. From his perspective, Luker was a tremendous historian who had opened his eyes to African American history. At one point, as things were coming to a head, he asked if he could give his professor a hug. Looking back on his encounter with a young Amani Whitfield, Luker remarked that "there was something about his grace that almost made me whole again."[4]

If Antioch wasn't for Whitfield, Colorado State University was. Leaving the Midwest for the West and coming into his own as a student, Whitfield found mentors in Arthur Worrall, an Americanist, and Kenneth Rock, a Europeanist. Both men saw something in him and encouraged him to do graduate work. Not wanting to write the Graduate Record Examinations, a standardized test for admission to most U.S. graduate programs, and interested in leaving the United States – in getting out of Dodge for a few years – Whitfield applied to Dalhousie University in Halifax, Nova Scotia, to study African history. With a couple of suitcases and a handful of books, Whitfield arrived in Halifax in the fall of 1997, not knowing how his intellectual journey would be at once propelled and re-routed. In his words, his thesis supervisor, Philip Zachernuk, gave him "the biggest intellectual ass kicking" of his life.[5] African history, in this case the intellectual history of West Africa in the late nineteenth and early twentieth century, cannot be reduced, Zachernuk insisted, to "African Nationalist" on the one hand and "British Imperialist" on the other. Pushing his student to move beyond inherited categories, especially binary categories, because they simplify more than they clarify, Zachernuk taught Whitfield an important lesson: The past must be understood on its own terms and in ways that "recover its complexity and provoke fresh understanding."[6]

Being Black in Nova Scotia, a province with a Black history that stretches back to the seventeenth century,[7] and living in the historically Black part of Halifax, on Gottingen Street not far from Uniacke Square, led Whitfield to think about Black Nova Scotian history. Where did Black Nova Scotians come from? he wondered. Where did they settle? What were their material conditions? What institutions did they build? And how did they navigate racism? Questions in tow, Whitfield spoke to Michael Cross, a pioneer in Canadian social history and a much loved professor whose dedication to students was "the stuff of urban legend."[8] Like Luker, Worrall, Rock, and Zachernuk before him, Cross saw something pretty special in the animated young man who couldn't stop talking. Telling him that he had a lot to offer, Cross encouraged Whitfield to study Canadian history at the doctoral level. Although Cross didn't supervise him, Whitfield would later say that the tall, angular, and activist historian was "like a father to me."[9] Supervised by David Sutherland and Judith Fingard, two generous historians of Nova Scotia who took him under their respective and capacious wings and who pushed him to write quickly – and then read every single word – Whitfield completed his thesis in just four years, if not a record then close to it. James W. St. G. Walker, the external examiner, remembers the thesis very clearly. Because Whitfield "was able to bring a thorough understanding of American slavery to African-Canadian history," he could "assess the experience of the refugees and enslaved African Americans who came to the Maritimes in terms of the American background that so profoundly influenced their lives and their relationships, both within their own communities and with the surrounding majority society."[10]

"Black American Refugees in Nova Scotia, 1813–1840" became *Blacks on the Border: The Black Refugees in British North America, 1815–1860,* Whitfield's first monograph. Published by the University of Vermont Press in 2006, *Blacks on the Border* was widely and warmly received. Indeed, reviewers struggled to find enough adjectives, calling it "timely," "important," "welcome," "wonderful," "richly detailed," "a must-read," and a "tour de force."[11] Nova Scotia, Whitfield argued, wasn't on the sleepy edge of the Atlantic world, a world dizzy with dreams of wealth and ideas of freedom; of people coming and going; of planters, merchants, traders, soldiers, and officials. It was very much a part of it, as were Prince Edward Island and New Brunswick. Crucially, Britain's Maritime colonies were also part of the Black Atlantic, a world marked by slavery and the slave trade and the subject of Whitfield's next book.[12]

Slavery is the most neglected aspect of pre-Confederation history.
                                                    – Harvey Amani Whitfield, 2020

That slavery existed in New France and British North America is not a new discovery. Calling it "a sombre and unattractive chapter" in Canadian history, T.W. Smith undertook the first study of slavery on the northern half of North America in the late 1890s.[13] Yet few historians followed his lead. Indeed, it wasn't until the 1950s that Marcel Trudel began what became *L'esclavage au Canada français*, a landmark, by any definition, in Canadian historical writing,[14] although not everyone welcomed it at the time. Because Trudel had challenged the myth of New France's "perfect homogeneity," a myth largely invented by Lionel Groulx,[15] he encountered both incredulity and reproach from some circles. *Slavery? In New France? Who are you to cheapen our history?*[16] But others welcomed *L'esclavage*, calling it "original" and "audacious."[17] A decade or so later, Robin Winks published *The Blacks in Canada: A History*, also an original and audacious book. And when it was included, 35 years later, in the *Literary Review of Canada's* list of Canada's 100 most important books, no one was surprised. But as Whitfield has observed, neither *L'esclavage au Canada français* nor *The Blacks in Canada* inspired research on slavery in Canada in any kind of sustained way. There were exceptions, of course. *The Hanging of Angélique: The Untold Story of Slavery in Canada and the Burning of Old Montreal* by Afua Cooper; *Done with Slavery: The Black Fact in Montreal, 1760–1840* by Frank Mackey; and *Bonds of Alliance: Indigenous and Atlantic Slaveries in New France* by Brett Rushforth are obvious examples,[18] as are the many articles on slavery and enslaved people in the Maritimes by Barry Cahill and Kenneth Donovan.[19] But as Donovan wrote in 2014, slavery isn't "a significant part" of the Canadian narrative, of the story Canadians like to tell themselves, in part because it "goes against the dominant image of Canada as a land of freedom."[20]

North to freedom? Yes. For some. But for others, it was north to bondage, the brilliant title of Whitfield's 2016 history of slavery in the Maritimes.[21] On the one hand, slavery is slavery, robbing individuals of their freedom and denying their worth as human beings. But on the other hand, slavery varied across time and space. In the Caribbean basin, in the southern colonies, and later in the southern states, it was characterized by sugar, rice, indigo, tobacco, and cotton plantations. A plantation owner might own 100-plus slaves, although most owned between 20 and 30. In the Maritimes, however, a master owned just one or two slaves, although some owned more. Nova Scotia's John Polhemus enslaved 10 people, making him one of the larger slave owners in the Maritimes. But if slavery was incidental to the larger economy, the labour performed by and the wealth generated by enslaved people was essential to individual family economies. Sometimes called family slavery, intimate slavery, or close-quarters slavery, owners and slaves lived under the same roof. And while there may have been "ties of affection" between an owner and a slave,[22] it also meant that enslaved people were "on call" 24/7, to cook, clean, or empty a chamber pot, and they or their family members could be beaten, raped, or sold.[23] Although there were no slave rebellions in the Maritimes – there was no Maritime equivalent to Nat Turner, for example – there was slave resistance, from slowing the pace of work to running away and from negotiating better work conditions to using the courts to win freedom.

Although intimately connected to slave societies in the West Indies,[24] the Maritimes were not themselves slave societies, but they were societies with slaves. Who were these enslaved men, women, and children? What were their names? Where did they come from? Who did they love? How did they love? What were they like? What skills did they have? When did they die? And where are they buried?

… putting flesh onto the bones of enslaved people in the Maritimes.
– Amani Whitfield, 2019

Writer Timothy Findley evocatively described the experience of doing archival research in his novel *The Wars*. "The boxes smell of yellow dust. You hold your breath. As the past moves under your fingertips, part of it crumbles. Other parts, you know you'll never find. This is what you have."[25] For Whitfield, it was that experience times ten. Unlike Findley's fictional biographer, he didn't have boxes of letters, photographs, and newspaper clippings to spread across tabletops in reading rooms. Instead, he had Black fragments in white archives.[26] Those fragments, moreover, were imperfect and imprecise: enslaved people were sometimes referred to as servants while free Blacks could be and were kidnapped, re-enslaved, and sold in the West Indies, a form of racist terrorism that made freedom precarious at best and dangerous at worst. Indeed, the line between freedom and unfreedom was a fine one. For example, when Lydia Jackson, a free Black woman in Guysborough Township, found herself abandoned, destitute, and desperate, she indentured herself as a servant, only to discover that she had been tricked by her indenturer, who then sold her into slavery. Jackson's story is unique insofar as it's documented. Yet historical sources, from the extraordinary to the everyday, from the Book of Negroes to probate records,[27] have a way of turning up. Patiently gathered, Whitfield's archival fragments, glimpses, and silences accumulated over time, filling banker boxes in his study. An idea took shape and a manuscript emerged.

Reading the individual entries is a strangely moving experience: This is all we will ever know about the 1,465 men, women, and children who were enslaved in the Maritimes. Some entries are longer. Others are shorter. Some give us real insight into the life of an enslaved person. Others are only a name and a date. And some are not even that. Bill, or Belfast, was 27 years old when, after 10 years of slavery in Nova Scotia, he ran away, attempting to board a ship bound for Newfoundland. Diana Bastian was only 15 when she died in childbirth after being "Deluded and Ruined at Government House by George More Esq. the naval officer and one of Governor Macarmick's Counsel," sexual violence being built into slavery. Indeed, some of the entries are difficult to read: Judy, or Jude, was beaten to death; Lydia Jackson was beaten with "tongs, sticks, pieces of rope &c. about the head and face"; and Jameson Davis, Blaise, and an unnamed woman were beaten in turn with a cudgel, a cane, and an "Iron flesh fork."

Archives are by definition capricious, sometimes generous and sometimes parsimonious, even cruel. They are especially unkind to historians researching the lives of enslaved people. As a result, Whitfield was unable locate the names of nearly 430 enslaved men, women, and children. In life, they were robbed by the inhumane and transatlantic traffic in human beings. In death, they have been robbed a second time, this time by history's indifference. To read entry after entry of unnamed slaves is heartbreaking, something novelist Lawrence Hill understood, the importance and power of one's name being a recurring theme in *The Book of Negroes* and a recurring concern for its protagonist, Aminata Diallo:

> In the [ship's] darkness, men repeated my name and called out their own as I passed. They wanted me to know them. Who they were. Their names. That they were alive, and would go on living.
> "Idrissa."
> "Keita."
> And so it went.

To publish his book in the United States, Hill changed its title to *Someone Knows My Name*.

> He repeated my name over and over, and then added, "I must hear you say it. Please. Say it. Say my name."
> "Chekura," I said.
> "Someone knows my name."[28]

Like *The Book of Negroes*, the *Dictionary of Enslaved Black People in the Maritimes* is also a moral project.[29] Decentring the narrative of discovery, exploration, and settlement; of Loyalists, governors, and officers; of the Odells, the Winslows, and the Robies, or the fine old Maritime families, Amani Whitfield has recovered 1,465 enslaved Black men, women, and children, giving them dignity and in some instances agency. "This book," he writes, "bears witness to their existence." Reading between the lines, it's not hard to imagine them asking, like the fictional Aminata Diallo asked, "How exactly does that man own us?"[30]

For that matter, how does anyone own anyone else? What web of violence, laws, assumptions, and practices makes that possible? The first recorded

African slave in New France may or may not have asked these questions, but he understood the impossibility of his situation. When France resumed control of the St. Lawrence River Valley in 1632, the enslaved boy who had been brought by the English three years earlier, in 1629, and who had been sold for 50 *écus* to a French man, was given to a new owner. A year later, he was given the name Olivier Le Jeune, his African name, the name given to him by his parents, having been stolen and discarded. When asked if he wished to be baptised, he said yes, but with biting insight into a world in which a white person could own a Black person, he added, "You say that by baptism I shall be like you: I am black and you are white, I must have my skin taken off then in order to be like you."[31]

Donald Wright
University of New Brunswick

NOTES

1 According to Ralph Luker's version of events, he told his class that "in eyes of the law, slaves had the same status as animals and were owned as property." Some students believed that he had called Black people animals. "Teacher studies options," *Springfield News Sun,* June 21, 1994.

2 Martin Gotlieb, "Protesting Antioch's Nature a Bit Naive," *Dayton Daily News,* June 24, 1994.

3 Eugene Genovese to Ralph Luker, July 24, 1993; Michael O'Brien to Ralph Luker, July 14, 1993; John Hope Franklin to Ralph Luker, July 16, 1993. Antioch College, Antiochiana, Ralph Luker biographical file.

4 Ralph E. Luker, "Some of My Children," *History News Network,* August 20, 1994. Available online at https://historynewsnetwork.org/blog/6878.

5 Amani Whitfield, personal communication with author, July 19, 2021.

6 Philip S. Zachernuk, *Colonial Subjects: An African Intelligentsia and Atlantic Ideas* (Charlottesville: University Press of Virginia, 2000), 9.

7 Although the evidence is imperfect, the first Black person in what is now Nova Scotia was likely Mathieu Da Costa who served as an interpreter between French explorers and traders and Indigenous Peoples. Meanwhile, the first recorded Black resident in what is now Nova Scotia was "La Liberté Le Neigre" in 1686 (underline in original). In 1693, assuming it is the same person, La Liberté is listed as being 40 years old and living with his wife, Cristine, age 35, and their four children. He owned one rifle. In 1707, he is listed with his wife, one boy fourteen or older, three boys younger than fourteen, one girl twelve or older, two girls younger than twelve, four cattle, eleven sheep, and five pigs. He no longer owned a rifle. In 1714, he is listed as living with his wife, four sons, and two daughters. One final point: The 1707 census includes "Arpents de terre en valeur,"

or cultivated land. Actually, it meant something even more specific: land that has been seeded. According to the census, La Liberté did not have any land seeded. Some Acadians in Port Royal had eight or ten or even twenty-five "arpents de terre en valeur," others one or two or even one-half, and yet others none. According to Greg Kennedy, "Most Acadian families in the early eighteenth century were not producing enough to feed themselves. Clearly they are working in other ways, and La Liberté had a reasonable amount of livestock, all things considered. It's difficult, therefore, to draw specific conclusions about his race, since other Acadian families were not really making a living from farming either." Greg Kennedy, personal communication with author, September 19, 2021. See also Greg Kennedy, *Something of a Peasant Paradise? Comparing Rural Societies in Acadie and the Loudunais, 1604–1755* (Montreal and Kingston: McGill-Queen's University Press, 2014), especially Chapter 3. For the censuses themselves, see "Acadie Recensements, 1671–1752," Library and Archives Canada. Available online at https://heritage.canadiana.ca/view/oocihm.lac_reel_c2572/1?r=0&s=2.

8   Peter Twohig, "Remembering Michael S. Cross," *The Acadiensis Blog,* October 23, 2019. Available online at https://acadiensis.wordpress.com/2019/10/23 /remembering-michael-s-cross/.

9   Harvey Amani Whitfield, "Black Refugees in Nova Scotia, 1813–1840," (Dalhousie University, PhD thesis, 2003), viii.

10   James W. St. G. Walker, personal communication with author, July 22, 2021. See also James W. St. G. Walker, *The Black Loyalists: The Search for a Promised Land in Nova Scotia and Sierra Leone, 1783–1870* (New York: Holmes and Maiers, 1976; Toronto: University of Toronto Press, 1992); and James W. St. G. Walker, "Myth, History and Revisionism: The Black Loyalists Revisited," *Acadiensis* 29, no. 1 (Autumn 1999): 88–105.

11   W. Bryan Rommel-Ruiz, *Journal of the Early Republic* 27, no. 3 (Fall 2007): 563, 565; Walter C. Rucker, *American Historical Review* 113, no. 4 (October 2008): 1143; Karolyn Smardz Frost, *H-Canada, H-Net Reviews,* July 2008. Available online at https://networks.h-net.org/node/3449/reviews/27332/frost-whitfield -blacks-border-black-refugees-british-north-america-1815; George H. Junne Jr., *Canadian Historical Review,* 89, no. 3 (September 2008): 412; Ken Donovan, *New England Quarterly,* 80, no. 4 (December 2007): 717.

12   See Winfried Siemerling, *The Black Atlantic Reconsidered: Black Canadian Writing, Cultural History, and the Presence of the Past* (Montreal and Kingston: McGill-Queen's University Press, 2015); and Barrington Walker, "Exhuming the Archive: Black Slavery and Freedom in the Maritimes and Beyond," *Acadiensis* 56, no. 2 (Summer/Autumn 2017): 196-204.

13   T.W. Smith, "The Slave in Canada," *Collections of the Nova Scotia Historical Society* 10 (1899): 1. Available online at https://archives.novascotia.ca/pdf/africanns /F90N85-SlaveInCanada.pdf.

14 Marcel Trudel, *L'esclavage au Canada français: histoire et conditions de l'esclavage*
(Québec: Les Presses Universitaires Laval, 1960). Although *L'esclavage au Canada français* broke new ground, some passages jar contemporary sensibilities.
Commenting on the culinary skills of an enslaved woman, Trudel wrote: "On
serait tenté de crier: vive l'esclavage!" That is, "One is tempted to cry out: long live
slavery!" (*L'esclavage*, 1960, 171). Forty-plus years and two editions later, neither
Trudel nor his colleague, Micheline D'Allaire, thought to remove the joke, if it
can be called that (*Deux siècles de l'esclavage au Québec*, 2004, 156; *Deux siècles de
l'esclavage au Québec,* 2009, 157). On the subject of illegitimate children, Trudel
wrote: "ou c'est le maître lui-même qui trouve amusant d'augmenter son cheptel
[livestock] à peu de frais" (*L'esclavage*, 1960, 262). Again, neither Trudel nor D'Allaire thought to raise the issue of consent in the second and third editions. Nor did
they remove the reference to livestock. (2004, 260; 2009, 258). In 2013, an Eng-
lish-language translation of the 2009 edition was published. Although he wanted
"to remain true to [Trudel's] original intention, which imparts a somewhat archaic
flavour to some passages in the book," translator George Tombs removed the reference to livestock: "masters could enjoy sexual relations with Amerindian or black
slave women living under the same roof, thereby increasing the overall number
of slaves at no additional cost" (*Canada's Forgotten Slaves*, 2013, 10, 205). Still on
the subject of sex, Trudel stated that four owners "ont cédé aux charmes de leurs
esclaves," or "yielded to the charms of their slaves" (*L'esclavage*, 1960, 262). This
sentence survived the 2004 edition (260), the 2009 edition (258), and the 2013
translation (205). Similarly, Trudel wrote: "Il importe surtout de noter qu'après
avoir goûté de l'exotique, les Canadiens reviennent, pour les secondes noces, au
menu normal" (*L'esclavage*, 1960, 286). In English, "It is important to note that
after having tasted the exotic, the Canadians returned, in their second marriage, to
a normal menu." In slightly altered forms, this sentence survived the 2004 edition
("… qu'après avoir goûté de l'exotisme," 287) and the 2009 edition ("… qu'après
avoir goûté à l'exotisme," 286). Because it was overly sexualized, Tombs altered the
phrase and removed the reference to "normal" in the 2013 translation: "whereas
once Canadians survived a first marriage with an Amerindian, they were more
likely to marry a white person the second time around" (226). (George Tombs,
personal communication with author, 27 September 2021.) A few sentences
later, Trudel referred to two Canadians who first married "sauvagesses," but "ne
reviennent pas à la même sauce," or "did not subsequently return to their own
kind, marrying a woman of French origin" (*L'esclavage,* 1960, 287). This sentence
survived the 2004 edition (287) but not the 2009 edition. It does not appear in
Canada's Forgotten Slaves. See Marcel Trudel avec la collaboration de Micheline
D'Allaire, *Deux siècles de l'esclavage au Québec* (Montréal: Hurtubise HMH, 2004);
Marcel Trudel avec la collaboration de Micheline D'Allaire, *Deux siècles de l'esclavage au Québec* (Québec: Édition Bibliothèque Québécoise, 2009); Marcel Trudel,

Canada's Forgotten Slaves: Two Hundred Years of Bondage, trans. George Tombs (Montréal: Véhicule Press, 2013).

15 Lionel Groulx often referred to the perfect ethnic, social, religious, and moral homogeneity of New France. See Lionel Groulx, *La naissance d'une race* (Montréal: Librairie d'Action canadienne-française, 1930), 22.

16 Marcel Trudel, *Memoirs of a Less Travelled Road: A Historian's Life* (Montreal: Véhicule Press, 2002), 152. See also Marcel Trudel and Mathieu d'Avignon, *Connaître pour le plaisir de connaître: Entretien avec l'historien Marcel Trudel sur la science historique et le métier d'historien au Québec* (Québec: Les Presses de l'Université Laval, 2005), 7–9, 25.

17 Jean Hamelin, *Revue d'histoire de l'Amerique française* 14, no. 4 (1961): 603.

18 See Afua Cooper, *The Hanging of Angélique: The Untold Story of Slavery in Canada and the Burning of Old Montréal* (Athens: University of Georgia Press, 2007); Frank Mackey, *Done with Slavery: The Black Fact in Montreal, 1760–1840* (Montreal and Kingston: McGill-Queen's University Press, 2010); and Brett Rushforth, *Bonds of Alliance: Indigenous and Atlantic Slaveries in New France* (Chapel Hill: University of North Carolina Press, 2012). See also Afua Cooper, Francoise Baylis, Camille Cameron, Ainsley Francis, Paul E. Lovejoy, David States, Shirley Tillotson, Harvey Amani Whitfield, and Norma Williams, *Report on Lord Dalhousie's History on Slavery and Race,* 2019. Available online at https://www.dal.ca /dept/ldp/findings.html.

19 See Barry Cahill "Habeas Corpus and Slavery in Nova Scotia: *R v Hecht Ex Parte Rachel, 1798,*" *University of New Brunswick Law Journal* 44 (1995): 179–209; Barry Cahill, "Slavery and the Judges of Loyalist Nova Scotia," *University of New Brunswick Law Journal* 43 (1994): 73–134; Kenneth Donovan, "Slavery and Freedom in Atlantic Canada's African Diaspora: Introduction," *Acadiensis* 43, no. 1 (Winter/Spring 2014): 109–15; Kenneth Donovan, "Female Slaves as Sexual Victims in Île Royale," *Acadiensis* 43, no. 1 (Winter/Spring 2014): 147–56; Kenneth Donovan, "Slaves in Cape Breton, 1713–1815," *Directions: Canadian Race Relations Foundation* 4, no. 1 (Summer 2007): 44-5; Kenneth Donovan, "Slaves in Île Royale, 1713–1758," *French Colonial History* 5 (2004): 25–42; Kenneth Donovan, "A Nominal List of Slaves and Their Owners in Île Royale, 1713–1760," *Nova Scotia Historical Review* 16 (1996): 151–62; Kenneth Donovan, "Slaves and Their Owners in Ile Royale, 1713–1760," *Acadiensis* 25, 1 (Autumn 1995): 3–32.

20 Donovan, "Slavery and Freedom in Atlantic Canada's African Diaspora: Introduction," 110. Marcel Trudel said much the same thing, according to his translator George Tombs: "I remember asking Trudel why this pioneering work had only just begun to spawn new studies and fiction about slavery in Canada. He shook his head wistfully, replying that this subject had long been a blind spot in the French Canadian psyche. But what of English Canada, I asked. Why had no comparable work on slavery in English Canada ever come out? Could there be some way of adapting my translation, so that it included as many references to slaves

belonging to English Canadian as to French Canadian owners? Otherwise readers of my translation might get the mistaken impression that slave owners in Canada had mainly been French-speaking, and rarely English-speaking! He seemed daunted by the amount of research such an adaptation would involve." Tombs, "Translator's Preface," in Trudel, *Canada's Forgotten Slaves,* 11.

21 See Harvey Amani Whitfield, *North to Bondage: Loyalist Slavery in the Maritimes* (Vancouver: UBC Press, 2016). See also Harvey Amani Whitfield, ed., *Black Slavery in the Maritimes: A History in Documents* (Peterborough: Broadview Press, 2018). Whitfield's many contributions to the Black history of Atlantic Canada are part of a remarkable record of books, articles, theses, and local histories. See Suzanne Morton and Donald Wright, "Black History in Atlantic Canada: A Bibliography," *Acadiensis* 50, no. 1 (Spring 2021): 223–75.

22 Whitfield, *North to Bondage,* 73.

23 Whitfield's reading of close-quarters slavery distinguishes *North to Bondage* from *L'esclavage au Canada français.* In his review of *Deux siècle de l'esclavage au Québec,* the largely unchanged 2004 edition of *L'esclavage au Canada français,* Brett Rushforth noted that Trudel's characterization of close-quarters slavery is dated, to say the least. For example, Trudel depicted "notre esclavage" as "tout humain," or humane, writing that its "atmosphère familiale," or familial nature, led to "l'affectation réciproque des maîtres and des esclaves," or mutual affection between masters and slaves. In fact, "Leur servitude mise à part, les esclaves du Canada français sont soumis à des conditions de vie qui ne diffèrent pas tellement de celles de leurs maîtres et ils participent aux sacrements de l'Église de la même façon que les personnes libres." In English, "Their servitude aside, slaves in Canada lived under conditions that differed very little from those of their masters and they participated in the sacraments of the Church in the same way as free people." See Brett Rushforth, *Canadian Historical Review* 82, no. 2 (2005): 373–5. See also Susanne Roethlisberger, "Black Slavery, Historians, and Textbooks: A Study of the Representation of Enslaved People of African Descent in Quebec's Historiography and History Textbooks" (McGill University, MA thesis, 2020); and Nelle Sawallisch, "Trudel's Legacies: For a Critical Understanding of Slavery in Quebec," *Zeitschrift für Kanada-Studien* 36 (2016): 86–101.

24 "Every spoonful of sugar, drop of molasses, and sip of rum that colonists consumed linked the Maritimes inextricably to West Indian slave labor, just as Maritime-shingled houses sheltered slaveholders and Atlantic cod fed enslaved people." Sarah Chute, "Bound to Slavery: Economic and Biographical Connections to Atlantic Slavery between the Maritimes and West Indies after 1783" (University of Vermont, MA thesis, 2021), 3–4. Similarly, Shirley Tillotson has argued that Nova Scotia's public finances and therefore its public works, its roads and bridges, for example, were dependent on customs and excise duties applied to slave-produced goods, including rum, coffee, sugar, and molasses. Shirley Tillotson, "A Region of Feeling: Bringing the History of Emotions to Political

Economy in Atlantic Canada," University of New Brunswick, W. Stewart MacNutt Lecture, November 25, 2020. See also Shirley Tillotson, "How (and How Much) King's College Benefited from Slavery in the West Indies, 1789–1854," May 6, 2019. Available online at https://ukings.ca/wp-content/uploads/2021/01 /202001TillotsonKingsSlaveryIndirectConnections_Secure.pdf; and Shirley Tillotson, "Importing the Plantation: The West Indies Trade and Nova Scotia's Public Revenue, 1789–1835," *Journal of the Royal Nova Scotia Historical Society*, forthcoming, 2022.

25 Timothy Findley, *The Wars* (Toronto: Clarke, Irwin, 1977), 11.

26 See Harvey Amani Whitfield, "White Archives, Black Fragments: Problems and Possibilities in Telling the Lives of Enslaved Black People in the Maritimes," *Canadian Historical Review* 101, no. 3 (September 2020): 323–45.

27 Prepared by the British in 1782, the Book of Negroes is a register of nearly 3,000 Black Americans, mostly free but some still enslaved, bound for Nova Scotia aboard British vessels. It includes names and personal details, including physical characteristics, occupations, and the names of former owners. Digitized, it is available online at https://archives.novascotia.ca/africanns/archives/?ID=26.

28 Lawrence Hill, *The Book of Negroes* (Toronto: Harper Collins, 2007), 66.

29 This *Dictionary* is the second dictionary of enslaved people in Canada. See Marcel Trudel, *Dictionnaire des esclaves et de leur propriétaires au Canada français* (Montréal: Hurtubise HMH, 1990).

30 Hill, *The Book of Negroes,* 134.

31 Reuben Gold Thwaites, ed., *The Jesuit Relations and Allied Documents,* vol. 5 (Cleveland: Burrows Brothers, 1897), 63.

Historical Overview: Black Slavery in the Maritimes

After the American Revolution, two Black men named Liberty arrived in the Maritimes. Ironically, they were both still enslaved. In one case, Captain Dunbar planned to take Liberty to Saint John, New Brunswick, from New York. According to British officials, Liberty "acknowledges to have been purchased by the Capt. at the West Indies 17 years ago."[1] What we also learn from this simple entry in the Book of Negroes, a listing of Black people whom the British had evacuated from New York, is that Captain Dunbar had purchased Liberty when he was only eight years old. Of course, we know nothing about Liberty's parents. Before being brought to the Maritimes, Liberty had lived in the West Indies (and possibly Africa before that) and New York.

In the other case, James Lysle (Lyle) enslaved Liberty and brought him to Nova Scotia via St. Augustine (East Florida). Previously, in 1782, Liberty was living in Savannah and had been sold to Matthew Lyle before being sold to James. Along with Liberty, a mother and daughter named Sarah and Pegg were also forced to move to Nova Scotia.[2] These slaves almost certainly noticed the large number of free Black Loyalists – those Black Americans who gained freedom during the American Revolution by escaping to British lines and sometimes serving and aiding the Crown's war effort – who were also part of the migration to Nova Scotia. Although Liberty, Sarah, and Pegg shared the Black Loyalists' background as American slaves, they differed from these free Blacks because they remained enslaved.

Biographical Sketches of Black Slaves and Black Atlantic Scholarship

The stories of these two men embody the essence of this biographical dictionary, which helps illuminate the lives of enslaved Black people in the Maritimes within the context of the Black Atlantic world.[3] In 1996, well before the emphasis on biography in Black Atlantic scholarship, Paul Lovejoy noted that "in studying slavery and the slave trade, biography can capture details of history ... By re-inserting individuals into the reality of slavery, biographies put flesh on the bones of the past."[4] This biographical dictionary offers 1,465 brief life histories of mostly enslaved Black people in the Maritimes,[5] making it the first scholarly attempt to collect and make concrete the individual lives of enslaved Black people who lived in this region. Although my work focuses on Black slavery, the biographical approach can also be applied to understanding the enslavement of Indigenous Peoples.[6]

The individual lives in this book show the remarkable range of the Black experience in the Atlantic world. The men, women, and children found in this dictionary came from various points of origin, including Africa, the West Indies, the Carolinas, the Chesapeake, and the northern states. Some of them were born in the Maritimes, which shows that there were generations of enslaved Black people in the region. Slaves worked in a variety of tasks and occupations that cannot be summed up by the production of staple crops like sugar, rice, or cotton. Maritime slaves also had a broad range of family ties, and they struggled to keep families together and raise children in the shadow of potential separation as relatives could be sold at any time. The broad cross-section of slaves who fit into the category "Maritime slaves" is incredibly diverse. They were able to survive slavery and in some cases eventually become free. The questions for historians are how can we do justice to these people and how can we best document their lives? My purpose is to encourage historians to take these names and study them further so that scholars can create a repository of knowledge about enslaved Black people in the Maritimes and how they were connected to the wider Black Atlantic.[7]

The slave biographies in this book are an important addition to the many impressive works about slavery that understandably focus on the collective experiences of enslaved people.[8] In his work *Africans in the Old South*, Randy Sparks notes that microhistory – the study of smaller topics or smaller units of history – allows scholars to challenge the dominant narrative about slavery.[9] If one thinks of slavery, the idea of Virginian tobacco plantations or Jamaican sugar estates understandably comes to the fore; but to focus solely on these regions helps erase the lived reality of the individuals who populate the pages of this book. Historian Simon Newman notes that within the British Atlantic world "slavery was defined, enforced, and experienced in dramatically different ways."[10] In the windswept and cold Maritimes, slavery found fertile ground that produced multiple generations of enslaved people who provided labour for their owners but who also produced food and goods that helped sustain the slave populations in the West Indies. Exploring the individual lives of enslaved people in the Maritimes tells the story of slavery outside of plantation societies (such as the West Indies, Virginia, or South Carolina), but also intimately connected to them, that powered the economies of the British, French, and other European empires.

There are 1,465 people documented in this book. Their stories have varying levels of detail; some are fleshed out through their interactions with white Maritime society, others had only the dimmest outline of their existence recorded. All, to some extent, had their lives silenced by the archives, in that the documentary evidence favours and illuminates the lives of wealthy or well-known people rather than the lives of enslaved people.[11] In a similar vein to *Slave Biographies: The Atlantic Database Network*, this book seeks to unearth the stories of men, women, and children who would not otherwise have found their way into historical works.[12] This book bears witness to their existence; it documents the lives of Maritimes slaves and highlights their connections to the wider Atlantic world. This book also helps us recognize that these enslaved Black people in the Maritimes had likes, dislikes, good traits, bad ones, and various levels of physical, spiritual, and intellectual talent. We must affirm the notion that all of these slaves were unique individuals, despite the efforts of their owners and the wider British Atlantic world to dehumanize them. They were people – and their actions to keep their families together and fight for their dignity are poignantly told in many of the biographies in this book. Regardless of the lack of available primary sources, their stories deserve sustained investigation. As Brett Rushforth reminds us in terms of his own work,

I have aimed, wherever possible, to recover the details of enslaved individuals' lives: their names, ages, friends, lovers, occupations, and, occasionally, their aspirations and fears. I believe that these portraits add an important dimension to my analysis, demonstrating the wide range of slaves' experiences and showing the limits of their opportunities. But telling their many stories is more than a narrative device. It reflects an ethical commitment to recognize the humanity of the enslaved, something their masters sought to deny. If their lives are useful because they illuminate the systems through which they passed, their value is intrinsic.[13]

Sometimes the best information we have about an enslaved person comes from a runaway advertisement. These documents usually left in-depth descriptions of runaway slaves.[14] For example, Bill was a slave from South Carolina who escaped from his owner Michael Wallace in 1794 following 10 years of bondage in Nova Scotia. Wallace published a runaway slave advertisement that described Bill's plan to escape:

RAN Away, on Thursday evening, the 18th inst. A Negro Man Servant, the property of the Subscriber, named Belfast; but who commonly goes by the name of Bill. – At the time of [the] elopement he was in the service of William Forsyth, Esq.; and had meditated an attempt to get on board a ship that night which lay in the harbour, bound to Newfoundland; but was frustrated. It is probable, however, he may still endeavor to escape that way, therefore, the masters of all coasters going along shore, or other vessels bound to sea, are hereby forewarned from carrying him off at their peril, as they will be prosecuted, if discovered, with the utmost rigour of the law. The above reward will be paid to any person or persons who shall apprehend and secure him, so that I may recover him again. He is a likely, stout-made fellow, of five feet eight or nine inches high, and about 27 years of age; of mild good countenance and features, smooth black skin, with very white teeth; is a native of South Carolina, speaks good English, and very softly, and has been in this province for ten years. When he went off, he wore an old Bath-Coating short coat, of a light colour, wore out at the elbows; brown cloth or trowsers, also much wore at the knees; a round hat, and an old black silk [handkerchief] about his neck – But as he had other [clothes] secreted in town, he may have changed his whole apparel. He will no doubt endeavor to pass for a free man, and possibly by some other name.[15]

Due to the wealth of detail provided by an owner desperate to find his enslaved property, Bill is among the more fleshed out characters in Maritime slavery. Still, we know little else about his life. Bill's intriguing life elicits many historical questions: Did he have any family in Nova Scotia? Was he married? What daily tasks did Bill do? How did he experience the American Revolution? How many different owners did he have before Michael Wallace? Why did he run away – mistreatment, hope of freedom, searching for a loved one, or all of the above?

In contrast to the comparative wealth of detail about Bill, several hundred entries in this book belong to slaves who remain nameless. In 1786, for example, an unnamed boy and an unnamed man (enslaved at one point to Charles McPherson) were sold at a public auction in New Brunswick.[16] The questions about these slaves are almost endless: Where were they from? What were their names? Was the man being sold the father of the boy? If they were father and son, what happened to the mother? These stories are fragmentary remains of the historical record, but they offer insight into unnamed slaves sold at a public auction. Also, the individual life stories of these slaves are similar to the biographical sketches throughout the rest of this book: They were everyday slaves. There was no Olaudah Equiano, Phillis Wheatley, or Domingos Alvares – people whose lives left a lasting imprint on the historical record and enabled historians to write full-length biographies.[17] And in many cases, the biographies in this dictionary might well raise more questions than they answer. Indeed, as this historical overview makes clear, even our best sources for Maritime slavery do not always record the actual names of slaves, thereby underlining how their owners viewed them – as human commodities to be purchased, traded, and bequeathed to relatives like livestock or real estate.

This work belongs to the growing field of biography and the Black Atlantic, which uses individual stories to re-centre understandings of the everyday reality of slavery.[18] The book offers information about slave names, age, gender, occupation, place of origin, location, and owner. Readers will also find information about slave families: how they survived, dealt with separation, and married free Blacks. This work required the use of not only primary sources, but also a range of secondary sources, including the work of Ken Donovan, David States, Raylene Fairfax, F.W. Harris, T.W. Smith, and Jim Hornby. Together, their work has allowed me to adhere to the words of Carlo Ginzburg: "If the sources offer us the possibility of reconstructing not only indistinct masses but also individual personalities, it would be absurd to ignore it. To extend the historic concept of the 'individual' in the direction of the lower classes is a worthwhile objective."[19]

The Contours of Maritime Slavery

The introduction and development of slavery in the New World is among the most important events in global history, resulting in the growth of a lucrative and exploitative labour system justified by perceived racial differences. Slavery existed throughout the New World, from Chile and Argentina in the south to Nova Scotia and Newfoundland in the north. It is not surprising that slavery played a part in Canadian history, but it is startling that it has not received more widespread attention from the general Canadian public and especially historians. Historian Ken Donovan notes that although various artists, writers, directors, and historians have worked on slavery, it "is not a significant part of the Canadian historical narrative." Studying slavery in Canada as opposed to, say, escaped American slaves, "goes against the dominant image of Canada as a land of freedom."[20] Slavery is one of the most neglected aspects of Canadian history. The focus, understandably, when discussing Black Canadian history has been on the Underground Railroad, the Black Loyalists, and other groups who found freedom under the British flag. Yet thousands of Black people were enslaved in the Maritimes, Quebec, and Upper Canada between the seventeenth and early nineteenth centuries (1605–1820s).

Black migration is one of the hallmarks of the history of the Maritimes. These migrations – coerced and voluntary – connected the Maritimes to the United States, Africa, the Caribbean, and Europe. Between 1605 and 1820, several thousand Black people settled in the Maritimes. These migrants included 3,000 Black Loyalists, possibly 1,500 to 2,000 Loyalist slaves, 550 Jamaican Maroons (from 1796 to 1800), several hundred slaves in Île Royale, an unknown number of New England Planter slaves (possibly up to 200), a small number of slaves brought up from the coastal slave trade, and about 3,200 Black refugees from the War of 1812.[21] We must understand the history of slavery within this larger context of migration throughout the British Empire, the Black Atlantic, and the African diaspora.

People of African descent have lived in the Maritimes since the early 1600s. These first Black inhabitants were not necessarily enslaved. Before 1605, for example, Mathieu Da Costa served as a paid translator between the Mi'kmaq and French. Da Costa's life story indicates that he had become familiar with the local Indigenous language through previous travels to Nova Scotia. In all likelihood he spoke multiple languages, including French and Mi'kmaw.[22] Other early Africans might have been servants, but they were not necessarily enslaved in the same way that Black people throughout the Atlantic world would have been during the 1700s. The first major incidence of slavery occurred in Île Royale (Cape Breton). Between 1713 and 1758, there were 266 slaves living there, and the vast majority of them were Black people. These slaves did not make up a large percentage of the colony's population.[23] They came from various regions, including the American colonies, the West Indies, and Africa. Most Île Royale masters only owned a few slaves. These slaves worked in the domestic sphere, which included washing clothes, cooking, gardening, cutting firewood, nursing, moving hay, and shovelling snow, and these were valuable tasks that allowed an owner's family to engage in other occupations. In several entries throughout this book the work patterns of Île Royale slaves are illuminated, especially the variety of tasks they undertook. In this northern outpost of the French Empire, therefore, there were small numbers of slaves per household, significant levels of interaction between owners and their slaves, and a mixed economic system where slaves acted as multi-occupational labourers as there were no slave-produced staples such as tobacco, cotton, rice, or sugar. Slavery did not dominate the economic or political structure as it did in South Carolina or Jamaica. This society with slaves would be expanded in the ensuing decades as English-speaking settlers, including the Loyalists, migrated to the Maritimes.[24]

Slaveholders and their slaves became much more common in Nova Scotia after the founding of Halifax in 1749. This growing town became an integral part of the trading system between Europe, North America, the West Indies, and Africa. This economic exchange included timber, fish, molasses, sugar, salt, and slaves. Maritime slaves helped to produce goods that sustained and strengthened the slave societies in the British Caribbean – societies that relied on those goods and others, particularly fish, from the Maritimes and New England. This trade resulted in slaves being brought into the region. In 1750 Captain Bloss, a Royal Navy officer, brought 16 slaves to Nova Scotia, possibly from Antigua. They built him "a very good house."[25] One year later, a Boston newspaper advertised "JUST arriv'd from Hallifax, and to be sold, Ten Hearty Strong Negro Men, mostly Tradesmen, such as Caulkers, Carpenters, Sailmakers, Ropemakers."[26] The skills of these slaves highlight the type of work that slaves were expected to do in both Boston and Halifax. In 1752, a Halifax merchant offered several slaves for sale in a Nova Scotian newspaper:

> Just imported, and to be sold by Joshua Mauger, at Major Lockman's store in Halifax, several Negro slaves, viz. A very likely Negro Wench, of about thirty five Years

of Age, a Creole born, has been brought up in a Gentleman's family, and capable of doing all sorts of Work belonging thereto, as Needle-Work of all sorts, and in the best Manner; also Washing, Ironing, Cookery, and every other Thing that can be expected from Such a Slave. Also, 2 Negro boys of about 12 or 13 Years old, likely, healthy, and well shap'd, and understand some English: likewise 2 healthy Negro slaves of about 18 Years of Age, of agreable tempers, and fit for any kind of business; and also a healthy Negro Man of about 30 years of age.[27]

Mauger – Maugerville, New Brunswick, is named after him – offered the slaves for sale in Halifax because some market for them clearly existed. He could have easily sold them in Charleston, New York, or Boston, but instead chose to offer them for sale in Nova Scotia. Similar to other documents about Maritime slavery, this source leads to more questions than answers. Why did Mauger carefully detail the skills of the female slave, but refrain from saying anything about the skills of the male slaves? How were these slaves related, if at all? Was the female slave the mother of the 12- and 13-year-old boys? The advertisement also has another imprint of Atlantic slavery on it – the commodification and dehumanization of Black bodies. We do not know any of these slaves' names, which is also true of Captain Bloss's slaves and the 10 enslaved men sold in Boston. Certainly, each one of these people had names that were known to their friends, family members, and owners. Unfortunately, their names have been mostly lost in the historical record.

Following the Acadian Expulsion, Governor Charles Lawrence offered the expropriated Acadian land to English-speaking settlers. The government further granted an additional 50 acres of land for each Black person brought into the colony, thereby encouraging slavery in the region. As a result, some of the New England Planters brought slaves to Nova Scotia. Between 1759 and 1774, approximately 8,000 Planters settled in Nova Scotia. Historians do not know the exact number of slaves who arrived in the Maritimes during this time, but it is clear that a number of prominent Planters owned slaves.[28] For example, in 1777 Simeon Perkins recorded in his diary that he had "settled with Mr. Mercer, and pay him for a Negro boy … The boys name is Jacob, which I have altered to Frank. He is about 10 or 11 years old."[29] Originally from Connecticut, Perkins served as a legislator in Nova Scotia's House of Assembly for many years (during the mid-1760s and from 1770 to 1799) as well as a local judge. His cold and indifferent description of the child slave leaves many questions for historians. Where were Jacob's parents? Did Perkins purchase the child away from his parents or had Mr. Mercer already sold them? What type of work did Perkins want this child to do? Did the child have any other relatives in the area? Planter slaves like Frank (or Jacob) and their owners were fully engaged in the larger British world, and Nova Scotia was hardly an outpost beyond the reaches of the Anglo-American world. In fact, the New England Planters's use of slaves and their strengthening of slavery in the Maritime colonies underlined their similarity to other slaveholding areas throughout New England and New York. Like slaves already in Île Royale, New England Planter slaves had close contact with their owners and worked in a mixed economy. Most slaves worked in a range of tasks, such as planting crops, repairing fences, cooking, cleaning, and caring for children. The character of New England Planter slavery was perpetuated and expanded by the subsequent arrival of Loyalist slaveowners and their slaves.[30]

Maritime slavery must be understood as part of several overlapping systems of Black labour exploitation throughout the British world. The majority of Maritime slaves came from the American colonies, including New England, the Middle Atlantic (New York, New Jersey, and Pennsylvania), the Chesapeake (Virginia, Maryland, Delaware), and the Deep South (South Carolina and Georgia). Some of these slaves were born in Africa and the Caribbean.[31] Quite often, they had lived in many places in the Atlantic world before coming to the Maritimes. In July 1784, for example, New York Loyalist Frederick William Hecht placed an advertisement in the *Royal St. John's Gazette* complaining that his "negro man slave, named Hector" had recently escaped. Hecht unwittingly left historians plenty of information about Hector, and thus scholars can partially reconstruct some of this slave's life. First, Hector worked as a cooper, so he had an important skill that would have been valuable in Saint John. Second, he had travelled throughout the Atlantic world and along the North American coast: Hecht noted "[Hector] came from St. Augustine [Florida] to this place, via New-York." Moreover, aside from being "very talkative," Hecht noted that Hector "speaks English much like the West-India negroes." This detail indicates that Hector might have been from Africa or almost certainly had lived in the Caribbean. Hector was also a well-travelled slave, having possibly lived in Africa, the West Indies, St. Augustine, briefly New York, and finally Saint John.[32] Once slaves like Hector arrived in the Maritimes, they used their traditions, family connections, and work experiences to navigate the living conditions of their new homes. In the Maritimes, they encountered a form of slavery that would have been familiar to those from New England and other northern colonies. At the outset of Loyalist settlement, most slaves lived briefly in Shelburne, but the poor land resulted in the town suffering from serious outmigration. As a result most slaves relocated with their owners – if they were not taken back to the United States – to the Annapolis region of western Nova Scotia and Saint John, though slaves also settled throughout the Maritimes.[33]

Slaves usually lived with their owners and worked alongside them doing a variety of tasks. The intimate nature of slave/slaveholder relationships in the Maritimes could, however, be a double-edged sword. In some cases living with their owners might result in better treatment, but it could just as easily become an abusive relationship if slaves did not have the comfort of a large slave community or distance provided by living in slave cabins. In some cases, intimate slavery resulted in a closer and benevolent (in paternalistic terms) relationship between owners and slaves. In her 1789 will, Anna Lillie carefully listed how she wanted her slave Casar treated after her death:

> It is also my will and intention that my black man Casar be free, and that the Sum of Ten Pounds be retained and left in the hands of my herein after named Executor, to be applied to the use of said Casar, in case of Sickness, or other necessity, at the discretion of my said Executor ... [I] do hereby bequeath to my [within?] named black Man Casar the Feather Bed + Bedstead whereupon he usually sleeps, and also the bed clothes and bedding belonging thereto.[34]

Of course, close quarters between slaveholders and their chattel did not stop certain slave owners from willingly breaking up families. In his will, Caleb Fowler seemed to care very little for his female slave and her daughter:

> I give [my wife Mary Fowler] my Negro Wench named Hannah to be hers as long as she remains my Widow and no longer. I order and it is my Will that the said Negro Wench Hannah and her Child Diana shall remain in my Family if they are disposed of before my son Caleb is Eighteen years old, then if my Children should wish to keep them, whoever they live with, shall allow a reasonable price for them or either of them, and in case the said Hannah does not behave herself well after my decease, I order her to be sold at the discretion of Executors ... and it is my Will that the said negro child Dianah [sic] shall remain with her Mother (if either is sold) until she is ten years old, then one of my said daughters as they two can agree to have her, which ever takes her to allow a reasonable price to be deducted our of their share or Legacy abovementioned for her.[35]

Fowler encouraged his children to separate a mother from her daughter when the girl was only 10. The will demonstrates how little some slaveholders cared about slaves who they claimed to be part of their "family." There is nothing in the will about Diana's father – unless Fowler was the father, which is possible. The intimacy of Maritime slavery comes through in many of the biographies in this book. Slaves were consistently in the orbit of their proprietors with little respite or hope to get distance between themselves and their owners. Most Maritime slaves had to live in the same house as their masters and as a result they were on call 24 hours a day.

The Maritimes began as a society with slaves and remained so until the end of slavery in the 1820s. Similar to New England (with the exception of the Narragansett region of Rhode Island), there were no large plantations, plantation overseers, slave gangs, Black drivers, or absentee owners. Most importantly, neither region produced any staple crop comparable to rice, cotton, tobacco, or sugar.[36] Yet both New England and the Maritime region used slave labour and maintained slaveholding connections and trading relationships with the British West Indies.

In understanding the work of slaves in the Maritime colonies, it is helpful to understand New England and the Maritimes as a connected and integrated region or borderland.[37] This was especially the case in terms of slavery and slave work. Slaves were multi-occupational labourers doing every possible task in the urban and rural landscape. They worked alongside their owners, free Blacks, and poor whites. The work of Maritime slaves did not define the economy, but their labour helped slaveholding families do better than those without the extra hands that slaves provided. Maritime farmers with slaves could clear more land and plant more crops, thus reaping greater harvests. It is no coincidence that slavery prospered and lasted the longest in those areas – the Annapolis Valley, for instance – where the most productive farming operations were located.[38] In addition to their farm labour, slaves helped to build the region's roads, homes, and churches, and they did every possible task within the shipping industry. The Maritimes did not have a staple crop or large numbers of slaves per household, but this should not lead one to the false conclusion that slave labour remained unimportant or even meaningless. In her foundational work, Joanne Pope Melish notes "that far from being a marginal or luxury item in the households of the wealthy, slaves were crucially important in performing the work that a household head would have performed in a purely subsistence, or pre-market, economy ... slaves contributed to the expansion and diversification of the New England economy."[39] Maritime slaves similarly contributed to the growth of the region through their work in the domestic, urban, and rural sectors of the economy. Taken together, they undertook an incredibly broad range of tasks and fulfilled multiple occupations.

Maritime slaves were multi-occupational as the nature of the regional economy required that they be prepared to do more than one task. In this sense, they again had much in common with their enslaved counterparts in New England. Historian Lorenzo Greene wrote "Not only was Negro labor in New England used in specific tasks, but many Negroes fell into the category of 'Jack of all trades,' that is, they were able to turn their hands to several different kinds of work."[40] Slave-for-sale or slave-wanted advertisements usually boasted or required that a slave was "fit for town and country" or could do "all kinds of work." These types of notices were widespread in the Maritimes and New England.[41] The advertisements are illuminating for the light they shed on the skilled and diversified nature of work that Maritime slaves performed. As the notices indicate, occupational diversity was inculcated in slaves from childhood. Women and young teenagers also served their owners in a variety of ways.[42] In 1786 the printer of the *Royal American Gazette* summed up the expectations of local slaves through the example of a young teenager: "A Healthy, stout, NEGRO BOY, about fourteen Years of Age. He has been brought up in a Gentleman's Family, is very handy at Farming, House-Work, or attending Table, is strictly honest, and has an exceeding good Temper."[43] In 1799 another slaveholder noted that his young male slave was "very active" and could "do all sorts of Farming work, and is a handy House Servant."[44] These two slaves were busy tilling the soil, cleaning the house, and waiting on their owners' families. They had to be adept at a range of tasks, from planting crops and clearing soil to cooking and childcare. Slave work continued to be diversified throughout the late eighteenth into the early nineteenth century. As multi-occupational labourers, slaves cleared forests, removed rocks, broke ground, planted crops, built shelters, cleaned houses, cooked, and nursed children. They had experience in different types of agricultural labour, but also remained responsible for various types of domestic labour.

The work that Maritime slaves performed must be understood within the American historiographical trend that might be summed up as capitalism and slavery. Prominent scholars, for instance, have emphasized, in Christy Clark-Pujara's words, the "Business of Slavery."[45] These scholars point out the many ways that plantation slave societies like Barbados were linked with more northern parts of the British Empire, such as New England and New York. These areas were connected through the production and use of slave-produced staple crops, finance networks, and various institutions throughout the northeast that invested in slavery. Without question, Maritime slavery was part of this network. Maritime owners maintained business connections with plantation societies in the West Indies and the United States. In 1786, for example, Nova Scotian resident John Chipman noted in his business records the price for "passage of [George Halliburton's] Negro Wench at Antigua."[46] A Nova Scotian businessman, Samuel Starr, noted the proceeds "of a Black man sold at St. Vincent."[47] In an 1801 account book, Virginian Loyalist turned large-scale New Brunswick slaveholder, Jacob Ellegood, recorded "Cash for sale of negroes in Virginia as rendered in your account £120. Virginia [currency] 100." Although Ellegood had left Virginia nearly 20 years earlier, he still sold slaves there. The document is silent as to the names of the slaves.[48] Historian T.W. Smith observed the business of slavery in several Maritime account books as Maritimers engaged in selling and trading slaves in the southern states and the West Indies:

> Probate records in 1769, already quoted, contain an item respecting the proceeds of the sale of a slave boy in Carolina by a Halifax business man. It is certain that on more than one occasion, and it is believed that on many occasions, slaves were taken from Shelburne or Halifax to the West Indies for sale; the account books of Benjamin DeWolfe, one of the earlier merchants of Windsor, show sales in the same islands of slaves from Hants County; and Lieutenant Clarkson's manuscript journal, though covering only the last few months of 1791, gives several instances

of schemes for carrying Negroes – not in every case slaves after human law – to the United States for the evident purpose of sale.[49]

An examination of regional newspapers shows how local businesspeople purchased slave-produced goods and sold them in Nova Scotia, New Brunswick, and Prince Edward Island.[50] On the flipside, slaves worked within the larger patterns and rhythms of the Maritime region's economy. The trade items that slaves helped to produce tied the Maritimes to the flow of commerce between England, the West Indies, the United States, and Africa. Specifically, slaves in the Maritimes provided products for the West Indian slave population in the same way that slaves in New England did for the islands.[51]

The Legal Status of Slavery

After the influx of American Loyalists and their slaves to the Maritimes, slavery was widespread and racism became increasingly entrenched. It is a mistake, however, to see the region as monolithically dedicated to both slavery and racism. Though slavery remained strong, it was highly contested by anti-slavery legislators, judges, lawyers, and religious groups such as the Quaker settlement at Beaver Harbour in Charlotte County. According to W.A. Spray, "At the top of their agreement in large letters were the words, 'No Slave Masters Admitted.'"[52] The number of slaves increased after the Loyalist influx, but slavery remained legally insecure because although it was recognized under common law as a form of private property it had no statutory basis (such as a slave code) in Nova Scotia or New Brunswick. In Prince Edward Island, an act that dealt with slave baptism gave statute recognition to slavery.[53] The tenuousness of slavery is highlighted by the numerous attempts by owners to gain statute protection for their property (in 1787, 1789, 1801, and 1808 in Nova Scotia, and in 1801 in New Brunswick). They were defeated each time.[54] Yet Maritime slavery seems to have lasted into the early 1820s, and owners constantly fought in the courts and legislatures to protect their alleged right to own slaves.

Between 1783 and 1785, a complex mix of American slaves from a wide range of locations – from East Florida to northern Massachusetts – settled in the Maritimes. Due to the limitations of evidence, scholars cannot give an exact number of Loyalist slaves in the Maritimes. Estimates range from about 1,500 to 2,000. The reason scholars cannot give an accurate number is due to the ambiguities in the documentation. It is not always explicit if an individual was actually enslaved.[55] Chattel slaves were often called "servants" – a practice that makes it difficult to distinguish between free Black servants and those who remained enslaved after arriving in the Maritimes. As Robin Winks noted, there "is no way to know how many of the several thousand Negroes in the Maritime provinces were slaves and how many were free." He believed that the reason for the indiscriminate usage of "slave" and "servant" reflected an increasing concern about the morality of slavery. He suggests that though "most 'servants' were slaves," others were either free Black children or indentured adults.[56]

Slaveowners and slaves struggled to redefine what slavery meant by partially relying on past experiences while confronting the new realities of settlement, climate, soil, and economy. Slaves, for instance, had to maintain and protect families and friendships while also performing labour for their owners. An example of how enslaved families attempted to stay together and protect themselves from their masters is the runaway advertisement for James, his wife Bet, and their children. In 1785, according to their owner Samuel Andrews, "A Man, his Wife, and two Children, *James, Bet, Frank, and Judy*" escaped.[57] He described them as all speaking good English and mentioned that James "is a carpenter by trade." This slave family absconded either because of their treatment at Andrews's hands or because he planned to sell them. It would have been easier for the family to run away separately, but the fact that the entire family escaped together underlines the importance of family ties. Unfortunately, Andrews recaptured them.[58]

In terms of labour, the transition from slavery in the American colonies to the Maritimes differed by slave. Those from New York or New England probably experienced the greatest continuity between their old and new homes, while those from South Carolina or Maryland faced more rigorous adjustments. The first years after the Loyalist influx to the Maritimes were devoted to defining a system of slavery that was complicated by the large population of free Black Loyalists, the lack of clarity regarding slavery's legal status, and the willingness of Loyalist slaves to abscond and challenge the emerging social order so that they could win freedom, gain autonomy, reunite, and protect their families from predatory owners.[59]

In the Maritimes after the American Revolution, the labels of "free," "servant," or "slave" could also change quickly if a person ran away or was re-enslaved. This is probably the most significant issue to understand about Black life in the late eighteenth and early nineteenth centuries. A Black person might arrive in New Brunswick as a slave only to escape from their owner before being recaptured and sold to the West Indies. Another individual could begin their sojourn in Nova Scotia as a free person, become subjected to indentured servitude, then be re-enslaved before eventually escaping and finally enjoying freedom in Sierra Leone. In 1792, approximately 1,200 Black people migrated from the Maritimes to Sierra Leone under the auspices of the British government and the leadership of Black Loyalist Thomas Peters and Royal Navy officer John Clarkson. The case of Lydia Jackson is instructive. Originally, she settled at Manchester (Guysborough Township) with other free Blacks. As a result of poverty and the desertion of her husband, Jackson indentured herself to a Loyalist for what she thought would be a short time. It turned out that this person had tricked Jackson into signing an indenture that essentially made her a servant for life. This man then sold Jackson as a slave to a Dr. Bulman (or Bolman). As the doctor's slave, Jackson suffered from brutal mistreatment. Bulman regularly beat "her with the tongs, sticks, pieces of rope &c. about the head and face." John Clarkson noted that eventually Jackson escaped to Halifax when her owner planned on "selling her to some planter in the West Indies to work as a slave." Lydia Jackson's story must be considered in the context of Clarkson's following comment: "I do not know what induced me to mention the above case as I have many others of a similar nature; for example, Scott's case, Mr. Lee, Senr. case, Smith's child, Motley Roads child, Mr. Farish's negro servant, &c."[60]

In the case of re-enslavement, historians can only speculate about how many Black people – whose stories never made it before a court – were kidnapped and sold to the West Indies.[61] The kidnapping of Black people in Nova Scotia became widespread enough that legislators attempted in 1789 to pass An Act for the Regulation and Relief of the Free Negroes within the Province of Nova Scotia. Although the bill failed, it noted that "attempts have been made to carry some of them out of the Province, by force and Strategem for the scandalous purpose of making property of them in the West Indies contrary to their will and consent."[62] Based on information from a local observer (possibly his brother John), the anti-slavery advocate Thomas Clarkson argued that whites reduced

> again to slavery those negroes who had so honourably obtained their freedom. They hired them as servants, and, at the end of the stipulated time, refused payment of their wages, insisting that they were slaves: in some instances they destroyed their tickets of freedom, and then enslaved the negroes for want of them; in several instances, the unfortunate Africans were taken onboard vessels, carried to the West Indies, and there sold for the benefit of their plunderers.[63]

The line between Black servants and Black slaves was extremely fluid and could easily be transgressed and manipulated. Even those Blacks who were indentured servants were often treated as slaves and consistently faced the fear of being sold to the West Indies or elsewhere. To what extent did white Loyalists distinguish between an indentured Black servant and a Black slave? More importantly, did indentured Black servants and slaves see each other as having different statuses? Black servants and Black slaves ran away together sometimes from the same master. For example, South Carolina Loyalist Nathaniel Bullern arrived in Nova Scotia as the owner of 10 slaves. Among these slaves were Jupiter and Clarinda. At some point, Bullern seems to have freed one of them but kept the other as a slave. In 1784, in a Nova Scotian newspaper, Bullern complained about the loss of "TWO NEGRO[ES] (Jupiter and

Clarinda) – the Property of Mr. Nath. Bullern, the One an [indented] Servant, the Other a Slave."[64] In running away together, Jupiter and Clarinda saw their status as similar if not the same. Although one was a servant and the other enslaved, they were both part of a world of "unfreedom" and sought to escape together.[65]

Several court cases in Shelburne in the 1780s and 1790s show how easily Black people could fall victim to re-enslavement, but also the ways in which they could go to court, defeat attempts at re-enslavement, and achieve freedom. The first years after the Loyalist influx were, at best, confusing and complicated in terms of the changing status of free Black, Black servant, and Black slave. Runaway advertisements included Black indentured servants and Black servants, but were these people essentially enslaved? It would, of course, depend on their masters, but Black servants operated in a world where they could easily be sold as slaves to the United States or the West Indies. Were their lives any different than their enslaved brethren? Again, the answer varied by individual circumstance.

The Nature of Maritime Slavery

There are three aspects of Maritime slavery that readers must understand regarding slave ownership, the notion of family slavery, and the agency of enslaved people. First, slaveholding reached into most socioeconomic classes of white society with artisans, small business owners, women, and small farmers possessing one or two slaves. For example, Thomas Bean and John DeMill were both registered as carpenters in Saint John. DeMill owned one male slave in his 20s, while Bean possessed a young teenager named Keziah (or Kezzia).[66] The prominence of the middle and artisanal classes in the ranks of slaveholders should not mask the reality that slave ownership remained widespread among the political and economic elite in New Brunswick and Nova Scotia. For example, Virginian Stair Agnew brought slaves to New Brunswick, where he served as a judge on the Inferior Court of Common Pleas and in the House of Assembly for many years.[67] Joshua Upham came to New Brunswick from Massachusetts and owned slaves. He served on the province's Supreme Court.[68] Cairo and Bella accompanied their owner James Peters to New Brunswick. The recipient of several land grants, Peters became a member of the House of Assembly and a magistrate.[69] New York Loyalist Thomas Barclay – though he complained about his relative poverty in Nova Scotia – also held several prominent positions and owned a few slaves.[70] The provincial government granted slave owner General Timothy Ruggles an enormous amount of land in Nova Scotia.[71] The most important point about regional slaveholders is that they cut across white society from the likes of Lieutenant-Governor John Wentworth to cabinet maker William Black. And while the ownership of slaves was widespread, it was uneven throughout the region. Specifically, Prince Edward Island's slaveholders were almost all part of the local elite. In Nova Scotia and New Brunswick, however, slave ownership was much more common, with small farmers and artisans regularly possessing slaves; but the economically prosperous still made up the majority of owners.

One understudied group of slaveowners is white women in the Maritimes, some of whom owned their slaves outright while others possessed them through marriage. They participated actively in the system of Maritime slavery. Recent research focusing on slave-owning women in the American South has elicited numerous insights about these women. As historian Stephanie E. Jones-Rogers argues, "Slave-owning women invested in, and profited from their financial ties to, American slavery and its marketplace."[72] Jones-Rogers also notes that when "we listen to what enslaved people had to say about white women and slave mastery, we find that they articulated quite clearly their belief that slave-owning women governed their slaves in the same ways that white men did; sometimes they were more effective at slave management or they used more brutal methods of discipline than their husbands did."[73] These insights hold true for some slave-owning Maritime women.

The relationship between Susan Barclay and Mertilla Dixon demonstrates how slave-owning women most often treated enslaved or re-enslaved Black women. During the American Revolution, after abandoning her master in Virginia, Mertilla Dixon migrated to Charleston and eventually went "into Colonel Fanning's Service" but also ended up working for a series of well-known Loyalists, including the Winslow and Barclay families. Mrs. Barclay employed her in Nova Scotia, but Dixon absconded from this woman because she repeatedly "threatened to ship her to the West Indies, and there to dispose of her as a Slave, and being fully persuaded that she was to be put on board a vessel, then ready for Sea, she has (about a fortnight since) taken refuge with her father Charles Dixon, in Birchtown and prays Your Honor's Protection, until Major Barclay, can prove his claim."[74] The actions of Mrs. Barclay speak to how white women also participated in the system of slavery and attempted to re-enslave Black people who had already earned their freedom.

Second, the close proximity of Maritime slaves and their owners resulted in the same type of "family" bondage that typified slavery in New England and most parts of the Middle Colonies. Historians have identified several ideas that undergirded North American slavery, including "patriarchalism," paternalism, and family slavery.[75] Each of these forms of social control can be found among slaveholders in the Maritimes. During the eighteenth century, patriarchalism was an important part of slaveholding ideology – especially in the southern states and Jamaica – and was generally founded on the notion that the master served as a father figure to his slaves. Masters demanded that slaves obey them, but also sometimes recognized their obligation to "provide" for their slaves.

As Philip Morgan notes, this seemingly benevolent casting of the master's role should not hide the realities of what patriarchalism meant; this included "governance, authority, rigid control, adjudication, unswerving obedience, and severe discipline." Yet words of caring for slaves should not necessarily be dismissed because they sometimes represented an "authentic, if deeply flawed, worldview." In the late eighteenth and early nineteenth centuries, paternalism replaced patriarchalism, meaning "more reciprocity" and "less authoritarianism." It also emphasized a master's "kindness toward his slaves."[76] While some owners did express genuine caring for their slaves, the reality is best summed up in Adam Rothman's review essay in which he argues "What planters said they thought they were doing for their slaves bears only a faint resemblance to what they were actually doing to their slaves."[77]

The best example of this delusional thinking in the Maritime colonies is the former Royal Governor of New Hampshire John Wentworth's treatment of his slaves. In 1784, after migrating to Nova Scotia, he decided to send 19 slaves to Suriname. Although Wentworth seems to have owned the slaves only for a short period of time, he "earnestly" implored their intended master, his relative Paul Wentworth, to take "care" of his slaves. Wentworth almost seemed to express sadness in sending them to a brutal form of slavery, but this hardly stopped him from doing it:

> I am much interested for them, insomuch that I have had them christened, and would rather have liberated them, than sent them to any Estate, that I was not assured of them being treated with care and humanity, which I shall consider as the only favor that can be done to me on this Occasion.[78]

The notion of obligations could also be turned against slaveholders. When one Maritime slaveowner tried to free an elderly slave, the old man replied "Master you eated when I was meat, and now you must pick me when I'm bone."[79] Moreover, interactions between slave and owner could be marked by compromise, negotiation, and less authoritarianism. Maritime slaves realized this possibility and attempted to twist and turn every situation to their advantage. This does not mean they always or even usually succeeded in getting what they wanted, be it freedom or perhaps a marriage partner from another family, but the opportunity existed and many slaves seized it.

Family slavery is the best way to understand the relationships and close interactions among the vast majority of Maritime slaves and slaveholders. Black slaves worked next to their owners, ate with them, and slept in the same houses. This proximity made slaves part of the household and family they served.[80] In the Maritimes, both slaves and slaveholders were explicitly conscious of the notion of belonging to a family. For instance, a "sickly" slave named Dinah, on her way from New York to Nova Scotia, commented that she had "always been in the family" of her owner.[81] Dinah's words reflected an expectation that her master should provide for her medical care after years of service. In 1787, Thomas Lester's slaves and a hired Black labourer ran away from his home in Waterborough, New Brunswick. Lester wrote that his two slaves, Sam and Beller, were siblings and "raised in the family."[82] British officials described John Barbarie's slave Plato as having been "Born in the Captain's Family."[83]

The notion of belonging to a family does not mean that slavery in New England or the Maritime colonies was benevolent or mild. Maritime slaveholders exploited Black labour and regularly broke apart Black families no matter how long slaves had been members (though clearly inferior ones) of their owner's family. As the historian William Piersen has argued, "While the closeness of master and bondsmen often created ties of deep and abiding affection, the duty of one to rule and of the other to obey led to unavoidable frustrations for both, frustrations which constantly chafed the ideal of paternalistic harmony."[84] The intimate interactions between Maritime slaves and slave owners were contradictory and ran the gamut from expressions and acts of true affection and kindness to violent and sadistic outbursts.[85]

There are numerous examples of slaveholders attempting to bestow gifts on their slaves, usually manumission, money, clothing, or literacy in a will. Often, slaveholders' decisions to give their former slaves freedom or money took effect only after the owner died. One can look at these actions from a cynical perspective as self-serving actions under the guise of benevolent mastery or an attempt to save their souls. Some slaveholders simply wanted to avoid having to support slaves as they got older and calculated that manumission and a small financial gift would actually be cheaper than several years of old-age care for superannuated enslaved people. Yet this cynical view does not take into account the actual bonds of affection and alliance that could develop between slaves and their owners. During the American Revolution, Patriots forced Reverend John Wiswall from his home in present-day Maine. As he travelled to Nova Scotia, he wrote a letter to one of his relatives and implored "Remember me to Dinah." Wiswall noted that she could live "where she pleases" until he could send her another message. Wiswall also bluntly stated that he was "determined not to sell her to any Body."[86] In his will, Amherst, Nova Scotia, resident Stephen Reed told his sons to "comfortably take care" of his slaves "during their natural lives."[87]

In other cases, slaveowners appreciated long terms of service from their slaves and wanted to give them support after freeing them. In 1819, Prince Edward Islander William Schurman left detailed instructions for his former slave Susannah: "That my Negro Servant Susannah Schurman shall be provided for in the family for as long as she wishes to remain in the family with meat, drink and clothing as long as she lives, but if it be her choice to leave the family my will is to give her fifty pounds lawful money of this Island."[88] Susannah had the choice to enjoy her freedom with a decent sum of money or to remain in familiar circumstances where her "family" would care for her until she died. The danger, of course, was the possibility that one of Schurman's executors would not follow through with his instructions. Another slaveowner, Isaac Bonnell, wanted "My Black Boys George, Tom, and Bob" to be taught to read the Bible, write, and promised them "new cloaths of Every Description." He also promised to free them once they reached adulthood.[89] Thomas Leonard manumitted his slave Phillis and her daughter, and he also instructed his executors to give them "fifty pounds."[90] Without any conditions, widow Ann Cosby gave "my black Woman named Rose, a Molotto Girl named Agatha, and my black Man named John Bulkley ... their full Freedom."[91] These examples of one aspect of slave and slaveowner relations show that caring and bonds of affection could develop within the confines of Maritime family slavery. But examples of affection between whites and Blacks were always tainted by the coercion of slavery. And the instances of kindness unfortunately pale in comparison to problematic offers of freedom, incidents of breaking slave families apart, and acts of gross physical violence.

Although a few owners freed slaves outright in their wills, others preferred to attach strict conditions to the possibility of freedom. By doing so, an owner could retain an authoritarian control while pretending to make an offer of freedom that could be withdrawn at a moment's notice. In 1799 George Cornwall held out the prospect of eventual release from bondage but threatened to punish his slaves if they did not show their appreciation for his alleged kindness by working in an "honest and orderly" manner. "I give to Charity my beloved wife," Cornwall provided, "all my Negro Slaves [requiring?] her to manumit and set them free by her will after her decease, but in case they do not behave as honest and orderly servants, I wish she would sell them as undeserving of her or my intended bounty towards them."[92] Nearly 10 years later, Charity Cornwall still owned three adult male slaves.[93]

The term "family slavery" understandably might make some readers uncomfortable. In using it, there is no suggestion that somehow slaves were equal to or even decently treated members of the master's extended family. Historian Wendy Warren describes the relationship between slaves and owners as a form of "intimate slavery." She argues "enslaved people were dependent members of the English *household*. But they were not part of the colonial English family."[94] This was certainly the case between Maritime slaveholders and their slaves. So it is accurate to refer to the relationship between Maritime slaves and their owners as family slavery or intimate slavery only if we understand the limitations of these relationships. I suggest another phrase to describe the interactions of slaves and owners: close-quarters slavery. This means simply that slaves and owners in the Maritimes knew each other well. They spent hours around each other every single day. There was no escape for a slave in Nova Scotia who spent the entire day working on a farm with their owner, only to be called to cooking duty at night, and emptying a chamber pot at three in the morning. Whatever term historians use, we must acknowledge the range of experiences slaves had with their owners. As the biographical sketches in this book demonstrate, the intimate interactions between Maritime slaves and slaveowners were complicated.

Third, and most importantly, slaves were far from powerless. Not only did they regularly negotiate aspects of their bondage, but they also exerted their agency through absconding. This was often done to keep their families from being separated. Local records are full of instances of children removed from their parents' care. As such, it is not surprising that some slave families decided to flee rather than see themselves torn apart. At times, running away could be an attempt to reunite families, while some slave families escaped to leave a violent or otherwise difficult situation. Other reasons for leaving included mistreatment or forced sexual relations between a master and slave. These families escaped to retain some sense of control over their lives. They ran away as families because of the importance of these relationships. They would have had a better opportunity to escape and hide as individuals, yet they preferred to remain together as families even if this lessened their chance of gaining permanent freedom.

The Gradual Ending of Slavery

Although slavery was not protected by statute law in Nova Scotia and New Brunswick, the lack of legislation to formally end the institution is striking when compared to the emancipation laws that neighbouring regions enacted. Indeed, every New England state along with Pennsylvania, New York, and New Jersey had adopted immediate or gradual emancipation by 1804, while Prince Edward Island legislators did not repeal the 1781 Slave Baptism Act until 1825.[95] In the other parts of British North America, Upper and Lower Canada, slavery was slowly abolished judicially and legislatively. In the late 1790s, Chief Justice James Monk issued a series of decisions that made "slavery virtually untenable in Lower Canada."[96] In 1793 the Upper Canada legislature passed "An Act to Prevent the further introduction of SLAVES," which banned importation of slaves and freed the children of slaves once they reached the age of 25.

Nova Scotia and New Brunswick did not adopt gradual emancipation because neither colony had statute law, such as a slave code that protected slavery, and therefore most legislators deemed it unnecessary. By the late 1780s, slaveholders realized that the basis for their ownership of Black property might be tenuous without a slave code. They attempted on several occasions to have legislation passed that would have given slavery statutory recognition. These bills were usually dressed up in the garb of either regulating the free Black population or enacting gradual emancipation but, according to Barry Cahill, sought not to "regulate Black persons [but rather] to regularize Black slavery."[97] Each bill protected the property of slaveholders and confirmed ownership of "Negro Slaves." In Nova Scotia, there were unpassed bills in 1787, 1789, 1801 (an attempt to set up a commission), and 1808, while in New Brunswick the slaveholder and politician Stair Agnew tried unsuccessfully to push through similar legislation in 1801.[98] The 1801 New Brunswick bill and the 1801 and 1808 Nova Scotia bills proposed gradual emancipation in the Maritimes. They were blocked because the majority of legislators in these colonies did not want slaveowners to be able to use these bills to give legal grounds for slavery or to receive compensation for emancipated slaves. As David Bell argues, the 1801 New Brunswick bill was simply an "ill-disguised attempt to give direct legislative recognition to the existence of slavery."[99] This was also the intent of the Nova Scotian bills.

Although the influx of Loyalist slaveowners and their slaves greatly expanded and strengthened slavery, it left the institution vulnerable. The categories of "slave," "servant," and "free Black" became contingent and unstable. Nova Scotia and New Brunswick did not have statute law related to slavery, leaving a space for Black and white people to negotiate and understand the perimeters of slavery. Slaveholders regularly went to court to retrieve runaway slaves or to re-enslave free Blacks, while slaves went to court to challenge owners' rights to hold them in bondage. From the moment they stepped onto the shores of the Maritimes, slaves took an active role in obtaining their own freedom by running away or finding sympathetic whites willing to support their claims in court. Until the mid-1790s, Nova Scotian judges sometimes returned escaped slaves to their supposed owners.[100] Subsequently, chief justices Thomas Strange and S.S. Blowers made it nearly impossible for owners to prove they held legal title to their slaves. They both assiduously avoided a direct ruling against slavery generally, instead opting to make it exceedingly difficult for individual owners to prove they could legally own slaves. In an 1800 brief regarding a slave case in New Brunswick, Solicitor-General Ward Chipman explained how this process worked in Nova Scotia. He highlighted the ways in which Nova Scotia had gradually made slavery seem untenable, at least from the point of view of some owners. His explanation for Nova Scotia's slow legal action against slavery was based mainly on his correspondence with Blowers. Chipman observed

that the general question respecting the slavery of Negroes has been often agitated there in different ways, but has never received a direct decision; that although the Court there has avoided an adjudication of the principal point, yet as they required the fullest proof of the master's claim in point of fact, it has been generally found very easy to succeed in favor of the Negro, by taking some exception collateral to the general question, and, therefore, that course has been taken.[101]

Chipman also recounted the case of a Black woman who had been placed in jail and brought to the court on a writ of habeas corpus and freed. The owner protested and Blowers baited the master by encouraging him to "try the right." The master brought an action against "a person who had received and hired the wench." Although the slaveholder produced a bill of sale that demonstrated purchase in New York, the master could not "prove that the seller had a legal right to dispose of her." Blowers directed the jury to find for the defendant and they did so.[102]

In contrast, the conservative legal and political culture of New Brunswick ensured that judges upheld slavery or at least left it alone.[103] Historian David Bell suggests that its judges were protesting the intellectual tides of the early nineteenth century, as illustrated by Nova Scotia's judicial elimination of slavery, the growing agitation against the slave trade, and the adoption of gradual or immediate emancipation in most northern states. They believed that a class of gentlemen connected to the Crown should rule society. From this perspective, ending slavery signalled not progressive social policy but rather another step toward a state of anarchy where people did not accept their God-given places in society.[104] Slavery in New Brunswick did not end until the early 1820s because the judiciary did not follow the footsteps of Strange and Blowers in Nova Scotia.

Eventually, slavery ended in the Maritimes because slaves pushed back against their owners and won their freedom with the help of local anti-slavery whites. They were supported in this endeavour by an increasingly broad swath of the white Maritime population during the early nineteenth century. The majority of politicians and everyday people were not willing to give statute recognition to slavery. Moreover, sympathetic whites harboured runaways and willingly challenged slaveholders in court. The supporters of slavery became an ever smaller and more isolated group. By the early 1800s, well-known slaveowners such as Stair Agnew, Joseph Clarke, James DeLancey, Jesse Gray, and Caleb Jones simply did not represent the majority of opinion in the region. Others who were inclined to own slaves could leave the Maritimes for the West Indies or the United States. In many ways the ending of slavery can be seen as a positive example of Black–white cooperation, where humanitarian impulses played an important role in destroying slavery.

But the other reason slavery ended is economic. The use of free Black labour, which began in the 1780s and expanded during the next 25 years, made chattel bondage unnecessary. This eventual switch to cheap Black labour, though, should not be seen as inevitable or easy. For slaveholders, the loss of a capital asset that could be sold out of the region represented a serious financial hit. If slavery had ended suddenly, the loss of human property would have been catastrophic for a slaveholder's financial standing. Yet, as we know, slavery did not end suddenly but rather very gradually and slowly, which gave slaveowners plenty of time to devise other methods to still benefit from their slaves. First, they sold slaves out of the region to the West Indies or the United States, which simply continued a well-trodden path embraced by slaveholders for decades. Second, in substituting forms of indentured servitude for chattel slavery, former owners could still benefit from their Black servants during some of their best and most productive years. Slaveowners usually freed slaves when they reached their 20s and in some cases not until they were 30.[105] Slaveholders also hired out slaves to other residents, which gave the owners another revenue stream.[106] They continued, therefore, to exploit Black people even after they were offered conditional freedom.[107] From the perspective of slaveholders, free Black labour was not necessarily as good as slave labour, which they could sell, but eventually it did serve as a decent substitute for those who had previously owned slaves. Once slavery had disappeared from the region, Black labour could be further exploited through a system of gross inequities and racial discrimination free from the stain of slavery on the region. Free Blacks and Black indentured servants did similar forms of labour – multi-occupational work ranging from farm labour to carpentry – to that which slaves had done. In the final analysis, slavery gradually ended in the Maritimes because of Black agency and growing numbers of anti-slavery whites (including sympathetic judges).

Maritime Black Culture

The Maritimes were home to a broad range of Black culture. North American slaves employed their traditions and beliefs to fashion autonomous spaces of material, oral, and expressive community. Conscious of their African heritage, Maritime slaves forged a slave culture within the parameters of their white environment. In New Brunswick, one slaveowner noted that his runaway "attempts to play the VIOLIN."[108] Violins held an important place in American slave culture and were prevalent in parts of West Africa. According to historian Sterling Stuckey, the violin became "the most important instrument of slave musicians and important among northern slaves as well."[109] The presence of an enslaved Black person playing the violin directly connects Black culture in the Maritimes to the wider culture of African and African American slaves in the Atlantic world.

Most Loyalist slaves were either from New England or the Middle Colonies, and they brought their experiences and traditions with them to the Maritimes. Throughout these regions, cultural activities such as Negro Election Day and the Pinkster Festival gained popularity. These events were multiracial; Black and white people participated, and local newspapers commented on each event. On Negro Election Day slaves elected an individual among them to a ceremonial office, and although this post was unofficial the person elected often exercised real influence among the Black population. On the other hand, Pinkster (originally a Dutch religious holiday that could be a day of rest or used for religious ceremonies like baptism) encompassed several days of traditional African dancing, sporting events, and the crowning of a king.[110] Aspects of these activities accompanied northern slaves to the Maritimes and were termed "Negro Frolicks" in Shelburne, which hardly captures the cultural significance of these celebrations. These "Frolicks" were banned in 1785 for two possible reasons. First, the festivals were loud and gave rise to what officials perceived of as rowdy behaviour. Second, slaveowners realized that these celebrations could have been spaces for increased solidarity among slaves and free Blacks or sites where slaves made elaborate runaway plans. Whatever the case, these dances embodied deeply held religious and spiritual values and were an expression of African aesthetics – something that was also reinforced by the presence of free Blacks.

There are two other aspects of slave culture that deserve attention: slave clothing and baptism. In an important article, Shane White and Graham White demonstrate how slaves used clothing to appropriate "items of elite apparel" to display "an almost bewildering variety in slave apparel" and to carve out a "surprising degree of social and cultural space."[111] Runaway advertisements in the Maritimes, for example, show that slaves built their own cultural space by appropriating fancier clothing than usually afforded to slaves.[112] These clothes could have held status meanings not only for the wider society but also within the Black community. Apparel represented the property individual slaves had been able to accumulate. Slaves' clothing offered them control over their own bodies by fashioning for public view the image they wanted others to see. Maritime slaves also lived in a community with a substantial free Black population. Perhaps, through the use of certain clothing, slaves were attempting to project how they thought free Blacks should appear. For example, Dinah escaped from her owner Robert Wilkins wearing, "a blue and white Ticking Petticoat, a purple and white Callico short Gown, and an old blue Cloak."[113] In another advertisement, James Hayt provided a lengthy description of the clothes and physical appearance of slave Abraham: "A Run-Away negro boy, about 16 years of age – he had on a short blue jacket, with sleeves lined with white swan skin, a scarlet waistcoat, two rows bright buttons, with a collar, nankeen breeches, thread stockings, new shoes, plated buckles, and [an] all round black hat. – He has a pleasant countenance, is very talkative, tall of his age, but well proportioned, and formerly belonged to Capt. John Hall, of Saint Andrews."[114] The opportunity to gain some modicum of control over their bodies and appearance made the use of clothing a significant part of Black culture and slave self-expression.

Slaves were baptized throughout the Maritimes. The records of these baptisms are scattered throughout township and church records. For instance, in 1793 "Jane, Dinah, Samuel, Negro children property of B. Belcher Esq." were baptized.[115] Masters and slaves probably had varied and complicated understandings of baptism's meaning. Slaveholders probably baptized their slaves to follow the Great Commission of making disciples throughout the world (Matthew 28:18–20).[116] Yet like their American cousins, Maritime slaveholders could also have used parts of the New Testament to justify slaveholding and their exploitation of Black labour (Ephesians 6:5–7).[117] According to Albert Raboteau, slaves might have believed that "baptism would raise their status and lead eventually to freedom for their children, if not themselves."[118] At the same time, those slaves from Africa or with parents from Africa might have seen baptism in light of their own traditions; for some African societies, water and rivers held an important place in individuals' religious understanding and could have purifying or regenerative purposes. The meaning of baptism could also have been a way to negotiate for better treatment *within* the system of slavery. In being baptized, slaves were asserting their humanity by claiming to have a relationship with the very same God their owners worshipped.

Value of Slaves

The pricing of slaves in the Maritimes is difficult to assess. There are not nearly enough documents recording slave prices to offer anything approaching an overall estimate of the value of slaves. It also remains unclear why owners assigned slaves certain prices or offered varying rewards for runaway slaves. Most documents simply mention the value of a slave and sometimes sex and age, but rarely anything about skill level. It is also not always clear whether the currency listed is in sterling, Halifax currency, or another legal tender. According to Julian Gwyn, "the par value between Halifax currency and sterling was H£1.11 [Halifax pounds] to £1.00."[119] He adds that, during the late 1780s, a common labourer's daily wage in the Annapolis Valley was 75 cents.[120] Despite Gwyn's helpful context, any assessment of slave prices is impressionistic; but it does provide insight into how slaveowners valued their slaves. And in the various documents, ranging from estate inventories to bills of sales to rewards for runaways, the price of slaves varied tremendously. In May 1783, for example, John Wilson offered "Two Guineas" reward for his young escaped male slave.[121] Slightly over one year later, in July 1784, Frederick William Hecht offered "Five Guineas" reward for Hector, who was a cooper.[122] Most adults were valued at between £25 and £60, with the majority worth around £30 or £40. The prices of slave children ranged from £5 (in 1786) to at least £50 (in 1804).[123] In 1779, for instance, before the Loyalist influx, one 12-year-old male slave named Abram commanded the price of £50.[124] In an estate inventory from 1796, on the other hand, a Halifax slaveowner listed his "black girl" named Sary as worth £30.[125] In 1804 in Annapolis County, the estate of Robert Dickson sold eight-year-old Percilla for £17 to William Robertson.[126] Four years later, Sarah Allen sold 14-year-old Bacchus to Titus Knapp for £30. The price of adult slaves also varied drastically over time and it is not exactly clear why one slave was worth more than another. In 1786, Richard Betts's slave Jane was valued at £35, while 10 years later Bethaser Creamer's slave Mary was valued at £60. Creamer also listed his adult male slave Benjamin as worth £60. In 1802, Dr. Bond purchased Kate for £40.[127] These sums must be set within the contextual reality that the Maritimes experienced a postwar depression from 1784 to at least 1792.

A study of individual slave prices within a household is more revealing.[128] The 1786 inventory of Richard Betts listed four slaves and their values: Toney, Prince (or Primus), and Jane were listed as worth £35, while Harry was priced at £40. It is not clear why Harry was worth more money. Perhaps he was a skilled slave, or the other slaves were older or more troublesome from the owner's perspective. We do not know. The total value of Betts's inventory was about £1053, while the combined value of the slaves was £145.[129] Thus, slaves accounted for 13.77 per cent of the total wealth of his estate. Annapolis County resident Joseph Totten's 1788 inventory listed five slaves, including two adults and three children. Totten recorded the three children as being worth a total of £15, or £5 for each individual child. His "Negro Wench" was valued at £60, while a "Negro Boy" cost about £50. Totten noted that the currency he used was "New York Money" to the total of £125, which he converted to about £78. Taken together, they were worth more than half a lot of land he owned in the town of Annapolis, which he valued at £150.[130] The precise age of Totten's adult slaves or the skills they possessed are unknown.[131] Betts and Totten made their wills during an economic downturn, and this probably affected the appraisal of their slaves. Both men lived relatively nearby one another, with Betts at Granville and Totten at Annapolis Royal. The low value that Totten placed on his child slaves might be indicative of a general attitude among local slaveholders that they cost their owners money and might not become productive for several years.

Some estate inventories reveal that, except for actual real estate, slaves were usually worth more than other property (ranging from furniture to livestock). For example, Totten's horse, wagon, three cows, case of pistols, and one silver watch were worth a total of £46, much less than his slaves, whose combined value was about £78. In 1801, a Yarmouth slaveholder purchased a seven-year-old slave named Jack for £39.[132] In comparison, Stephen Reed's 1801 inventory lists four oxen and one heifer as worth £35.[133] In the late 1780s in Shelburne, Jesse Gray sold Mary Postell in the same town for 100 bushels of potatoes, and Benjamin Douglas purchased a 22-year-old female for £50 (Halifax currency) in another region of Nova Scotia. The prices of Loyalist slaves varied over time and place.[134]

Slavery, Sources, and the Methodological Problems of the Book of Negroes

Sources are always challenging for historians of slavery in the New World. We are quite often left documents written by slaveholders, government officials, and other white people who viewed slaves in a mostly disparaging light. Yet American slaves did leave some written and oral sources such as slave narratives and the Works Progress Administration (WPA) interviews of the 1930s.[135] Southern slaveowners left a rich trove of diaries, court records, letters, newspapers, and government documents that historians have used to carefully ferret out enslaved peoples' actions, aspirations, culture, and work patterns. Although slavery in the Maritimes is intimately connected to the experience of enslaved people in New England and other more southern colonies, there is far less documentation. Maritime historians do not have the source material available to scholars of American or Caribbean slavery, such as the papers of George Washington, the Butler Plantation Papers, Thomas Thistlewood's incredibly disturbing diary, or the *Southern Agriculturist*. The lack of documentation for enslaved people in the Maritimes is even more spartan than in neighbouring New England, where scholars may consult narratives of Venture Smith or James Mars. In the Maritimes, narratives of Black people focus on the lives of Black Loyalists or free Blacks such as Boston King or David George.[136] However, the petition of Black Loyalist Thomas Peters discusses the plight of his enslaved counterparts.[137] Two enslaved people, Zimri Armstrong and Isaac Willoughby, petitioned the government in 1785 and 1834 respectively. Armstrong described how a white family had re-enslaved him, while Willoughby outlined the history of his family's enslavement and asked the government for financial support.[138] And in contrast to New England, where there is copious documentation especially about well-known female slaves such as Phillis Wheatley and Elizabeth Freeman, the Maritime archive silences the experiences of Black women. Maritime sources do regularly hint at the relationship between slaveholders and enslaved Black people, but there is no equivalent to Rhode Island master James McSparran's records or Connecticut slaveowner Joshua Hempstead's decades-long diary detailing his relationship with his slaves.[139] Maritime scholars of slavery must carefully examine existing sources to understand the lives of everyday slaves.

Since the archive silences the experiences of slave women specifically and enslaved Black people generally,[140] scholars must read sources meticulously and against the grain to recover the history of individual slaves to understand the complex everyday lives and motives of slaves. In the Maritimes, without the benefit of sources like Hempstead's diary, scattered documentation must be pieced together, including runaway slave advertisements, slave for sale notices, government sources, bills of sale, court proceedings, probate records, and church documents. These sources can be supplemented with township books and oral traditions, which were recorded in the late nineteenth and early twentieth centuries. The major drawback to these sources is the lack of enslaved Black voices, which can be difficult to glean unless carefully ferreted out through a white intermediary. The few times we can hear slave voices – in court records, diaries, or oral traditions – are extraordinarily enticing, but they offer somewhat limited glimpses into what slaves thought or said. One way to recover the ideas, thoughts, and feelings of Maritime slaves is through their actions and interactions with slaveowners, the court system, and each other. These are hardly perfect sources, but they do say much about what slaves faced and how they attempted to better their lives.

Perhaps the most important source we have in trying to piece together Black lives and voices is the Book of Negroes, a listing by British officials of the names and places of origins of free and enslaved Black Americans who were evacuated to Nova Scotia from New York during the spring and autumn of 1783.[141] But this magnificent source must be treated with great care and trepidation. It does not, for instance, come even close to listing the total number of slaves who came to the Maritimes with their Loyalist owners. The enslaved people of Caleb Jones and James DeLancey, for example, who both owned about five or six slaves each, are not listed in the Book of Negroes. The slaves that southern Loyalists brought up to the region from East Florida are also not included. [142] In addition, the Book of Negroes is not simply a record of free Blacks and Loyalist slaves; it also contains hints about how Black people were easily re-enslaved before they arrived in the Maritimes or once they got there. The sliding scales of slavery and freedom defy and challenge historians to acknowledge these textured and multilayered experiences of free Blacks and slaves. The line between Black slaves and Black servants, for instance, could be ambiguous and easily manipulated. During the evacuation of New York, British officials noted that Samuel Ives had been "sold to Captain Grayson by Jonathan Eilbeck of New York who it does not appear had any right to sell him as he was the property [of] Capt. Talbot of Virginia from whence he was brought by the troops 5 years ago and had a pass from Sir Henry Clinton which Mr. Eilbeck destroyed."[143]

As discussed earlier, whites regularly attempted to re-enslave free Blacks in the Maritimes, as the court records in Shelburne make abundantly clear. And even the possession of a General Birch Certificate (GBC) could not guarantee a Black person's protection from re-enslavement. In 1787, a free Black named Dick Hill had been unlawfully placed onboard a schooner to be sent to the West Indies as a slave. Hill, incredibly, had a GBC, and even though Shelburne officials sent a letter to Captain McDonald warning him "you must therefore not take this Negro away ... as you will be answerable in case the Negro is taken away" the records indicate "the [vessel] was got underway and almost out of the Harbour."[144]

Another aspect of this problem is that the Book of Negroes listed free Blacks as being in the "possession" of a white Loyalist even if they had a GBC.[145] As a result of all of these factors, free Black people were incredibly vulnerable to re-enslavement or the loss of their freedom. So, it is not accurate to see those listed as free in the Book of Negroes as truly free or forever free. Their freedom was tenuous at best and could be taken away at any instance.

This problem of re-enslavement or loss of freedom is poignantly illustrated in the story of Thomas Rogers's "Negroes," who each held a GBC that should have guaranteed their freedom. Less than a year after their arrival, Rogers placed an unusually lengthy runaway notice complaining about the loss of his "Negroes," who he described as "belonging to the subscriber." The runaway advertisement demonstrates the lengths that escaped unfree people were willing to go to obtain their freedom:

> HARBOURED, or otherwise CONCEALED. THE following Negroes belonging to the subscriber, viz. Edward Morris, an elderly negro about five feet five inches high, by trade a mason, has a remarkable wound in his forehead which shews a hole resembling a bullet shot, is a celebrated methodist preacher among the negroes, was bred at Fairfield in Connecticut; also Charity his wife, a half bred Indian of the tribe on Long Island, province of New York, and a small boy about seven years of age, son of the said wench by an Indian father. Andrew Bush, a comely stout negro, remarkable high forwarded, generally called the Widow's Peek, formerly the property of Doctor Bush, in Connecticut, is a remarkable *good miller*, which practice he has been used all his life to, also his wife Eanus, a yellow mustee [octoroon or a person of mixed ancestry]. And, Peter Cock, a young negro, comely countenance.[146]

Thomas Rogers continued his runaway notice with a long accusatory epistle about runaway servants and slaves. He identified one of the major difficulties facing Loyalist slaveholders, stating that "for the better security of indented servants, slaves, &c there [should be] a law of the province enacting that any person harbouring, concealing, or otherwise encouraging indented servants, apprentices or slaves from their master or their service, for every such offence shall forfeit the sum of ten pounds, &c." The problem, as Rogers saw it, rested on New Brunswick's failure to have enacted laws preventing local residents from protecting fugitive slaves and runaway indentured servants. Rogers also noted that "a certain Mr. Dibble, has encouraged some of the aforesaid servants." Dibble apparently had told Rogers's unfree Black servants to lodge a complaint with local magistrates "to have them liberated," but it failed mostly due to John Coffin, who "judiciously" decided in Rogers's favour. Without question, Edward Morris, his wife, and the other unfree labourers were quite capable of wanting their freedom without encouragement from Dibble, but certainly his help would have been appreciated. Rogers claimed that Dibble had enticed his "indebted" servants away "under pretense of purchasing them, but which [Rogers] ... informs him, [Mr.?] Dibble, that he will not have any bargain, or other negociation whatever touching the above servants, with him, and hereby once more forwarns him from farther harbouring, concealing, or otherwise said negroes from returning to their duty."[147]

Although each of these runaways had GBCs, which guaranteed their freedom, Rogers claimed that they were unfree labourers.[148] In less than one year from their arrival in New Brunswick, they had gone from being listed in the Book of Negroes as free Black Loyalists with GBCs to unfree indentured servants, and the next step easily could have been enslavement (if they were not already being treated as slaves). Reflecting on white treatment of free Blacks, Black American Baptist preacher David George noted that "White people in Nova Scotia" had "treated many of us as bad as though we (free Blacks) had been slaves."[149] Edward Morris, his wife Charity, their child Peter Cock, Andrew Bush, and his wife had lost their freedom and were being treated, as David George noted, like slaves despite their legal status as free. They absconded from Rogers because he had deprived them of their freedom and planned to do worse, such as break up their families through sale. Perhaps these people realized that they were about to be re-enslaved by an unscrupulous master or sold to the West Indies, and this is precisely why they absconded as a group. It was also rather common for white Loyalists not to pay wages they owed to Black workers – in effect re-enslaving them.

It is certainly plausible that Thomas Rogers had turned his free Black servants into de facto slaves by not paying any wages, and this might have resulted in their decision to abscond. Another possible reason behind their escape is that Rogers might have taken and sold some of their children. Charity Morris had three children when she left New York in 1783.[150] But by May 1784, the runaway notice only mentions one of her children with Edward Morris. What happened to the other two? Had they died earlier in the winter or had Rogers illegally sold them to the West Indies? Black children were at extreme risk for re-enslavement, and without the intervention of the local authorities they could easily be sold to the West Indies. Another example of this process occurred in November 1791 when two young Black boys faced re-enslavement by their alleged owners, whom they regarded as having no right to their service as slaves. In the first case, a Black woman named Susannah Connor "came here personally into Court" and complained that John Harris intended to take her son out of the province. Her son (Robert Gemmel or Gammel) worked as Harris's indentured apprentice. The court ordered Harris to come in immediately and answer for his alleged plans. Harris readily admitted that he planned to leave the province, but claimed that the only reason he planned to take the boy was because there were no other available owners to teach Gemmel the art of butchery. The court cancelled the indenture. If Susannah Connor had not intervened on behalf of her son, Gemmel would have been taken out of the province – to the United States or elsewhere – and no doubt enslaved. In the other case, a sympathetic local citizen told the court that Timothy Mahan "detains, a Negro Boy, who he hath attempted to sell, and Dispose of, without having property therein." The court ordered Mahan to appear before it along with the five-year-old John Simmons. Mahan claimed that Simmons's parents had given him the boy three years earlier. The court found that Mahan had treated the child "kindly, and humanely," but ruled that Simmons's parents had no right to give him away and Mahan had no "property in the said Boy." What is unclear is whether Mahan originally stole the child from his parents, as saying they gave the child to him was certainly a convenient answer. Nevertheless, the boy escaped sale to another owner. The cases of Robert Gemmel, John Simmons, and Charity Morris's children underline the tenuous nature of the line between slavery and freedom that Black people faced in the Maritimes, even – and perhaps especially – if they were small children.[151]

In escaping from Rogers, his "servants" were asserting their freedom and autonomy. Rogers's runaway advertisement also illuminates the problematic nature of using the Book of Negroes uncritically. According to it, some of Rogers's "Negroes" should have been guaranteed their freedom through the possession of a General Birch Certificate, but they clearly lost what little freedom they might have had in New Brunswick. Without Rogers's runaway advertisement, historians would likely not know that these people possessed freedom certificates yet were actually re-enslaved. Slaves and indentured Black servants regularly married and ran away together, underlining the similarity of their status and the dangerous situation they confronted in a society that sometimes allowed their sale to the West Indies. The prevention of Black people being sold out of the region as slaves depended almost wholly on the government's willingness to enforce certain laws and Black people's ability to escape and find sustenance among other free people of African descent or anti-slavery whites. The Book of Negroes is one of the best sources for early North American history and historiography, but it must be treated with great care as it represents not an end point or final say about an individual; rather, it documents many individual lives that must be carefully traced (if possible) to truly understand what happened to them once they arrived in the Maritimes.

A Note on the Biographical Entries

This book is not inclusive of every slave who lived in the Maritimes. Historians will continue to find bills of sale, probate records, and other sources that will add more names. Yet it is the most complete listing of enslaved Black people in the Maritimes to date. The many nameless slaves mentioned in this book present a methodological issue. It is possible that some of them have been counted twice. It is also possible that many enslaved people are forever lost to history because a bill of sale was not preserved or an individual slave did not get baptized or become the subject of a runaway slave advertisement. What we know about Maritime slavery is fragmentary, sometimes resting on a runaway notice or brief mention in a diary. The place of origin of many of these slaves is not completely clear. Sometimes we only find a reference to where a slave came from right before settling in the Maritimes. In other words, a slave who lived in New York for 10 years before coming to Saint John might have been born in the West Indies or Africa or South Carolina. Despite these challenges, the evidence of slave life presented in this book far outweighs the absence of evidence.[152]

Before readers delve into this biographical dictionary, it is essential to understand the humanity of these enslaved people. The system of slavery was inhumane, exploitative, and exceedingly brutal. It turned human beings into commodities, undeserving of even the most basic form of human dignity. One must never underestimate the fear and violence that formed the basis of slavery. Yet it is a mistake to assume that enslaved people had no agency or ability to determine certain aspects of their lives. To put it bluntly, slaves had cards that they could play against their owners. They rarely had good cards to play, but that did not mean they could never win a hand. Maritime slaves had agency in their dealings with individual owners. They could run away, demand better treatment, work listlessly until given what they wanted, and negotiate their own freedom. Although it is easy to imagine all slaves as having had the same experiences and as having been passive victims, this biographical dictionary tells a different story.

NOTES

1   Book of Negroes, Sir Guy Carleton Papers, RG 1, Nova Scotia Archives (NSA), Halifax; for an online version, see https://novascotia.ca/archives/africanns /BN.asp.

2   Loyalists from Saint Augustine bound to Chedabucto, July 1784, Chipman Papers, Muster Master General's Office, Loyalist Musters, MG 23, D 1, ser. I, vol. 24, NSA. This document spells the last name as Lysle, but it is most likely Lyle; see Harriet Cunningham Hart, *History of the County of Guysborough, Nova Scotia* (1877; repr. Guysborough: Guysborough Historical Society, 2016), 250–2. Liberty's relationship to Sarah and Pegg is not clear.

3   In using the term "Black Atlantic," I mean the overlapping experiences of Black people that transcended national boundaries and borders along the Atlantic Ocean. The emphasis is on placing the history of Black people in a broader Atlantic context rather than one based in national or imperial boundaries. In the Black

Atlantic, as a result of the Atlantic slave trade, people of African descent trans-
mitted culture, language, traditions, labour experiences, and eventually resistance
to slavery from various points on the African coast to diverse slave societies in
the New World. The classic study on this subject is Paul Gilroy, *The Black Atlantic: Modernity and Double Consciousness* (Cambridge: Harvard University Press,
1993). For an important Canadian perspective, see Winfried Siemerling, *The Black
Atlantic Reconsidered: Black Canadian Writing, Cultural History, and the Presence
of the Past* (Montreal and Kingston: McGill-Queen's University Press, 2015).

4 Paul Lovejoy, "Biography as Source Material: Towards a Biographical Archive of
Enslaved Africans," in *Source Material for Studying the Slave Trade and the Afri-
can Diaspora: Papers from a Conference of the Centre of Commonwealth Studies,
University of Stirling, April 1996* (Stirling, UK: University of Stirling, 1996), 119.

5 Although the vast majority of individuals in this book were slaves, a few of them
either suffered re-enslavement or were free people who were married to slaves (or
the free children of slaves). I also included the story of a free Black man named
Pero who laboured for a slave owner named Jesse Gray, a southern Loyalist who
settled in Nova Scotia. During his employment, Gray severely beat Pero with 100
lashes. Despite being technically free, Pero was treated little better than his enslaved brethren. Gray's actions were so outrageous that local authorities charged
him, but the grand jury refused to indict him; see *R v. Gray*, November 9, 1786,
Shelburne, RG 60, vol. 27, no. 27.2, NSA.

6 On Indigenous biographies, see Robert S. Grumet, ed., *Northeastern Indian Lives,
1632–1816* (Amherst: University of Massachusetts Press, 1996).

7 Marcel Trudel, *Canada's Forgotten Slaves: Two Centuries of Bondage*, trans.
George Tombs (Montreal: Vehicule Press, 2013).

8 The study of regional slavery has grown tremendously in the last 30 years. These
works include, but are not limited to, the following: Franco Paz and Harvey Amani Whitfield, "On the Edge of Freedom: The Re-enslavement of Elizabeth Watson
in Nova Scotia," in *In Search of Liberty: African American Internationalism in the
Nineteenth-Century Atlantic World*, eds. Ronald Angelo Johnson and Ousmane K.
Power Greene (Athens: University of Georgia Press, 2021), 17–39; Harvey Amani Whitfield, "White Archives, Black Fragments: Problems and Possibilities in
Telling the Lives of Enslaved Black People in the Maritimes," *Canadian Historical
Review* 101, no. 3 (September 2020): 322–45; Harvey Amani Whitfield, ed., *Black
Slavery in the Maritimes: A History in Documents* (Peterborough, ON: Broadview
Press, 2018); Catherine M.A. Cottreau-Robins, "Exploring the Landscape of Slav-
ery in Loyalist Era Nova Scotia," in *The Consequences of Loyalism: Essays in Honor
of Robert M. Calhoon*, eds. Rebecca Brannon and Joseph S. Moore (Columbia:
University of South Carolina Press, 2019), 122–34; Harvey Amani Whitfield,
"Runaway Advertisements and Social Disorder in the Maritimes: A Preliminary Study," in *Violence, Order, and Unrest: A History of British North America,
1749–1876*, eds. Elizabeth Mancke et. al. (Toronto: University of Toronto Press,

2019), 214–35; Afua Cooper, "'Deluded and Ruined': Diana Bastian – Enslaved African Canadian Teenager and White Male Privilege," *Brock Education Journal* 27 (2017): 26–34; Harvey Amani Whitfield, "The African Diaspora in Atlantic Canada: History, Historians, and Historiography," *Acadiensis* 46, no. 1 (Winter/ Spring 2017): 213–32; Harvey Amani Whitfield, *North to Bondage: Loyalist Slavery in the Maritimes* (Vancouver: University of British Columbia Press, 2016); Catherine Cottreau-Robins, "Searching for the Enslaved in Nova Scotia's Loyalist Landscape," *Acadiensis* 43, no. 1 (Winter/Spring, 2014): 125–36; Catherine (Katie) Cottreau-Robins, "The Loyalist Plantation: An Interdisciplinary Approach to Early African-Nova Scotian Settlement," *Journal of the Royal Nova Scotia Historical Society* 17 (2014): 32–56; Ken Donovan, "Slavery and Freedom in Atlantic Canada's African Diaspora: Introduction," *Acadiensis* 43, no. 1 (Winter/Spring 2014): 109–115; Heather MacLeod-Leslie, "Archaeology and Atlantic Canada's African Diaspora," *Acadiensis* 43, no. 1 (Winter/Spring, 2014): 137–45; Ken Donovan, "Female Slaves as Sexual Victims in Île Royale," *Acadiensis* 43, no. 1 (Winter/ Spring, 2014): 147–56; Jennifer Harris, "Black Life in a Nineteenth Century New Brunswick Town," *Journal of Canadian Studies* 46, no. 1 (Winter 2012): 138–66; Harvey Amani Whitfield, "The Struggle over Slavery in the Maritime Colonies," *Acadiensis* 41, no. 2 (Summer/Autumn 2012): 17–44; Harvey Amani Whitfield, "Slavery in English Nova Scotia," *Journal of the Royal Nova Scotia Historical Society* 13 (2010): 23–40; Harvey Amani Whitfield and Barry Cahill, "Slave Life and Slave Law in Colonial Prince Edward Island, 1769–1825," *Acadiensis* 38, no. 2 (Summer/Autumn, 2009): 29–51; Harvey Amani Whitfield, "Black Loyalists and Black Slaves in Maritime Canada," *History Compass* 5, no. 6 (November 2007): 1980–97; Kenneth Donovan, "Slaves and Their Owners in Île Royale, 1713–1760," *Acadiensis* 25, no. 1 (Autumn 1995): 3–32; Kenneth Donovan, "A Nominal List of Slaves and Their Owners in Île Royale, 1713–1760," *Nova Scotia Historical Review* 16 (1996): 151–62; Kenneth Donovan, "Slaves in Île Royale, 1713–1758," *French Colonial History* 5 (2004): 25–42; D.G. Bell, "Slavery and the Judges of Loyalist New Brunswick," *University of New Brunswick Law Journal*, 31 (1982): 9–42; Barry Cahill, "Habeas Corpus and Slavery in Nova Scotia: *R v. Hecht, ex parte Rachel*, 1798," *University of New Brunswick Law Journal*, 44 (1995): 179–209; Barry Cahill, "Slavery and the Judges of Loyalist Nova Scotia," *University of New Brunswick Law Journal*, 43 (1994): 73–135; Robin W. Winks, *The Blacks in Canada: A History* (New Haven: Yale University Press, 1971); W.A. Spray, *The Blacks in New Brunswick* (Fredericton: Brunswick Press, 1972); T.W. Smith, "The Slave in Canada," *Collections of the Nova Scotia Historical Society*, 10 (1899): 1–161; and I. Allen Jack, "The Loyalists and Slavery in New Brunswick," *Proceedings of the Royal Society of Canada* 4 (1898): 137–85. Dalhousie University and King's College both committed to uncovering their histories with slavery, and I helped out with some of the research; see https://www.dal.ca/dept/ldp/findings.html and https://ukings .ca/administration/public-documents/slavery-scholarly-inquiry. Generally, on the growth and development of Black history in the Maritimes, see Suzanne Morton and Donald Wright, "Black History in Atlantic Canada: A Bibliography," *Acadiensis: Journal of the History of the Atlantic Region*, 50 (Spring 2021): 223–275.

 9 Randy J. Sparks, *Africans in the Old South: Mapping Exceptional Lives across the Atlantic World* (Cambridge: Harvard University Press, 2016), 4; see also Sigurdur Gylfi Magnusson, "What Is Microhistory?" *History News Network*, https://historynewsnetwork.org/article/23720.

10 Simon Newman, *A New World of Labor: The Development of Plantation Slavery in the British Atlantic* (Philadelphia: University of Pennsylvania Press, 2013), 3. In using the phrase "British Atlantic world," I mean the connections of trade and migration between the Americas, Africa, and Britain that linked Britain, its colonies, and other trading outposts.

11 R.G.S. Carter, "Of Things Said and Unsaid: Power, Archival Silences, and Power in Silence," *Archivaria* 61 (Spring 2006): 215–33; David Thomas, Simon Fowler, and Valerie Johnson, *The Silence of the Archive* (London: Facet Publishing, 2017).

12 Eve M. Kahn, "New Databases Offer Insights Into the Lives of Escaped Slaves," *New York Times*, February 18, 2016, https://www.nytimes.com/2016/02/19/arts/design/new-databases-offer-insights-into-the-lives-of-escaped-slaves.html?searchResultPosition=1; Slave Biographies, http://history.msu.edu/research/projects/data-archives/slave-biographies; SHADD Biography Project, http://www.tubmaninstitute.ca/the_shadd_collection; Runaway Slaves in Britain, https://www.runaways.gla.ac.uk; Freedom on the Move, http://freedomonthemove.org; and also on Facebook Live, May 4, 2018: "The Study of Slavery and Abolition in the Digital Age," Gilder Lehrman Center for the Study of Slavery, Resistance, and Abolition, https://www.facebook.com/GilderLehrmanCenter/videos/the-glc-presents-the-study-of-slavery-and-abolition-in-the-digital-age-part-2/1036696489815929; https://enslaved.org.

13 Brett Rushforth, *Bonds of Alliance: Indigenous and Atlantic Slaveries in New France* (Chapel Hill: University of North Carolina Press, 2012), 13.

14 On runaway advertisements and how historians have used them, see Shane White, "The Allure of the Advertisement: Slave Runaways in and around New York City," *Journal of the Early Republic* 41, no. 4 (December 2020): 611–33; Harvey Amani Whitfield, "Runaway Advertisements and Social Disorder in the Maritimes: A Preliminary Study," in *Violence, Order, and Unrest: A History of British North America, 1749–1876*, eds. Elizabeth Mancke et. al. (Toronto: University of Toronto Press, 2019), 214–35; Antonio T. Bly, *Escaping Bondage: A Documentary History of Runaway Slaves in Eighteenth-Century New England, 1700–1789* (Lanham, MD: Lexington, 2013); John Hope Franklin and Loren Schweninger, *Runaway Slaves: Rebels on the Plantation* (Oxford: Oxford University Press, 1999); Billy G. Smith, "Black Women Who Stole Themselves in Eighteenth-Century America," in *Inequality in Early America*, eds. Carla Gardina Pestana and Sharon V. Salinger (Lebanon, NH: University Press of New England,

1999), 134–59; David Waldstreicher, "Reading the Runaways: Self-Fashioning, Print Culture, and Confidence in Slavery in the Eighteenth-Century Mid-Atlantic," *William and Mary Quarterly* 56, no. 2 (1999): 243–72; Amani Marshall, "'They Will Endeavor to Pass for Free': Enslaved Runaways' Performances of Freedom in Antebellum South Carolina," *Slavery and Abolition* 31, no. 2 (2010): 161–80; Amani Marshall, "'They Are Supposed To Be Lurking About The City': Enslaved Women Runaways in Antebellum Charleston," *South Carolina Historical Magazine* 115, no. 3 (2014): 188–212.

15 *Weekly Chronicle*, March 15, 1794. In this context, "likely" meant that the slave was likely to be profitable.

16 *Royal Gazette*, July 4, 1786.

17 Vincent Carretta, *Equiano, the African: Biography of a Self-Made Man* (New York: Penguin, 2005); Vincent Carretta, *Phillis Wheatley: Biography of a Genius in Bondage* (Athens: University of Georgia Press, 2011); James H. Sweet, *Domingos Alvares, African Healing, and the Intellectual History of the Atlantic World* (Chapel Hill: University of North Carolina Press, 2011).

18 Lisa A. Lindsay and John Wood Sweet, eds., *Biography and the Black Atlantic* (Philadelphia: University of Pennsylvania Press, 2013); Jon F. Sensbach, *Rebecca's Revival: Creating a Black Christianity in the Atlantic World* (Cambridge: Harvard University Press, 2005); Clifton Crais and Pamela Scully, *Sara Baartman and Hottentot Venus: A Ghost Story and a Biography* (Princeton: Princeton University Press, 2009); Robin Law and Paul Lovejoy, *The Biography of Mahommah Gardo Baquaqua: His Passage from Slavery to Freedom in the Atlantic World* (Princeton: Markus Weiner, 2001). On history and biography, see "*AHR* Roundtable: Historians and Biography," *American Historical Review* 144, no. 3 (June 2009): 573–661. An excellent recent example written for a popular and academic audience is Ibram X. Kendi and Keisha N. Blain, eds., *Four Hundred Souls: A Community History of African America, 1619–2019* (New York: One World, 2021).

19 Carlo Ginzbburg, *The Cheese and the Worms: The Cosmos of a Sixteenth Century Miller* (New York: Penguin Books, 1982), xx, cited in Sparks, *Africans*, 3.

20 Donovan, "Slavery and Freedom in Atlantic Canada's African Diaspora," 110.

21 Whitfield, "African Diaspora in Atlantic Canada," 213–32. On the difficulty of counting slaves in the Maritimes, see discussion later in this introduction.

22 John Johnston, "Research Note: Mathieu Da Costa along the Coasts of Nova Scotia: Some Possibilities," *Journal of the Royal Nova Scotia Historical Society* 4 (2001): 152–64.

23 Kenneth Donovan estimates that slaves represented about 3 per cent of the population of Louisbourg, the capital of Île Royale; see Donovan, "Slaves in Île Royale, 1713–1758," 27. Ninety per cent of Île Royale slaves were Black, while 10 per cent were Indigenous. We do not know very much about Indigenous slavery in the Maritimes aside from Donovan's important work, but also see the pathbreaking article by Ruma Chopra, "Maroons and Mi'kmaq in Nova Scotia, 1796–1800,"

Acadiensis 46, no. 1 (Winter/Spring 2017): 5–23; on Indigenous slavery in Canada broadly, see Brett Rushforth, *Bonds of Alliance: Indigenous and Atlantic Slaveries in New France* (Chapel Hill: University of North Carolina Press, 2012) and Allan Greer, *Property and Dispossession: Natives, Empires, and Land in Early Modern North America* (Cambridge: Cambridge University Press, 2018).

24 Donovan, "Slaves and Their Owners in Île Royale, 1713–1760," 3–32; Donovan, "Nominal List of Slaves and Their Owners in Île Royale, 1713–1760," 151–62; Donovan, "Slaves in Île Royale, 1713–1758," 25–42; Donovan, "Female Slaves as Sexual Victims in Île Royale," 147–56.

25 Letter from Governor Cornwallis about Captain Bloss, RG 1, vol. 35, doc. 25, NSA. Ken Donovan notes that a schooner brought nine slave men, the property of Captain Bloss, to Nova Scotia from Antigua; see Donovan, "Slaves in Île Royale, 1713–1758," 32.

26 *Boston Post Boy*, September 23, 1751; *Boston Post Boy*, August 8, 1750. It is clear that Captain Bloss and Benjamin Hallowell knew each other.

27 *Halifax Gazette*, May 30, 1752.

28 From her preliminary research, historian Karolyn Smardz Frost argues that there may have been as many as 200 Planter slaves (private conversation, February 26, 2015, Wolfville, NS).

29 Harold A. Innis, ed., *The Diary of Simeon Perkins, 1766–1780* (Toronto: Champlain Society, 1948), 143.

30 T. Stephen Henderson and Wendy G. Robicheau, eds., *Nova Scotia Planters in the Atlantic World, 1759–1830* (Fredericton: Acadiensis Press, 2012); Lucille H. Campey, *Planters, Paupers, and Pioneers: English Settlers in Atlantic Canada* (Toronto: Dundurn Press, 2010); George Rawlyk and Gordon T. Stewart, *A People Highly Favoured of God: The Nova Scotia Yankees and the American Revolution* (Toronto: Macmillan, 1972); Margaret Conrad, ed., *Making Adjustments: Change and Continuity in Planter Nova Scotia, 1759–1800* (Fredericton: Acadiensis Press, 1991); Margaret Conrad and Barry Moody, eds., *Planter Links: Community and Culture in Colonial Nova Scotia* (Fredericton: Acadiensis Press, 2001); Margaret Conrad, ed., *They Planted Well: New England Planters in Maritime Canada* (Fredericton: Acadiensis Press, 1988); Margaret Conrad, ed., *Intimate Relations: Family and Community in Planter Nova Scotia, 1759–1800* (Fredericton: Acadiensis Press, 1995).

31 Whitfield, *North to Bondage*, 19–35.

32 *Saint John Gazette*, July 15, 1784.

33 Whitfield, *North to Bondage*, 36–45.

34 Anna Lillie, 1789, Halifax County, RG 48, Probate Records, NSA.

35 Caleb Fowler, 1793, Annapolis County, RG 48, Probate Records, NSA.

36 On slave work in New England and the North more broadly, see Jared Hardesty, *Black Lives, Native Lands, White Worlds: A History of Slavery in New England* (Amherst: University of Massachusetts Press, 2019); Allegra di Bonaventura, For

Adam's Sake: A Family Saga in Colonial New England (New York: W.W. Norton, 2013); Christy Clark-Pujara, *Dark Work: The Business of Slavery in Rhode Island* (New York: New York University Press, 2016); Jared Hardesty, *Unfreedom: Slavery and Dependence in Eighteenth-Century Boston* (New York: New York University Press, 2016); Jared Hardesty, "'The Negro at the Gate': Enslaved Labor in Eighteenth-Century Boston," *New England Quarterly* 87, no. 1 (March 2014): 72–98; C.S. Manegold, *Ten Hills Farm: The Forgotten History of Slavery in the North* (Princeton: Princeton University Press, 2010); William D. Piersen, *Black Yankees: The Development of an Afro-American Subculture in Eighteenth-Century New England* (Amherst: University of Massachusetts Press, 1988); Lorenzo J. Greene, *The Negro in Colonial New England* (1942; reprint New York: Atheneum, 1968); Ira Berlin, *Many Thousands Gone: The First Two Centuries of Slavery in North America* (Cambridge: Harvard University Press, 1998), 177–94; Robert K. Fitts, *Inventing New England's Slave Paradise: Master/Slave Relations in Eighteenth-Century Narragansett, Rhode Island* (New York: Garland, 1998); Joanne P. Melish, *Disowning Slavery: "Race" and Gradual Emancipation in New England* (Ithaca, NY: Cornell University Press, 1998); 1–49; and Peter Benes, ed., *Slavery/Antislavery in New England – The Dublin Seminar for New England Folklife Annual Proceedings, 2003* (Boston: Boston University, 2005).

37 John G. Reid, *Essays on Northeastern North America, Seventeenth and Eighteenth Centuries* (Toronto: University of Toronto Press, 2008); see also the various essays in Stephen J. Hornsby and John G. Reid, eds., *New England and the Maritime Provinces: Connections and Comparisons* (Montreal and Kingston: McGill-Queen's University Press, 2005).

38 Graeme Wynn, "1800–1810: Turning the Century," in *The Atlantic Region to Confederation: A History*, eds. Phillip A. Buckner and John G. Reid (Toronto: University of Toronto Press, 1994), 211.

39 Melish, *Disowning Slavery*, 18.

40 Greene, *Negro in Colonial New England*, 119.

41 Robert E. Desrochers, "Slave-For-Sale Advertisements and Slavery in Massachusetts, 1704–1781," *William and Mary Quarterly* 59, no. 3 (July 2002): 623–64.

42 On slave-for-sale advertisements, see Whitfield, *Black Slavery in the Maritimes*, 23–71.

43 *Royal American Gazette*, June 19, 1786.

44 *Royal Gazette*, June 11, 1799.

45 Clark-Pujara, *Dark Work*, 10 (quoted words are the title of one of the chapters); Sven Beckert, *Slavery's Capitalism: A New History of American Economic Development* (Philadelphia: University of Pennsylvania Press, 2016); Edward Baptist, *The Half Has Never Been Told: Slavery and the Making of American Capitalism* (New York: Basic Books, 2014); Wendy Warren, *New England Bound: Slavery and Colonization in Early America* (New York: W.W. Norton, 2016).

46 John Chipman Invoice, 1786, John Chipman Collection, 1900.353-CHI/I, Esther Clark Wright Archives, Acadia University.

47 Karolyn Smardz Frost, "Before the Loyalists: Planting Slavery in Nova Scotia, 1759–1776" (unpublished paper, 2018), 4.

48 Lt. Col. Jacob Ellegood, Saunders Family Fonds, Accounting 4–34, Harriet Irving Library, University of New Brunswick.

49 Smith, "Slave in Canada," 119.

50 *Royal Gazette*, July 1, 1800; *Royal Gazette*, August 17, 1787; *Royal Gazette*, April 8, 1794; *Royal Gazette*, October 4, 1796.

51 On the flow of commerce from the Maritimes to the West Indies and other places, see Wynn, "1800–1810," 210–14; Ann Gorman Condon, "1783–1800: Loyalist Arrival, Acadian Return, Imperial Reform," in Buckner and Reid, eds., *Atlantic Region to Confederation*, 206–9; Julian Gwyn, *Excessive Expectations: Maritime Commerce and Economic Development of Nova Scotia, 1740–1870* (Montreal and Kingston: McGill-Queen's University Press, 1998), 15–42; and Hornsby and Reid, eds., *New England and the Maritime Provinces*.

52 Spray, *Blacks in New Brunswick*, 17; James MacGregor, *A Letter to a Clergyman Urging Him to Set Free a Black Girl He Held in SLAVERY* (Halifax: A. Henry, 1788).

53 An Act, declaring that Baptism of SLAVES shall not exempt them from BONDAGE, 1781, CO 228, Colonial Office Acts No. 1, Prince Edward Island, 1770–1781, MS 1–66, Public Archives and Records Office, Prince Edward Island (PAROPEI), Charlottetown, Prince Edward Island.

54 *Journal and Proceedings of the House of Assembly* (JHOA) (Halifax: King's Printer, 1787), pp. 17, 22, NSA; An Act for the Regulation and Relief of the Free Negroes Within the Province of Nova Scotia, In Council, April 2, 1789, RG 5, Series U, Unpassed Bills, 1762–1792, NSA; *JHOA*, 1801, p. 72, NSA; A Bill relating to Negroes, February 6, 1801, Legislative Assembly Records, RS 24, S 14-B 9, Provincial Archives of New Brunswick (PANB), Fredericton; An Act for regulating Negro Servants within and throughout this Province, 1808, RG 5, ser. U, Unpassed Bills, NSA.

55 Whitfield, *North to* Bondage, 10–12, 119–20.

56 Winks, *Blacks in Canada*, 45–6.

57 *Nova Scotia Packet and General Advertiser,* October 5 and 12, 1785.

58 Whitfield, *Black Slavery in the Maritimes*, 42.

59 For a full listing of works related to the Black Loyalists, see Whitfield, *North to Bondage*, 132–4.

60 C.B. Fergusson, ed., *Clarkson's Mission to America, 1791–1792* (Halifax: Public Archives of Nova Scotia, 1971), 90.

61 Fergusson, *Clarkson's Mission to America*, 90.

62 An Act for the Regulation and Relief of the Free Negroes Within the Province of Nova Scotia, In Council, April 2, 1789, RG 5, ser. U, box 1, 1762–1792, NSA.

63 Thomas Clarkson "Some Account of the New Colony at Sierra Leone," *American Museum; or Universal Magazine* (May 1792), 229–30.

64 *Nova Scotia Gazette and Weekly Chronicle*, September 21, 1784. In the Book of Negroes (Sir Guy Carleton Papers, RG 1, NSA), Clarinda (age 19) and Jupiter (age 33) are listed one after the other. Clarinda seems to have been the property of Henry Boyd before becoming the property of Dr. Bullern. The way Bullern wrote his runaway advertisement makes it somewhat unclear exactly which one remained enslaved.

65 Hardesty, *Unfreedom*.

66 Esther Clark Wright, *The Loyalists of New Brunswick* (1955; reprint, Moncton: Moncton Publishing Company Limited, 1972), 259, 276; Book of Negroes, Sir Guy Carleton Papers, RG 1, NSA.

67 W.O. Raymond, "The Negro in New Brunswick," *Neith* 1, no. 1 (February 1903): 33.

68 Ann Gorman Condon, *The Envy of the American States: The Loyalist Dream for New Brunswick* (Fredericton: New Ireland Press, 1984), 191; Sharon Dubeau, *New Brunswick Loyalists: A Bicentennial Tribute* (Agincourt: Generation Press, 1983), 2, 147; J.W. Lawrence, *Foot-Prints* (Saint John: J & A McMillan, 1883), 58–9.

69 Book of Negroes, Sir Guy Carleton Papers, RG 1, NSA; Dubeau, *New Brunswick Loyalists,* 114.

70 Book of Negroes, Sir Guy Carleton Papers, RG 1, NSA; Shelburne County Tax Assessment for the year 1787, Shelburne County Archives and Genealogical Society (SCAGS), Shelburne, NS. Simeon Perkins noted that Major Barclay "came After two Black men, one of them David by name, belongs to Major Barcla [*sic*]"; see C.B Fergusson, ed., *The Diary of Simeon Perkins, 1790–1796* (Toronto: Champlain Society, 1961), 104. Barclay also attempted to re-enslave Mertilla Dixon (as discussed in this introduction).

71 Book of Negroes, Guy Carleton Papers, RG 1, NSA.

72 Stephanie E. Jones-Rogers, *They Were Her Property: White Woman as Slave Owners in the American South* (New Haven, CT: Yale University Press, 2019), xvii.

73 Jones-Rogers, *They Were Her Property,* xv–xvi.

74 Complaint of Mertilla Dixon, RG 34–321 file M 97, NSA.

75 Good discussions of family slavery include Piersen, *Black Yankees*, and Melish, *Disowning Slavery*. The literature on paternalism includes Eugene D. Genovese and Elizabeth Fox-Genovese, *The Mind of the Master Class: History and Faith in the Southern Slaveholders' Worldview* (New York: Cambridge University Press, 2005); Eugene D. Genovese and Elizabeth Fox-Genovese, *Fatal Self Deception: Slaveholding Paternalism in the Old South* (New York: Cambridge University Press, 2011); Eugene D. Genovese, *The World the Slaveholders Made: Two Essays in Interpretation* (New York: Pantheon Books, 1969); Eugene D. Genovese, *Roll, Jordan, Roll: The World the Slaves Made* (New York: Pantheon Books, 1974); James Oakes, *The Ruling Race: A History of American Slaveholders* (New York:

Knopf, 1982); Philip D. Morgan, *Slave Counterpoint: Black Culture in the Eighteenth-Century Chesapeake and Lowcountry* (Chapel Hill: University of North Carolina Press, 1998); and Lacy K. Ford, *Deliver Us From Evil: The Slavery Question in the Old South* (New York: Oxford University Press, 2009).

76 Morgan, *Slave Counterpoint*, 276, 275, 284–96; see also Philip D. Morgan, "Three Planters and Their Slaves: Perspectives on Slavery in Virginia, South Carolina, and Jamaica, 1750–1790," in *Race and Family in the Colonial South*, ed. Winthrop D. Jordan (Jackson: University Press of Mississippi, 1987), 37–79.

77 Adam Rothman, "Elizabeth Fox-Genovese, Eugene Genovese, and the Proslavery Worldview," *Reviews in American History* 41 (September 2013): 568.

78 John Wentworth to Paul Wentworth or his attorney, February 24, 1784, Wentworth Letters, vol. 49, NSA.

79 Smith, "Slave in Canada," 89.

80 Piersen, *Black Yankees*, 25–36.

81 Book of Negroes, Sir Guy Carleton Papers, RG 1, NSA.

82 *Royal Gazette*, July 10, 1787.

83 Book of Negroes, Sir Guy Carleton Papers, RG 1, NSA.

84 Piersen, *Black Yankees*, 36.

85 On the range of relations between slaves and owners in Boston, see Jared Hardesty, *Unfreedom*, Chapter 3.

86 Wiswall to Morice, January 15, 1776, Journal of Rev. John Wiswall, Acadia University Library, Wolfville, NS.

87 Stephen Reed, 1801, Cumberland County, RG 48, Probate Records, NSA.

88 Will of William Schurman, 1819, RG 62, ser. 1, lib. 1, fol. 130, PAROPEI.

89 Isaac Bonnell, 1806, Annapolis County, RG 48, Probate Records, NSA.

90 Thomas Leonard, 1788, Kings County, RG 48, Probate Records, NSA.

91 Ann Cosby, 1788, Annapolis County, RG 48, Probate Records, file C 11, NSA.

92 George Cornwall, 1799, Annapolis County, RG 48, Probate Records, NSA.

93 Petition of John Taylor and others, Negro proprietors, December 1807, RG 5 A, box 14, doc. 49, NSA.

94 Warren, *New England Bound*, 157.

95 AN ACT *to repeal an Act made and passed in the twenty-first year of his late Majesty's reign intituled* "An Act, *declaring that* Baptism *of* SLAVES *shall not exempt them from* BONDAGE," CO 228, Colonial Office Acts, #4, Prince Edward Island, 1812–1829, MS nos. 181–278, PAROPEI.

96 Winks, *Blacks in Canada*, 102.

97 Cahill, "Slavery and the Judges," 87.

98 *Journal and Proceedings of the House of Assembly* (JHOA), 1787, NSA; An Act for the Regulation and Relief of the Free Negroes Within the Province of Nova Scotia, In Council, April 2, 1789, RG 5, ser. U, Unpassed Bills, 1762–1792, NSA; *JHOA*, July 16, 1801, NSA; A Bill relating to Negroes, February 6, 1801, Legislative Assembly Records, RS 24, S 14-B 9, Provincial Archives of New Brunswick

(PANB), Fredericton, New Brunswick. There is another version of this bill – A Bill relating to Negroes [read 1st time – 2nd 12 February 1801 + ordered to be committed, 13th February 1801, progress. Withdrawn]; An Act for regulating Negro Servants within and throughout this Province, 1808, RG 5, Series U, Unpassed Bills, NSA.

99   Bell, "Judges of Loyalist New Brunswick," 21.

100   Carole Watterson Troxler, "Re-enslavement of Black Loyalists: Mary Postell in South Carolina, East Florida, and Nova Scotia," *Acadiensis* 37, no. 2 (Summer/ Fall, 2008): 70–85; *R. v. Gray*, April to November 1791, Shelburne County Court of General Sessions of the Peace, RG 60, vol. 1, #49.4, NSA.

101   Jack, "The Loyalists and Slavery," 181.

102   Cahill, "Habeas Corpus and Slavery," 179–209; *Hecht v. Moody*, 1799, RG 39 C, Halifax, vol. 81, NSA.

103   *Royal Gazette*, February 18, 1800.

104   Bell, "Judges of Loyalist New Brunswick," 31. On early Saint John, see D.G. Bell, *Early Loyalist Saint John: The Origin of New Brunswick Politics, 1783–1786* (Fredericton: New Ireland Press, 1983); see also David Bell, *Loyalist Rebellion in New Brunswick: A Defining Conflict for Canada's Political Culture* (Halifax: Formac, 2013).

105   Isaac Bonnell, 1806, Annapolis County, RG 48, Probate Records, NSA; Jacob Troop, 1805, Annapolis County, RG 48, Probate Records, NSA; George Cornwall, 1799, Annapolis County, RG 48, Probate Records, NSA.

106   Smith, "Slave in Canada," 116.

107   *Examiner*, February 11, 1881. The original memorandum book has not survived.

108   *Royal Gazette*, July 10, 1787.

109   Sterling Stuckey, *Slave Culture: Nationalist Theory and the Foundations of Black America* (New York: Oxford University Press, 1987), 21.

110   James Oliver Horton and Lois E. Horton, *In Hope of Liberty: Culture, Community and Protest among Northern Free Blacks, 1700–1860* (New York: Oxford University Press, 1997), 22–4, 30–3; for excellent work on these festivals, see Piersen, *Black Yankees*, 117–40; Shane White, "'It Was a Proud Day': African Americans, Festivals, and Parades in the North, 1741–1834," *Journal of American History* 81, no. 1(1994): 13–50; and Joseph P. Reidy, "Negro Election Day and Black Community Life in New England, 1750–1860," *Marxist Perspectives* 1 (Fall 1978): 102–17. On Christianity and other cultural beliefs and activities, see Graham Russell Hodges, *Root & Branch: African Americans in New York & East Jersey, 1613–1863* (Chapel Hill: University of North Carolina Press, 1999), 115–28.

111   Shane White and Graham White, "Slave Clothing and African-American Culture in the Eighteenth and Nineteenth Centuries," *Past and Present* 148, no.1 (August 1995): 150, 155.

112   *Royal Gazette*, October 12, 1787; *Royal Gazette*, August 21, 1787.

113   *Nova Scotia Packet and General Advertiser*, August 3, 1786.

114 *Royal Gazette* (New Brunswick), October 12, 1787.

115 Cornwallis Township Book, June 1793, p. 8, MG 4, vol. 18–18A, NSA; also see St. Paul's Anglican Church Baptismal Records, Amelia Byers, John Byers, Edward Byers, William Byers, 1795, PAROPEI.

116 Matthew 28:18–20 – "Then Jesus came to them and said, 'All authority in heaven and on earth has been given to me. Therefore go and make disciples of all nations, baptizing them in the name of the Father and of the Son and of the Holy Spirit, and teaching them to obey everything I have commanded you. And surely I am with you always, to the very end of the age.'"

117 Ephesians 6:5–7 – "Slaves, obey your earthly masters with respect and fear, and with sincerity of heart, just as you would obey Christ. Obey them not only to win their favor when their eye is on you, but as slaves of Christ, doing the will of God from your heart. Serve wholeheartedly, as if you were serving the Lord, not people."

118 Albert J. Raboteau, *Canaan Land: A Religious History of African Americans* (Oxford: Oxford University Press, 1999), 16.

119 Gwyn, *Excessive Expectations*, 32; see also John J. McCusker, *Money and Exchange in Europe and America, 1600–1775: A Handbook* (Chapel Hill: University of North Carolina Press, 1978).

120 Gwyn, *Excessive Expectations*, 23.

121 *Nova Scotia Gazette and Weekly Chronicle*, May 20, 1783.

122 *Saint John Gazette*, July 15, 1784.

123 Smith, "Slave in Canada," 66–7; Joseph Totten, 1788, Annapolis County, RG 48, Probate Records, NSA.

124 Bill of Sale, Colchester County, Register of Deeds, vol. 1, p. 468, NSA.

125 Smith, "Slave in Canada," 94.

126 Sale of a Slave, MG 100, vol. 103, #F3a, NSA.

127 Smith, "Slave in Canada," 67, 94, 64.

128 Sources consulted for this section include Smith, "Slave in Canada," 62–7, 94; *Douglass v. MacNeill*, 1791, Halifax County, RG 39 C, vol. 62, no. 62, NSA; *R. v. Gray*, November 1786, Shelburne County, RG 60, vol. 27, #27.2, NSA; Slavery in Colchester, Sale of Slave, September 29, 1779, F 142, NSA; Richard Betts, 1786 Annapolis County, RG 48, Probate Records, NSA; Joseph Totten, 1788, Annapolis County RG 48, Probate Records, NSA; J.R. Campbell, *A History of the County of Yarmouth, Nova Scotia* (Saint John, NB: J. & A. McMillan, 1876), 145; *Daily Sun* (Saint John), August 29, 1890; *Times* (Moncton), October 27, 1880; Sale of a Slave, MG 100, vol. 103, #F3a, NSA; Bill of Sale, Colchester County, Register of Deeds, vol. 1, p. 468, NSA; Richard Wilson slave sale, August 19, 1793, NSA; and Thomas Chandler slave sale, January 27, 1792, NSA.

129 Richard Betts, 1786 Annapolis County, RG 48, Probate Records, NSA.

130 McCusker, *Money and Exchange*, 165. Also see John J. McCusker, *How Much Is That in Real Money? A Historical Price Index for Use as a Deflator of Money Values*

in the Economy of the United States (Worcester, MA: American Antiquarian Society, 1992).

131 Joseph Totten, 1788, Annapolis County, RG 48, Probate Records, NSA.

132 Campbell, A History of the County of Yarmouth, Nova Scotia, 145.

133 Stephen Reed, 1801, Cumberland County, RG 48, Probate Records, NSA.

134 Douglass v. MacNeill, 1791, Halifax, RG 39 C, vol. 62, no. 62, NSA; R. v. Gray, November 9, 1786, Shelburne, RG 60, vol. 27, #27.2, NSA.

135 See, for example, https://www.loc.gov/collections/slave-narratives-from-the -federal-writers-project-1936-to-1938/articles-and-essays/introduction-to -the-wpa-slave-narratives/wpa-and-the-slave-narrative-collection.

136 Vincent Carretta, ed., Unchained Voices: An Anthology of Black Authors in the English-Speaking World of the Eighteenth Century (1996; expanded edition, Lexington: University Press of Kentucky, 2004).

137 Thomas Peters to Lord Grenville, "The Humble Petition of Thomas Peters, A Negro," 1790, FO 4/1, C 308757, National Archives (NA), London, United Kingdom.

138 Petition of Isaac Willoughby, February 8, 1834, RG 5, ser. P, NSA; Zimri Armstrong, Saint John's County, no. 78, F 1024, RS 108, Land Petitions, PANB.

139 Melish, Disowning Slavery, 11–49; Bonaventura, For Adam's Sake.

140 Carter, "Of Things Said and Unsaid: Power, Archival Silences, and Power in Silence," 215–33; Thomas, Fowler, and Johnson, Silence of the Archive; Marisa J. Fuentes, Dispossessed Lives: Enslaved Women, Violence, and the Archive (Philadelphia: University of Pennsylvania Press, 2016), 1–12; Stephanie E. Smallwood, Saltwater Slavery: A Middle Passage from Africa to American Diaspora (Cambridge: Harvard University Press, 2007), Chapters 1 and 2; Brian Connolly and Marisa Fuentes, "Introduction: From Archives of Slavery to Liberated Futures?" History of the Present: A Journal of Critical History 6 (Fall 2016): 105–16. The entire edition of this journal is devoted to a series of quality essays about slavery and the archive.

141 Graham Russell Hodges, The Black Loyalist Directory: African Americans in Exile after the American Revolution (New York: Garland, 1996); for an appendix of enslaved Black people who went to the Maritimes according to the Book of Negroes, see Whitfield, North to Bondage, 121–30, as well as Book of Negroes, Sir Guy Carleton Papers, RG 1, NSA.

142 Carole Watterson Troxler, "Uses of the Bahamas by Southern Loyalist Exiles," in The Loyal Atlantic: Remaking the British Atlantic in the Revolutionary Era, eds. Liam Riordan and Jerry Bannister (Toronto: University of Toronto Press, 2012), 200.

143 Book of Negroes, Sir Guy Carleton Papers, RG 1, NSA.

144 Paper Respecting Dick Hill, a Free Negro Man sent to West Indies from Shelburne in Joshua Wises Schooner Commanded by Captain McDonald, 1787, RG 60, Shelburne #25.3, NSA.

145 Book of Negroes, Sir Guy Carleton Papers, RG 1, NSA. There is a column in the Book of Negroes called "Names of the Persons in Whose Possession They Now

Are"; see, for example, https://archives.novascotia.ca/africanns/book-of-negroes
/page/?ID=19. It is the column right before the page break, and most of the time
this column is filled out but occasionally it is not.

146 *Royal Saint John's Gazette* (New Brunswick), May 13, 1784. It is interesting to note
that the Book of Negroes states that Edward (or Ned) Morris was only 36, but in
this runaway advertisement he is described as elderly. The age in the Book of
Negroes may be an error.

147 *Royal Saint John's Gazette*, May 13, 1784.

148 *Royal Saint John's Gazette*, May 13, 1784.

149 David George, "An Account of the Life of Mr. DAVID GEORGE, from Sierra Leone in Africa; given by himself in a Conversation with Brother RIPPON of London, and Brother [Samuel] PEARCE [1766–1799] of Birmingham," in Carretta,
Unchained Voices, 340.

150 Book of Negroes, Sir Guy Carleton Papers, RG 1, NSA.

151 General Sessions at Shelburne, Nova Scotia, November 1 and 3, 1791, Shelburne
Records, MG 4, vol. 141, NSA.

152 There is a significant number of "UNNAMED" enslaved people, although they
remain a minority. We have tried to provide as much information about such
persons as possible. Entries listed under "ADULT FEMALE SLAVE OF [SLAVE-
HOLDER]," "ADULT MALE SLAVE OF [SLAVEHOLDER]," and "CHILD
SLAVE" come from the 1807 Digby petition; other enslaved people whose names
we do not know are listed under "UNNAMED" or "UNNAMED [BOY/CHILD/
GIRL/MAN/PERSON/WOMAN]."

BIOGRAPHICAL DICTIONARY OF ENSLAVED
BLACK PEOPLE IN THE MARITIMES

1. AARON (c. 1783, age 15) – Enslaved to Oliver Hicks, who migrated to the Maritimes after the American Revolution, Aaron was possibly from New York. British officials described him as a "stout boy." Source: Book of Negroes.

2. ABIGAIL [spelled **ABIGILL** in the Book of Negroes] (c. 1783, age 7) – Enslaved to Jacob Beeber, Abigail went to the Maritimes from New York. British officials described her as a "likely girl." Source: Book of Negroes.

3. ABIGAIL (c. 1783, age 20) – Enslaved to Stephen Sneadon, who migrated to the Maritimes after the American Revolution with one other slave. British officials in New York described Abigail as a "stout wench." Source: Book of Negroes.

4. ABRAHAM (c. 1746) – Abraham was enslaved to the Connecticut Regiment during the siege and takeover of Louisbourg. Source: Kenneth Donovan, "A Nominal List of Slaves and Their Owners in Île Royale, 1713–1760," *Nova Scotia Historical Review* 16 (1996): 151–62, esp. 156.

5. ABRAHAM (c. 1783, age 21) – Enslaved to Massachusetts Loyalist Gideon White, who settled in Shelburne, Nova Scotia, Abraham, according to the Book of Negroes, was "allowed to go with Mr. Edwards to Nova Scotia." British officials in New York described him as a "stout man." Source: Book of Negroes.

6. ABRAHAM (c. 1783, age 10) – Abraham was enslaved to John Nash, who migrated to the Maritimes after the American Revolution with a few other slaves. British officials described him as a "fine boy." Source: Book of Negroes.

7. ABRAHAM (c. 1783, age 21) – Enslaved to Captain McLeod, Abraham went to Nova Scotia from New York and was possibly from New York. British officials described him as a "stout fellow" and "The Captain's Property." Source: Book of Negroes.

8. ABRAHAM (c. 1784) – John Wentworth sent Abraham and 18 other slaves from Nova Scotia to his "relation" Paul Wentworth in Suriname. Wentworth described these slaves as "American born or well seasoned, and are perfectly stout, healthy, sober, orderly, Industrious, & obedient." Wentworth had the slaves christened and claimed to be concerned for their welfare. He noted "Abraham has been used to Cattle and to Attend in the House, etc." Source: John Wentworth to Paul Wentworth or his attorney, February 24, 1784, Wentworth Letters, vol. 49, Nova Scotia Archives (hereafter NSA), Halifax.

9. ABRAHAM (c. 1787, age 16) – In 1787, James Hayt placed an advertisement for his teenage runaway slave named Abraham. The advertisement described him as a "Run-Away negro boy, about 16 years of age – he had on a short blue jacket, with sleeves lined with white swan skin, a scarlet waistcoat, two rows bright buttons, with a collar, nankeen breeches, thread stockings, new shoes, plated buckles, and [an] all round black hat. – He has a pleasant countenance, is very talkative, tall of his age, but well proportioned, and formerly belonged to Capt. John Hall, of Saint Andrews." Source: *Royal Gazette*, October 12, 1787.

10. ABRAHAM (c. 1797) – Abraham was enslaved to Munson Jarvis, who sold him along with a woman named Lucy to Abraham de Peyster in Saint John, New Brunswick. Source: David Russell Jack, "General John Watts de Peyster," *Acadiensis* 7, no. 3 (July 1907): 290.

11. ABRAM (c. 1779, age 12) – Born in Maryland, Matthew Harris brought Abram to Nova Scotia and settled in Pictou. In 1779, he sold Abram to one Matthew Archibald. The bill of sale tells historians two things: First, Abram is probably being sold away from his family (if his mother had not already been sold at an earlier date and we know nothing about his father – unless Harris himself fathered Abram). Second, men and women of relatively modest means could own slaves, as Matthew Archibald and Matthew Harris were a tanner and yeoman, respectively. At age 12, Abram had already been a slave in Maryland and Nova Scotia. Moreover, he had been sold at least once before he became a teenager. Source: Colchester County, Register of Deeds, vol. 1, p. 468, NSA.

12. ABSALOM (c. 1783/1784) – Absalom was enslaved to Captain Isaac Young in Digby, Nova Scotia. Young's slaves were from New York. Source: T.W. Smith, "The Slave in Canada," *Collections of the Nova Scotia Historical Society* 10 (1899): 25.

13. ACHABEE (c. 1783, age 60) – Achabee was enslaved to Dr. Nathaniel Bullern, who migrated from South Carolina to Nova Scotia with a total of 10 slaves. Bullern's slaves elucidate the nature of family connections and kinship networks in the region. His oldest slaves, Achabee and Catharina, were both 60 at the end of the American Revolution. Jenny and Prince were 40 and 30, respectively. Bullern also owned another male slave in his early 30s and three females ranging in ages 19 to 25. His two youngest slaves were an infant named Sarah and a 6 year old. It is unclear who the parents of these children were, but it is possible that one or both parents were among Bullern's slaves. British officials in New York described Achabee as a "stout fellow." Source: Book of Negroes.

14. ACHEURY, MAGDELAINE (c. 1735) – Magdelaine gave birth to a boy named Philippe in Île Royale. Source: Donovan, "Nominal List of Slaves and Their Owners," 153.

15. JACQUES (c. 1735) – Jacques was Philippe's father and Magdelaine's husband. Source: Donovan, "Nominal List of Slaves and Their Owners," 153.

16. PHILIPPE (c. 1735) – Philippe was Magdelaine's son. Source: Donovan, "Nominal List of Slaves and Their Owners," 153.

17. PHILIPPE (c. 1735) – Philippe was Phillippe's godfather. Source: Donovan, "Nominal List of Slaves and Their Owners," 153.

18. MARIE JEANNE (c. 1735) – Marie Jeanne was Phillippe's godmother. Source: Donovan, "Nominal List of Slaves and Their Owners," 153.

19. ADAM (c. 1779) – New York Loyalist Daniel Shatford bequeathed Adam to his wife in Halifax. Source: Smith, "Slave in Canada," 14.

20. ADELAISE (c. 1750s) – Adelaise was enslaved to Jean Laborde, a wealthy merchant who owned several slaves. Source: Kenneth Donovan, "Slaves in Île Royale, 1713–1758," French Colonial History 5 (2004): 32.

21. ADULT FEMALE SLAVE OF JOHN BASTEIT (c. 1807) – Basteit owned an unnamed woman and an unnamed child. It is likely that the adult female slave was the mother of the child slave, but there is no mention of an adult male slave in Basteit's household. It is possible that Basteit was the father of the child slave. Basteit signed the 1807 Digby slaveholder petition. Source: Petition of John Taylor and Others, Negro Proprietors, to the General Assembly, December 1807, RG 5 A, box 14, doc. 49, NSA.

22. ADULT FEMALE SLAVE OF THOMAS CORNWELL (c. 1807) – Cornwell owned three unnamed slaves, including one adult female and two children. The adult female slave might have been the mother of the child slaves, but that is not clear. There is no mention of a male slave, so it is possible that Cornwell fathered the children. Cornwell signed the 1807 Digby slaveholder petition, which in part stated "Your petitioners are far from pretending to advocate Slavery as a System. With the creation of that System they had nothing to do … But, unfortunately for your petitioners, owing to certain doubts now entertained by The Kings Courts of Law in this Province, such property is rendered wholly untenable by your petitioners, whose Negro Servants are daily leaving their service and setting your petitioners at defiance." Source: Petition of John Taylor and Others, Negro Proprietors, to the General Assembly, December 1807, RG 5 A, box 14, doc. 49, NSA.

23. ADULT FEMALE SLAVE OF EBENEZER CUTLER (c. 1807) – Cutler owned an unnamed child and an unnamed adult female. It is likely that the female slave was the mother of the child slave. Due to the lack of a male slave in the household, it is possible that Cutler fathered the child. Cutler signed the 1807 Digby slaveholder petition. Source: Petition of John Taylor and Others, Negro Proprietors, to the General Assembly, December 1807, RG 5 A, box 14, doc. 49, NSA.

24. ADULT FEMALE SLAVE OF FREDERICK DEVOUE (c. 1807) – Devoue owned one unnamed male and one unnamed female slave and signed the 1807 Digby slaveholder petition. Source: Petition of John Taylor and Others, Negro Proprietors, to the General Assembly, December 1807, RG 5 A, box 14, doc. 49, NSA.

25. ADULT FEMALE SLAVE OF ISAAC HATFIELD (c. 1807) – Hatfield owned a total of five unnamed slaves and signed the 1807 Digby slaveholder petition. Source: Petition of John Taylor and Others, Negro Proprietors, to the General Assembly, December 1807, RG 5 A, box 14, doc. 49, NSA.

26. ADULT FEMALE SLAVE OF ISAAC HATFIELD (c. 1807) – Hatfield owned a total of five unnamed slaves and signed the 1807 Digby slaveholder petition. Source: Petition of John Taylor and Others, Negro Proprietors, to the General Assembly, December 1807, RG 5 A, box 14, doc. 49, NSA.

27. ADULT FEMALE SLAVE OF NICHOLAS JAMES (c. 1807) – James owned four slaves, including three children. It is likely that the female slave was the mother of the three children. James signed the 1807 Digby slaveholder petition. Source: Petition of John Taylor and Others, Negro Proprietors, to the General Assembly, December 1807, RG 5 A, box 14, doc. 49, NSA.

28. ADULT FEMALE SLAVE OF SIMEON JONES (c. 1807) – Jones owned two slaves and signed the 1807 Digby slaveholder petition. Source: Petition of John Taylor and Others, Negro Proprietors, to the General Assembly, December 1807, RG 5 A, box 14, doc. 49, NSA.

29. ADULT FEMALE SLAVE OF SAMUEL MELANSON (c. 1807) – Melanson owned one unnamed female and one unnamed child slave, and it is likely that the adult female was the mother of the child slave while Melanson may have fathered the child. He signed the 1807 Digby slaveholder petition. I am thankful to Colby Gaudet for sharing his research with me that corrected my previous mistranslation of the Acadian last name. Source: Petition of John Taylor and Others, Negro Proprietors, to the General Assembly, December 1807, RG 5 A, box 14, doc. 49, NSA; Colby Gaudet, "Suivant la coutume du Pays": Practices of Slavery among the Acadians of Southern Nova Scotia, 1780–1844," (unpublished manuscript, April 2021).

30. ADULT FEMALE SLAVE OF BELONEY MELANSON (c. 1807) – Melanson owned one unnamed female and an unnamed child, and it is likely that the female was the mother of the child slave. Melanson signed the 1807 Digby slaveholder petition. I am thankful to Colby Gaudet for sharing his research with me that corrected my previous mistranslation of the Acadian last name. Source: Petition of John Taylor and Others, Negro Proprietors, to the General Assembly, December 1807, RG 5 A, box 14, doc. 49, NSA; Colby Gaudet, "Suivant la coutume du Pays": Practices of Slavery among the Acadians of Southern Nova Scotia, 1780–1844," (unpublished manuscript, April 2021).

31. ADULT FEMALE SLAVE OF JAMES MOODY (c. 1807) – Moody, a well-known Loyalist from New Jersey, also had several other slaves in his household that possibly constituted a family. The adult slaves were probably born in New Jersey, while the child slaves were undoubtedly born in Nova Scotia. In 1807, Moody owned eight slaves: two adult males, one adult female, and five children. Moody signed the 1807 Digby slaveholder petition. Source: Petition of John Taylor and Others, Negro Proprietors, to the General Assembly, December 1807, RG 5 A, box 14, doc. 49, NSA.

32. ADULT FEMALE SLAVE OF JOHN POLHEMUS (c. 1807) – Polhemus owned 10 slaves, which makes him one of the largest slaveholders in the history of the Maritimes. His household consisted of three male slaves, two female slaves, and five child slaves. He expanded his holding of slaves over time since, according to the Book of Negroes, he arrived in Nova Scotia with only two slaves. It is possible, however, that some of them were not recorded in the Book of Negroes. Polhemus signed the 1807 Digby slaveholder petition. Sources: Petition of John Taylor and Others, Negro Proprietors, to the General Assembly, December 1807, RG 5 A, box 14, doc. 49, NSA; Book of Negroes.

33. ADULT FEMALE SLAVE OF JOHN POLHEMUS (c. 1807) – Polhemus owned 10 slaves, which makes him one of the largest slaveholders in the history of the Maritimes. His household consisted of three male slaves, two female slaves, and five child slaves. He expanded his holding of slaves over time since, according to the Book of Negroes, he arrived in Nova Scotia with only two slaves. It is possible, however, that some of them were not recorded in the Book of Negroes. Polhemus signed the 1807 Digby slaveholder petition. Sources: Petition of John Taylor and Others, Negro Proprietors, to the General Assembly, December 1807, RG 5 A, box 14, doc. 49, NSA; Book of Negroes.

34. ADULT FEMALE SLAVE OF BETHIAH PURDY (c. 1807) – Purdy signed the 1807 Digby slaveholder petition. Source: Petition of John Taylor and Others, Negro Proprietors, to the General Assembly, December 1807, RG 5 A, box 14, doc. 49, NSA.

35. ADULT FEMALE SLAVE OF ELIJAH PURDY (c. 1807) – Purdy owned one male and two female slaves and signed the 1807 Digby slaveholder. Source: Petition of John Taylor and Others, Negro Proprietors, to the General Assembly, December 1807, RG 5 A, box 14, doc. 49, NSA.

36. ADULT FEMALE SLAVE OF ELIJAH PURDY (c. 1807) – Purdy owned one male and two female slaves and signed the signed the 1807 Digby slave-holder. Source: Petition of John Taylor and Others, Negro Proprietors, to the General Assembly, December 1807, RG 5 A, box 14, doc. 49, NSA.

37. ADULT FEMALE SLAVE OF HENRY RUTHERFORD (c. 1807) – Rutherford owned four slaves. It is possible that these slaves were a family as they consisted of an adult male, adult female, and two children. Rutherford signed the 1807 Digby slaveholder petition. Source: Petition of John Taylor and Others, Negro Proprietors, to the General Assembly, December 1807, RG 5 A, box 14, doc. 49, NSA.

38. ADULT FEMALE SLAVE OF JOHN TAYLOR (c. 1807) – Taylor owned two adult male slaves, two adult female slaves, and two child slaves. He signed the 1807 Digby slaveholder. Source: Petition of John Taylor and Others, Negro Proprietors, to the General Assembly, December 1807, RG 5 A, box 14, doc. 49, NSA.

39. ADULT FEMALE SLAVE OF JOHN TAYLOR (c. 1807) – Taylor owned two adult male slaves, two adult female slaves, and two child slaves. He signed the 1807 Digby slaveholder. Source: Petition of John Taylor and Others, Negro Proprietors, to the General Assembly, December 1807, RG 5 A, box 14, doc. 49, NSA.

40. ADULT FEMALE SLAVE OF EDWARD THORNE (c. 1807) – Thorne owned two adult slaves – one male and this woman – and he signed the 1807 Digby slaveholder petition. Source: Petition of John Taylor and Others, Negro Proprietors, to the General Assembly, December 1807, RG 5 A, box 14, doc. 49, NSA.

41. ADULT FEMALE SLAVE OF FREDERICK WILLIAMS (c. 1807) – Williams owned two male slaves, one female slave, and three child slaves. The number of child slaves demonstrates that Williams had intentions of expanding and contin-uing slaveholding in Nova Scotia. He signed the 1807 Digby slaveholder petition. Source: Petition of John Taylor and Others, Negro Proprietors, to the General Assembly, December 1807, RG 5 A, box 14, doc. 49, NSA.

42. ADULT FEMALE SLAVE OF MR. WINNIETT (c. 1807) – Winniett owned three adult slaves and one child slave and signed the 1807 Digby slave-holder petition. Source: Petition of John Taylor and Others, Negro Proprietors, to the General Assembly, December 1807, RG 5 A, box 14, doc. 49, NSA.

43. ADULT MALE SLAVE OF F.L. BÖHME (c. 1807) – Böhme owned two male slaves and a child slave. There is no mention of any female slaves or who the mother of the child might have been. Böhme signed the 1807 Digby slaveholder petition. Source: Petition of John Taylor and Others, Negro Proprietors, to the General Assembly, December 1807, RG 5 A, box 14, doc. 49, NSA.

44. ADULT MALE SLAVE OF F.L. BÖHME (c. 1807) – Böhme owned two male slaves and a child slave. There is no mention of any female slaves or who the mother of the child might have been. Böhme signed the 1807 Digby slaveholder petition. Source: Petition of John Taylor and Others, Negro Proprietors, to the General Assembly, December 1807, RG 5 A, box 14, doc. 49, NSA.

45. ADULT MALE SLAVE OF HARRY DOUCET (c. 1807) – Doucet signed the 1807 Digby slaveholder petition. I am thankful to Colby Gaudet for sharing his research with me that corrected my previous mistranslation of the Acadian last name. Source: Petition of John Taylor and Others, Negro Proprietors, to the General Assembly, December 1807, RG 5 A, box 14, doc. 49, NSA; Colby Gaudet, "Suivant la coutume du Pays": Practices of Slavery among the Acadians of Southern Nova Scotia, 1780–1844," (unpublished manuscript, April 2021).

46. ADULT MALE SLAVE OF FREDERICK DEVOUE (c. 1807) – Devoue owned one male and one female slave and signed the 1807 Digby slaveholder petition. Source: Petition of John Taylor and Others, Negro Proprietors, to the General Assembly, December 1807, RG 5 A, box 14, doc. 49, NSA.

47. ADULT MALE SLAVE OF ISAAC HATFIELD (c. 1807) – Hatfield owned a total of five slaves and signed the 1807 Digby slaveholder petition. Source: Petition of John Taylor and Others, Negro Proprietors, to the General Assembly, December 1807, RG 5 A, box 14, doc. 49, NSA.

48. ADULT MALE SLAVE OF ISAAC HATFIELD (c. 1807) – Hatfield owned a total of five slaves and signed the 1807 Digby slaveholder petition. Source: Petition of John Taylor and Others, Negro Proprietors, to the General Assembly, December 1807, RG 5 A, box 14, doc. 49, NSA.

49. ADULT MALE SLAVE OF ELIZABETH JAMES (c. 1807) – James signed the 1807 Digby slaveholder petition. Source: Petition of John Taylor and Others, Negro Proprietors, to the General Assembly, December 1807, RG 5 A, box 14, doc. 49, NSA.

50. ADULT MALE SLAVE OF SIMEON JONES (c. 1807) – Jones signed the 1807 Digby slaveholder petition. Source: Petition of John Taylor and Others, Negro Proprietors, to the General Assembly, December 1807, RG 5 A, box 14, doc. 49, NSA.

51. ADULT MALE SLAVE OF JAMES MOODY (c. 1807) – A well-known Loyalist from New Jersey, Moody had several other slaves in his household that possibly constituted a family. The adult slaves were probably born in New Jersey, while the child slaves were undoubtedly born in Nova Scotia. In 1807 Moody owned eight slaves: two adult males, one adult female, and five children. Moody signed the 1807 Digby slaveholder petition. Source: Petition of John Taylor and Others, Negro Proprietors, to the General Assembly, December 1807, RG 5 A, box 14, doc. 49, NSA.

52. ADULT MALE SLAVE OF JAMES MOODY (c. 1807) – A well-known Loyalist from New Jersey, Moody had several other slaves in his household that possibly constituted a family. The adult slaves were probably born in New Jersey, while the child slaves were undoubtedly born in Nova Scotia. In 1807, Moody owned eight slaves: two adult males, one adult female, and five children. Moody signed the 1807 Digby slaveholder petition. Source: Petition of John Taylor and Others, Negro Proprietors, to the General Assembly, December 1807, RG 5 A, box 14, doc. 49, NSA.

53. ADULT MALE SLAVE OF JOHN POLHEMUS (c. 1807) – Polhemus owned 10 slaves, which makes him one of the largest slaveholders in the history of the Maritimes. His household consisted of three male slaves, two female slaves, and five child slaves. He expanded his holding of slaves over time since, according to the Book of Negroes, he arrived in Nova Scotia with only two slaves. It is possible, however, that some of them were not recorded in the Book of Negroes. Polhemus signed the 1807 Digby slaveholder petition. Sources: Petition of John Taylor and Others, Negro Proprietors, to the General Assembly, December 1807, RG 5 A, box 14, doc. 49, NSA; Book of Negroes.

54. ADULT MALE SLAVE OF JOHN POLHEMUS (c. 1807) – Polhemus owned 10 slaves, which makes him one of the largest slaveholders in the history of the Maritimes. His household consisted of three male slaves, two female slaves, and five child slaves. He expanded his holding of slaves over time since, according to the Book of Negroes, he arrived in Nova Scotia with only two slaves. It is possible, however, that some of them were not recorded in the Book of Negroes. Polhemus signed the 1807 Digby slaveholder petition. Sources: Petition of John Taylor and Others, Negro Proprietors, to the General Assembly, December 1807, RG 5 A, box 14, doc. 49, NSA; Book of Negroes.

55. ADULT MALE SLAVE OF ELIJAH PURDY (c. 1807) – Purdy owned one male slave and two female slaves and signed the signed the 1807 Digby slaveholder. Source: Petition of John Taylor and Others, Negro Proprietors, to the General Assembly, December 1807, RG 5 A, box 14, doc. 49, NSA.

56. ADULT MALE SLAVE OF HENRY RUTHERFORD (c. 1807) – Rutherford owned four slaves, and it is possible that these slaves were a family as they consisted of an adult male, adult female, and two children. Rutherford signed the 1807 Digby slaveholder petition. Source: Petition of John Taylor and Others, Negro Proprietors, to the General Assembly, December 1807, RG 5 A, box 14, doc. 49, NSA.

57. ADULT MALE SLAVE OF ANDREW SNODGRASS (c. 1807) – Snodgrass owned just the one slave, and he signed the 1807 Digby slaveholder petition. Source: Petition of John Taylor and Others, Negro Proprietors, to the General Assembly, December 1807, RG 5 A, box 14, doc. 49, NSA.

58. ADULT MALE SLAVE OF JOHN TAYLOR (c. 1807) – Taylor owned two male slaves, two female slaves, and two child slaves and signed the 1807 Digby slaveholder petition. Source: Petition of John Taylor and Others, Negro Proprietors, to the General Assembly, December 1807, RG 5 A, box 14, doc. 49, NSA.

59. ADULT MALE SLAVE OF JOHN TAYLOR (c. 1807) – Taylor owned two male slaves, two female slaves, and two child slaves and signed the 1807 Digby slaveholder petition. Source: Petition of John Taylor and Others, Negro Proprietors, to the General Assembly, December 1807, RG 5 A, box 14, doc. 49, NSA.

60. ADULT MALE SLAVE OF EDWARD THORNE (c. 1807) – Thorne owned two adult slaves and signed the 1807 Digby slaveholder petition. Source: Petition of John Taylor and Others, Negro Proprietors, to the General Assembly, December 1807, RG 5 A, box 14, doc. 49, NSA.

61. ADULT MALE SLAVE OF JOHN VROOM (c. 1807) – Vroom owned three slaves, including two children. He did not own a female slave, so either he purchased these children from another owner or Vroom owned a female slave who died or was sold. Vroom signed the 1807 Digby slaveholder petition. Source: Petition of John Taylor and Others, Negro Proprietors, to the General Assembly, December 1807, RG 5 A, box 14, doc. 49, NSA.

62. ADULT MALE SLAVE OF FREDERICK WILLIAMS (c. 1807) – Williams owned two male slaves, one female slave, and three child slaves. The number of child slaves demonstrates that Williams had intentions of expanding and continuing slaveholding in Nova Scotia. He signed the 1807 Digby slaveholder petition. Source: Petition of John Taylor and Others, Negro Proprietors, to the General Assembly, December 1807, RG 5 A, box 14, doc. 49, NSA.

63. ADULT MALE SLAVE OF FREDERICK WILLIAMS (c. 1807) – Williams owned two male slaves, one female slave, and three child slaves. The number of child slaves demonstrates that Williams had intentions of expanding and continuing slaveholding in Nova Scotia. He signed the 1807 Digby slaveholder petition. Source: Petition of John Taylor and Others, Negro Proprietors, to the General Assembly, December 1807, RG 5 A, box 14, doc. 49, NSA.

64. ADULT MALE SLAVE OF MR. WINNIETT (c. 1807) – Winniett owned three adult slaves and one child slave and signed the 1807 Digby slaveholder petition. Source: Petition of John Taylor and Others, Negro Proprietors, to the General Assembly, December 1807, RG 5 A, box 14, doc. 49, NSA.

65. ADULT MALE SLAVE OF MR. WINNIETT (c. 1807) – Winniett owned three adult slaves and one child slave and signed the 1807 Digby slaveholder petition. Source: Petition of John Taylor and Others, Negro Proprietors, to the General Assembly, December 1807, RG 5 A, box 14, doc. 49, NSA.

66. AGATHA (c. 1788) – Agatha was enslaved to Ann Cosby at Annapolis Royal, Nova Scotia, who owned two other slaves and freed them in her 1788 will: "I do also give and devise unto my black Woman named Rose, a Molotto Girl named Agatha, and my black Man named John Bulkley ... their full Freedom." Source: Ann Cosby, 1788, Annapolis County, RG 48, Probate Records, File C 11, NSA.

67. AGGY (slave? c. 1784) – Aggy was possibly enslaved to Captain Daniel McNeill (also spelled MacNeil and McNeil), who migrated to Country Harbour with other southern Loyalists. The majority of these Loyalists and their slaves were from North Carolina, South Carolina, and Georgia. They had settled briefly in East Florida before moving to Nova Scotia. Black people at Country Harbour were either slaves or "quasi-free" and subject to re-enslavement. Abolitionist Thomas Clarkson explained the phenomenon of re-enslavement: "It was not long till these loyalists, many of whom had been educated with all the ideas of the justice of slavery, the inferiority of negroes, and the superiority of white men, that are universal in the southern provinces of America, began to harass and oppress the industrious black settlers, and even wantonly to deprive them of the fruits of their labour, expelling them from the lands they had cleared." Clarkson continued by noting that whites reduced "again to slavery those negroes who had so honourably obtained their freedom. They hired them as servants, and, at the end of the stipulated time, refused payment of their wages, insisting that they were slaves: in some instances they destroyed their tickets of freedom, and then enslaved the negroes for want of them; in several instances, the unfortunate Africans were taken onboard vessels, carried to the West Indies, and there sold for the benefit of their plunderers." At Country Harbour, Black people were listed on the musters as the "Servants" of a white Loyalist, which meant it was very easy for them to be re-enslaved if they were not already enslaved. Sources: Thomas Clarkson, "Some Account of the New Colony at Sierra Leone," American Museum; or *Universal Magazine* (May 1792), 229–30; Settlers at Country Harbour, Ward Chipman Papers, Muster Master General's Office, Loyalist Musters, 1776–1785, MG 23, D1, ser. I, vol. 24, 1–470, Library and Archives Canada (LAC). Note: Ellen Wilson believed that the information Clarkson used came from Thomas Peters; see Ellen Wilson, *The Loyal Blacks* (New York: Capricorn Books, 1976), 181.

68. ALEXANDER (slave? c. 1784) – Alexander was possibly enslaved to George Westphal, who planned to settle near Halifax and who had six Black people living in his household. Source: Loyalists and Disbanded Troops at Cole Harbour, Chipman Papers, Muster Master General's Office, Loyalist Musters, 1776–1785, MG 23, D1, ser. I, vol. 24, LAC.

69. ALLEN, BARBARRY (c. 1783, age 22) – Barbarry was enslaved to Humphrey Winters, who migrated to the Maritimes from New York and Virginia. British officials at New York described her as a "healthy stout wench." Source: Book of Negroes.

70. ALLEN, FREELOVE (slave? c. 1796) – Possibly enslaved, Freelove Allen lived in Prince Edward Island. She was convicted of theft and sentenced to death. She or a number of white women petitioned that she be pardoned and sent or sold to the West Indies. Source: Harvey Amani Whitfield and Barry Cahill, "Slave Life and Slave Law in Colonial Prince Edward Island, 1769–1825," Acadiensis 38, no. 2 (Summer/ Autumn, 2009): 50.

71. ALLEN, JOHN (slave? c. 1796) – Possibly enslaved, John Allen was the husband of Freelove Allen and was charged with robbing the home of Colonel Robert Gray. Source: Whitfield and Cahill, "Slave Life and Slave Law," 50.

72. AMABLE, LOUIS (c. 1757, age 12) – Enslaved to Jean Loppinot, Louis lived with another female slave and helped care for Loppinot's large family. Sources: Donovan, "Nominal List of Slaves and Their Owners," 160; Kenneth Donovan, "Slaves and Their Owners in Île Royale, 1713–1760," Acadiensis 25, no. 1 (Autumn 1995): 28–29.

73. AMBRELLA (slave? c. 1784) – Ambrella was possibly enslaved to George Westphal, who planned to settle nearby Halifax and who had six Black people living in his household. Source: Loyalists and Disbanded Troops at Cole Harbour, Chipman Papers, Muster Master General's Office, Loyalist Musters, 1776–1785, MG 23, D1, ser. I, vol. 24, LAC.

74. AMBROSE, JOHN (slave? c. 1784) – John was possibly enslaved to Mr. Currie, who settled at Country Harbour, Nova Scotia. The majority of these Loyalists and their slaves were from North Carolina, South Carolina, and Georgia. They had settled briefly in East Florida before moving to Nova

Scotia. Black people at Country Harbour were either slaves or "quasi-free" and subject to re-enslavement. Abolitionist Thomas Clarkson explained the phenomenon of re-enslavement: "It was not long till these loyalists, many of whom had been educated with all the ideas of the justice of slavery, the inferiority of negroes, and the superiority of white men, that are universal in the southern provinces of America, began to harass and oppress the industrious black settlers, and even wantonly to deprive them of the fruits of their labour, expelling them from the lands they had cleared." Clarkson continued by noting that whites reduced "again to slavery those negroes who had so honourably obtained their freedom. They hired them as servants, and, at the end of the stipulated time, refused payment of their wages, insisting that they were slaves: in some instances they destroyed their tickets of freedom, and then enslaved the negroes for want of them; in several instances, the unfortunate Africans were taken onboard vessels, carried to the West Indies, and there sold for the benefit of their plunderers." At Country Harbour, Black people were listed on the musters as the "Servants" of a white Loyalist, which meant it was very easy for them to be re-enslaved if they were not already enslaved. Sources: Clarkson, "Some Account of the New Colony at Sierra Leone," 229–30; Settlers at Country Harbour, Chipman Papers, Muster Master General's Office, Loyalist Musters, 1776–1785, MG 23, D1, ser. I, vol. 24, LAC. Note: Ellen Wilson believed that the information Clarkson used came from Thomas Peters; see Wilson, *Loyal Blacks*, 181.

75. AMORETTA (c. 1783, age 50) – Enslaved to Charles Morris, who purchased her from a man in Charleston, Amoretta migrated with Morris to the Maritimes with one other slave. British officials in New York described her as a "stout wench." Source: Book of Negroes.

76. ANDREW (c. 1783, age 9) – Andrew was enslaved to Lieutenant Cox, with whom he migrated to the Maritimes from New York after the American Revolution. British officials described him as a "likely boy." The officials also noted that Lieutenant Cox had "brought him [as a] child from North Carolina after picking him up in [the woods]." Source: Book of Negroes.

77. ANDREW (c. 1808) – Andrew was probably enslaved to Captain Jacob Smith in Woodstock, New Brunswick. Source: Smith, "Slave in Canada," 87.

78. ANGELIQUE (c. 1749) – Angelique was enslaved to Jacques Prevost and had an infant child. By 1754, the Prevost family had purchased two more slaves. Source: Donovan, "Slaves and Their Owners in Île Royale, 1713–1760," 11.

79. INFANT SON (c. 1749) – The infant child of Angelique. Source: Donovan, "Slaves and Their Owners in Île Royale, 1713–1760," 11.

80. ANGELIQUE (c. 1754) – This enslaved person gave birth to a son. Source: Ken Donovan, "Female Slaves as Sexual Victims in Île Royale," Acadiensis 43, no. 1 (Winter /Spring, 2014): 150.

81. PIERRE (c. 1754) – The infant son of Angelique. Source: Donovan, "Female Slaves as Sexual Victims in Île Royale," 150.

82. ANGELIQUE (c. 1759) – Angelique was the enslaved woman of a widow named Madame Carrerot. Source: Donovan, "Nominal List of Slaves and Their Owners," 160.

83. ANN (c. 1784) – John Wentworth sent Ann and 18 other slaves from Nova Scotia to his "relation" Paul Wentworth in Suriname. Wentworth described these slaves as "American born or well seasoned, and are perfectly stout, healthy, sober, orderly, Industrious, & obedient." Wentworth had the slaves Christened and claimed to be concerned for their welfare. He also claimed that the female slaves "promise well to increase their numbers." Source: John Wentworth to Paul Wentworth or his attorney, February 24, 1784, Wentworth Letters, vol. 49, NSA.

84. ANNA (c. 1783, age 20) – Enslaved to John Speir, who migrated to the Maritimes after the American Revolution, Anna was possibly from New Jersey. British officials in New York recorded that Speir had purchased Anna from another owner. These same officials described her as a "stout wench." Source: Book of Negroes.

85. ANNE (c. 1784) – Anne was enslaved to John Todd at Chedabucto, Nova Scotia, who owned several other slaves. These slaves were probably from Georgia, South Carolina, East Florida, or another southern state. Source: Loyalists from Saint Augustine to Chedabucto, July 1784, Chipman Papers, Muster Master General's Office, Loyalist Musters, 1776–1785, MG 23, D1, ser. I, vol. 24, LAC.

86. ANNIE (c. 1783, age 17) – Enslaved to Colonel Edward Cole, Annie spent the first part of her life in Rhode Island before being evacuated with her owner to New York. British officials in New York described her as an "ordinary wench." She eventually settled with Cole in Parrsboro, Nova Scotia. Interestingly, she is not listed in the Parrsboro township book that lists the rest of Cole's slaves, which suggests that she might have died, fled, or been sold. Sources: Book of Negroes; Parrsboro Township Book, Esther Clark Wright Archives (ECWA), Acadia University, Wolfville, Nova Scotia.

87. ANSON (c. 1783, age 21) – Enslaved to Lieutenant McDonald, who migrated to the Maritimes after the American Revolution with one other slave,

Anson was possibly from New York. British officials in New York described him as a "stout fellow." Source: Book of Negroes.

88. ANTHONY (slave? c. 1783) – In his diary, New England Planter and Liverpool resident Simeon Perkins commented that "Mr. Granadine's Negro Man Anthony & Negro woman Hagar Arrive with Prince Snow at Evening from Shelburn to Live with me, per agreement for 50 dollars from the first of December to the first of May, for which I agreed to allow him 50 dollars. I have a letter from Mr. Granadine." Anthony and Hagar were probably enslaved to Granadine (various ways of spelling this name) and he hired them out to Perkins for several months. Source: D.C. Harvey, ed., Diary of Simeon Perkins, 1780–1789 (Toronto: Champlain Society, 1958), 211.

89. ANTOINE (c. 1742) – Antoine was enslaved to Louisbourg merchant Louis Jouet, who owned numerous slaves. Source: Donovan, "Nominal List of Slaves and Their Owners," 154.

90. ANTOINE (slave/indentured servant? c. 1750) – Antoine left Louisbourg on a vessel headed to France. Described as a "mulatto," Antoine "was listed as a 'voluntary passenger.'" His status in Louisbourg is unclear. Perhaps he was an indentured servant or a slave who was allowed to travel to France. Source: Donovan, "Slaves and Their Owners in Île Royale, 1713–1760," 31.

91. APPOLON, MARIE (c. 1758) – Marie was an enslaved woman in Île Royale. Source: Donovan, "Nominal List of Slaves and Their Owners," 160.

92. ARMSTRONG, ZIMRI (c. 1785) – During the 1780s, Zimri Armstrong petitioned the governor of New Brunswick. Armstrong had "agread" to work for Samuel Jarvis for two years as long as Jarvis paid for his passage to New Brunswick and purchased the freedom of Armstrong's family, who were slaves. During his indenture, Samuel Jarvis had transferred control of Armstrong to his brother and returned to the United States. According to Armstrong, Samuel Jarvis "left me destitute of both Cloaths and provisions in a Strange Country … [and] had sold my wife and family." Armstrong then petitioned the provincial government, stating that he should be freed from Jarvis's service. Governor Thomas Carleton, however, showed scant concern for the slave or free Black population in New Brunswick and the provincial council had little interest in helping Armstrong. The only option for Armstrong was to pursue his complaint through the court system, which he lacked the resources to do. In this instance, Armstrong lost his family and his own freedom for a period of years. Source: Zimri Armstrong, Saint John's County, no. 78, F 1024, RS 108, Land Petitions, Provincial Archives of New Brunswick (PANB), Fredericton, New Brunswick.

93. WIFE OF ZIMRI ARMSTRONG (c. 1785) – This woman was sold away from her husband along with her child or children; the source does not make clear how many children or if they were other types of relatives like nieces or cousins. Source: Zimri Armstrong, Saint John's County, no. 78, F 1024, RS 108, Land Petitions, PANB.

94. UNNAMED CHILD OF ZIMRI ARMSTRONG (c. 1785) – This child was sold with his or her mother away from the father; the source does not make clear how many children Armstrong had. Source: Zimri Armstrong, Saint John's County, no. 78, F 1024, RS 108, Land Petitions, PANB.

95. ARNY (c. 1742) – An enslaved man from Guadeloupe, Arny was sold by Captain Pierre Cosset to Julian Bannier for 800 livres. Source: Donovan, "Slaves and Their Owners in Île Royale, 1713–1760," 8.

96. ASAR (c. 1738) – Asar was enslaved to Julien Grandchamp, who purchased him to work at his inn. As historian Ken Donovan notes, the Grandchamp family also purchased an Indigenous slave named Louis after obtaining Asar. Source: Donovan, "Slaves and Their Owners in Île Royale, 1713–1760," 15.

97. ASH, AMY (slave? c. 1784) – Amy was possibly an enslaved person who settled at Belle Vue in Beaver Harbour. Although these people might have been nominally free, they were regularly subjected to re-enslavement. Source: Loyalists at Belle Vue, Chipman Papers, Muster Master General's Office, Loyalist Musters, 1776–1785, MG 23, D1, ser. I, vol. 24, LAC.

98. ASH, JACK (slave? c. 1784) – Jack was possibly an enslaved person who settled at Belle Vue in Beaver Harbour. Although these people might have been nominally free, they were regularly subjected to re-enslavement. Source: Loyalists at Belle Vue, Chipman Papers, Muster Master General's Office, Loyalist Musters, 1776–1785, MG 23, D1, ser. I, vol. 24, LAC.

99. ASH, JAMES (slave? c. 1784) – James was possibly an enslaved person who settled at Belle Vue in Beaver Harbour. Although these people might have been nominally free, they were regularly subjected to re-enslavement. Source: Loyalists at Belle Vue, Chipman Papers, Muster Master General's Office, Loyalist Musters, 1776–1785, MG 23, D1, ser. I, vol. 24, LAC.

100. AUGUSTUS, CAESAR (c. 1788) – Caesar Augustus married Darias Snider at St. George's Anglican church in Sydney, Cape Breton. Source: September 4, 1788, St. George's Sydney, MG 4, no. 147, NSA.

101. DARIAS SNIDER, DARIAS (c. 1788) – Darius was the wife of Caesar Augustus. Source: September 4, 1788, St. George's Sydney, MG 4, no. 147, NSA.

102. AUGUSTUS, ELISABETH (slave? c. 1792, infant) – Elizabeth was the child of Caesar Augustus and Darias Snider, who died in infancy. Source: March 20, 1792, St. George's Sydney, MG 4, no. 147, NSA.

103. BACCHUS (c. 1808, age 14) – Bacchus was enslaved to Titus Knapp, who had bought him from Sarah Allen for £30. She described Bacchus as a "Mulato Boy." Source: Smith, "Slave in Canada," 67.

104. BARBE (c. 1748, age 25) – Barbe was enslaved to Jean Pierre Roma, who had planned to settle in Prince Edward Island but went instead to Louisbourg in 1732; he owned 12 slaves. Sources: Donovan, "Slaves and Their Owners in Île Royale, 1713–1760," 10; Donovan, "Female Slaves as Sexual Victims in Île Royale," 149.

105. MARIE (c. 1748/1749) – Marie was the infant daughter of John Pierre Roma's slave Barbe. Sources: Donovan, "Slaves and Their Owners in Île Royale, 1713–1760," 10; Donovan, "Female Slaves as Sexual Victims in Île Royale," 149.

106. BARNY (slave? c. 1784) – Possibly enslaved to Michael Houseal, a Loyalist from Maryland, Barny lived with three other Black people who were also possibly slaves. Houseal remained in Nova Scotia until at least 1800, when he decided to move to England. In that same year, he attempted to hire out a young Black female as an indentured servant. Source: Loyalists and Disbanded Troops at Cole Harbour, Chipman Papers, Muster Master General's Office, Loyalist Musters, 1776–1785, MG 23, D1, ser. I, vol. 24, LAC; *Royal Gazette*, June 24, 1800.

107. BATHSHEBA (c. 1788) – Bathsheba was enslaved to Mr. Hecht (possibly Frederick William Hecht); her daughter Hagar was baptized in 1788. Source: List of Baptisms, November 23, 1788, Records of the Anglican Church, Digby Township Book, MG 4, vol. 23, item 3, NSA.

108. HAGAR (c. 1788) – The daughter of Bathsheba and enslaved to Mr. Hecht, Hagar was baptized in 1788. Source: List of Baptisms, November 23, 1788, Records of the Anglican Church, Digby Township Book, MG 4, vol. 23, item 3, NSA.

109. BASS, JOHN (slave? c. 1796) – Possibly enslaved, John Bass was charged with robbing the home of Colonel Robert Gray. Source: Whitfield and Cahill, "Slave Life and Slave Law," 50.

110. BASTIAN, DIANA (c. 1792, age 15) – An Anglican Church recorder memorialized the sad life of young teenager Diana Bastian (her surname has

been spelled various ways: Bustian, Bastian, and Bestian) in this burial record. His extraordinary account highlights the brutal life of Bastian, but also
her refusal to allow George More (who was much older than Bastian) and
his powerful friends to dehumanize her. The church's documentation illuminates the way one young enslaved girl fought against her tormentor: "Buried
Diana Bastian a Negro Girl belonging to Abraham Cuyler [former mayor
of Albany, New York], Esq. in the 15th year of her Age, she was Deluded
and Ruined at Government House by George More Esq. the Naval officer
and one of Governor Macarmick's Counsel by whom she was pregnant with
Twins and delivered [of], but one of them; She most earnestly implored the
favour of Mr. More's Brother Justice's to be admitted to her oath, concerning
her pregnancy by him, but was refused that with every other assistance by
him & them." Source: September 15, 1792, Burial Record 1785–1827, St. George's Anglican Church, Sydney.

111. UNNAMED CHILD (c. 1792) – The infant child of Bastian. Source: September
15, 1792, Burial Record 1785–1827, St. George's Anglican Church, Sydney.

112. BAZLEY, SCIPIO (c. 1783, age 30) – Enslaved to Reverend John Beardsley, who migrated to the Maritimes after the American Revolution with two
other slaves, Scipio was possibly from Connecticut. British officials described
him as a "stout fellow." Source: Book of Negroes.

113. BEARDSLEY, DINAH (c. 1783, age 35) – Enslaved to Reverend John
Beardsley, who migrated to the Maritimes after the American Revolution with
two other slaves, Dinah was possibly from Connecticut. British officials noted
that Dinah "says she is his own property [Beardsley's] having always been in
the Family." The officials also described her as a "sickly wench." Source: Book of
Negroes.

114. BEARDSLEY, PETER (c. 1783, age 24) – Enslaved to Reverend John
Beardsley, who migrated to the Maritimes after the American Revolution
with two other slaves, Peter was possibly from Connecticut. British officials
described him as a "stout fellow." Source: Book of Negroes.

115. BELLA (c. 1783, age 14) – Enslaved to James Peters, who migrated to the
Maritimes from New York, Bella was probably from New York. British officials
in New York described her as a "stout wench." Source: Book of Negroes.

116. BELLA (c. 1790, age 1) – Bella was enslaved to Benjamin James; in 1790,
when a local church in Granville baptized her, she was listed as the "property of
Benjamin James." Source: Register of Baptisms and Marriages for the Three Districts of the
Township of Granville, Granville Township Book, MG 4, vol. 34, item 3, NSA.

117. BELLA (c. 1788) – Bella was enslaved to Joseph Totten, who, in his will, gave three Black children away to his daughters but not the other slaves, which means that a slave family was probably broken up; for instance, Totten stated: "I give and bequeath my Negro Girl Slave named Bella [?] to my daughter Jane." Source: Joseph Totten, 1788, Annapolis County, RG 48, Probate Records, NSA.

118. BELLER (c. 1787, age 16) – Enslaved to Thomas Lester, who, in a runaway slave advertisement, commented that Beller and Sam (her brother) had been "raised in the family." Lester described Beller as "between a black and mulatto, 16 years old, midling tall and slim, is raw bon'd has a scar between her eye and temple, is slow in her speech, has a black cover'd hat with white lining, and lived formerly with Judge Peters at Saint John." This person might be the same individual as entry 115. Source: *Royal Gazette* (New Brunswick), July 10, 1787.

119. BEN (c. 1783, age 11) – Ben was enslaved to James Dunn, who migrated to the Maritimes from New York. Before evacuating New York, James Dunn owned at least four slaves in Norfolk, Virginia. Escaping the onslaught of the rebels, Dunn and his slaves went to New York City. In 1783, as the last Loyalists were evacuated, Dunn lost three slaves. According to his Loyalist claim, "One, Lucy, staid in the Fleet when Claimant went on Shore, but afterwards going on Shore was taken by a Rebel Colonel." British officials in New York described Ben as a "fine boy." Sources: Book of Negroes; James Dunn, Loyalist Claims Commission, AO12/55/31, NSA.

120. BEN (c. 1783, age 22) – Ben was enslaved to John Wilson, who, in a runaway slave advertisement, noted: "ABSCONTED himself on Thursday last from on Board the Transport Ship FRIENDS, a Negro Lad named Ben, he is 22 Years of Age, five feet four Inches high, of a remarkable dark complection Slender made, with a thin face and Large Lips, he has a Sore on one of his little fingers; and took with him three sailors Jackets and may pass for a Sailor. I hereby request all master of Vessels not to Ship him as he is my own property; and I forewarn any Person from harbouring or imploying him, as I shall [prosecute] them, who conceal him from me, and will give the above reward to them who may take him and bring him on board my Ship." Source: *Nova Scotia Gazette and Weekly Chronicle*, May 20, 1783.

121. BEN (c. 1786, age 30) – Enslaved to Maryland Loyalist Captain Caleb Jones, in 1786 Ben attempted to run away on two separate occasions. The first runaway notice described Ben thusly: "RUN away, a negro man named BEN, about thirty years of age, the property of Capt. Jones, had on when he went away a light brown jacket, a plad waistcoat, corduroy breeches, white stockings, and a round hat; is about five feet six inches high, stout and well set, has very black thick lips." A few months later, Ben escaped again with a group of Jones's slaves. Source: *Royal Gazette*, March 7, 1786 and July 25, 1786.

122. BEN (c. 1785) – Enslaved to Governor Patterson of Prince Edward Island, Ben became part of the Jupiter Wise conspiracy to steal rum, have a party, and escape to Boston. Ben commented when approached by other conspirators that he had long wanted to run away from Patterson. Sources: *King v. Jupiter Wise*, 1786, Public Archives and Records Office, Prince Edward Island (PAROPEI); Henry Holman, "Slaves and Servants on Prince Edward Island: The Case of Jupiter Wise," *Acadiensis* 12, no. 1 (1982): 100–4; Jim Hornby, *Black Islanders* (Charlottetown: Institute of Island Studies, 1991), 15–19.

123. BENJAMIN? (c. 1787) – Benjamin (name is not clear on baptismal record), an enslaved infant, was baptized in Cornwallis, Nova Scotia. Source: List of Baptisms, October 21, 1787, Cornwallis Township Book, MG 4, vol. 18-18 A, item 3, NSA.

124. BENJAMIN (c. 1746) – Benjamin was enslaved to the Connecticut Regiment during the siege and takeover of Louisbourg. Source: Donovan, "Nominal List of Slaves and Their Owners," 156.

125. BENJAMIN (c. 1783, age 21) – Enslaved to Mr. Coulson, who purchased him from a widow in South Carolina, Benjamin went to the Maritimes from New York when Coulson migrated there with one other slave. British officials described Benjamin as a "stout fellow." Source: Book of Negroes.

126. BENJAMIN (c. 1796) – Enslaved to Balthazar (Bethaser) Creamer in Preston, Nova Scotia, Benjamin lived with an adult female slave and a young girl. They were probably a family. Apparently, after Creamer's 1796 will and before its 1797 revision, the French war vessel *Raison* captured and "carried" off Benjamin. The estate of Balthazar Creamer valued him at £60 before reducing it to £40 after he had been kidnapped. Perhaps the estate's executors hoped to get some sort of compensation from the government. Source: Smith, "Slave in Canada," 94.

127. MARY (c. 1796) – Enslaved to Balthazar Creamer in Preston, Nova Scotia, Mary was valued at £60 in Creamer's estate inventory. She might have been married to Creamer's adult slave Benjamin and been the mother of Sary. Allegedly, she ran away from the Creamer family, but this might have happened after the kidnapping of her husband and death of her daughter. Source: Smith, "Slave in Canada," 94.

128. SARY (c. 1796) – Enslaved to Balthazar Creamer in Preston, Nova Scotia, Sary was valued at £30 in Creamer's 1796 estate inventory. She might have been the daughter of Creamer's adult slaves named Benjamin and Mary. Sary died within a year of the original estate inventory. Source: Smith, "Slave in Canada," 94.

129. BENSON, LYDIA (c. 1790) – Enslaved to New York Loyalist Christopher Benson, who lived in Granville, Nova Scotia, Lydia married John Moses. Source: Register of Baptisms and Marriages for the Three Districts of the Township of Granville, Granville Township Book, MG 4, vol. 34, item 3, NSA.

130. MOSES, JOHN (c. 1790) – Enslaved to Christopher Benson, John was married to Lydia Benson. Source: Register of Baptisms and Marriages for the Three Districts of the Township of Granville, Granville Township Book, MG 4, vol. 34, item 3, NSA.

131. BERRY, WILLIAM (c. 1780s/1790s?) – William was enslaved to John Lent, who arrived with other Loyalists in Shelburne in 1783. According to oral tradition, William became unhappy about not having a wife and convinced Lent to purchase a woman named Dinah. They had a daughter who died at age 106 in 1893. William apparently lived to be 98 years old and was from Long Island, New York. Sources: *The Times*, February 3, 1893; Sharon Robart-Johnson, *Africa's Children: The History of Blacks in Yarmouth, Nova Scotia* (Toronto: Natural Heritage Books, 2009), 141.

132. DINAH (c. 1780s/1790s?) – Dinah was enslaved to John Lent and married to his slave William Berry. Source: *The Times*, February 3, 1893.

133. MCKINNON, HESTER (c. 1780s/1790s?) – Enslaved to John Lent, and the daughter of William Berry and Dinah, Hester was named after the Lent's housekeeper, who was in charge of the slaves. She died at age 106 in 1893. Sources: *The Times*, February 3, 1893; Robart-Johnson, *Africa's Children*, 153.

134. BERTRAM, ANTHONY (c. 1784) – Anthony Bertram was probably enslaved to Nathan Hubbill in Chedabucto, Nova Scotia. Source: Loyalists from Saint Augustine to Chedabucto, Chipman Papers, Muster Master General's Office, Loyalist Musters, 1776–1785, MG 23, D1, ser. I, vol. 24, LAC.

135. BESS (c. 1805) – Bess was enslaved to Annapolis merchant Joshua F. de St. Croix who, in his will, freed his "faithfull servant" and directed his sons to pay Bess £10 per year for the rest of her life. Source: Will of Joshua F de St. Croix, Annapolis County, RG 48, Probate Records, NSA.

136. BET (c. 1783, age 5) – Enslaved to Samuel Davenport, who migrated to the Maritimes after the American Revolution with another enslaved child, Bet was from New York. British officials at New York described her as a "fine girl." Source: Book of Negroes.

137. BET (c. 1783, age 10) – Enslaved to John de Young, Bet went to the Maritimes with Young when he migrated from New York. British officials described her as a "stout girl." Source: Book of Negroes.

138. BETSEY (c. 1784, age 2) – Betsey was enslaved to John Grant, who was originally from Scotland and who, after serving the British army near Ticonderoga during the Seven Years War, settled in Queens County, Long Island. After the American Revolution, he settled in Nova Scotia with a large family and nine slaves. These enslaved people might have been a family unit. Sources: Catherine M.A. Cottreau-Robins, "Exploring the Landscape of Slavery in Loyalist Era Nova Scotia," in *The Consequences of Loyalism: Essays in Honor of Robert M. Calhoon*, eds., Rebecca Brannon and Joseph S. Moore (Columbia: University of South Carolina Press, 2019), 131–2; also Smith, "Slave in Canada," 93–4.

139. BETT (c. 1789) – Enslaved to Lord Dunmore in Nassau, Bett escaped to Shelburne, Nova Scotia, and then to Halifax. Dunmore appointed George and Robert Ross of Shelburne to capture Bett and send her back to the Bahamas. Source: Marion Robertson, *King's Bounty: A History of Early Shelburne* (Halifax: Nova Scotia Museum, 1983), 95.

140. BETTS (c. 1783, age 30) – Enslaved to Captain Longstreet, who migrated to the Maritimes after the American Revolution, Betts was probably from New Jersey. British officials described her as an "ordinary wench." Source: Book of Negroes.

141. BETTY (c. 1761) – Betty was enslaved to the Evans family of Massachusetts, who moved to Nova Scotia in the early 1760s. Source: Isaiah W. Wilson, *A Geography and History of the County of Digby* (Halifax: Holloway Bros. Printers, 1900), 302.

142. BETTY (c. 1783, age 20) – Enslaved to Nathaniel Dickenson, Betty was moved to the Maritimes after the American Revolution along with two other slaves. She was probably from New Jersey. British officials in New York described her as a "stout wench." Source: Book of Negroes.

143. BETTY (c. 1783, age 20) – Enslaved to Conrad Hendricks, who migrated to the Maritimes after the American Revolution, Betty and her infant were probably from New Jersey. British officials at New York described her as a "stout wench." Source: Book of Negroes.

144. UNNAMED INFANT CHILD (c. 1783) – This infant was enslaved to Conrad Hendricks and was moved to the Maritimes after the American Revolution along with his or her mother Betty. Source: Book of Negroes.

145. BETTY (c. 1783, age 26) – Enslaved to Edward Beattie, Betty went to the Maritimes after the American Revolution with Beattie and her two enslaved children. She was from New York. British officials described her as a "likely wench." Source: Book of Negroes.

146. SARAH (c. 1783, age 1 – precisely 11 months) – Sarah was enslaved to Edward Beattie. British officials noted that she had been "born [after] Edward Beattie bought Betty" and they described her as a "fine child." Source: Book of Negroes.

147. JACK (c. 1783, age 4) – Enslaved to Edward Beattie, British officials noted that Jack had been "born [after] Edward Beattie bought Betty" and these officials described him as a "fine boy." Source: Book of Negroes.

148. BETTY (slave? c. 1784) – Betty settled at Belle Vue in Beaver Harbour and was possibly a slave. Although these people might have been nominally free, they were regularly subjected to re-enslavement. Source: Roll of Loyalists Settled at Belle Vue in Beaver Harbour, Chipman Papers, Muster Master General's Office, Loyalist Musters, 1776–1785, MG 23, D1, ser. I, vol. 24, LAC.

149. BETTY (c. 1802) – Betty was enslaved to Virginia Loyalist Jacob Ellegood, who owned several slaves – some of whom were part of the same slave family. Ellegood served in the New Brunswick legislative assembly and also owned a large farm. He was the brother-in-law of John Saunders, who served as chief justice of the New Brunswick Supreme Court and who was also from Virginia. Source: Will of Jacob Ellegood, York County, New Brunswick, 1802, PANB.

150. BETTY ANNA (c. 1789) – Enslaved to Captain William Booth, who was stationed in Shelburne during the late 1780s, Betty Anna was probably from Grenada, where Booth's brother-in-law was a planter and merchant. She worked as a domestic in Booth's household. On June 3, 1789, Booth wrote that he had "sent Betty on board the ship for Grenada by way of New Providence [Bahamas] – gave her two shifts a complete white dress and a new Striped short Gown, Blankets, Nightcap, Bread and Cheese, &c – She had also an old, yellow striped short gown and petticoat of the same with a hat." Booth claimed he had "no further use for her" in Shelburne. Source: William Booth, *Remarks and Rough Memorandums: Captain William Booth, Corps of Royal Engineers, Shelburne, Nova Scotia, 1787, 1789* (Shelburne: Shelburne Country Arhives and Geoealogical Sociaty, 2008), 90–1.

151. BILL (c. 1783, age 15) – Bill was enslaved to Lieutenant McLeod, who migrated to the Maritimes after the American Revolution with another slave. British officials at New York described Bill as a "likely boy." Source: Book of Negroes.

152. BILL (c. 1783, age 12) – Enslaved to Aury Van Voorst, who migrated to the Maritimes after the American Revolution, Bill was probably from New Jersey. British officials at New York described him as a "likely boy." Source: Book of Negroes.

153. BILL (c. 1783, age 26) – Enslaved to William Black, who migrated to the Maritimes from New York, Bill was from New York. British officials described him as a "stout fellow." Source: Book of Negroes.

154. BILL (c. 1783, age 25) – Enslaved to William Douglas, who settled in the Maritimes after the American Revolution, Bill was possibly from New York. British officials in New York described him as a "stout ugly fellow." Source: Book of Negroes.

155. BILL (c. 1787) – Bill was enslaved to Sarah Grant of Annapolis, Nova Scotia, who listed him in her estate inventory as worth £35 – which was more than she valued her other slave Caesar. Source: Sarah Grant, 1787, Annapolis County, Nova Scotia, RG 48, NSA.

156. BILL [or **BELFAST**] (c. 1794, age 27) – A native of South Carolina, Bill attempted to escape from his owner Michael Wallace while in the service of William Forsyth. After spending 10 years enslaved in Nova Scotia, Bill carefully planned to escape from his owner. Wallace's runaway advertisement illuminates how Bill meticulously attempted to escape his owner for good. "RAN Away, on Thursday evening, the 18th inst. a Negro Man Servant, the property of the Subscriber, named Belfast; but who commonly goes by the name of Bill.–––––––– At the time of the elopement he was in the service of William Forsyth, Esq; and had meditated an attempt to get on board a ship that night which lay in the harbour, bound to Newfoundland; but was frustrated: It is probable, however, he may still endeavour to escape that way, therefore, the masters of all coasters going along shore, or other vessels bound to sea, are hereby forewarned from carrying him off at their peril, as they will be prosecuted, if discovered, with the utmost rigour of the law. The above reward will be paid to any person or persons who shall apprehend and secure him, so that I may recover him again. He is likely, stout-made fellow, of five feet eight or nine inches high, and about 27 years of age; of mild good countenance and features, smooth black skin, with very white teeth; is a native of South Carolina, speaks good English, and very softly, and has been in this province for ten years. When he went off, he wore an old Bath-Coating short coat, of a light colour, wore out at the elbows; brown cloth or duffil[?] trowsers, also much wore at the knees; a round hat, and an old black silk [handkerchief] about his neck: – But as he had other cloaths secreted in town, he may have changed his whole apparel. He will no doubt endeavour to pass for a free man, and possibly by some other name." Source: *Weekly Chronicle*, March 15, 1794.

157. BINA (c. 1783–84, age 17) – Enslaved to John Nash, who settled at Cheda-bucto, Nova Scotia, Bina was described by British officials as a "likely wench." Source: Loyalists from Saint Augustine to Chedabucto, Chipman Papers, Muster Master General's Office, Loyalist Musters, 1776–1785, MG 23, D1, ser. I, vol. 24, LAC.

158. POMPEY (c. 1783) – Pompey was the son of Bina and also enslaved to John Nash. Source: Book of Negroes.

159. BLACK BILL (c. 1780s) – Enslaved to William Schurman (or Schurmann) in Prince Edward Island, Black Bill was originally from New York and he lived with a few other slaves in PEI. Source: Whitfield and Cahill, "Slave Life and Slave Law," 36.

160. BLACK CATO (c. ?) – Enslaved to Jesse Oakes of Bridgetown, Nova Scotia, Black Cato was valued at £45 by Oakes and lived with one other slave. Source: F.W. Harris, "The Negro Population of the County of Annapolis," Paper read at the Annual Meeting of the Historical Association of Annapolis Royal, November 11, 1920, PANS, 16.

161. BLACK CHARLES (c. 1810s) – Black Charles was possibly enslaved to the Easson family of Annapolis, Nova Scotia. This family had trading inter-ests in Jamaica. Given the substantial number of slaves in Annapolis in the late eighteenth century and the lack of a surname, it seems likely that at some point in Charles's life that he had been enslaved. Source: Easson Family Fonds, MG 1 vol. 3478 no. A199, NSA, https://archives.novascotia.ca/africanns/archives/?ID=66.

162. BLACK JACK (c. 1792) – Enslaved to William Bulmer, Black Jack was manumitted on his owner's death. Source: Smith, "Slave in Canada," 18.

163. BLACK JAMES (c. ?) – Enslaved to Jesse Oakes of Bridgetown, Nova Scotia, Black James was valued at £10 by Oakes and lived with one other slave. Source: Harris, "Negro Population of the County of Annapolis," 15.

164. BLACK JEFF (c. 1780s?) – Enslaved to Dr. Harris, who resided in Truro, Nova Scotia. Source: Smith, "Slave in Canada," 56.

165. BLACK PETER (slave? c. 1798–1803?) – Black Peter was possibly en-slaved in Kings County, Nova Scotia, because, as stated on an undated scrap of paper, "Black Peter now lives with Esq. John Chipman, helps him [haul] ship timber." Source: Undated Loose Paper, RG 34-316, 1798–1803, Kings County Proceedings of the Sessions, NSA.

166. BLACK MAN (slave? c. 1790) – In 1790, a Mr. Chalmer sent his "Blk. Man, belonging to his schooner to Shelburne." Source: Charles Bruce Fergusson, ed., *The Diary of Simeon Perkins*, 1790–1796 (Toronto: The Champlain Society, 1961), 51.

167. BLACK MAN (slave? c. 1792) – Simeon Perkins noted "We have the Black Caulker on ye *Minerva*" and the next day he commented "the Blk man Caulkg." Source: Fergusson, *Diary of Simeon Perkins*, 1790–1796, 198.

168. BLACK MARY (c. 1810s) – Black Mary was possibly enslaved to the Easson family of Annapolis, Nova Scotia. This family had trading interests in Jamaica. Given the substantial number of slaves in Annapolis in the late eighteenth century and the lack of a surname, it seems likely that at some point in Mary's life that she had been enslaved. Source: Easson Family Fonds, MG 1 vol. 3478 no. A199, NSA, https://archives.novascotia.ca/africanns/archives/?ID=66.

169. BOB (c. 1783, age 15) – Enslaved to Adjutant Cunningham, who migrated to the Maritimes from New York, Bob was possibly from New York. British officials described him as a "likely boy." Source: Book of Negroes.

170. BOB (c. 1783, age 19) – Enslaved to James Fraser, who migrated to the Maritimes from New York with a young female slave, Bob was probably from South Carolina. British officials described him as a "stout fellow." Source: Book of Negroes.

171. BOB (c. 1783, age 7) – Enslaved to Isaac Cooper, who migrated to the Maritimes from New York, Bob was possibly from Delaware, but it is unclear. British officials described him as a "fine boy." Source: Book of Negroes.

172. BOB (slave? c. 1784) – Bob was possibly enslaved to Lieutenant Cornwall, who migrated to Country Harbour with other southern Loyalists. The majority of these Loyalists and their slaves were from North Carolina, South Carolina, and Georgia. They had settled briefly in East Florida before moving to Nova Scotia. Black people at Country Harbour were either slaves or "quasi-free" and subject to re-enslavement. Abolitionist Thomas Clarkson explained the phenomenon of re-enslavement: "It was not long till these loyalists, many of whom had been educated with all the ideas of the justice of slavery, the inferiority of negroes, and the superiority of white men, that are universal in the southern provinces of America, began to harass and oppress the industrious black settlers, and even wantonly to deprive them of the fruits of their labour, expelling them from the lands they had cleared." Clarkson continued by noting that whites reduced "again to slavery those negroes who had so honourably obtained their freedom. They hired them as servants, and, at the end of the stipulated time, refused payment of their wages, insisting that they were slaves: in some instances they destroyed their tickets of freedom, and then enslaved the negroes for want of them; in several instances, the unfortunate Africans were taken onboard vessels, carried to the West Indies, and there sold for the benefit of their plunderers." At Country Harbour, Black people were listed on the musters as the "Servants" of a white Loyalist, which meant it was very easy for them to be re-enslaved if they were not already enslaved. Sources: Clarkson, "Some Account of the New Colony at Sierra Leone," 229–30; Settlers at Country Harbour, Chipman Papers, Muster Master General's Office, Loyalist Musters, 1776–1785, MG 23, D1, ser. I, vol. 24, LAC. Note: Ellen Wilson believed that the information Clarkson used came from Thomas Peters; see Wilson, *Loyal Blacks*, 181.

173. BOB (c. 1806, age 12) – Isaac Bonnell owned three young male slaves who he wanted to free once they reached 24 years of age. In his will, Bonnell clearly expressed some sentimental attachment to his young slaves. He not only intended to free them, but also to provide them with some basic necessities such as clothing. He also wanted them to have a rudimentary understanding of the Bible, because that would help them in early nineteenth-century society. These slaves would not gain their freedom until their mid-20s, which meant that Bonnell's family would continue to exploit their labour for many years. There is no mention of these slaves' biological parents, which means that they could have died or been sold. In discussing his slaves, Bonnell noted it was "My Desire is that My Black Boys George, Tom, & Bob – be Taught to Read [?] in the Bible & to write Legible hand & that they be Sett at Liberty as they [?] Arrive to the Age of Twenty four years. Each to be allow'd [?] of good new Cloathes of Every Description Beside their Common wearing apparel. George Was Born in November 1790. Tom Was born in May 1792. And Bob Was Born in February 1794." Source: Isaac Bonnell, 1806, Annapolis County, RG 48, Probate Records, NSA.

174. BOB (c. 1797) – Bob ran away from Robert Guthrie in New Brunswick. Gutherie noted that Bob stood about five feet five inches high and detailed his clothing and apparel. He made no mention of Bob's personality, work, or colour. Source: *Saint John Gazette*, January 6, 1797.

175. BOLTON, JENNY (c. 1783, age 11) – Enslaved to Mr. Potts, who migrated to the Maritimes after the American Revolution, Jenny was possibly from Virginia. Her likely parents, Thom Bolton and Anny Bolton, were headed to Shelburne in the same boat as Jenny, but they were free. It is possible that Mr. Potts owned all of them and freed Thom and Anny while continuing to enslave Jenny because he knew the parents would never leave their daughter and he could continue to exploit their labour. This is an example of how slaveowners continued to exploit Black families even when some of the members were technically free. British officials in New York described Jenny as a "stout girl." Source: Book of Negroes.

176. BOSTON (c. 1783, age 30) – Enslaved to William Briggs, who migrated to the Maritimes from New York, Boston was described by British officials in New York as a "stout fellow." Source: Book of Negroes.

177. BOURDETT, HARRY (c. 1783, age 18) – Enslaved to Oliver Bourdett, who migrated to the Maritimes after the American Revolution with one other enslaved teenager, Harry was described by British officials at New York as a "stout fellow." Source: Book of Negroes.

178. BREDE, LOUIS (c. 1735) – Louis was a French slave, who served on the crew of *King George*. Source: Donovan, "Nominal List of Slaves and Their Owners," 153.

179. BRINKERHOFF, JACK (c. 1783, age 26) – Enslaved to Lieutenant Cooper, who migrated to the Maritimes from New York, Jack was described by British officials as an "ordinary fellow." Source: Book of Negroes.

180. BRINNA [or **BINNA**] (slave? c. 1784) – Brinna was possibly enslaved to Lieutenant Cornwall, who migrated to Country Harbour with other southern Loyalists. The majority of these Loyalists and their slaves were from North Carolina, South Carolina, and Georgia. They had settled briefly in East Florida before moving to Nova Scotia. Black people at Country Harbour were either slaves or "quasi-free" and subject to re-enslavement. Abolitionist Thomas Clarkson explained the phenomenon of re-enslavement: "It was not long till these loyalists, many of whom had been educated with all the ideas of the justice of slavery, the inferiority of negroes, and the superiority of white men, that are universal in the southern provinces of America, began to harass and oppress the industrious black settlers, and even wantonly to deprive them of the fruits of their labour, expelling them from the lands they had cleared." Clarkson continued by noting that whites reduced "again to slavery those negroes who had so honourably obtained their freedom. They hired them as servants, and, at the end of the stipulated time, refused payment of their wages, insisting that they were slaves: in some instances they destroyed their tickets of freedom, and then enslaved the negroes for want of them; in several instances, the unfortunate Africans were taken onboard vessels, carried to the West Indies, and there sold for the benefit of their plunderers." At Country Harbour, Black people were listed on the musters as the "Servants" of a white Loyalist, which meant it was very easy for them to be re-enslaved if they were not already enslaved. Sources: Clarkson, "Some Account of the New Colony at Sierra Leone," 229–30; Settlers at Country Harbour, Chipman Papers, Muster Master General's Office, Loyalist Musters, 1776–1785, MG

23, D1, ser. I, vol. 24, LAC. Note: Ellen Wilson believed that the information Clarkson used came from Thomas Peters; see Wilson, *Loyal Blacks*, 181.

181. BRISTOL (c. 1783, age 35) – Enslaved to Isaac Brown, who migrated to the Maritimes after the American Revolution, Bristol was probably from New Jersey. British officials in New York noted Dr. Brown's father had purchased him when he was 1 year old. These same officials described him as a "stout fellow." Source: Book of Negroes.

182. BRISTOL (slave? c. 1784) – Possibly an enslaved person belonging to Joseph Russell, who planned to settle near Halifax. Russell had three other Black people in his household. Source: Loyalists and Disbanded Troops at Cole Harbour, Chipman Papers, Muster Master General's Office, Loyalist Musters, 1776–1785, MG 23, D1, ser. I, vol. 24, LAC.

183. BRISTOL (c. 1798) – Enslaved to James Moody, Bristol had a daughter named Sylvia who was baptized in 1798. Both of these people might have been included in Moody's listing of slaves from the 1807 Digby petition, but this is unclear. Source: List of Baptisms, April 1, 1798, Records of the Anglican Church, Digby Township Book, NSA.

184. SYLVIA (c. 1798) – Enslaved to James Moody, Sylvia was the child of Bristol. Both Sylvia and Bristol might have been included in Moody's listing of slaves from the 1807 Digby petition, but this is unclear. Source: List of Baptisms, April 1, 1798, Records of the Anglican Church, Digby Township Book, NSA.

185. BRITAIN, HAGAR (c. 1783, age 41) – Enslaved to Captain Drummond, who migrated to the Maritimes after the American Revolution, Hagar was possibly from New York. British officials noted Captain Drummond had purchased her from another owner. The officials described her as an "ordinary wench." Source: Book of Negroes.

186. BROADSTREET, CESAR (slave? c. 1788) – Cesar was baptized along with several other Black people in New Brunswick. The recorder listed him as the servant of Peter Ryerson (though it is difficult to read his master's name). Source: Early Parish Records, New Brunswick, September 14, 1788, possibly PANB; this repository did not stamp this document, so it is unclear if it is from PANB, NBM, or the UNB Loyalist Collection.

187. BROSS, RACHEL (c. 1799) – Enslaved to Frederick William Hecht, Rachel was brought before S.S. Blowers, the chief justice of the Nova Scotia Supreme Court, on a writ of habeas corpus. Hecht claimed her as a slave and attempted to prove he rightfully owned her, but Blowers determined that Hecht could not prove that the person he purchased Bross from had the right to sell her. Sources: *Hecht v. Moody*, 1799, RG 39 C, Supreme Court of Nova Scotia, Halifax, vol. 81, NSA; Barry Cahill, "Habeas Corpus and Slavery in Nova Scotia: *R v. Hecht, ex parte Rachel*, 1798," *University of New Brunswick Law Journal*, 44 (1995): 179–209.

188. BRUCE, BETSY (c. 1783, age 13) – Betsy was enslaved to William Wilson, who migrated to the Maritimes from New York with three other slaves. She was originally from Virginia. British officials described her as a "fine girl ¾ white." They also noted "these three persons [Betsy, Hilley, and Jenny] appear to be the property of William Wilson, they having fallen to him in consequence of a marriage settlement between him and Elizabeth Nansberg, Virginia." Source: Book of Negroes.

189. BRUCE, JENNY (c. 1783, age 15) – Jenny was enslaved to William Wilson, who migrated to the Maritimes from New York with three other slaves. She was originally from Virginia. British officials described her as a "fine girl ¾ white." Source: Book of Negroes.

190. BRUTUS (c. 1787) – Brutus was enslaved to Margaret Murray in Halifax, Nova Scotia, who agreed to free him at age 21. Murray owned two other slaves named Marianne and Flora. Sources: Will of Margaret Murray, 1787, Halifax County, NSA; Smith, "Slave in Canada," 91–2.

191. BUCK (c. 1812) – In his will, William Wanton (a founder of the University of New Brunswick) simply noted "Unto my late negro Slave and Servant Buck (to whom I have some time since given his freedom) the sum of one hundred dollars, to be paid to him as soon after my death (if he should so long live) as my dear wife should see fit." Source: Will of William Wanton, 1812, Saint John County, PANB.

192. BULKLEY, JOHN (c. 1788) – John was enslaved to Ann Cosby at Annapolis Royal, who freed three slaves in her 1788 will: "I do also give and devise unto my black Woman named Rose, a Molotto Girl named Agatha, and my black Man named John Bulkley … their full Freedom." Source: Ann Cosby, 1788, Annapolis County, RG 48, Probate Records, File C 11, NSA.

193. BUSH, ANDREW (free/possibly re-enslaved c. 1783–84, age 25) – Originally from Connecticut, where Dr. Hubbard owned him, Andrew escaped and possessed a General Birch Certificate (GBC). After arriving in the Maritimes, Thomas Rogers re-enslaved or took away Bush's freedom along with several other allegedly free Black Loyalists from Connecticut. Rogers's advertisement is an extremely important source because of the way it illuminates slave life, family structure, and occupation, often with remarkable detail: "HARBOURED, or otherwise CONCEALED, THE following Negroes belonging to the subscriber, viz. Edward Morris, an elderly negro about five feet five inches high, by trade a mason, has a remarkable wound in his forehead which shews a hole resembling a bullet shot, is a celebrated Methodist preacher among the negroes, was bred at Fairfield in Connecticut; also Charity his wife, a half bred Indian of the tribe on Long Island, province of New York, and a small boy about eleven years of age, son of the said wench by an Indian father. Andrew Bush, a comely stout negro, remarkable high forwarded, generally called the Widow's Peek, formerly the property of Doctor Bush in Connecticut, is a remarkable good miller, which practice he has been used all his life to, also his wife Eanus, a yellow mustee. And Peter Cock, a young negro, comely countenance, bandy with one leg, and has spent best part of the last six months at the house and in the neighbourhood of a person named White Raymond, in or near the lower cove, at Parr." Sources: Book of Negroes, *Royal Saint John's Gazette* (New Brunswick), May 13, 1784. For an in-depth description of this story of re-enslavement (which included Charity Morris, Edward Morris, Peter Cox, Eanus Deaton, and a few children), see Harvey Amani Whitfield, ed., *Black Slavery in the Maritimes: A History in Documents* (Peterborough: Broadview Press, 2018), 37–40.

194. BUTLER, JAMES (c. 1795) – Enslaved to James Etheridge, James married a free Black woman named Susanna in Granville, Nova Scotia in 1795. Source: James Butler and Susanna Marriage, 1795, Granville Township Book, NSA.

195. BYERS [or **BYARS**], **AMELIA** (c. 1800) – Colonel Robinson owned Amelia and her husband Jack along with their children. Originally from Virginia, she probably arrived in Prince Edward Island as part of the Loyalist influx to the Maritimes. In 1800, her owner recorded his decision to conditionally offer Jack and Amelia their freedom: "19th July 1800 – I was under the necessity of telling my servants, Jack and Amelia to get them to go to Prince Town – that at the end of one year, if they behaved themselves well (of which I was to be the judge) and that neither Mrs. _____ or myself wanted either of them, I would give them their liberty; that is to say, only for themselves two, not liberty for any children they now have or may hereafter have. But I also told them that if they or either of them misbehaved, they forfeit all expectations thereto. I also told them as long as either of us wanted them, they were not to look for or expect their liberty, but to remain slaves as long as we or either of us, thought proper."

Although Robinson owned Jack and Amelia, it is clear that his slaves also had agency in gaining their freedom. Slavery was complicated, and it is far too simple to assume that slaves had no cards they could play. For example, there are various types of negotiation coexisting in Robinson's note. The first sentence of his entry is profoundly revealing. Robinson wrote that he was "under the necessity" of telling his slaves about their impending move to Prince Town. Why did he feel compelled to tell them anything? They were his slaves after all. Yet the first sentence demonstrates that Robinson felt like he could not just tell his slaves what to do. Robinson did not simply make Amelia and Jack leave their home, but rather he explained to them – that is, negotiated with the two slaves – as to why they should go to Prince Town.

Indeed, Robinson had to sweeten the deal or face two discontented or resistant slaves. He offered freedom to the couple while simultaneously denying it to their children, but this gave the slaves a chance to seize their own freedom. As historian Ira Berlin argues, slaves could negotiate their freedom, but it "was a complicated business." Robinson had most of the advantages, including an understanding of the law and more material resources than his slaves. His notation left little doubt as to his goal of controlling his slaves' behaviour by placing demeaning demands on them. Indeed, like many slaveholders who offered conditional manumission throughout North America, Robinson could not "resist squeezing [his] slaves one last time." But Jack and Amelia were far from helpless. They could call upon a reservoir of knowledge about their owners and "the support of family and community." The tenor of Robinson's note reveals a man trying to convince himself that he still controlled his slaves by attempting to put various types of restrictions on Jack and Amelia's potential freedom. Yet his slaves did in some ways control their path to freedom if "they behaved themselves." They knew how to please Robinson and his wife after years of service to them. The enslaved couple could use this knowledge to obtain freedom. Yet the continued enslavement of their children presented financial challenges that required the couple to slowly build up enough money to purchase their children's liberty. Jack and Amelia's opportunity for freedom is an example of the negotiations that took place between slaveholders and slaves throughout the Atlantic world, including the Maritime colonies. These two slaves did not have the best cards to play, but they did have cards and could win a hand against their owners that might well result in freedom or the amelioration of certain conditions. Sources: Ira Berlin, *Many Thousands Gone: The First Two Centuries of Slavery in North America* (Cambridge: Harvard University Press, 1998) 235; *Examiner*, February 11, 1881; Whitfield and Cahill, "Slave Life and Slave Law in Colonial Prince Edward Island," 29–51; Hornby, *Black Islanders*, 34–40.

196. BYERS, EDWARD (c. 1800) – Edward was a son of Jack and Amelia Byers. Sources: *Examiner*, February 11, 1881; Whitfield and Cahill, "Slave Life and Slave Law in Colonial Prince Edward Island," 35–6; Hornby, *Black Islanders*, 34–40.

197. BYERS, JOHN [JACK] (c. 1800) – John was enslaved to Colonel Robinson, who also owned John's wife Amelia (see entry) along with their children. Sources: *Examiner*, February 11, 1881; Whitfield and Cahill, "Slave Life and Slave Law in Colonial Prince Edward Island," 35–6; Hornby, *Black Islanders*, 34–40.

198. BYERS, JOHN (c. 1800) – John was a son of Jack and Amelia Byers. Sources: *Examiner*, February 11, 1881; Whitfield and Cahill, "Slave Life and Slave Law in Colonial Prince Edward Island," 35–6; Hornby, *Black Islanders*, 34–40.

199. BYERS, PETER [BLACK PETER] (c. 1800) – Peter was a son of Jack and Amelia Byers. He is one of the few enslaved persons, if not the only enslaved person, from the Maritimes that has an entry in the *Dictionary of Canadian Biography*. In 1815, he was charged with theft and as a result lost his life. Sources: *Examiner*, February 11, 1881; Whitfield and Cahill, "Slave Life and Slave Law in Colonial Prince Edward Island," 35–6; Hornby, *Black Islanders*, 34–40; H.T. Holman, "BYERS, PETER, known as Black Peter," in *Dictionary of Canadian Biography*, vol. 5, University of Toronto/Université Laval, 2003–, http://www.biographi.ca/en/bio/byers_peter_5E.html.

200. BYERS, WILLIAM (c. 1800) – William was a son of Jack and Amelia Byers. Sources: *Examiner*, February 11, 1881; Whitfield and Cahill, "Slave Life and Slave Law in Colonial Prince Edward Island," 35–6; Hornby, *Black Islanders*, 34–40.

201. BYNA (c. 1776) – Nova Scotia farmer Joseph Wilson bequeathed Byna and Sylla to his relatives. Source: Smith, "Slave in Canada," 15.

202. CAMPBELL, SANCHO (c. 1780s?) – Sancho was enslaved to Colonel Joseph Robinson, who settled in Prince Edward Island, and he allegedly saved the Robinson family from being eaten by sharks. He lived to the age of 105. Sources: Smith, "Slave in Canada," 69; Whitfield and Cahill, "Slave Life and Slave Law," 36.

203. CAPITRAN [CAPTAIN?] (c. 1749) – Capitran was enslaved to Louis Delort, who also owned several other slaves. Source: Donovan, "Nominal List of Slaves and Their Owners," 158.

204. CAPTAIN (c. 1783, age 15) – Enslaved to John Graff, British officials described Captain as a "stout lad." Source: Book of Negroes.

205. CARIB (c. 1750s) – Enslaved to Pierre Boullot, Carib lived with a few other slaves. Source: Donovan, "Slaves in Île Royale, 1713–1758," 35.

206. CARO [CAIRO] (c. 1783, age 20) – In 1783, British officials described Caro as a "stout wench." In his 1806 will, New York Loyalist James Peters bequeathed Caro to his wife, but noted that if she remarried Caro could be freed. However, Peters made clear that due to her "long and faithful" service that his family should make sure that Caro would be cared for throughout the rest of her life: "It is my will that she be kindly treated and provided with every necessary that may contribute to render her comfortable and happy in her declining years." Sources: Book of Negroes; Will of James Peters, 1806/1820, Queens County, PANB.

207. CASAR (c. 1783, age 16) – Enslaved to Oliver Bourdett, who migrated to the Maritimes after the American Revolution with one other enslaved teenager, Casar was described by British officials at New York as a "stout fellow." Source: Book of Negroes.

208. CASAR (c. 1783, age 40) – Enslaved to Richard Jenkins, who migrated to the Maritimes after the American Revolution with two other slaves, Casar was described by British officials in New York as a "thin fellow." Source: Book of Negroes.

209. CASAR (c. 1783, age 26) – Enslaved to John Hicks, who migrated to the Maritimes after the American Revolution, Casar was probably from New York. British officials in New York described him as a "stout fellow." Source: Book of Negroes.

210. CASAR (c. 1783, age 27) – Enslaved to Mrs. Johnson, who migrated to the Maritimes after the American Revolution with another teenaged slave, Casar was described by British officials in New York as a "stout fellow." Source: Book of Negroes.

211. CASAR (c. 1783, age 25) – Enslaved to Cornelius Van Dine, who went to the Maritimes after the American Revolution, Casar was from New Jersey. British officials in New York described him as a "stout fellow." Source: Book of Negroes.

212. CASAR (c. 1789) – Casar was enslaved to Massachusetts Loyalist Anna Lillie (or Ann Lilie), whose husband died after they arrived in Nova Scotia. She was extremely fond of Casar. In her will, she freed Casar, left him money, and his favourite bed. During slavery some owners and enslaved individuals held truly affectionate feelings for one another. This should not blind us to other examples of cruelty between masters and slaves. The relationships between slaves and owners were remarkably multifaceted and ran the spectrum from affectionate feelings to depraved cruelty. As Lillie wrote in her will, "It is also my will and intention that my black man Casar be free, and that the Sum of Ten Pounds be retained and left in the hands of my herein after named Executor, to be applied to the use of said Casar, in case of Sickness, or other necessity, at the discretion of my said Executor ... I the aforementioned Anna Lillie do hereby bequeath to my [within?] named black Man Casar the Feather Bed + Bedstead whereupon he usually sleeps, and also the bed clothes and bedding belonging thereto." Source: Anna Lillie, 1789, Halifax County, RG 48, Probate Records, NSA.

213. CAESAR (c. 1784) – Enslaved to the Departments of the Army and Navy. Caesar settled at Chedabucto, Nova Scotia. Although not common, some Black people were enslaved to the Departments of the Army and Navy. Source: Loyalists from Saint Augustine to Chedabucto, Chipman Papers, Muster Master General's Office, Loyalist Musters, 1776–1785, MG 23, D1, ser. I, vol. 24, LAC.

214. CAESAR (slave? c. 1784) – Possibly enslaved to Michael Houseal, a Loyalist from Maryland, Caesar lived with three other Black people who also might have been slaves. Houseal remained in Nova Scotia until at least 1800, when he decided to return to England. In that same year, he attempted to hire out a young Black female as an indentured servant. Sources: Loyalists and Disbanded Troops at Cole Harbour, Chipman Papers, Muster Master General's Office, Loyalist Musters, 1776–1785, MG 23, D1, ser. I, vol. 24, LAC; *Royal Gazette*, June 24, 1800.

215. CAESAR (c. 1787) – Enslaved to Sarah Grant, Caesar was described by British officials in New York in 1783 as an "ordinary fellow." In her will and inventory, Grant listed Caesar as a "Negro Man" worth £30. Sources: Book of Negroes; Will of Sarah Grant, 1787, Annapolis County, RG 48, NSA.

216. CAESAR (slave? c. 1784) – Caesar was probably enslaved to well-known Loyalist Edward Winslow in the Maritimes, along with two other men. Source: Accounts of Edward Winslow, 1783–84, June 17, 1784, Winslow Papers (online), https://www.lib.unb.ca/winslow/fullrecord.cgi?id=500&level=2&BACKSTR=fields=Title%2CCreator _name%2CSubject%2CSource%2CETC_Sequence&order_by=Identifier&level=2&Creator _name=&Title=&Subject=Caesar&Source=&Keyword=.

217. CAESAR, JUBA (c. 1800–1845, age 63 in 1845) – Juba was enslaved to the Shey family in Hants County, Nova Scotia, who described him as a "faithful servant" and buried him in the family plot. Source: David States, "Presence and Perseverance: Blacks in Hants County, Nova Scotia, 1871–1914" (MA thesis, Saint Mary's University, 2002), 33.

218. CATHARINA (c. 1783, age 60) – Enslaved to Dr. Nathaniel Bullern, who migrated from South Carolina to Nova Scotia with a total of 10 slaves. Bullern's slaves also indicate several different possibilities of family connections and kinship networks. His oldest slaves, Achabee and Catharina, were both 60 at the end of the American Revolution. Jenny and Prince were 40 and 30, respectively. Bullern also owned another male slave in his early 30s and three females ranging in ages 19 to 25. His two youngest slaves were an infant named Sarah and a 6 year old. It is unclear who the parents of these children were, but it is possible that one or both parents were among Bullern's slaves. British officials in New York described Catharina as an "old stout wench." Source: Book of Negroes.

219. CATHERINE/CATHERINA (c. 1796, age 2) – Catherine/Catherina was an enslaved toddler, who Jonathan Fowler of Digby sold to John Crosscup of Granville. The bill of sale says nothing about the child's parents. Source: Slave Bill of Sale, Chesley Papers, MG 1, Vol. 177, Doc. 75, NSA.

220. CATHERINE (c. 1802, age 5) – In 1802 Prince Edward Island slaveholder Thomas Haszard, originally from Rhode Island, sold Catherine and another mixed-race child – he described them as "molatta" – to his relatives. The bill of sale says nothing about either of the children's parents. Source: Declaration by Thomas [Haszard] re. selling mulatto children, Nov. 1802," acc. 2702, Smith Alley Collection, ser. 22, no. 878, PAROPEI.

221. CATHERINE FRANÇOISE (c. 1740, age 7) – Enslaved to the wife of M. Rodrigue, Catherine Françoise worked as a house servant. Source: Donovan, "Nominal List of Slaves and Their Owners," 155.

222. CATHERINE FRANÇOISE (c. 1733, age 7) – Catherine Françoise was enslaved to Marie Anne de Bell Isle of Île Royale. Source: Donovan, "Nominal List of Slaves and Their Owners," 153.

223. CATHERINE (c. 1749) – Enslaved to Blaisse Cassaignoles, Catherine was sold to a former slave whom she married (Jean Baptiste Cupidon). Source: Donovan, "Slaves and Their Owners in Île Royale, 1713–1760," 29.

224. CATO [CATTO] (c. 1745) – Cato was enslaved to William Pepperell, one of the military leaders of the 1745 siege of Louisbourg. Source: Donovan, "Slaves and Their Owners in Île Royale, 1713–1760," 24.

225. CATO (c. 1745) – Cato was an enslaved man under the command of John Storer during the 1745 siege of Louisbourg. Source: Donovan, "Nominal List of Slaves and Their Owners," 157.

226. CATO (c. 1781) – Enslaved to Richard Wenman, Cato laboured as a house servant and escaped briefly before being recaptured. Wenman promised to free Cato if he served Wenman's daughter for an extra two years. Source: Smith, "Slave in Canada," 91; Judith Fingard, "Wenman, Richard," *Dictionary of Canadian Biography*, http://www .biographi.ca/en/bio/wenman_richard_4F.html.

227. CATO (c. 1783, age 25) – Cato was enslaved to John Bridgewater, who migrated to the Maritimes after the American Revolution. British officials in New York noted that Bridgewater had "bought him 18 years ago out of a Guinea Ship at New York." These same officials described Cato as a "stout fellow." Source: Book of Negroes.

228. CATO (slave? c. 1784) – Cato was possibly enslaved to Lieutenant James Boisseau, who migrated to Country Harbour with other southern Loyalists. The majority of these Loyalists and their slaves were from North Carolina, South Carolina, and Georgia. They had settled briefly in East Florida before moving to Nova Scotia. Black people at Country Harbour were either slaves or "quasi-free" and subject to re-enslavement. Abolitionist Thomas Clarkson explained the phenomenon of re-enslavement: "It was not long till these loyalists, many of whom had been educated with all the ideas of the justice of slavery, the inferiority of negroes, and the superiority of white men, that are universal in the southern provinces of America, began to harass and oppress the industrious black settlers, and even wantonly to deprive them of the fruits of their labour, expelling them from the lands they had cleared." Clarkson continued by noting that whites reduced "again to slavery those negroes who had so honourably obtained their freedom. They hired them as servants, and, at the end of the stipulated time, refused payment of their wages, insisting that they were slaves: in some instances they destroyed their tickets of freedom, and then enslaved the negroes for want of them; in several instances, the unfortunate Africans were taken onboard vessels, carried to the West Indies, and there sold for the benefit of their plunderers." At Country Harbour, Black people were listed on the musters as the "Servants" of a white Loyalist, which meant it was very easy for them to be re-enslaved if they were not already enslaved. Sources: Clarkson, "Some Account of the New Colony at Sierra Leone," 229–30; Settlers at Country Harbour, Chipman Papers, Muster Master General's Office, Loyalist Musters, 1776–1785, MG 23, D1, ser. I, vol. 24, LAC. Note: Ellen Wilson believed that the information Clarkson used came from Thomas Peters; see Wilson, *Loyal Blacks*, 181.

229. CELIA (c. 1784) – John Wentworth sent Celia and 18 other slaves from Nova Scotia to his "relation" Paul Wentworth in Suriname. Wentworth described these slaves as "American born or well seasoned, and are perfectly stout, healthy, sober, orderly, Industrious, & obedient." Celia was listed as a child. Source: John Wentworth to Paul Wentworth or his attorney, February 24, 1784, Wentworth Letters, vol. 49, NSA.

230. CEASER (c. ?) – Ceasar was enslaved to the Bovyer family, who brought him and a few other slaves to Prince Edward Island. Their homestead consisted of 100 cleared acres and livestock such as horses, cattle, sheep, and hogs. Their slaves, including Ceaser, were responsible for the tasks associated with farming on the Island. Source: Orlo Jones and Doris Muncey Haslam, eds., *An Island Refuge: Loyalists and Disbanded Troops on the Island of Saint John* (Charlottetown: Abegweit Branch United Empire Loyalists, 1983), 43.

231. CEASOR (c. 1783, age 30) – Ceasor was enslaved to Peter Ryerson, who migrated to the Maritimes from New York with a child slave. British officials in New York described him as a "stout man." This might be the same person as Cesar Broadstreet (see entry), but we cannot be sure. Source: Book of Negroes.

232. UNNAMED BOY (c. 1783, age 9) – Enslaved to Peter Ryerson, this unnamed boy was possibly the son of Ceasor. Source: Book of Negroes.

233. CESAR (c. 1758) – Cesar was an enslaved person in Île Royale. Source: Donovan, "Nominal List of Slaves and Their Owners," 160.

234. CESARD (c. 1734, age 12) – In 1734, Captain Charles Le Roy sold Cesard to Île Royale merchant Louis Lachaume for 350 livres. Cesard had been sold away from the West Indies and there is no mention of his family. Source: Donovan, "Slaves and Their Owners in Île Royale, 1713–1760," 8.

235. CEZAR (c. 1750s) – Cezar was enslaved to Jean Laborde, an exceedingly wealthy merchant who owned several slaves; there might well have been at least two Cezars in Île Royale. Source: Donovan, "Slaves in Île Royale, 1713–1758," 32.

236. CHANCE (c. 1781) – Enslaved to Samuel Mack, Chance ran away from his owner in 1781. Source: Harris, "Negro Population of the County of Annapolis," 18.

237. CHARITY (c. 1783, age 21) – Enslaved to John Bennett, who migrated to the Maritimes after the American Revolution, Charity was described by British officials as a "stout lad." Source: Book of Negroes.

238. CHARLES (c. 1733, age 18) – Enslaved to Charles Benoist, Charles, like most Île Royale slaves, worked as a domestic for the Benoist family. Source: Donovan, "Slaves and Their Owners in Île Royale, 1713–1760," 3.

239. CHARLES (c. 1750, age 18) – Charles was enslaved to Captain Dagat. Source: Donovan, "Nominal List of Slaves and Their Owners," 159.

240. CHARLES (c. 1783, age 23) – Enslaved to James Alexander, who migrated to the Maritimes after the American Revolution, Charles was probably from

Georgia or South Carolina. British officials in New York described him as a "stout fellow." Source: Book of Negroes.

241. CHARLES (c. 1783, age 10) – Enslaved to Samuel Stretch, who migrated to the Maritimes after the American Revolution, Charles was described by British officials as a "fine boy." Source: Book of Negroes.

242. CHARLES (c. 1783/1784) – Enslaved to Captain Isaac Young in Digby, Nova Scotia, Charles and Young's other slaves were from New York. Source: Smith, "Slave in Canada," 25.

243. CHARLES (slave? c. 1784) – Charles was possibly enslaved to Lieutenant James Boisseau, who migrated to Country Harbour with other southern Loyalists. See entry for Cato regarding these Loyalists. Sources: Clarkson, "Some Account of the New Colony at Sierra Leone," 229–30; Settlers at Country Harbour, Chipman Papers, Muster Master General's Office, Loyalist Musters, 1776–1785, MG 23, D1, ser. I, vol. 24, LAC. Note: Ellen Wilson believed that the information Clarkson used came from Thomas Peters; see Wilson, *Loyal Blacks*, 181.

244. CHARLES (c. 1784) – Charles was enslaved to John Nash, who settled at Chedabucto, Nova Scotia. Source: Loyalists from Saint Augustine to Chedabucto, Chipman Papers, Muster Master General's Office, Loyalist Musters, 1776–1785, MG 23, D1, ser. I, vol. 24, LAC.

245. CHARLES (c. 1794) – Charles was enslaved to Azariah Pritchard (or Pretchard), who placed a runaway advertisement in the *Quebec Gazette* describing Charles as being multilingual – speaking English, some French, and "Micmac." Before living in Quebec, Pritchard had settled in New Brunswick after the War. Sources: Charmaine Nelson "Special Issue: Expanding and Complicating the Concept of Creolization," *African and Black Diaspora: An International Journal* 12, no. 3 (2019): 267; Gregory Palmer, *Biographical Sketches of Loyalists of the American Revolution* (Westport: Meckler Publishing, 1984), 705.

246. CHARLES (c. 1804) – Charles was enslaved to James DeLancey, whose estate valued him at £18. Source: George DeLancey Hanger, "The Life of Loyalist Colonel James DeLancey," *Nova Scotia Historical Review* 3, no. 2 (1983): 53.

247. CHARLES (c. 1828, age 20) – Charles was enslaved to the Ormsby family on Prince Edward Island. In the Montserrat slave registry of 1828 a notation was made that listed four slaves of the Ormsby household who were living in Prince Edward Island: "I Matthew William Blake (for Catharine Ormsby) do swear that the Return now by me delivered to be registered contains to the best of my knowledge and belief a true faithful and accurate account and description of all the Slaves belonging to Catharine Ormsby and being within this Island (Save and Except the following Slaves of the Names as follows Charles Male Black Twenty Years, Mary Jane Female Black Thirteen Years, Fanny Female Coloured Eleven Years, Edward Male Black Eight Years, residing with Mr. Ormsby at Prince Edward Island)." Source: Montserrat Slave Register, December 3, 1828, T_71_450, p. 285, The National Archives (TNA), Kew, UK. I must thank Mr. Neil How of the Montserrat National Trust, Montserrat, West Indies, for sharing this document with me.

248. CHARLES JOSEPH (c. 1729, age 10) – Enslaved to Governor St. Ovide in Île Royale, Charles Joseph came from the West Indies and lived with one other child slave. Source: Donovan, "Nominal List of Slaves and Their Owners," 152.

249. CHARLOT (c. 1794) – Charlot was enslaved to Abel Michener. According to local tradition, the Michener family kept their slaves until 1834. Source: States, "Presence and Perseverance: Blacks in Hants County," 36.

250. CHARLOTTE (c. 1749) – Enslaved to Robert Duhaget in Île Royale. Source: Donovan, "Nominal List of Slaves and Their Owners," 157.

251. CHARLOTTE (c. 1749) – Enslaved to Michel De la Valliere in Île Royale. Source: Donovan, "Nominal List of Slaves and Their Owners," 159.

252. CHARLOTTE (c. 1784) – Charlotte was possibly enslaved to Captain Marshall, who migrated to Country Harbour with other southern Loyalists. The majority of these Loyalists and their slaves were from North Carolina, South Carolina, and Georgia. They had settled briefly in East Florida before moving to Nova Scotia. Black people at Country Harbour were either slaves or "quasi-free" and subject to re-enslavement. Abolitionist Thomas Clarkson explained the phenomenon of re-enslavement: "It was not long till these loyalists, many of whom had been educated with all the ideas of the justice of slavery, the inferiority of negroes, and the superiority of white men, that are universal in the southern provinces of America, began to harass and oppress the industrious black settlers, and even wantonly to deprive them of the fruits of their labour, expelling them from the lands they had cleared." Clarkson continued by noting that whites reduced "again to slavery those negroes who had so honourably obtained their freedom. They hired them as servants, and, at the end of the stipulated time, refused payment of their wages, insisting that they were slaves: in some instances they destroyed their tickets of freedom, and then enslaved the negroes for want of them; in several instances, the unfortunate Africans were taken onboard vessels, carried to the West Indies, and there sold for the benefit of their plunderers." At Country Harbour, Black people were listed on the musters as the "Servants" of a white Loyalist, which meant it was very easy for them to be re-enslaved if they were not already enslaved. Sources: Clarkson, "Some Account of the New Colony at Sierra Leone," 229–30; Settlers at Country Harbour, Chipman Papers, Muster Master General's Office, Loyalist Musters, 1776–1785, MG 23, D1, ser. I, vol. 24, LAC. Note: Ellen Wilson believed that the information Clarkson used came from Thomas Peters; see Wilson, *Loyal Blacks*, 181.

253. CHARLOTTE (c. 1784) – Charlotte was possibly enslaved to Captain Hamilton, who migrated to Country Harbour with other southern Loyalists. The majority of these Loyalists and their slaves were from North Carolina, South Carolina, and Georgia. They had settled briefly in East Florida before moving to Nova Scotia. Black people at Country Harbour were either slaves or "quasi-free" and subject to re-enslavement. Abolitionist Thomas Clarkson explained the phenomenon of re-enslavement: "It was not long till these loyalists, many of whom had been educated with all the ideas of the justice of slavery, the inferiority of negroes, and the superiority of white men, that are universal in the southern provinces of America, began to harass and oppress the industrious black settlers, and even wantonly to deprive them of the fruits of their labour, expelling them from the lands they had cleared." Clarkson continued by noting that whites reduced "again to slavery those negroes who had so honourably obtained their freedom. They hired them as servants, and, at the end of the stipulated time, refused payment of their wages, insisting that they were slaves: in some instances they destroyed their tickets of freedom, and then enslaved the negroes for want of them; in several instances, the unfortunate Africans were taken onboard vessels, carried to the West Indies, and there sold for the benefit of their plunderers." At Country Harbour, Black people were listed on the musters as the "Servants" of a white Loyalist, which meant it was very easy for them to be re-enslaved if they were not already enslaved. Sources: Clarkson, "Some Account of the New Colony at Sierra Leone," 229–30; Settlers at Country Harbour, Chipman Papers, Muster Master General's Office, Loyalist Musters, 1776–1785, MG 23, D1, ser. I, vol. 24, LAC. Note: Ellen Wilson believed that the information Clarkson used came from Thomas Peters; see Wilson, *Loyal Blacks*, 181.

254. CHARLOTTE (c. 1787) – Charlotte was an enslaved female of the Walker family. She lived with another slave named Nancy and was baptized in Wilmot, Nova Scotia. Source: List of Baptisms, September 3, 1787, Cornwallis Township Book, NSA.

255. CHARLOTTE (c. 1788) – Enslaved to John Whidden, Charlotte was baptized in Cornwallis, Nova Scotia. Source: List of Baptisms, February 26, 1788, Cornwallis Township Book, NSA.

256. CHASE, POMPEY (c. 1783, age 28) – Enslaved to Reuben Chase, who purchased him from Jacob Sharpe of Boston, Pompey migrated to the Maritimes from New York. British officials described him as a "stout fellow." Source: Book of Negroes.

257. CHILD SLAVE OF F.L. BÖHME (c. 1807) – Böhme owned two male slaves and a child slave. There is no mention of any female slaves or who the mother of the child might have been. Böhme signed the 1807 Digby slaveholder petition. Source: Petition of John Taylor and Others, Negro Proprietors, to the General Assembly, December 1807, RG 5 A, box 14, doc. 49, NSA.

258. CHILD SLAVE OF THOMAS CORNWELL (c. 1807) – Thomas Cornwell owned three slaves – one female and two children. The female slave might have been the mother of the child slaves, but that is unclear. There is no mention of a male slave, so it is possible that Cornwell fathered the children. Cornwell signed the 1807 Digby slaveholder petition. Source: Petition of John Taylor and Others, Negro Proprietors, to the General Assembly, December 1807, RG 5 A, box 14, doc. 49, NSA.

259. CHILD SLAVE OF THOMAS CORNWELL (c. 1807) – Thomas Cornwell owned three slaves – one female and two children. The female slave might have been the mother of the child slaves, but that is unclear. There is no mention of a male slave, so it is possible that Cornwell fathered the children. Cornwell signed the 1807 Digby slaveholder petition. Source: Petition of John Taylor and Others, Negro Proprietors, to the General Assembly, December 1807, RG 5 A, box 14, doc. 49, NSA.

260. CHILD SLAVE OF EBENEZER CUTLER (c. 1807) – Ebenezer Cutler owned two slaves – one child and an adult female. It is possible that the female slave was the mother of the child slave, while Cutler might have fathered the child. There is no mention of a male slave in the household. Cutler signed the 1807 Digby slaveholder petition. Source: Petition of John Taylor and Others, Negro Proprietors, to the General Assembly, December 1807, RG 5 A, box 14, doc. 49, NSA.

261. CHILD SLAVE OF SAMUEL DOUCET (c. 1807) – Samuel Doucet lived near his relative Harry Doucet and owned two slaves – one child and an adult male; it is unclear if the adult male and the child were related. Doucet signed the 1807 Digby slaveholder petition. Source: Petition of John Taylor and Others, Negro Proprietors, to the General Assembly, December 1807, RG 5 A, box 14, doc. 49, NSA.

262. CHILD SLAVE OF SAMUEL MELANSON (c. 1807) – Samuel Melanson owned two slaves – one female and one child. It is possible that the adult female was the mother of the child slave, but this is unclear. It is possible Melanson fathered the child. Melanson signed the 1807 Digby slaveholder petition. Source: Petition of John Taylor and Others, Negro Proprietors, to the General Assembly, December 1807, RG 5 A, box 14, doc. 49, NSA.

263. CHILD SLAVE OF BELONEY MELANSON (c. 1807) – B. Melanson owned two slaves – one female and one child. It is possible that the adult female was the mother of the child slave, but this is unclear. It is possible Melanson was the father of the child. Melanson signed the 1807 Digby slaveholder petition. Source: Petition of John Taylor and Others, Negro Proprietors, to the General Assembly, December 1807, RG 5 A, box 14, doc. 49, NSA.

264. CHILD SLAVE OF MR. WINNIETT (c. 1807) – Mr. Winniett owned four slaves – three adults and one child. Winniett signed the 1807 Digby slaveholder petition. Source: Petition of John Taylor and Others, Negro Proprietors, to the General Assembly, December 1807, RG 5 A, box 14, doc. 49, NSA.

265. CHILD SLAVE OF JOHN POLHEMUS (c. 1807) – John Polhemus owned 10 slaves, which makes him one of the largest slaveholders in the history of the Maritimes. His household consisted of three male slaves, two female slaves, and five child slaves. He also seems to have expanded his holding of slaves over time. According to the Book of Negroes, he arrived in Nova Scotia with only two slaves. It is possible, however, that some of them were not recorded in the Book of Negroes. Polhemus signed the 1807 Digby slaveholder petition. Sources: Petition of John Taylor and Others, Negro Proprietors, to the General Assembly, December 1807, RG 5 A, box 14, doc. 49, NSA; Book of Negroes.

266. CHILD SLAVE OF JOHN POLHEMUS (c. 1807) – John Polhemus owned 10 slaves, which makes him one of the largest slaveholders in the history of the Maritimes. His household consisted of three male slaves, two female slaves, and five child slaves. He also seems to have expanded his holding of slaves over time. According to the Book of Negroes, he arrived in Nova Scotia with only two slaves. It is possible, however, that some of them were not recorded in the Book of Negroes. Polhemus signed the 1807 Digby slaveholder petition. Sources: Petition of John Taylor and Others, Negro Proprietors, to the General Assembly, December 1807, RG 5 A, box 14, doc. 49, NSA; Book of Negroes.

267. CHILD SLAVE OF JOHN POLHEMUS (c. 1807) – John Polhemus owned 10 slaves, which makes him one of the largest slaveholders in the history of the Maritimes. His household consisted of three male slaves, two female slaves, and five child slaves. He also seems to have expanded his holding of slaves over time. According to the Book of Negroes, he arrived in Nova Scotia with only two slaves. It is possible, however, that some of them were not recorded in the Book of Negroes. Polhemus signed the 1807 Digby slaveholder petition. Sources: Petition of John Taylor and Others, Negro Proprietors, to the General Assembly, December 1807, RG 5 A, box 14, doc. 49, NSA; Book of Negroes.

268. CHILD SLAVE OF JOHN POLHEMUS (c. 1807) – John Polhemus owned 10 slaves, which makes him one of the largest slaveholders in the history of the Maritimes. His household consisted of three male slaves, two female slaves, and five child slaves. He also seems to have expanded his holding of slaves over time. According to the Book of Negroes, he arrived in Nova Scotia with only two slaves. It is possible, that that some of them were not recorded in the Book of Negroes. Polhemus signed the 1807 Digby slaveholder petition. Sources: Petition of John Taylor and Others, Negro Proprietors, to the General Assembly, December 1807, RG 5 A, box 14, doc. 49, NSA; Book of Negroes.

269. CHILD SLAVE OF JOHN POLHEMUS (c. 1807) – John Polhemus owned 10 slaves, which makes him one of the largest slaveholders in the history of the Maritimes. His household consisted of three male slaves, two female slaves, and five child slaves. He also seems to have expanded his holding of slaves over time. According to the Book of Negroes, he arrived in Nova Scotia with only two slaves. It is possible, however, that some of them were not recorded in the Book of Negroes. Polhemus signed the 1807 Digby slaveholder petition. Sources: Petition of John Taylor and Others, Negro Proprietors, to the General Assembly, December 1807, RG 5 A, box 14, doc. 49, NSA; Book of Negroes.

270. CHILD SLAVE OF JOHN BASTEIT (c. 1807) – John Basteit owned two slaves – one woman and one child. It is possible that the female slave was the mother of the enslaved child, but there is no mention of an adult male slave in Basteit's household. It is possible that Basteit fathered the child. Basteit signed the 1807 Digby slaveholder petition. Source: Petition of John Taylor and Others, Negro Proprietors, to the General Assembly, December 1807, RG 5 A, box 14, doc. 49, NSA.

271. CHILD SLAVE OF ISAAC BONNETT [or **BONNELL**] (c. 1807) – Isaac Bonnell owned two child slaves. There is no mention of these children's parents. It is possible they died or were sold away. Bonnell signed the 1807 Digby slaveholder petition. It should be noted that the two child slaves mentioned in the petition could be the same children Bonnell mentioned in his will. Please see entries for George, Bob, and Tom. However, if this is the case, then why are these children the only two slaves listed in his household for the petition? It could mean that one of the slave children had died or been sold. Bonnell did not intend to free any of them until they were 24 years of age. Source: Petition of John Taylor and Others, Negro Proprietors, to the General Assembly, December 1807, RG 5 A, box 14, doc. 49, NSA.

272. CHILD SLAVE OF ISAAC BONNETT [or **BONNELL**] (c. 1807) – Isaac Bonnell owned two child slaves. There is no mention of these children's parents. It is possible they died or were sold away. Bonnell also signed the 1807 Digby slaveholder petition. It should be noted that the two child slaves mentioned in the petition could be the same children Bonnell mentioned in his will. Please see entries for George, Bob, and Tom. However, if this is the case, then why are these children the only two slaves listed in his household for the petition? It could mean that one of the slave children had died or been sold. Bonnell did not intend to free any of them until they were 24 years of age. Source: Petition of John Taylor and Others, Negro Proprietors, to the General Assembly, December 1807, RG 5 A, box 14, doc. 49, NSA.

273. CHILD SLAVE OF NICHOLAS JAMES (c. 1807) – Nicholas James owned four slaves – three children and one female. It is probable that the female slave was the mother of the three children. The father of the children might have lived with Elizabeth James (possibly the daughter of Nicholas James). James signed the 1807 Digby petition. Source: Petition of John Taylor and Others, Negro Proprietors to the General Assembly, December 1807, RG 5 A, box 14, doc. 49, NSA.

274. CHILD SLAVE OF NICHOLAS JAMES (c. 1807) – Nicholas James owned four slaves – three children and one female. It is probable that the female slave was the mother of the three children. The father of the children might have lived with Elizabeth James (possibly the daughter of Nicholas James). James signed the 1807 Digby petition. Source: Petition of John Taylor and Others, Negro Proprietors, to the General Assembly, December 1807, RG 5 A, box 14, doc. 49, NSA.

275. CHILD SLAVE OF NICHOLAS JAMES (c. 1807) – Nicholas James owned four slaves – three children and one female. It is probable that the female slave was the mother of the three children. The father of the children might have lived with Elizabeth James (possibly the daughter of Nicholas James). James signed the 1807 Digby petition. Source: Petition of John Taylor and Others, Negro Proprietors, to the General Assembly, December 1807, RG 5 A, box 14, doc. 49, NSA.

276. CHILD SLAVE OF JOHN VROOM (c. 1807) – Loyalist John Vroom owned three slaves, including two children. He did not own a female slave, so either he purchased these children from another owner or Vroom owned a female slave who had died or was sold. Vroom signed the 1807 Digby slaveholder petition. Source: Petition of John Taylor and Others, Negro Proprietors, to the General Assembly, December 1807, RG 5 A, box 14, doc. 49, NSA.

277. CHILD SLAVE OF JOHN VROOM (c. 1807) – Loyalist John Vroom owned three slaves, including two children. He did not own a female slave, so either he purchased these children from another owner or Vroom owned a female

slave who had died or was sold. Vroom signed the 1807 Digby slaveholder petition. Source: Petition of John Taylor and Others, Negro Proprietors, to the General Assembly,
December 1807, RG 5 A, box 14, doc. 49, NSA.

278. CHILD SLAVE OF ISAAC HATFIELD (c. 1807) – Isaac Hatfield owned
a total of five slaves. Hatfield signed the 1807 Digby slaveholder petition. Source:
Petition of John Taylor and Others, Negro Proprietors, to the General Assembly, December
1807, RG 5 A, box 14, doc. 49, NSA.

279. CHILD SLAVE OF JAMES MOODY (c. 1807) – James Moody was a
well-known Loyalist from New Jersey, and there were several other slaves in
his household that possibly constituted a family. The adult slaves were probably
born in New Jersey, while the child slaves were undoubtedly born in Nova Scotia. In 1807, Moody owned eight slaves: two adult males, one adult female, and
five children. Moody signed the 1807 Digby slaveholder petition. Source: Petition
of John Taylor and Others, Negro Proprietors, to the General Assembly, December 1807, RG 5
A, box 14, doc. 49, NSA.

280. CHILD SLAVE OF JAMES MOODY (c. 1807) – James Moody was a
well-known Loyalist from New Jersey, and there were several other slaves in
his household that possibly constituted a family. The adult slaves were probably
born in New Jersey, while the child slaves were undoubtedly born in Nova Scotia. In 1807, Moody owned eight slaves: two adult males, one adult female, and
five children. Moody signed the 1807 Digby slaveholder petition. Source: Petition
of John Taylor and Others, Negro Proprietors, to the General Assembly, December 1807, RG 5
A, box 14, doc. 49, NSA.

281. CHILD SLAVE OF JAMES MOODY (c. 1807) – James Moody was a
well-known Loyalist from New Jersey, and there were several other slaves in
his household that possibly constituted a family. The adult slaves were probably
born in New Jersey, while the child slaves were undoubtedly born in Nova Scotia. In 1807, Moody owned eight slaves: two adult males, one adult female, and
five children. Moody signed the 1807 Digby slaveholder petition. Source: Petition
of John Taylor and Others, Negro Proprietors, to the General Assembly, December 1807, RG 5
A, box 14, doc. 49, NSA.

282. CHILD SLAVE OF JAMES MOODY (c. 1807) – James Moody was a
well-known Loyalist from New Jersey, and there were several other slaves in
his household that possibly constituted a family. The adult slaves were probably
born in New Jersey, while the child slaves were undoubtedly born in Nova Scotia. In 1807, Moody owned eight slaves: two adult males, one adult female, and
five children. Moody signed the 1807 Digby slaveholder petition. Source: Petition

of John Taylor and Others, Negro Proprietors, to the General Assembly, December 1807, RG 5 A, box 14, doc. 49, NSA.

283. CHILD SLAVE OF JAMES MOODY (c. 1807) – James Moody was a well-known Loyalist from New Jersey, and there were several other slaves in his household that possibly constituted a family. The adult slaves were probably born in New Jersey, while the child slaves were undoubtedly born in Nova Scotia. In 1807, Moody owned eight slaves: two adult males, one adult female, and five children. Moody signed the 1807 Digby slaveholder petition. Source: Petition of John Taylor and Others, Negro Proprietors, to the General Assembly, December 1807, RG 5 A, box 14, doc. 49, NSA.

284. CHILD SLAVE OF MARGARET MOODY (c. 1807) – Margaret Moody signed the 1807 Digby slaveholder petition. Source: Petition of John Taylor and Others, Negro Proprietors, to the General Assembly, December 1807, RG 5 A, box 14, doc. 49, NSA.

285. CHILD SLAVE OF HENRY RUTHERFORD (c. 1807) – Henry Rutherford owned four slaves, and it is possible that these slaves were a family as they consisted of an adult male, adult female, and two children. Rutherford signed the 1807 Digby slaveholder petition. Source: Petition of John Taylor and Others, Negro Proprietors, to the General Assembly, December 1807, RG 5 A, box 14, doc. 49, NSA.

286. CHILD SLAVE OF HENRY RUTHERFORD (c. 1807) – Henry Rutherford owned four slaves, and it is possible that these slaves were a family as they consisted of an adult male, adult female, and two children. Rutherford signed the 1807 Digby slaveholder petition. Source: Petition of John Taylor and Others, Negro Proprietors, to the General Assembly, December 1807, RG 5 A, box 14, doc. 49, NSA.

287. CHILD SLAVE OF JOHN TAYLOR (c. 1807) – John Taylor owned two adult male slaves, two adult female slaves, and two child slaves. He signed the 1807 Digby slaveholder. Source: Petition of John Taylor and Others, Negro Proprietors, to the General Assembly, December 1807, RG 5 A, box 14, doc. 49, NSA.

288. CHILD SLAVE OF JOHN TAYLOR (c. 1807) – John Taylor owned two adult male slaves, two adult female slaves, and two child slaves. He signed the 1807 Digby slaveholder. Source: Petition of John Taylor and Others, Negro Proprietors, to the General Assembly, December 1807, RG 5 A, box 14, doc. 49, NSA.

289. CHILD SLAVE OF FREDERICK WILLIAMS (c. 1807) – Frederick Williams owned two male slaves, one female slave, and three child slaves. The number of child slaves demonstrates that Williams had intentions of expanding and continuing slaveholding in Nova Scotia. He signed the 1807 Digby slaveholder petition. Source: Petition of John Taylor and Others, Negro Proprietors, to the General Assembly, December 1807, RG 5 A, box 14, doc. 49, NSA.

290. CHILD SLAVE OF FREDERICK WILLIAMS (c. 1807) – Frederick Williams owned two male slaves, one female slave, and three child slaves. The number of child slaves demonstrates that Williams had intentions of expanding and continuing slaveholding in Nova Scotia. He signed the 1807 Digby slaveholder petition. Source: Petition of John Taylor and Others, Negro Proprietors, to the General Assembly, December 1807, RG 5 A, box 14, doc. 49, NSA.

291. CHILD SLAVE OF FREDERICK WILLIAMS (c. 1807) – Frederick Williams owned two male slaves, one female slave, and three child slaves. The number of child slaves demonstrates that Williams had intentions of expanding and continuing slaveholding in Nova Scotia. He signed the 1807 Digby slaveholder petition. Source: Petition of John Taylor and Others, Negro Proprietors, to the General Assembly, December 1807, RG 5 A, box 14, doc. 49, NSA.

292. CHLOE (c. ?) – Possibly enslaved to the Bains family, Chloe, according to oral tradition, was extremely light-skinned and preferred to distinguish herself from slaves and people of colour. Source: Smith, "Slave in Canada," 89–90.

293. CHLOE (c. 1809) – Chloe was enslaved to Jonathan Shearman in Nova Scotia who, in his will, told his wife and daughter to care for Chloe for the rest of her life if she remained with the family. Source: Smith, "Slave in Canada," 17.

294. CHLOE (c. 1801) – Nova Scotian politician and merchant Benjamin Belcher owned several slaves in Cornwallis, including Chloe. Belcher noted: "I give my Negro man named Jack and my Negro boy Samuel and Negro boy James and Negro Girl called Chloe to my son Benjamin and his Heirs." The relationship between Jack, Samuel, James, and Chloe is unclear. Jack might have been the father or another relative or simply fictive kin. In his will, Belcher left strict directions for his heirs about the slaves, noting that he was "for ever charging them my children unto whom I have entrusted these Negro people with never to sell barter or exchange them or any of them under any pretension except it is for whose bad [?] Offences as will render them not safe to be kept in the Family and that to be adjudged of by three Justices of the Peace in said Township and in such case as their order they may be sold and disposed of. And I further request as soon as these young Negroes shall be capable to be taught to read, they shall be learnt the word of God." Source: Will of Benjamin Belcher, 1801, Kings County, Will Book, vol. 1, 222–27, NSA.

295. CIPIO (c. 1759) – Enslaved to Reverend John Cleaveland, Cipio was from New England. Source: Donovan, "Nominal List of Slaves and Their Owners," 160.

296. CLAIRE (c. 1749) – Claire was enslaved to Leon Fautoux. Source: Donovan, "Nominal List of Slaves and Their Owners," 158.

297. CLARINDA (c. 1783–84, age 19) – Clarinda was enslaved to Dr. Nathaniel Bullern, who migrated from South Carolina to Nova Scotia with a total of 10 slaves. Bullern's slaves also indicate several different possibilities of family connections and kinship networks. His oldest slaves, Achabee and Catharina, were both 60 at the end of the American Revolution. Jenny and Prince were 40 and 30 respectively. Bullern also owned another male slave in his early 30s and three females ranging in ages 19 to 25. His two youngest slaves were an infant named Sarah and a 6 year old. It is unclear who the parents of these children were, but it is possible that one or both parents were among Bullern's slaves. In 1784, Bullern placed a runaway advertisement in the local paper complaining that Clarinda had escaped with a man named Jupiter. In the advertisement, Bullern lists one of them as an indented servant and the other as a slave. It is not clear whether Jupiter or Clarinda had become indentured as opposed to enslaved, but this might have been a difference of degree rather than kind as they both absconded from Bullern: "RUN AWAY 8th September, TWO NE-GRO – the Property of Mr. Nath Bullern, the One an intended Servant, the other a Slave; the Man had on when he went away a [?] Hatt, a blue Coat, about 6 feet high, answered to the name of JUPITER – The woman had on a short red Bays Bedgown, answers to the name Clarinda." Sources: Book of Negroes; *Nova Scotia Gazette and Weekly Chronicle*, September 21, 1784.

298. CLARINDA (c. 1788) – Clarinda was enslaved to Joseph Totten who, in his will, gave three Black children away to his daughters but not the other slaves, which means that a slave family was probably broken up. In his will, Totten stated: "I give and bequeath Negro Girl Slave named Clarinda to my Daughter Phebe Totten." Source: Will of Joseph Totten, 1788, Annapolis County, RG 48, Probate Records, NSA.

299. CLEVELAND (c. 1800s?) – Cleveland was enslaved to Charles Dixon in New Brunswick, who paid £60 for Cleveland but ended up freeing him allegedly to "set a Christian example." This might be true, but it is likely that the same Charles Dixon owned other slaves. Source: James Snowdon, "Dixon, Charles," *Dictionary of Canadian Biography*, vol. 5, http://www.biographi.ca/en/bio/dixon_charles_5E.html.

300. CLO (c. 1791) – Clo was enslaved to Richard McHeffey, who bequeathed her to his wife. Source: Smith, "Slave in Canada," 16.

301. CLORIN (c. 1749) – Clorin was enslaved to Madame Lartigue. Source: Donovan, "Nominal List of Slaves and Their Owners," 157.

302. COFFIN, PAUL (c. 1783, age 29) – Paul was enslaved to Major Coffin, who was part of Edmund Fanning's King's American Regiment. Coffin had purchased Paul from Mr. Greentree. Paul migrated to the Maritimes from New York along with Coffin's two other slaves. British officials in New York described him as a "stout labourer." Source: Book of Negroes.

303. COLE, TAMAR (c. 1787) – Enslaved to Edmund Crawley at Halifax, Nova Scotia, Tamar had several children – including Sophia. Crawley decided that the children would be divided among his nephews and nieces (except Sophia) at Halifax and would become free at age 36. Source: Smith, "Slave in Canada," 59.

304. SOPHIA (c. 1787) – Sophia was a child of Tamar Cole and enslaved to Edmund Crawley. Source: Smith, "Slave in Canada," 59.

305. UNNAMED CHILD (c. 1787) – This unnamed person was the child of Tamar Cole and enslaved to Edmund Crawley. Source: Smith, "Slave in Canada," 59.

306. UNNAMED CHILD (c. 1787) – This unnamed person was the child of Tamar Cole and enslaved to Edmund Crawley. Source: Smith, "Slave in Canada," 59.

307. UNNAMED CHILD (c. 1787) – This unnamed person was the child of Tamar Cole and enslaved to Edmund Crawley. Source: Smith, "Slave in Canada," 59.

308. UNNAMED CHILD (c. 1787) – This unnamed person was the child of Tamar Cole and enslaved to Edmund Crawley. Source: Smith, "Slave in Canada," 59.

309. COLLINS (slave? c. 1784) – Collins was possibly enslaved to F.H. Flieger, who planned to settle in nearby Halifax. Source: Loyalists and Disbanded Troops at Cole Harbour, Chipman Papers, Muster Master General's Office, Loyalist Musters, 1776–1785, MG 23, D1, ser. I, vol. 24, LAC.

310. COLLINS, MARY (c. 1783, age 28) – Enslaved to David Phillips, Mary migrated from New York to the Maritimes with her young daughter. British officials described her as a "stout wench." Source: Book of Negroes.

311. HANNA (c. 1783, age 2) – The daughter of Mary Collins, Hanna was enslaved to David Philips. British officials described her as "mulatto." Source: Book of Negroes.

312. COLLY (slave? c. 1784) – Possibly enslaved to George Westphal, who planned to settle in nearby Halifax, Colly was one of six Black people living in

Westphal's household. Source: Loyalists and Disbanded Troops at Cole Harbour, Chipman Papers, Muster Master General's Office, Loyalist Musters, 1776–1785, MG 23, D1, ser. I, vol. 24, LAC.

313. CONGO, CATHERINE (c. 1749) – Catherine was enslaved to Louisbourg merchant Bernard Detcheverry and his wife Jeanne. Source: Donovan, "Nominal List of Slaves and Their Owners," 157.

314. COTTRESS, JOHN (c. 1791) – Enslaved to Mr. Greggs [?] Farish, British abolitionist John Clarkson attempted to purchase and free John so that he could go to Sierra Leone. Source: C.B. Fergusson, ed., *Clarkson's Mission to America, 1791–1792* (Halifax: Public Archives of Nova Scotia, 1971), 57, 73.

315. COURTNEY, AMANDA (c. 1783, age 16) – Enslaved to Courtney Taylor, Amanda migrated to the Maritimes from New York with one other slave and was from South Carolina. She had been "Purchased from Captain Irwin of Charlestown." British officials described her as a "stout wench." Source: Book of Negroes.

316. COX [or **COCK**], **PETER** (free/possibly re-enslaved c. 1783–84, age 24) – Before arriving in New Brunswick, Cox was the slave of John Lloyd in Stamford, Connecticut. He left his owner during the American Revolution and the British government gave him a GBC. Cox ran away with several other former slaves from Connecticut (Charity Morris, Edward Morris, Andrew Bush, and Eanus Deaton) whom Rogers also attempted to re-enslave. Rogers described Cox as "a young negro, comely countenance." Sources: Book of Negroes; *Royal Saint John's Gazette* (New Brunswick), May 13, 1784. Please see entry on Andrew Bush for a lengthy description of this runaway advertisement.

317. COVENHOVEN, VAUGHN (slave? c. 1783, age 19) – Possibly enslaved to Captain Coggle, who migrated to the Maritimes from New York with one other slave, Vaughn was perhaps from New Jersey. British officials noted that he was "formerly slave to Peter Covenhoven, Middletown, New Jersey; captured by Col. Hyde's detachment in 1779 & afterwards purchased by Capt. Coggle." Source: Book of Negroes.

318. COWS (c. 1783, age 22) – Enslaved to Mr. Van Horn (possibly Lawrence Van Horn), who migrated to the Maritimes after the American Revolution with another slave, Cows was possibly from New Jersey. British officials at New York described him as an "ordinary fellow." Source: Book of Negroes.

319. CROMWELL (c. 1773) – In 1773, Cromwell escaped from his owner Jacob Hurd in Nova Scotia. Hurd described Cromwell as short, thick, and strong. Source: Smith, "Slave in Canada," 12.

320. CRUDEN, HENRY (c. 1783, age 13) – Enslaved to Colonel Thomson, Henry, according to the Book of Negroes, was given to Colonel Thomson by Colonel Cruden. British officials in New York described him as a "stout boy." Source: Book of Negroes.

321. CUFFEE (c. 1745) – Enslaved to Mr. Monis, Cuffee was from Massachusetts and he came to Louisbourg during the siege of 1745. Source: Donovan, "Nominal List of Slaves and Their Owners," 156.

322. CUFFEY (c. 1745) – Cuffey served under the command of Captain Samuel Lumbert at the siege of Louisbourg. Source: Donovan, "Nominal List of Slaves and Their Owners," 156.

323. CUPIDON, JEAN BAPTISTE (c. 1749) – Enslaved to Louis Delort and originally from Africa, Jean Baptiste eventually gained his freedom. In 1753, Jean Baptiste purchased the freedom of Catherine for 500 livres (which was done through installments and a sum upfront) and married her. Source: Donovan, "Slaves and Their Owners in Île Royale, 1713–1760," 29.

324. CURRY (c. 1784) – Enslaved to Georgia Loyalist John Todd at Chedabucto, Nova Scotia, along with several other slaves, Curry and the other slaves were probably from Georgia or East Florida. Source: Loyalists from Saint Augustine to Chedabucto, Chipman Papers, Muster Master General's Office, Loyalist Musters, 1776–1785, MG 23, D1, ser. I, vol. 24, LAC.

325. CYRUS (slave? c. 1784) – Possibly enslaved to Michael Houseal, a Loyalist from Maryland, Cyrus lived with three other Black people, who were also possibly slaves. Houseal remained in Nova Scotia until at least 1800, when he decided to return to England. In that same year, he attempted to hire out a young Black female as an indentured servant. Sources: Loyalists and Disbanded Troops at Cole Harbour, Chipman Papers, Muster Master General's Office, Loyalist Musters, 1776–1785, MG 23, D1, ser. I, vol. 24, LAC; *Royal Gazette*, June 24, 1800.

326. CYRUS (c. 1784) – Cyrus was an enslaved person who belonged to John Nash, who settled at Chedabucto, Nova Scotia. Source: Loyalists from Saint Augustine to Chedabucto, Chipman Papers, Muster Master General's Office, Loyalist Musters, 1776–1785, MG 23, D1, ser. I, vol. 24, LAC.

327. CYRUS (c. 1784) – John Wentworth sent Cyrus and 18 other slaves from Nova Scotia to his "relation" Paul Wentworth in Suriname. Wentworth described these slaves as "American born or well seasoned, and are perfectly stout, healthy, sober, orderly, Industrious, & obedient." Wentworth had the slaves

Christened and claimed to be concerned for their welfare. He also noted "All the men are expert in boats." Source: John Wentworth to Paul Wentworth or his attorney, February 24, 1784.

328. DANIEL (c. 1783, age 13) – Enslaved to William Black, who migrated to the Maritimes after the American Revolution, Daniel was probably from New York. His owner was a cabinet-maker. British officials at New York described him as a "stout boy." Source: Book of Negroes.

329. DAPHNE (c. 1784) – John Wentworth sent Daphne and 18 other slaves from Nova Scotia to his "relation" Paul Wentworth in Suriname. Wentworth described these slaves as "American born or well seasoned, and are perfectly stout, healthy, sober, orderly, Industrious, & obedient." Wentworth had the slaves Christened and claimed to be concerned for their welfare. He also claimed that the female slaves "promise well to increase their numbers." Source: John Wentworth to Paul Wentworth or his attorney, February 24, 1784.

330. DAVE (c. 1787) – In 1787 at Granville, Nova Scotia, Loyalist Christopher Benson sold an adult male named Squire and a boy named Dave. It is possible that these slaves were father and son. Source: Harris, "Negro Population of the County of Annapolis," 17.

331. DAUPHINE (c. 1759) – An enslaved woman working in Île Royale, Dauphine laboured as a cook. Source: Donovan, "Slaves in Île Royale, 1713–1758," 33.

332. DAWSON, ELIZABETH (c. 1784) – Elizabeth Dawson was enslaved to John Stewart at Chedabucto, Nova Scotia. The muster described her and possibly her husband (or brother) as "his property," meaning John Stewart owned them both. Source: Loyalists from Saint Augustine to Chedabucto, Chipman Papers, Muster Master General's Office, Loyalist Musters, 1776–1785, MG 23, D1, ser. I, vol. 24, LAC.

333. DAWSON, PETER (c. 1784) – Peter was enslaved to John Stewart at Chedabucto, Nova Scotia. Source: Loyalists from Saint Augustine to Chedabucto, Chipman Papers, Muster Master General's Office, Loyalist Musters, 1776–1785, MG 23, D1, ser. I, vol. 24, LAC.

334. DAVID (slave? c. 1784) – David was possibly enslaved to Lieutenant McKethan, who migrated to Country Harbour with other southern Loyalists, David and the majority of these Loyalists and their slaves were from North Carolina, South Carolina, and Georgia. They had settled briefly in East Florida before moving to Nova Scotia. Black people at Country Harbour were either slaves or "quasi-free" and subject to re-enslavement. Abolitionist Thomas Clarkson explained the phenomenon of re-enslavement: "It was not long till these loyalists, many of whom had been educated with all the ideas of the justice of slavery, the inferiority of negroes, and the superiority of white men, that are universal in the southern provinces of America, began to harass and oppress the industrious black settlers, and even wantonly to deprive them of the fruits of their labour, expelling them from the lands they had cleared." Clarkson continued by noting that whites reduced "again to slavery those negroes who had so honourably obtained their freedom. They hired them as servants, and, at the end of the stipulated time, refused payment of their wages, insisting that they were slaves: in some instances they destroyed their tickets of freedom, and then enslaved the negroes for want of them; in several instances, the unfortunate Africans were taken onboard vessels, carried to the West Indies, and there sold for the benefit of their plunderers." At Country Harbour, Black people were listed on the musters as the "Servants" of a white Loyalist, which meant it was very easy for them to be re-enslaved if they were not already enslaved. Sources: Clarkson, "Some Account of the New Colony at Sierra Leone," 229–30; Settlers at Country Harbour, Chipman Papers, Muster Master General's Office, Loyalist Musters, 1776–1785, MG 23, D1, ser. I, vol. 24, LAC. Note: Ellen Wilson believed that the information Clarkson used came from Thomas Peters; see Wilson, *Loyal Blacks*, 181.

335. DAVID (c. 1791) – Liverpool resident Simeon Perkins mentioned that two Black men named David and William who were possibly enslaved to Major Barclay and Mr. Simmons, respectively. Source: Fergusson, *Diary of Simeon Perkins, 1790–1796*, 104.

336. DAVIS, JAMESON (c. 1786) – During the American Revolution, Moses Reed and Jameson Davis were the property of Peter Green. They worked on his farm in Bute County, North Carolina. During the Loyalist occupation of Charleston, these men and an elderly slave "ran away from Mr. Green, who was a Rebell." The older man died, but Davis and Reed both made it to Charleston, where they worked for the British. After the evacuation of Charleston, they accompanied other southern Loyalists to St. Augustine, before eventually settling in Country Harbour, Nova Scotia, as free labourers for Colonel (or Captain) Hamilton. Molly Sinclair had been born in Charleston and lived with her master, James Sinclair, for most of her life. During the Revolution, she "was taken, with the other Plantation Negros" to Charleston. She migrated to St. Augustine before settling in Country Harbour with Colonel Hamilton. Her fellow servant, Phebe Martin, was the slave of Rebel William Martin. During the war, she ran away to Ninety-Six, South Carolina, and gained her freedom. After a short time in St. Augustine, she removed to Nova Scotia and also "lived with [Colonel?] Hamilton."

Although these Black Loyalists were free subjects of His Majesty, they found that freedom in the Maritime colonies could be fleeting at best. Moses Reed and Jameson Davis were "two years in the Service of Colonel Hamilton" and "received no wages." Phebe Martin claimed that she "was never [Hamilton's] slave, or ever received any Wages from him." After two years of being re-enslaved, these captive labourers resorted to escaping from their would-be master by travelling to distant Halifax where they hoped to be safe. At this point Hamilton, along with Captain Daniel McNeil, organized what can only be termed a slave patrol, which attempted to recapture the escaped labourers. The slave catchers found the four runaways, put them in irons, and locked them in a ship's hold, but not before they beat Jameson Davis with a "Cudgell." Molly Sinclair recalled "she was Chained to Moses Reed when put on the vessell." The re-enslaved men and women were taken to Shelburne, but before they could be shipped away local officials got word of their condition and ordered McNeil to bring them ashore for an enquiry and court investigation. McNeil claimed that he had been told to take the re-enslaved Black Loyalists to Shelburne and give them to a Mr. Dean, who "was to give him a Receipt for them, and, as he understood, was to carry them to the Bahamas." After hearing the testimony of the four men and women along with McNeil's statement, the Shelburne court considered whether the Blacks were the rightful property of Hamilton (there was no evidence such as a bill of sale) or should go free. The majority of the court, five in favour of freeing them and two against, decided that "the aforesaid Negros" would be allowed to "go where they pleased." Source: Special Sessions at Shelburne, Nova Scotia, August 5, 1786, Shelburne Records, MG 4, Vol. 141, NSA. There were two Hamilton's, one a captain and the other a colonel; also see, Carole Watterson Troxler, "Hidden from History: Black Loyalists at Country Harbour, Nova Scotia," in *Moving On: Black Loyalists in the Afro-Atlantic World*, ed., John W. Pulis (New York: Garland, 1999). This book chapter builds on several other earlier works by Troxler, including Carole Watterson Troxler, "Refuge, Resistance, and Reward: The Southern Loyalists' Claim on East Florida," *Journal of Southern History* 55 (1989): 582–90; Carole Watterson Troxler, "Loyalist Refugees and the British Evacuation of East Florida, 1783–1785," *Florida Historical Quarterly* 60 (July 1981): 1–28; Carole Watterson Troxler, "The Migration of Carolina and Georgia Loyalists to Nova Scotia and New Brunswick" (PhD diss., University of North Carolina, Chapel Hill, 1974).

337. DAVIS, PERO (c. 1786) – Southern Loyalist Jesse Gray re-enslaved several Black Loyalists in Shelburne, including Mary Postell (see her entry). But he also brutally beat Pero Davis, who seems to have been free or nominally free. Davis went to the local justice of the peace to report the act of violence: "Personally Appear'd this fifth day of November 1786 Pero Davis who being Sworn did Depose and say that sum time in the month of May Last the day he Does not Recolect, he being out [in] Argyle in said County in the Imploy of one Jesse Gray, he was by the said Jesse Gray Most Severly Beat with a Cowskin to the number of one hundred Lashes Round his Body in the gratest violence he Could Lay on in so much that he Cut the body of the Deponent in several Places." Gray's actions were so outrageous that local authorities charged him, but the grand jury refused to indict him. Although legally free, it is quite clear that Jesse Gray treated Pero Davis as a slave. Source: *King v. Jesse Gray*, November 9, 1786, Shelburne, vol. 27, no. 27.2, RG 60, NSA.

338. DEAL (c. 1787–1788) – Enslaved to Reverend Daniel Cock, who owned this young slave girl (and her mother at one point), the ownership of this slave resulted in James MacGregor condemning Cock in a famous 1788 pamphlet entitled *A Letter to a Clergyman Urging him to set free a Black Girl he held in SLAVERY*. Sources: Alan Wilson, *Highland Shepherd: James MacGregor, Father of the Scottish Enlightenment in Nova Scotia* (Toronto: University of Toronto Press, 2015), 74–75; James MacGregor, "A Letter to a Clergyman Urging him to set free a Black Girl he held in SLAVERY (1788)"; Barry Cahill, "Mediating a Scottish Enlightenment Ideal: The Presbyterian Dissenter Attack on Slavery in Late Eighteenth-Century Nova Scotia," in *Myth, Migration and the Making of Memory: Scotia and Nova Scotia, c. 1700–1990*, eds. Marjory Harper and Michael E. Vance (Halifax: Fernwood Publishing, 1999).

339. DEAL'S MOTHER (c. 1787–1788) – Reverend Daniel Cock owned this woman and allegedly sold her as she was "unruly" and "sullen." Sources: Wilson, *Highland Shepherd*, 74–75; MacGregor, "Letter to a Clergyman"; Cahill, "Mediating a Scottish Enlightenment Ideal."

340. DEATON, EANUS [or **UNUS**] (c. 1783–84, age 27) – The Book of Negroes described Eanus as a quadroon and sickly. She held a GBC, but Eanus was listed as being in the "possession" of Thomas Rogers who probably re-enslaved her. Before the war, she had been the slave of William Bush in Horseneck, Connecticut. In New Brunswick, she married Andrew Bush (if she had not done so earlier) and ran away from Thomas Rogers along with her husband as well as Charity Morris, Edward Morris, a child, and Peter Cock (or Cox). The runaway advertisement described Eanus and her husband thusly: "Andrew Bush, a comely stout negro, remarkable high forwarded, generally called the Widow's Peek, formerly the property of Doctor Bush, in Connecticut, is a remarkable *good miller*, which practice he has been used all his life to, also his wife Eanus, a yellow mustee [octoroon or a person of mixed ancestry]." Sources: Book of Negroes; *Royal Saint John's Gazette* (New Brunswick), May 13, 1784. For an in-depth description of this story of re-enslavement (which included Charity Morris, Edward Morris, Peter Cox, Eanus Deaton, and a few children) see, Whitfield, *Black Slavery in the Maritimes*, 37–40.

341. DEVOTION, PHILIP (c. 1744) – Philip was an enslaved man under the command of John Storer. Source: Donovan, "Nominal List of Slaves and Their Owners," 157.

342. DIANA/DINAH (c. 1783–84, age 20 in 1783) – Enslaved to Richard Jenkins, Diana/Dinah was probably from New York. Jenkins brought her to

Shelburne, Nova Scotia. British officials in New York described her as a "stout wench." In 1784, she was indicted for stealing several articles from one Bernard Kean. Sources: Book of Negroes; *Indictment, the King v. Diana, a Negro Woman*, 1784, RG 60, vol. 3, 3.1, NSA.

343. DIANA (c. 1783, age 7) – Enslaved to Captain Frink, who migrated to the Maritimes from New York, Diana was from New York. British officials described her as a "likely girl" who had been purchased from Mrs. Beadle of Staten Island. Source: Book of Negroes.

344. DIANA (c. 1783, age 22) – Diana was enslaved to Dr. Nathaniel Bullern, who migrated from South Carolina to Nova Scotia with a total of 10 slaves. Bullern's slaves also indicate several different possibilities of family connections and kinship networks. His oldest slaves, Achabee and Catharina, were both 60 at the end of the American Revolution. Jenny and Prince were 40 and 30 respectively. Bullern also owned another male slave in his early 30s and three females ranging in ages 19 to 25. His two youngest slaves were an infant named Sarah and a 6 year old. It is unclear who the parents of these children were, but it is possible that one or both parents were among Bullern's slaves. British officials in New York described Diana as an "ordinary wench." Source: Book of Negroes.

345. DIANA (c. 1783, age 22) – Enslaved to Colonel Robertson, who migrated to the Maritimes after the American Revolution, Diana was described by British officials in New York as a "likely wench." Source: Book of Negroes.

346. DIANA (c. 1801) – Nova Scotian politician and merchant Benjamin Belcher owned several slaves in Cornwallis, including Diana. Belcher noted in his will[?] "I give my Negro Girl Diana to my daughter Elizabeth Belcher Sheffield" and left strict directions for his heirs about the slaves, noting that he was "for ever charging them my children unto whom I have entrusted these Negro people with never to sell barter or exchange them or any of them under any pretension except it is for whose bad [?] Offences as will render them not safe to be kept in the Family and that to be adjudged of by three Justices of the Peace in said Township and in such case as their order they may be sold and disposed of. And I further request as soon as these young Negroes shall be capable to be taught to read, they shall be learnt the word of God." This is probably the same slave that Belcher had baptized in 1793. Source: Will of Benjamin Belcher, 1801, Kings County, NSA.

347. DIANNAH [DIANA] (slave? c. 1784) – Diannah was possibly enslaved to Captain Daniel McNeill (also spelled MacNeil and McNeil), who migrated to Country Harbour with other southern Loyalists. The majority of these Loyalists and their slaves were from North Carolina, South Carolina, and Georgia. They had settled briefly in East Florida before moving to Nova Scotia. Black people at Country Harbour were either slaves or "quasi-free" and subject to re-enslavement. Abolitionist Thomas Clarkson explained the phenomenon of re-enslavement: "It was not long till these loyalists, many of whom had been educated with all the ideas of the justice of slavery, the inferiority of negroes, and the superiority of white men, that are universal in the southern provinces of America, began to harass and oppress the industrious black settlers, and even wantonly to deprive them of the fruits of their labour, expelling them from the lands they had cleared." Clarkson continued by noting that whites reduced "again to slavery those negroes who had so honourably obtained their freedom. They hired them as servants, and, at the end of the stipulated time, refused payment of their wages, insisting that they were slaves: in some instances they destroyed their tickets of freedom, and then enslaved the negroes for want of them; in several instances, the unfortunate Africans were taken onboard vessels, carried to the West Indies, and there sold for the benefit of their plunderers." At Country Harbour, Black people were listed on the musters as the "Servants" of a white Loyalist, which meant it was very easy for them to be re-enslaved if they were not already enslaved. Sources: Clarkson, "Some Account of the New Colony at Sierra Leone," 229–30; Settlers at Country Harbour, Chipman Papers, Muster Master General's Office, Loyalist Musters, 1776–1785, MG 23, D1, ser. I, vol. 24, LAC. Note: Ellen Wilson believed that the information Clarkson used came from Thomas Peters; see Wilson, *Loyal Blacks*, 181.

348. DICK (c. 1783, age 11) – Enslaved to John Moore, who migrated to the Maritimes after the American Revolution, Dick was probably from North Carolina. British officials in New York described him as a "likely boy." Source: Book of Negroes.

349. DICK (c. 1783, age 27) – Enslaved to Benjamin Douglas (also spelled Douglass), Dick ran away from his owner in 1783. The advertisement offers a few interesting details about Dick's life, but not as much as other advertisements that describe occupation, family, and personality type: "RUN away on the 27th inst. A Negro Man, named, Dick, (belonging to Mr. BENJAMIN DOUGLASS, late Ensign in the King's Carolina Rangers) about five feet eight inches high Stout Made, had on when he went away a red coat turn'd up with blue, white Waistcoat and Breeches, Aged about Twenty Seven Years." Source: *Nova Scotia Gazette and Weekly Chronicle*, December 9, 1783.

350. DICK (slave? c. 1784) – This might be the same Dick who ran away from Benjamin Douglas (see entry above) because Captain Marshall possessed a man named Dick and he served with Ensign Douglass. Dick was possibly enslaved to Captain Marshall, who migrated to Country Harbour with other southern Loyalists. The majority of these Loyalists and their slaves were from North Carolina, South Carolina, and Georgia. They had settled briefly in East Florida before moving to Nova Scotia. Black people at Country Harbour were either slaves or "quasi-free" and subject to re-enslavement. Abolitionist Thomas Clarkson explained the phenomenon of re-enslavement: "It was not long till these loyalists, many of whom had been educated with all the ideas of the justice of slavery, the inferiority of negroes, and the superiority of white men, that are universal in the southern provinces of America, began to harass and oppress the industrious black settlers, and even wantonly to deprive them of the fruits of their labour, expelling them from the lands they had cleared." Clarkson continued by noting that whites reduced "again to slavery those negroes who had so honourably obtained their freedom. They hired them as servants, and, at the end of the stipulated time, refused payment of their wages, insisting that they were slaves: in some instances they destroyed their tickets of freedom, and then enslaved the negroes for want of them; in several instances, the unfortunate Africans were taken onboard vessels, carried to the West Indies, and there sold for the benefit of their plunderers." At Country Harbour, Black people were listed on the musters as the "Servants" of a white Loyalist, which meant it was very easy for them to be re-enslaved if they were not already enslaved. Sources: Clarkson, "Some Account of the New Colony at Sierra Leone," 229–30; Settlers at Country Harbour, Chipman Papers, Muster Master General's Office, Loyalist Musters, 1776–1785, MG 23, D1, ser. I, vol. 24, LAC. Note: Ellen Wilson believed that the information Clarkson used came from Thomas Peters; see Wilson, *Loyal Blacks*, 181.

351. DICK (c. 1790, age 20) – Dick was enslaved to Andrew Reynolds who, in a runaway advertisement, described Dick as speaking good English and the clothing he took with him. Source: *Nova Scotia Gazette*, August 17, 1790.

352. DICK (c. 1799) – In New Brunswick, at the turn of the century, Dick and Gill ran away from their owners. Their masters placed a joint advertisement in the local paper, which described the slaves' physical appearance and apparel: "RANAWAY on Sunday the 11th instant, two Negro Men named GILL and DICK, the property of the subscribers. – Gill is a dark mulatto, with short wooly hair; is about five feet six inches high; stout made; has square shoulders, bow legs, and walks clumsily. – Had on when he went away a homespun coat, and vest a mixture of black and white, half lapelled; trowsers twilled homespun, a smutty brown, and considerably worn – he also took with him two striped vests, and sundry other articles of clothing. DICK is a short thick set fellow, about 5 feet 4 inches high; remarkably black; has a scar on his cheek and another on his chin. – He had on and took with him a variety of cloathing – among other articles, a short coat without skirts; the color a mixture of blue with hemlock; nankeen overhails, &c." Source: *Royal Gazette* (New Brunswick), August 20, 1799.

353. DINAH (c. 1760s/1770s) – Dinah was enslaved to Reverend Seccombe in Chester, Nova Scotia. A well-known Baptist preacher, Seccombe came from Massachusetts and brought a few slaves with him. Source: Alexandra Montgomery, "An Unsettled Plantation: Nova Scotia's New Englanders and the Creation of a British Colony, 1759–1776," (Dalhousie University, MA Thesis, 2012), 44.

354. DINAH (c. 1776) – Dinah was enslaved to Reverend John Breynton, who sold her to Peter Shey of Hants County, Nova Scotia. Source: States, "Presence and Perseverance: Blacks in Hants County," 36.

355. DINAH (c. 1783) – During the American Revolution, Patriots forced Reverend John Wiswall from his home in present-day Maine. As he travelled to Nova Scotia, he wrote a letter to one of his relatives and implored "Remember me to Dinah." Wiswall noted that she could live "where she pleases" until he could send her another message. Wiswall also bluntly stated that he was "determined not to sell her to any Body." Source: Wiswall to Morice, January 15, 1776, Journal of Rev. John Wiswall, Acadia University Library, Wolfville, Nova Scotia.

356. DINAH (c. 1783, age 26) – In 1783, British officials described Dinah as a "stout wench." In 1786 Dinah absconded from her owner Robert Wilkins. In the runaway advertisement, Wilkins described Dinah as wearing "when she went away, a blue and white Ticking Petticoat, a purple and white Callico short Gown, and an old blue Cloak." Sources: Book of Negroes; *Nova Scotia Packet and General Advertiser*, August 3, 1786.

357. DINAH (c. 1783, age 28) – Dinah was enslaved to Captain Hornbrook, who migrated to the Maritimes after the American Revolution with her and a child named Cato (who was probably Dinah's son). She might have been from New York. British officials at New York described her as a "stout wench." Source: Book of Negroes.

358. CATO (c. 1783, age 2) – Described as an infant, Cato was enslaved to Captain Hornbrook who migrated to the Maritimes with Dinah (likely his mother). Source: Book of Negroes.

359. DINAH (c. 1783, age 38) – Enslaved to Lawrence Van Buskirk, who migrated to the Maritimes from New York after the American Revolution with one other slave, Dinah was from New York. British officials described her as a "stout wench." Source: Book of Negroes.

360. DINAH (c. 1791) – Dinah was enslaved to John Ditmars and was baptized in Nova Scotia. Source: List of Baptisms, December 19, 1791, Records of the Anglican Church, Digby Township Book, NSA.

361. DINAH [SINAH?] (c. 1791) – Enslaved to Edward Jones, Dinah was baptized at Clements, Nova Scotia. Source: List of Baptisms, December 19, 1791, Records of the Anglican Church, Digby Township Book, NSA.

362. DINAH (c. 1793) – New Brunswick resident Richard Wilson sold Dinah for £40 to Peter Hall of Windsor, Nova Scotia. About 10 months later, Wilson sold Dinah's daughter Violet for £11 to Peter Hall as well. Source: Dinah Bill of Sale, August 1793–1794, NSA; this document does not have a stamp indicating the proper archive.

363. VIOLET (c. 1794) – The enslaved daughter of Dinah, Violet was almost immediately sold away from her mother by Peter Hall to Charles Dixon. Source: Dinah Bill of Sale, August 1793–1794; the bill of sale for Violet is attached to the original bill of sale May 1794, NSA. This document does not have a stamp indicating the proper archive.

364. DINAH (c. 1806, age 26) – In 1806, John Ryan placed a warning in the local New Brunswick paper for people not to help his slave run away. In many years of research on slavery in the Maritimes, this author has never come across a similar advertisement: "CAUTION. THE Subscriber hereby cautions all persons against attempting in future to seduce from his Service his Female Negro Slave DINAH, (for whom he has a good legal title) as he is determined to punish by all legal ways and means, every offender of that description. And that no one may plead ignorance of the person of the Slave in excuse, he informs all concerned, that she is about 26 years of age – 4 feet 9 inches high – has a small scar upon her forehead – and lately belonged to Mr. JAMES TAYLOR, of Maugerville." Source: *Royal Gazette* (New Brunswick), December 24, 1806.

365. DIXON, MERTILLA (c. 1791) – In 1791, Mertilla Dixon filed a complaint in Shelburne, Nova Scotia, against the powerful Barclay family. Originally from Virginia, Dixon escaped to British lines and eventually went to Charleston with one John Serjant. After working for a series of well-known Loyalists, including Colonel Fanning and Edward Winslow, Dixon eventually worked as a domestic for Major Thomas Barclay and his wife (the sister of James DeLancey) and came to Nova Scotia with them. Apparently, Mrs. Barclay "threatened to ship her to the West Indies, and there dispose of her as a Slave, and being fully persuaded that she was to be put on board of a vessel, then ready for Sea, she has (about a fortnight since) taken refuge with her father Charles Dixon, in Birch Town, and prays Your Honor's protection, until Major Barclay, can prove his claim to [her]." Source: Complaint of Mertilla Dixon, RG 34-321 M 97 file, NSA.

366. DONNEL, PETER (c. 1784, age 29) – Enslaved to James Driscoll, who migrated to the Maritimes from New York, Peter was described by British officials as an "ordinary fellow." Source: Book of Negroes.

367. DOROTHY (c. 1783, age 5) – Enslaved to Widow Conley, who migrated to the Maritimes from New York, it is not clear where Dorothy originated. Source: Book of Negroes.

368. DOROTHY (c. 1784) – John Wentworth sent Dorothy and 18 other slaves from Nova Scotia to his "relation" Paul Wentworth in Suriname. Wentworth described these slaves as "American born or well seasoned, and are perfectly stout, healthy, sober, orderly, Industrious, & obedient." Wentworth had the slaves Christened and claimed to be concerned for their welfare. He also claimed that the female slaves "promise well to increase their numbers." Source: John Wentworth to Paul Wentworth or his attorney, February 24, 1784.

369. DOROTHY (c. 1815) – New York Loyalist Sarah Cory (widow of Griffin Cory who died in 1780) freed multiple slaves in her will. Cory's will stated (she was illiterate): "I give and direct my servant girl [Dorothy] with all her Children to be free from slavery with her bed and [bedding]." It is difficult to know how many children were actually freed, but it must have been at least two. Source: Will of Sarah Cory, Queens County, 1815, PANB.

370. UNNAMED CHILD OF DOROTHY (c. 1815) – This child was enslaved to Sarah Cory. Source: Will of Sarah Cory, Queens County, 1815, PANB.

371. UNNAMED CHILD OF DOROTHY (c. 1815) – This child was enslaved to Sarah Cory. Source: Will of Sarah Cory, Queens County, 1815, PANB.

372. DOWNAN, JEREMIAH (slave? c. 1784) – Jeremiah was possibly enslaved to Ensign McDougald, who migrated to Country Harbour with other southern Loyalists. The majority of these Loyalists and their slaves were from North Carolina, South Carolina, and Georgia. They had settled briefly in East Florida before moving to Nova Scotia. Black people at Country Harbour were either slaves or "quasi-free" and subject to re-enslavement. Abolitionist Thomas Clarkson explained the phenomenon of re-enslavement: "It was not long till these loyalists, many of whom had been educated with all the ideas of the justice of slavery, the inferiority of negroes, and the superiority of white men, that are universal in the southern provinces of America, began to harass and oppress the industrious black settlers, and even wantonly to deprive them of the fruits of their labour, expelling them from the lands they had cleared." Clarkson continued by noting that whites reduced "again to slavery those negroes who had so honourably obtained their freedom. They hired them as servants, and, at the end of the stipulated time, refused payment of their wages, insisting that they were slaves: in some instances they destroyed their tickets of freedom, and then enslaved the negroes for want of them; in several instances, the unfortunate Africans were taken onboard vessels, carried to the West Indies, and there sold for the benefit of their plunderers." At Country Harbour, Black people were listed on the musters as the "Servants" of a white Loyalist, which meant it was very easy for them to be re-enslaved if they were not already enslaved. Sources: Clarkson, "Some Account of the New Colony at Sierra Leone," 229–30; Settlers at Country Harbour, Chipman Papers, Muster Master General's Office, Loyalist Musters, 1776–1785, MG 23, D1, ser. I, vol. 24, LAC. Note: Ellen Wilson believed that the information Clarkson used came from Thomas Peters; see Wilson, *Loyal Blacks*, 181.

373. DUNLAP, JACK (c. 1783, age 9) – Enslaved to Mr. Lowerhele, who migrated to the Maritimes from New York, Jack was described by British officials as a "fine boy." Source: Book of Negroes.

374. EDWARD (c. 1790) – Enslaved to John Polhemus, Edward was baptized in Annapolis, Nova Scotia. The recorder noted that he and two other slaves belonged to John Polhemus, but it is unclear if this person is included in the 1807 Digby slaveholder petition in which Polhemus noted he owned 10 slaves. Source: Register of Baptisms, February 1790, St. Luke's Anglican Church, Annapolis Royal, Annapolis County, MG 4, vol. 4, NSA.

375. EDWARD (c. 1828, age 8) – Enslaved to the Ormsby family of Prince Edward Island, Edward was included in the Montserrat slave registry of 1828 as it contains a notation that listed four slaves of the Ormsby household who were living in Prince Edward Island: "I Matthew William Blake (for Catharine Ormsby) do swear that the Return now by me delivered to be registered contains to the best of my knowledge and belief a true faithful and accurate account and description of all the Slaves belonging to Catharine Ormsby and being within this Island (Save and Except the following Slaves of the Names as follows Charles Male Black Twenty Years, Mary Jane Female Black Thirteen Years, Fanny Female Coloured Eleven Years, Edward Male Black Eight Years, residing with Mr. Ormsby at Prince Edward Island)." Source: December 13, 1828, Montserrat Slave Register, T_71_450 page 285, TNA. This author must thank Mr. Neil How of the Montserrat National Trust, Montserrat, West Indies, for sharing this document.

376. EDWARDS, CATHERINE (slave? c. 1806–7) – Catherine was probably enslaved to Shelburne merchant George Ross, who ignored a writ of habeas corpus to bring her to court. Source: Barry Cahill, "Slavery and the Judges of Loyalist Nova Scotia," University of New Brunswick Law Journal 43 (1994): 117.

377. ELENORA (c. 1784) – John Wentworth sent Elenora and 18 other slaves from Nova Scotia to his "relation" Paul Wentworth in Suriname. Wentworth described these slaves as, "American born or well seasoned, and are perfectly stout, healthy, sober, orderly, Industrious, & obedient." Elenora was listed as a child. Source: John Wentworth to Paul Wentworth or his attorney, February 24, 1784.

378. ELIZABETH (c. 1783, age 24) – Enslaved to John Norris, who migrated to the Maritimes after the American Revolution with a few other slaves, Elizabeth was described by British officials as a "stout wench." Source: Book of Negroes.

379. ELIZABETH (c. 1783, age 26) – Enslaved to Captain Hicks, who migrated to the Maritimes after the American Revolution with several slaves, including an infant named Tim, Elizabeth was possibly from Pennsylvania. British officials in New York described her as a "stout wench." Source: Book of Negroes.

380. TIM (c. 1783, age 6 months) – Tim was the son of Elizabeth and also enslaved to Captain Hicks. Source: Book of Negroes.

381. ELIZABETH (c. 1783, age 24) – Enslaved to Francis Wood, who migrated to the Maritimes after the American Revolution, Elizabeth was described by British officials at New York as a "stout wench." Source: Book of Negroes.

382. UNNAMED CHILD (c. 1783) – This child was enslaved to Francis Wood, who migrated to the Maritimes with this child's mother, Elizabeth. Source: Book of Negroes.

383. ELIZABETH (slave? c. 1797) – Elizabeth and Esther were baptized in New Brunswick and both listed as "Black Adults of Mr. Lawton and Mr. Longmire." The wording indicates that they were probably slaves. Source: Parish Records, Maugerville, FCLCRN4C3R4, Unclear Archive, probably PANB or New Brunswick Museum; the author can share the photocopies of these baptismal records with anyone interested in seeing them.

384. EMANUAL (c. 1783, age 26) – Enslaved to Lieutenant Colonel Moncrief, who migrated to the Maritimes from New York, and accompanied by Emanual's wife and child who were apparently free (born in Jamaica). British officials in New York described him as "stout." Source: Book of Negroes.

385. EPHRAHIM (c. 1745) – Enslaved to the Connecticut Regiment during the siege and takeover of Louisbourg. Source: Donovan, "Nominal List of Slaves and Their Owners," 156.

386. ESTHER (c. 1783, age 18) – Enslaved to Bartholomew Crannell, who migrated to the Maritimes from New York, Esther was probably from New York. British officials described her as a "stout wench." Source: Book of Negroes.

387. ESTHER (slave? c. 1797) – Elizabeth and Esther were baptized in New Brunswick and both listed as "Black Adults of Mr. Lawton and Mr. Longmire." The wording indicates that they were probably slaves. Source: Parish Records of Maugerville, PANB.

388. ESTIENNE, JEAN BAPTISTE (c. 1742, age 20) – Enslaved to the Brothers of Charity, Jean Baptiste was baptized in 1742 while two slaves served as godfather and godmother. He worked at the King's Hospital, but ended up as a refugee following the siege of Louisbourg. Eventually, he returned with Brother Gregoire Chomey. In 1750, Jean Baptiste attempted to escape, but he was discovered and forced to remain in Louisbourg. Source: Donovan, "Slaves and Their Owners in Île Royale, 1713–1760," 17.

389. GODFATHER NAMED ESTIENNE (c. 1742) – This enslaved man was present at Jean Baptiste Estienne's baptism. The Brothers of Charity probably owned him. Source: Donovan, "Nominal List of Slaves and Their Owners," 155.

390. GODMOTHER NAMED MARIE (c. 1742) – This enslaved woman was present at Jean Baptiste Estienne's baptism. Source: Donovan, "A Nominal List of Slaves and Their Owners," 155.

391. ETHERINGTON, WILLIAM (slave? c. 1783, age 13) – British officials in New York noted William was "sold by Capt. Munro, British Legion, to John Van Winkle which had no right to do." Source: Book of Negroes.

392. ÉTIENNE (c. 1728, age 14) – Étienne was enslaved to Jean Seigneur, who purchased her to replace a woman named Louise. Seigneur's repeated rape of Louise was the "clearest case of sexual exploitation in the Louisbourg records." As the replacement for Louise, Étienne worked at Seigneur's inn and probably as his domestic. Source: Donovan, "Slaves and Their Owners in Île Royale, 1713–1760," 20–21.

393. EVE (c. 1783, age 56) – Enslaved to Francis Howse (or House), who migrated to the Maritimes after the American Revolution, Eve was described by British officials at New York as a "stout wench." Source: Book of Negroes.

394. EVE (c. 1783, age 64) – Enslaved to Henry Guest, who migrated to the Maritimes after the American Revolution, Eve was probably from Pennsylvania or Africa. British officials at New York described her as a "stout wench." Source: Book of Negroes.

395. EVE (c. 1780s?) – New Yorker John Rapalje sent "a Negro wench named Eve and her daughter Sukey" to George Leonard in New Brunswick. He noted that Eve "is an excellent hand at all sorts of housework [except cooking] … and one of the best servants for washing we ever had." Source: W.O. Raymond, "The Negro in New Brunswick," *Neith* (February 1903), 31.

396. SUKEY (c. 1780s) – The daughter of Eve, Sukey came to New Brunswick along with her mother. Source: Raymond, "Negro in New Brunswick," 31.

397. FAIRWEATHER, FRANK (c. 1783, age 10) – Enslaved to Thomas Fairweather, who migrated to the Maritimes from New York with no other slaves, Frank was probably from Connecticut. British officials described him as a "fine boy." Source: Book of Negroes.

398. FAME, JOHN (c. 1770) – John was enslaved to Joseph Gerrish. Source: Smith, "Slave in Canada," 14; David W. States and Karolyn Smardz Frost, "University of King's College, Nova Scotia: Direct Connections to Slavery, Section 5: King's College Students and Slavery Selected Biographies," unpublished manuscript, December 4, 2020, p. 9.

399. FANNY (c. 1790) – Enslaved to John Burbidge, Fanny was the mother of several slaves – including Peter, Hannah, and Flora. And, most likely, she was the mother of Burbidge's other slaves: Charleston, Samuel, and Rosanna. Burbidge had Fanny's children baptized. In 1790, he drew up manumission papers dictating that Fanny be freed in seven years, while her children were expected to be slaves until the age of 30. Burbidge also wanted the slaves to be taught to read and planned to give them clothes. Source: Arthur Eaton, *The History of Kings County; Heart of the Acadian Land* (Salem: The Salem Press Company, 1910), 234.

400. HANNAH (c. 1783, infant) – Enslaved to John Burbidge, Hannah was baptized in 1783 in Cornwallis, Nova Scotia. Source: List of Baptisms, September 28, 1783, Cornwallis Township Book, NSA.

401. PETER (c. 1786, infant) – Peter was enslaved to John Burbidge and was baptized in 1786. Source: List of Baptisms, July 2, 1786, Cornwallis Township Book, NSA.

402. FLORA (c. 1788) – Enslaved to John Burbidge, Flora lived with a few other slaves. Source: List of Baptisms, August 3, 1788, Cornwallis Township Book, NSA.

403. CHARLESTON (c. 1792) – Enslaved to John Burbidge, who owned several other slaves, Charleston was baptized at Cornwallis, Nova Scotia, on Burbidge's instructions. Source: List of Baptisms, February 13, 1792, Cornwallis Township Book, NSA.

404. SAMUEL (c. 1794, infant) – Enslaved to John Burbidge, Samuel was baptized one month after his birth. Source: List of Baptisms, February 1794, Cornwallis Township Book, NSA.

405. ROSANNA (c. 1796) – Enslaved to John Burbidge, Rosanna was baptized. Source: List of Baptisms, July 3, 1796, Cornwallis Township Book, NSA.

406. FANNY (c. 1783, age 22) – Enslaved to Mary Rinn, Fanny migrated to the Maritimes from New York with seven other slaves. She was previously owned by Marianna Jones, who gave her to Mary Rinn. British officials described her as a "sick wench." Source: Book of Negroes.

407. FANNY (c. 1828, age 11) – Fanny was enslaved to the Ormsby family of Prince Edward Island. In the Montserrat slave registry of 1828, a notation was made that listed four slaves of the Ormsby household who were living in Prince Edward Island: "I Matthew William Blake (for Catharine Ormsby) do swear that the Return now by me delivered to be registered contains to the best of my knowledge and belief a true faithful and accurate account and description of all the Slaves belonging to Catharine Ormsby and being within this Island (Save and Except the following Slaves of the Names as follows Charles Male Black Twenty Years, Mary Jane Female Black Thirteen Years, Fanny Female Coloured Eleven Years, Edward Male Black Eight Years, residing with Mr. Ormsby at Prince Edward Island)." Source: December 13, 1828, Montserrat Slave Register, T_71_450 page 285, TNA. I must thank Mr. Neil How of the Montserrat National Trust, Montserrat, West Indies, for sharing this document with me.

408. FIBBY (slave? c. 1784) – Fibby was possibly enslaved to Captain Daniel McNeill (also spelled MacNeil and McNeil), who migrated to Country Harbour with other southern Loyalists. The majority of these Loyalists and their slaves were from North Carolina, South Carolina, and Georgia. They had settled briefly in East Florida before moving to Nova Scotia. Black people at Country Harbour were either slaves or "quasi-free" and subject to re-enslavement. Abolitionist Thomas Clarkson explained the phenomenon of re-enslavement. "It was not long till these loyalists, many of whom had been educated with all the ideas of the justice of slavery, the inferiority of negroes, and the superiority of white men, that are universal in the southern provinces of America, began to harass and oppress the industrious black settlers, and even wantonly to deprive them of the fruits of their labour, expelling them from the lands they had cleared." Clarkson continued by noting that whites reduced "again to slavery those negroes who had so honourably obtained their freedom. They hired them as servants, and, at the end of the stipulated time, refused payment of their wages, insisting that they were slaves: in some instances they destroyed their tickets of freedom, and then enslaved the negroes for want of them; in several instances, the unfortunate Africans were taken onboard vessels, carried to the West Indies, and there sold for the benefit of their plunderers." At Country Harbour, Black people were listed on the musters as the "Servants" of a white Loyalist, which meant it was very easy for them to be re-enslaved if they were not already enslaved. Sources: Clarkson, "Some Account of the New Colony at Sierra Leone," 229–30; Settlers at Country Harbour, Chipman Papers, Muster Master General's Office, Loyalist Musters, 1776–1785, MG 23, D1, ser. I, vol. 24, LAC. Note: Ellen Wilson believed that the information Clarkson used came from Thomas Peters; see Wilson, *Loyal Blacks*, 181.

409. FILLIS (c. 1779) – Enslaved to William Haliburton in Hants County, Nova Scotia, Fillis was sold by Haliburton to the West Indies for £35. Source: States, "Presence and Perseverance: Blacks in Hants County," 34.

410. FILLIS (c. 1784, age 13) – Fillis was enslaved to John Grant, who was originally from Scotland; after serving the British army near Ticonderoga during the Seven Years War, Grant settled in Queens County, Long Island. After the American Revolution, he settled in Nova Scotia with a large family and nine slaves. These enslaved people might have been a family unit. Source: Cottreau-Robins, "Landscape of Slavery in Loyalist Era Nova Scotia," 131–2; see also Smith, "Slave in Canada," 93–4.

411. FLORA (c. 1769) – In Hants County the local court convicted Flora of stealing items from John Cunningham and sentenced her to 25 lashes. Source: States, "Presence and Perseverance: Blacks in Hants County," 41.

412. FLORA (c. 1786, age 27) – Flora was brought to New Brunswick after the American Revolution. In 1786, she participated in a mass escape with four other slaves from their owner Maryland Loyalist Caleb Jones: "RAN AWAY FROM the subscriber living at the Nashwakshis, in the county of York, between the 15th and 21st days of this instant July [June?], the following bound Negro slaves, viz., ISAAC about 30 years old, born on Long Island near New-York, had on when he went away, a short blue coat, round hat and white trowsers. BEN, about 35 years old, had on a Devonshire Kersey jacket lined with Scotch plad, corduroy breeches, and round hat. FLORA, a wench about 27 years old, much pitted with the small-pox, she had on a white cotton jacket and petticoat. ALSO NANCY about 24 years old, who took with her a Negro child, about four years old called LIDGE. The four last mentioned Negroes were born in Maryland, and lately brought to this country." Source: *Royal Gazette* (New Brunswick), July 25, 1786.

413. FLORA (c. 1787) – Enslaved to Margret Murray of Halifax, Flora lived with two other slaves including a child named Brutus. Murray freed the two adult slaves, Flora and Marianne, in her will. Sources: Will of Margaret Murray, 1787, Halifax County, NSA; Smith, "Slave in Canada," 91.

414. FLORA (c. 1780s) – Flora was enslaved to Hannah Lee in Marblehead, Massachusetts, and was probably enslaved to the Robie family in Halifax. When Hannah Lee died, she did not free Flora, but gave her several items. Flora went to Halifax to live with Mrs. Lee's granddaughter, Mary Bradstreet Robie, who owned Flora's daughter. Clearly, the Robies knew that Flora would come and serve them because she wanted to be with her child. Source: G. Patrick O'Brien, "'Unknown and Unlamented': Loyalist Women in Nova Scotia from Exile to Repatriation, 1775–1800" (PhD diss., University of South Carolina, 2019), 203–6; O'Brien to Whitfield and Chute, private correspondence, December 17, 2020.

415. FLORA'S DAUGHTER (c. late 1770s, early 1780s) – This unnamed daughter was enslaved to the Robie family, who fled Massachusetts and arrived in Halifax in 1775. This child was the daughter of a woman named Flora who was enslaved in Massachusetts to Hannah Lee, the grandmother of Mary Bradstreet Robie. It seems that Lee gave Flora's daughter to the Robie family before they migrated to Halifax. Source: O'Brien, "Loyalist Women in Nova Scotia from Exile to Repatriation," 203–6; O'Brien to Whitfield and Chute, private correspondence, December 17, 2020.

416. PRINCE (c. late 1780s) – Prince was probably enslaved. In Halifax, Mary Robie wrote: "A fine day. Received an addition to the family. A little black presented us by Mrs. Flora." When the Robies went back to Massachusetts in the late 1780s, the family was concerned that locals would look down on them because Prince was enslaved. Source: O'Brien, "Loyalist Women in Nova Scotia from Exile to Repatriation," 203–6; O'Brien to Whitfield and Chute, private correspondence, December 17, 2020.

417. FLORIMELL (c. 1776) – Florimell was enslaved to an unknown owner, who placed a runaway advertisement for her in the *Nova Scotia Gazette*. This advertisement describes her clothing, that she wore men's shoes, had facial scars (possibly indicating African birth), and spoke broken English. Sources: Charmaine Nelson "Special Issue: Expanding and Complicating the Concept of Creolization," *African and Black Diaspora: An International Journal* 12 (2019): 267; *Nova Scotia Gazette*, July 9, 1776.

418. FORTUNE (c. 1783, age 9) – Fortune was an enslaved boy of Major Coffin, who migrated to the Maritimes after the American Revolution with Fortune and a teenage female slave. Fortune was from South Carolina. British officials in New York noted that Fortune became the property of Major Coffin "by the marriage to Mrs. Coffin," who was from South Carolina. These same officials described him as a "likely boy." Source: Book of Negroes.

419. FORTUNE, RICHARD (c. 1790) – In his will, slaveowner Joseph Fairbanks freed his "old and faithful servant, Richard Fortune." Source: Smith, "Slave in Canada," 84.

420. FRACTION, PRINCE (c. 1783) – Enslaved to Edward Trigler, who purchased Prince from James Stokes of New York, Prince was described by British officials as "stout" but blind in the left eye. Source: Book of Negroes.

421. FRANCES (slave? c. 1762) – One of two young Black girls who were baptized at St. Paul's Church in Halifax, it is likely that both Frances and the other young Black girl were slaves. Source: Smith, "Slave in Canada," 85.

422. [Last name unclear], FRANCES (c. 1799, age 28) – Frances was enslaved to Reuben Tucker, from whom he absconded during the summer of 1799. In the runaway advertisement, Tucker described Frances as speaking good English and having a pleasant countenance. Source: *Royal Gazette*, July 9, 1799.

423. FRANCIS (c. 1784) – Francis was enslaved to Charles Montagu, who served as Royal Governor of South Carolina. Montagu freed Francis shortly before his death. The notation reveals a man saddened by his fate of only having one slave when he certainly had more back in South Carolina. Montagu wrote: "I have only one Negro, named Francis. He is to have his freedom." Source: Smith, "Slave in Canada," 91.

424. FRANÇOIS (c. 1742) – Ken Donovan's work to discover the fascinating story of François is a masterpiece of historical research. Using the records of Martinique's Superior Council and correspondence with Louisbourg officials, Donovan illuminates how François ended up in Louisbourg and eventually married and had a modicum of independence that most other slaves did not enjoy. In 1740, the commissaire-ordonnateur requested a slave to serve as executioner. Martinique's Superior Council decided to send François, who had been convicted of murdering a small Black child (he was given a choice of going to Île Royale or being executed). The Intendant of Martinique purchased François and allowed him to practise the skills necessary to be an executioner. Once in Louisbourg, the government provided François with 300 livres per year, rations, and purchased a wife for him. As Donovan states, "Clearly, François and his bride, although still slaves, were granted a measure of independence." Source: Donovan, "Slaves and Their Owners in Île Royale," 19.

425. UNNAMED WIFE (c. 1743) – The wife of François the executioner. Source: Donovan, "Slaves and Their Owners in Île Royale," 19.

426. FRANÇOIS (c. 1749) – Enslaved to Antoine Castaing. Source: Donovan, "Nominal List of Slaves and Their Owners," 158.

427. FRANÇOIS ANTHOINE MARIE (c. 1735, age 14) – Enslaved to François Lessene dit Francoeur. Source: Donovan, "Nominal List of Slaves and Their Owners," 153.

428. FRANÇOISE (slave; c. 1749) – Enslaved to merchant Louis Jouet, Françoise lived in a household with several other slaves. Source: Donovan, "Nominal List of Slaves and Their Owners," 154.

429. FRANCOISE (c. 1752) – From the Island of Dominique, Francoise came to Île Royale to work for her owner's sister Marie Cheron, who had partially inherited a St. Domingue plantation that she eventually sold for a "net value of 75,000 livres." Source: Donovan, "Slaves and Their Owners in Île Royale," 14.

430. FRANÇOISE (c. 1757) – Francoise was an enslaved woman who gave birth to a daughter. Source: Donovan, "Female Slaves as Sexual Victims in Île Royale," 150.

431. MARIE JEANNE (c. 1757) – The infant of Françoise. Source: Donovan, "Female Slaves as Sexual Victims in Île Royale," 150.

432. FRANK (c. 1784) – Frank was probably enslaved to well-known Loyalist Edward Winslow in the Maritimes along with two other men. Source: Accounts of Edward Winslow, 1783–84, June 17, 1784, Winslow Papers (online), https://www.lib.unb.ca/winslow/fullrecord.cgi?id=500&level=2&BACKSTR=fields=Title%2Ccreator_name%2CSubject%2CSource%2CETC_Sequence&order_by=Identifier&level=2&Creator_name=&Title=&Subject=Caesar&Source=&Keyword=.

433. GAMBO (c. 1745) – Colonel Samuel Moore brought Gambo to serve with him in Louisbourg. Source: Donovan, "Nominal List of Slaves and Their Owners," 156.

434. GASSANAULT, JEAN (c. 1734) – Jean was enslaved to B. Cassaignolles. Source: Donovan, "Nominal List of Slaves and Their Owners," 153.

435. GEMMEL, ROBERT (c. 1791) – Robert Gemmel almost suffered re-enslavement and sale out of Nova Scotia, but it was prevented by his mother named Susannah Connor, who "came here personally into Court" and complained that one John Harris intended to take her son out of the province. Her son [Robert Gemmel or Gammel] worked as Harris's indentured apprentice. The court ordered Harris to come in immediately and answer for his alleged plans. Harris readily admitted that he planned to leave the province, but claimed that the only reason he planned to take the boy was because there were no other available owners to teach Gemmel the art of butchery. The court cancelled the indenture. If Susannah Connor had not intervened on behalf of her son, Gemmel would have been taken out of the province – to the United States or elsewhere – and no doubt enslaved. The case of Robert Gemmel underlines the tenuous nature of the line between slavery and freedom that Black people faced in the Maritimes, even – perhaps especially – if they were small children. Source: General Sessions at Shelburne, Nova Scotia, November 1, 1791, Shelburne Records, MG 4, vol. 141, NSA.

436. GEORGE (c. 1783, age 13) – Enslaved to Captain Philips, George was described by British officials as a "stout boy." Source: Book of Negroes.

437. GEORGE (slave? c. 1784) – George was possibly enslaved to Lieutenant Boisseau, who migrated to Country Harbour with other southern Loyalists. The majority of these Loyalists and their slaves were from North Carolina, South Carolina, and Georgia. They had settled briefly in East Florida before moving to Nova Scotia. Black people at Country Harbour were either slaves or "quasi-free" and subject to re-enslavement. Abolitionist Thomas Clarkson explained the phenomenon of re-enslavement: "It was not long till these loyalists, many of whom had been educated with all the ideas of the justice of slavery, the inferiority of negroes, and the superiority of white men, that are universal in the southern provinces of America, began to harass and oppress the industrious black settlers, and even wantonly to deprive them of the fruits of their labour, expelling them from the lands they had cleared." Clarkson continued by noting that whites reduced "again to slavery those negroes who had so honourably obtained their freedom. They hired them as servants, and, at the end of the stipulated time, refused payment of their wages, insisting that they were slaves: in some instances they destroyed their tickets of freedom, and then enslaved the negroes for want of them; in several instances, the unfortunate Africans were taken onboard vessels, carried to the West Indies, and there sold for the benefit of their plunderers." At Country Harbour, Black people were listed on the musters as the "Servants" of a white Loyalist, which meant it was very easy for them to be re-enslaved if they were not already enslaved. Sources: Clarkson, "Some Account of the New Colony at Sierra Leone," 229–30; Settlers at Country Harbour, Chipman Papers, Muster Master General's Office, Loyalist Musters, 1776–1785, MG 23, D1, ser. I, vol. 24, LAC. Note: Ellen Wilson believed that the information Clarkson used came from Thomas Peters; see Wilson, *Loyal Blacks*, 181.

438. GEORGE (c. 1806, age 16) – Isaac Bonnell owned three young male slaves whom he wanted to free once they reached the age of 24. In this will, Bonnell clearly expressed some sentimental attachment to his young slaves. He not only intended to free them, but also to provide them with some basic necessities such as clothing. He also wanted them to have a rudimentary understanding of the Bible, because that would help them in early nineteenth-century society. These slaves would not gain their freedom until their mid-20s, which meant that Bonnell's family would continue to benefit from their labour for many years. There is no mention of these slaves' biological parents, which means that they could have died or been sold. We simply do not have enough information to know. In discussing his slaves, Bonnell noted it was "My Desire is that My Black Boys George, Tom, & Bob –be Taught to Read [?] in the Bible & to write Legible hand & that they be Sett at Liberty as they [?] Arrive to the Age of Twenty four years. Each to be allow'd [?] of good new Cloathes of Every Description Beside their Common wearing apparel. George Was Born in November 1790. Tom Was born in May 1792. And Bob Was Born in February 1794." Source: Will of Isaac Bonnell, 1806, Annapolis County, RG 48, Probate Records, NSA.

439. GEORGE (c. 1783) – Enslaved to Richard Jenkins, the Book of Negroes described George as the 14-year-old "Property of Richard Jenkins" and a "stout boy" in 1783. Eight years later, Jenkins complained to a local court in Shelburne that George had absconded from his home in nearby Green Harbour. Richard Jenkins claimed that John Stewart, another farmer in the same township, had attempted to "inveigle and Entice" George to escape. In court, George testified that he had absconded from Jenkins because he feared being blamed for his master's herring nets being "cast off their moorings" into the harbour. As he attempted to escape, George had run into Stewart, who "gave him some Bread, and Lobsters, and desired him to make the best of his way to Shelburne." He also reported, "John Stewart hath frequently advised, and persuaded this Deponent, to run away from his said master." Although George did not get away and his would-be friend John Stewart had to face court proceedings, this practical abolitionist had certainly tried to help George obtain freedom. This is possibly the same George that was owned by Richard Jenkins (see entry for George Jolly). Sources: Book of Negroes; Shelburne Records, MG 4, vol. 141, NSA; Summons for Richard Jenkins against John Stuart [or Stewart] on Information + Complaint for Inveigling the Servant of the Said Richard, RG 60, Shelburne County, 48.4, NSA.

440. GEORGES (c. 1713) – Enslaved to the first governor of Île Royale, Pasteur de Costebelle, Georges might have been the first enslaved Black person in Île Royale. Source: Donovan, "Nominal List of Slaves and Their Owners," 152.

441. GIBB, FRANK (c. 1783, age 9) – Enslaved to Robert Gibbs, who migrated to the Maritimes from New York. Frank was from New York. British officials described him as a "fine boy." Source: Book of Negroes.

442. GIBLINE, JAMES (slave? c. 1784) – James was possibly enslaved to Ensign Campbell, who migrated to Country Harbour with other southern Loyalists. The majority of these Loyalists and their slaves were from North Carolina, South Carolina, and Georgia. They had settled briefly in East Florida before moving to Nova Scotia. Black people at Country Harbour were either slaves or "quasi-free" and subject to re-enslavement. Abolitionist Thomas Clarkson explained the phenomenon of re-enslavement: "It was not long till these loyalists, many of whom had been educated with all the ideas of the justice of slavery, the inferiority of negroes, and the superiority of white men, that are universal in the southern provinces of America, began to harass and oppress the industrious black settlers, and even wantonly to deprive them of the fruits of their labour, expelling them from the lands they had cleared." Clarkson continued by noting that whites reduced "again to slavery those negroes who had so honourably obtained their freedom. They hired them as servants, and, at the end of the stipulated time, refused payment of their wages, insisting that they were slaves: in some instances they destroyed their tickets of freedom, and then enslaved the negroes for want of them; in several instances, the unfortunate Africans were taken onboard vessels, carried to the West Indies, and there sold for the benefit of their plunderers." At Country Harbour, Black people were listed on the musters as the "Servants" of a white Loyalist, which meant it was very easy for them to be re-enslaved if they were not already enslaved. Sources: Clarkson, "Some Account of the New Colony at Sierra Leone," 229–30; Settlers at Country Harbour, Chipman Papers, Muster Master General's Office, Loyalist Musters, 1776–1785, MG 23, D1, ser. I, vol. 24, LAC. Note: Ellen Wilson believed that the information Clarkson used came from Thomas Peters; see Wilson, *Loyal Blacks*, 181.

443. GIBSON, JOHN (c. 1785, age 25) – Enslaved to Jesse Noble, John attempted to escape from his owner. Noble claimed that Gibson's alias was John Boocher. Source: *Nova Scotia Gazette*, July 19, 1785.

444. GILL (c. 1783, age 8) – Enslaved to Benjamin Lester, who went to the Maritimes with four other slaves, Gill was from New York. It is possible that this Gill is the same as the one who ran away from his owner in 1799. British officials in New York described him as a "stout boy." Source: Book of Negroes.

445. GILL (c. 1784) – Gill was enslaved to Mr. Henderson, who settled at Chedabucto, Nova Scotia. Source: Loyalists from Saint Augustine to Chedabucto, Chipman Papers, Muster Master General's Office, Loyalist Musters, 1776–1785, MG 23, D1, ser. I, vol. 24, LAC.

446. GILL (c. 1799) – In New Brunswick, at the turn of the century, Gill and Dick ran away from their owners. The owners placed a joint advertisement in the local paper, which described the slaves' physical appearance and apparel: "RANAWAY on Sunday the 11th instant, two Negro Men named GILL and DICK, the property of the subscribers. – Gill is a dark mulatto, with short wooly hair; is about five feet six inches high; stout made; has square shoulders, bow legs, and walks clumsily. – Had on when he went away a homespun coat, and vest a mixture of black and white, half lapelled; trowsers twilled homespun, a smutty brown, and considerably worn – he also took with him two striped vests, and sundry other articles of clothing. DICK is a short thick set fellow, about 5 feet 4 inches high; remarkably black; has a scar on his cheek and another on his chin. – He had on and took with him a variety of cloathing – among other articles, a short coat without skirts; the color a mixture of blue with hemlock; nankeen overhails, &c." Source: *Royal Gazette* (New Brunswick), August 20, 1799.

447. GLOSTER, JOHN (c. 1745) – John was enslaved to Theodore Atkinson, who served on the governing council of New Hampshire. Atkinson sent John to serve with New Hampshire troops in Louisbourg. Source: Donovan, "Slaves and Their Owners in Île Royale," 23.

448. GOODMAN, CHARLES (c. 1783, age 11) – Enslaved to Isaac Goodman, who migrated to the Maritimes from New York, Charles was from Rhode Island. British officials in New York described him as a "stout man." Source: Book of Negroes.

449. GRANDCOMBE (c. 1732, age 45) – Enslaved to the Marquis de Sennett in Île Royale. Grandcombe came from Guadeloupe. Source: Donovan, "Nominal List of Slaves and Their Owners," 152.

450. GRANT, JAMES (c. 1798) – Enslaved to Jeremiah Northup, James attempted to escape. His owner described him as "smart" and likely." Source: Smith, "Slave in Canada," 62.

451. GRIFFITH, JACK (c. 1783) – Jack was enslaved to Robert Griffith, who migrated to the Maritimes from New York. Source: Book of Negroes.

452. GUY (c. 1785) – Enslaved to Captain Callbeck, Guy attempted to escape along with several other slaves during the Jupiter Wise conspiracy. Sources: *King v. Jupiter Wise*, 1786, PAROPEI; Holman, "Slaves and Servants on Prince Edward Island," 100–4; Hornby, *Black Islanders*, 15–19.

453. HAGAR (c. 1759) – Hagar was enslaved to merchant and politician Malachy Salter, who was originally from Boston and moved to Halifax and served in the legislative assembly. In 1759, he sent his wife a letter where he commented about his two slaves: Hagar and Jack. He seemed impressed with Hagar, noting that she "behaved better than ever." Jack, however, refused to comply with Salter's commands. Salter complained that "Jack is Jack still," and as a result he beat Jack almost every day with a whip or stick. He implored his wife to purchase "a negro boy" possibly to replace Jack, who he referred to as an "Idle, deceitfull, villain." Source: Malachy Salter to Mrs. Salter, September 2, 1759, MG 100, vol. 217, no. 27f, NSA.

454. HAGAR [misspelled **HARGAR**] (c. 1783, age 17) – Enslaved to Widow Brown, who migrated to the Maritimes after the American Revolution, Hagar was from New York. British officials in New York described her as an "ordinary wench." Source: Book of Negroes.

455. HAGAR (slave? c. 1780s) – In his diary, New England Planter and Liverpool resident Simeon Perkins commented "Mr. Granadine's Negro Man Anthony & Negro woman Hagar Arrive with Prince Snow at Evening from Shelburn to Live with me, per agreement for 50 dollars from the first of December to the first of May, for which I agreed to allow him 50 dollars. I have a letter from Mr. Granadine." It seems that Anthony and Hagar were enslaved to Granadine (or Grandine – it has different spellings) and he hired them out to Perkins for several months. In 1788, Perkins described the work of Hagar: "This day I Saw the thin Skin of a hogs Kidney fat manifactured into exceeding fine white Leather. It has the Same Appearance as the finest Leather Gloves, Commonly imported by the Name of Kid Gloves. It was done by our Black woman, Hagar. The process is Very Simple, being done by Laying it about 3 weeks in Common Soft Soap." Source: Harvey, *Diary of Simeon Perkins*, 1780–1789, 211, 413.

456. HALN [or **HAHN**], **ANTHONY** (c. 1783, age 27) – Enslaved to Nicholas Beckle, who migrated to the Maritimes from New York after the American Revolution, Anthony was described by British officials in New York as a "stout negro." Source: Book of Negroes.

457. HAM (c. 1783, age 15) – Enslaved to Ensign Hubbard, who migrated to the Maritimes after the American Revolution, Ham was possibly from Connecticut. British officials in New York described him as a "likely boy." Source: Book of Negroes.

458. HAMILTON, LUKE (c. 1798) – Enslaved to Justice Joshua Upham, the court ordered Luke to be executed for the murder of a girl named West. Source: J.W. Lawrence, *Foot-Prints* (Saint John: J & A McMillan, 1883), 58–9.

459. HAMMON, OTHELLOW (slave? c. 1827) – Probably enslaved to Gabriel Deveber, a former sheriff in New Brunswick, Othellow was briefly mentioned by DeVeber in his will (which left him £5). Deveber referred to Othellow and James as "my black boys," which indicates they grew up in his household and were probably enslaved at some point. Source: Will of Gabriel Deveber, Sunbury County, 1827, PANB.

460. HANNAH (c. 1783, age 14) – Enslaved to George Thomas, who migrated to the Maritimes from New York with another slave, Hannah was from South Carolina. British officials described her as a "fine girl." Source: Book of Negroes.

461. HANNAH (c. 1783, age 23) – Enslaved to John Patton, who migrated to the Maritimes after the American Revolution, Hannah was described by British officials in New York as a "stout wench." Source: Book of Negroes.

462. HANNAH (c. 1783, age 21) – Enslaved to Patrick Wall, who migrated to the Maritimes after the American Revolution with two other slaves, Hannah was from Massachusetts. British officials in New York described her as a "stout pockmarked wench." Source: Book of Negroes.

463. HANNAH (c. 1783, age 19) – An enslaved woman of Lieutenant Brackenback, who migrated to the Maritimes after the American Revolution, Hannah brought her child with her. British officials in New York described her as an "ordinary wench." Source: Book of Negroes.

464. JOSEPH (c. 1783, infant) – The son of Hannah and also enslaved to Lieutenant Brackenback, Joseph was described by British officials in New York as "naturally the Lieutenant's property." Source: Book of Negroes.

465. HANNAH (c. 1784) – Enslaved to John Grant in Chedabucto, Hannah was described as "his property [Grant's]." Source: Loyalists from Saint Augustine to Chedabucto, Chipman Papers, Muster Master General's Office, Loyalist Musters, 1776–1785, MG 23, D1, ser. I, vol. 24, LAC.

466. HANNAH (c. 1788) – Enslaved to Lieutenant Colonel Joseph Barton in Digby, Nova Scotia, along with her two children, Hannah and the male child were listed as worth £18, while the unnamed girl was listed as worth £6. The probate record does not mention an adult male slave. Source: Will of Joseph Barton, Digby 1788, NSA (kindly provided by Allistair Barton).

467. WILLIAM (c. 1788) – William was the son of Hannah and also enslaved to Lieutenant Colonel Joseph Barton in Digby, Nova Scotia. Source: Will of Joseph Barton, Digby 1788, NSA (kindly provided by Allistair Barton).

468. UNNAMED GIRL (c. 1788) – This unnamed child was the daughter of Hannah and also enslaved to Lieutenant Colonel Joseph Barton in Digby, Nova Scotia. Source: Will of Joseph Barton, Digby 1788, NSA (kindly provided by Allistair Barton).

469. HANNAH (c. 1793) – In his will, unlike some Nova Scotian slaveholders who freed slaves after their death, Caleb Fowler wanted to bequeath Hannah and her daughter to his family; but he would have allowed the sale of Diana once she reached the age of 10: "I give [my wife Mary Fowler] my Negro Wench named Hannah to be hers as long as she remains my Widow and no longer. I order and it is my Will that the said Negro Wench Hannah and her Child Diana shall remain in my Family if they are disposed of before my son Caleb is Eighteen years old, then if my Children should wish to keep them, whoever they live with, shall allow a reasonable price for them or either of them, and in case the said Hannah does not behave herself well after my decease, I order her to be sold at the discretion of Executors … and it is my Will that the said negro child Dianah [her name is spelled two different ways in the same will] shall remain with her Mother (if either is sold) until she is ten years old, then one of my said daughters as they two can agree to have her, which ever takes her to allow a reasonable price to be deducted out of their share or Legacy abovementioned for her." Fowler's will is an example of how slaveowners were more than willing to sell children away from their mothers. Fowler's relatives had unlimited power over Hannah and her daughter. Not surprisingly, there is no mention of Hannah's husband or the father of her child. Perhaps Fowler or one of his relatives fathered Diana. There was no avenue open for Hannah and her child to achieve liberty except to run away. Slaveholding families such as the Fowlers used a combination of coercion, terror, violence, and threats when dealing with slaves who were part of their family. In 1795, it seems that Hannah married one John Tallow with the permission of Caleb Fowler's executors. Source: Will of Caleb Fowler, 1793, Annapolis County, RG 48, Probate Records, NSA; Granville Township Book, NSA.

470. DIANA (c. 1793, age under 10) – The daughter of Hannah, Diana was enslaved to Caleb Fowler. See above entry. Sources: Will of Caleb Fowler, 1793, Annapolis County, RG 48, Probate Records, NSA; Granville Township Book, NSA.

471. TALLOW, JOHN (c. 1780s) – Enslaved to Joshua F. de St. Croix, who was a native of New York and had "sailed for Nova Scotia in one of his own vessels, with his family and slaves." This source indicates that there were at least two or more slaves on his ship. He also owned a slave named Bess. John eventually became free, purchased a large farm, and started a family. In 1795, John eventually married Hannah who had been enslaved to the Fowler family. Sources: Elizabeth Ruggles Coward, *Bridgetown Nova Scotia: Its History to 1900* (Kentville: Kentville Publishing, 1955), 33; Will of Caleb Fowler, 1793, Annapolis County, RG 48, Probate Records, NSA; Granville

Township Book, NSA; Karolyn Smardz Frost, "King's College, Nova Scotia: Direct Connections with Slavery" (unpublished paper submitted to King's College President William Lahey, October 2019), 3. I am thankful to Karolyn for sharing her research.

472. HANNAH (c. 1805, age 11) – In his will, Jacob Troop declared that 11-year-old Hannah would remain enslaved until her thirtieth birthday (1824). Surely Troop knew of the *DeLancey* decision (1803–4), which limited the rights of slaveholders in Nova Scotia. Thus, the fact that he remained committed to enslaving a young girl for nearly two more decades speaks to the fact that he saw slavery lasting for the foreseeable future. At the very same time, every state in New England as well as New York and New Jersey had adopted immediate or gradual emancipation. Troop also planned to divide Hannah's work between his five daughters: "At the Death of my Beloved wife Anna, the Black girl Hannah if [she serves] as a Faithful Servant till she is Thirty years of Age she is then to have her freedom, but if she is not Thirty years of Age at the Death of my Beloved wife Anna, then her service is to be divided equally among my five Daughters till she arrives to the age of Thirty, being now eleven years of age." Source: Will of Jacob Troop, 1805, Annapolis County, RG 48, Probate Records, NSA.

473. HANNIBAL (c. 1783, age 11) – Enslaved to Benjamin Lester, who went to the Maritimes with several other slaves, Hannibal was from New York. British officials in New York described him as a "stout boy." Source: Book of Negroes.

474. HARRIET (slave? c. 1810, age 13) – Harriet was described as a "mulatto girl" who had been accused of stealing "a piece of ribbon, value ninepence," in Yarmouth. She pled not guilty. The jury declared her guilty, and the court sentenced Harriet "to receive 12 lashes on the bare back and the sheriff was ordered to perform the same as soon as possible." It is unknown if Harriet was enslaved. Sources: George Stayley Brown, *Yarmouth, Nova Scotia: A Sequel to Campbell's History* (Boston: Rand Avery Company, 1888), 331; Robart-Johnson, *Africa's Children*, 42.

475. HARRIET (c. 1804) – Harriet was enslaved to James DeLancey, whose estate valued her at £25. Source: Hanger, "Life of Loyalist Colonel James DeLancey," 52–3.

476. HARRIM, CATHERINE (slave? c. 1827) – Gabriel Deveber, a former sheriff in New Brunswick, briefly mentioned this person in his will saying he left her £5. He referred to her as "my black woman," which has connotations of enslavement. It is possible she had been his slave and he freed her at some point and left her money (which regularly occurred among slaveholders in the Maritimes). Source: Will of Gabriel Deveber, 1827, Sunbury County, PANB.

477. HARRIS, CATO (c. 1770) – Cato Harris was enslaved to Joseph Gerrish and was later sold along with two other slaves for £150. Source: Smith, "Slave in Canada," 13; States and Smardz Frost, "Section 5: King's College Students and Slavery Selected Biographies," 9.

478. HARRY (c. 1783, age 12) – Enslaved to Samuel Peters, who went to the Maritimes after the American Revolution, Harry was from Connecticut. British officials in New York described him as a "fine boy." Source: Book of Negroes.

479. HARRY (c. 1783, age 30) – Enslaved to Johannis (or John) Ackerman, who migrated to the Maritimes after the American Revolution with two other slaves, Harry was probably from New Jersey. British officials at New York described him as an "ordinary fellow." Source: Book of Negroes.

480. HARRY (c. 1783, age 23) – Enslaved to John Anderson, who migrated to the Maritimes from New York also with an enslaved teenage boy, Harry was born on Staten Island. British officials in New York described him as "stout" and the former property of Medcalf Eden. Source: Book of Negroes.

481. HARRY (c. 1783, age 23) – Enslaved to Major Coffin, who was part of Edmund Fanning's King's American Regiment, Harry had been purchased by Coffin from Mr. Greentree. Harry came to the Maritimes from New York along with Coffin's two other slaves. British officials in New York described him as a "stout labourer." Source: Book of Negroes.

482. HARRY (c. 1784, age 7) – Harry was enslaved to John Grant, who was originally from Scotland and who, after serving the British army near Ticonderoga during the Seven Years War, settled in Queens County, Long Island. After the American Revolution, he settled in Nova Scotia with a large family and nine slaves. These enslaved people might have been a family unit. Source: Cottreau-Robins, "Landscape of Slavery in Loyalist Era Nova Scotia," 131–2; see also Smith, "Slave in Canada," 93–4.

483. HARRY (slave? c. 1784) – Possibly enslaved to Michael Houseal, a Loyalist from Maryland, Harry lived with three other Black people who were also possibly slaves. Houseal remained in Nova Scotia until at least 1800, when he decided to return to England. In that same year, he attempted to hire out a young Black female as an indentured servant. Sources: Loyalists and Disbanded Troops at Cole Harbour, Chipman Papers, Muster Master General's Office, Loyalist Musters, 1776–1785, MG 23, D1, ser. I, vol. 24, LAC; *Royal Gazette*, June 24, 1800.

484. HARRY (c. 1786) – Enslaved to Annapolis County resident Richard Betts (a Loyalist from New York), Harry was part of the 1786 inventory of Richard

Betts that listed four slaves and their values. According to the document, Toney, Prince (or Primus), and Jane were listed as worth £35 while Harry commanded the price of £40. It is not clear why Harry was worth more money. Perhaps he was a skilled slave or the other slaves were older or more troublesome. The relationship of each slave to the other slaves is unclear – if they were a family or totally unrelated. The total value of Betts's inventory was about £1,053, while the combined value of the slaves was £145. Thus, slaves accounted for 13.77 per cent of the total wealth of his estate. Source: Inventory of Richard Betts, 1786, Annapolis County, RG 48, NSA.

485. HAWKINS, CAESAR (c. 1797) – Enslaved to Mr. Willet of Granville, Nova Scotia, Caesar married an enslaved woman named Jane Japean. Source: March 11, 1797, Granville Township Book, NSA.

486. JAPEAN, JANE (c. 1797) – Enslaved to Mrs. Amberman in Granville, Nova Scotia, Jane married Caesar Hawkins. Source: March 11, 1797, Granville Township Book, NSA.

487. HAZARD, SAMUEL (c. 1770) – Samuel Hazard was enslaved to Joseph Gerrish and was later sold along with two other slaves for £150. Source: Smith, "Slave in Canada," 13; States and Smardz Frost, "Section 5: King's College Students and Slavery Selected Biographies," 9.

488. HEAD, JAMES (slave? c. 1827) – Gabriel Deveber, a former sheriff in New Brunswick, briefly mentioned James in his will, saying he left him £5. Deveber referred to Othellow and James as "my black boys," which indicates they grew up in his household. Although 1827 seems too late for people to still be enslaved, it was still possible. Source: Will of Gabriel Deveber, 1827, Sunbury County, PANB.

489. HECTOR (c. 1749) – Enslaved to the Brothers of Charity in Louisbourg. Source: Donovan, "Nominal List of Slaves and Their Owners," 155.

490. HECTOR (c. 1758) – Enslaved to the Morin family, Joseph dit Hector (this means he preferred the name Hector) was allowed to marry Victoire. They were the only enslaved couple in Louisbourg allowed to marry. Source: Donovan, "Slaves and Their Owners in Île Royale," 30.

491. VICTOIRE (c. 1754, age 13) – Victoire was enslaved to the Morin family. She was allowed to marry Joseph dit Hector. They were the only enslaved couple in Louisbourg allowed to marry. Sadly, she died five weeks after the wedding. Source: Donovan, "Slaves and Their Owners in Île Royale," 30–1.

492. HECTOR (c. 1784) – Enslaved to Frederick William Hecht who, after Hector escaped, placed an advertisement in a local paper that described Hector as a cooper and speaking English like a "West-India [Negro]." This meant he might have been from Africa or certainly the Caribbean. In his lifetime, Hector had lived in the West Indies, St. Augustine (Florida), New York, and New Brunswick. Source: *Saint John Gazette*, July 15, 1784.

493. HENRY (c. 1784) – John Wentworth sent Henry and 18 other slaves from Nova Scotia to his "relation" Paul Wentworth in Suriname. Wentworth described these slaves as "American born or well seasoned, and are perfectly stout, healthy, sober, orderly, Industrious, & obedient." Wentworth had the slaves Christened and claimed to be concerned for their welfare. He also noted that the male slaves "are expert in boats." Source: John Wentworth to Paul Wentworth or his attorney, February 24, 1784.

494. HERBERT, CHARLES (c. 1783, age 50) – Enslaved to Loyalist John Herbert, who migrated to the Maritimes after the American Revolution with seven other slaves, Charles was from Virginia. British officials described him as "nearly worn out." John Herbert's eight slaves indicate the possibilities of family formation. The exact nature of the family structure among his slaves is unclear, but the ages of the slaves do indicate some form of familial or kinship network. His oldest slaves, Charles and Rose, were ages 50 and 45, respectively. London and Hanna were 30 and 40 years old at the end of the war. Herbert's other slaves ranged in ages 5 to 16. Sources: Book of Negroes; John Herbert, Loyalist Claims Commission, AO12/55/18, NSA. On the confusing listing of Herbert's slaves in the Book of Negroes, see Harvey Amani Whitfield, North to Bondage: Loyalist Slavery in the Maritimes (Vancouver: University of British Columbia Press, 2016), 145.

495. HERBERT, DAVID (c. 1783, age 5) – Enslaved to Loyalist John Herbert, who migrated to the Maritimes after the American Revolution with seven other slaves, David was from Virginia. John Herbert's eight slaves indicate the possibilities of family formation. The exact nature of the family structure among his slaves is unclear, but the ages of the slaves do indicate some form of familial or kinship network. His oldest slaves, Charles and Rose, were ages 50 and 45, respectively. London and Hanna were 30 and 40 years old at the end of the war. Herbert's other slaves ranged in ages 5 to 16. Sources: Book of Negroes; John Herbert, Loyalist Claims Commission, AO12/55/18, NSA. On the confusing listing of Herbert's slaves in the Book of Negroes, see Whitfield, *North to Bondage*, 145.

496. HERBERT, HANNA (c. 1783, age 40) – Enslaved to Loyalist John Herbert, who migrated to the Maritimes after the American Revolution with seven other slaves, Hanna was from Virginia. John Herbert's eight slaves indicate the possibilities of family formation. The exact nature of the family structure among his slaves is unclear, but the ages of the slaves do indicate some form of familial or kinship network. His oldest slaves, Charles and Rose, were ages 50 and 45, respectively. London and Hanna were 30 and 40 years old at the end of the war. Herbert's other slaves ranged in ages 5 to 16. Sources: Book of Negroes; John Herbert, Loyalist Claims Commission, AO12/55/18, NSA. On the confusing listing of Herbert's slaves in the Book of Negroes, see Whitfield, *North to Bondage*, 145.

497. HERBERT, ISAAC (c. 1783, age 11) – Enslaved to Loyalist John Herbert, who migrated to the Maritimes after the American Revolution with seven other slaves, Isaac was from Virginia. John Herbert's eight slaves indicate the possibilities of family formation. The exact nature of the family structure among his slaves is unclear, but the ages of the slaves do indicate some form of familial or kinship network. His oldest slaves, Charles and Rose, were ages 50 and 45, respectively. London and Hanna were 30 and 40 years old at the end of the war. Herbert's other slaves ranged in ages 5 to 16. Sources: Book of Negroes; John Herbert, Loyalist Claims Commission, AO12/55/18, NSA. On the confusing listing of Herbert's slaves in the Book of Negroes, see Whitfield, *North to Bondage*, 145.

498. HERBERT, JENNY (c. 1783, age 9) – Enslaved to Loyalist John Herbert, who migrated to the Maritimes after the American Revolution with seven other slaves, Jenny was from Virginia. British officials noted that she was Herbert's property and she had left Virginia at the same time Dunmore left. John Herbert's eight slaves indicate the possibilities of family formation. The exact nature of the family structure among his slaves is unclear, but the ages of the slaves do indicate some form of familial or kinship network. His oldest slaves, Charles and Rose, were ages 50 and 45, respectively. London and Hanna were 30 and 40 years old at the end of the war. Herbert's other slaves ranged in ages 5 to 16. Sources: Book of Negroes; John Herbert, Loyalist Claims Commission, AO12/55/18, NSA. On the confusing listing of Herbert's slaves in the Book of Negroes, see Whitfield, *North to Bondage*, 145.

499. HERBERT, LONDON (c. 1783, age 30) – Enslaved to Loyalist John Herbert, who migrated to the Maritimes after the American Revolution with seven other slaves, London was from Virginia. John Herbert's eight slaves indicate the possibilities of family formation. The exact nature of the family structure among his slaves is unclear, but the ages of the slaves do indicate some form of familial or kinship network. His oldest slaves, Charles and Rose, were ages 50 and 45, respectively. London and Hanna were 30 and 40 years old at the end of the war. Herbert's other slaves ranged in ages 5 to 16. Sources: Book of Negroes; John Herbert, Loyalist Claims Commission, AO12/55/18, NSA. On the confusing listing of Herbert's slaves in the Book of Negroes, see Whitfield, *North to Bondage*, 145.

500. HERBERT, ROSE (c. 1783, age 45) – Enslaved to Loyalist John Herbert, who migrated to the Maritimes after the American Revolution with seven other slaves, Rose was from Virginia. British officials described her as an "ordinary wench." John Herbert's eight slaves indicate the possibilities of family formation. The exact nature of the family structure among his slaves is unclear, but the ages of the slaves do indicate some form of familial or kinship network. His oldest slaves, Charles and Rose, were ages 50 and 45, respectively. London and Hanna were 30 and 40 years old at the end of the war. Herbert's other slaves ranged in ages 5 to 16. Sources: Book of Negroes; John Herbert, Loyalist Claims Commission, AO12/55/18, NSA. On the confusing listing of Herbert's slaves in the Book of Negroes, see Whitfield, *North to Bondage*, 145.

501. HERBERT, VENUS (c. 1783, age 16) – Enslaved to Loyalist John Herbert, who migrated to the Maritimes after the American Revolution with seven other slaves, Venus was from Virginia. John Herbert's eight slaves indicate the possibilities of family formation. The exact nature of the family structure among his slaves is unclear, but the ages of the slaves do indicate some form of familial or kinship network. His oldest slaves, Charles and Rose, were ages 50 and 45, respectively. London and Hanna were 30 and 40 years old at the end of the war. Herbert's other slaves ranged in ages 5 to 16. Sources: Book of Negroes; John Herbert, Loyalist Claims Commission, AO12/55/18, NSA. On the confusing listing of Herbert's slaves in the Book of Negroes, see Whitfield, *North to Bondage*, 145.

502. HERCULES (slave? c. 1784) – Hercules was possibly enslaved to Lieutenant Joel Hudson, who migrated to Country Harbour with other southern Loyalists. The majority of these Loyalists and their slaves were from North Carolina, South Carolina, and Georgia. They had settled briefly in East Florida before moving to Nova Scotia. Black people at Country Harbour were either slaves or "quasi free" and subject to re-enslavement. Abolitionist Thomas Clarkson explained the phenomenon of re-enslavement: "It was not long till these loyalists, many of whom had been educated with all the ideas of the justice of slavery, the inferiority of negroes, and the superiority of white men, that are universal in the southern provinces of America, began to harass and oppress the industrious black settlers, and even wantonly to deprive them of the fruits of their labour, expelling them from the lands they had cleared." Clarkson continued by noting that whites reduced "again to slavery those negroes who had so honourably obtained their freedom. They hired them as servants, and, at the end of the stipulated time, refused payment of their wages, insisting that they were slaves: in some instances they destroyed their tickets of freedom, and then enslaved the negroes for want of them; in several instances, the unfortunate Africans were taken onboard vessels, carried to the West Indies, and there sold for the benefit of their plunderers." At Country Harbour, Black people were listed on the musters as the "Servants" of a white Loyalist, which meant it was very easy for them to be re-enslaved if they were not already enslaved. Sources: Clarkson, "Some Account of the New Colony at Sierra Leone," 229–30; Settlers at Country Harbour, Chipman Papers, Muster Master General's Office, Loyalist Musters, 1776–1785, MG 23, D1, ser. I, vol. 24, LAC. Note: Ellen Wilson believed that the information Clarkson used came from Thomas Peters; see Wilson, *Loyal Blacks*, 181.

503. HILL, DICK (c. 1787) – In 1787, a free Black man named Dick Hill had been unlawfully placed on board a schooner to be sent to the West Indies as a slave. Hill, incredibly, had a General Birch Certificate, which allegedly guaranteed his freedom. Unfortunately, the historical record is full of other examples of Black people who, like Dick Hill, were re-enslaved and sold to the West Indies. Source: Paper Respecting Dick Hill, a Free Negro Man sent to West Indies from Shelburne in Joshua Wises Schooner Commanded by Captain McDonald, 1787, Shelburne, RG 60, #25.3, NSA.

504. HOMENY, CUFFE (c. 1746) – Enslaved to Moses Pearson, Cuffe served under him during the siege and takeover of Louisbourg. Source: Donovan, "Nominal List of Slaves and Their Owners," 157.

505. HOPEFIELD SR., RICHARD (c. 1792, age 40) – Richard Hopefield was the husband of a female slave named Statia and the father of Richard Hopefield, Jr. In 1792, he attempted to take his family away from Joseph Clarke, but they were recaptured. Clarke described Hopefield as "about 5 feet 9 inches high – very active, and supposed to be near 40 years of age. – Had on when he went off a fearnought grey short coat and trowsers with white metal buttons – a new felt hat, & c." Hopefield and his family were involved in one of the lengthiest sagas about slavery and re-enslavement in New Brunswick history. In 1805, anti-slavery attorney Samuel Denny Street went before the New Brunswick Supreme Court and filed for a writ of habeas corpus for Richard Hopefield, Jr., who had allegedly been detained by Stair Agnew "for the space of Three years and fifty five Days." The case focused on Patience (also known as Stacey or Statia) who had been brought to New Brunswick as a slave, eventually married Richard Hopefield, Sr., and had several children including the younger Hopefield whom Agnew claimed to own. During the case, Hopefield, Sr., gave a deposition that outlined his personal life history. Born in Virginia, Hopefield served his owner during the American Revolution before escaping to the British. Shortly thereafter he married Patience and had several children, including Richard Hopefield, Jr., who was born in New Brunswick. Hopefield claimed that his wife "had been put on board a vessel by one Phineas Lovitt [a member of the House of Assembly] in order as the deponent was informed

to send her to the West Indies to be sold – when she was relanded by order of Governor Carleton who set her at liberty." It seems that Patience and
Hopefield lived together for several years as free people before Joseph Clarke
"forcibly seized" her. In 1792, Joseph Clarke placed an advertisement in the
local paper complaining about the loss of a female slave named "STATIA" and
her 5-year-old son and 15-month-old daughter. Clarke also noted that she
had run away with an indentured servant named Dick Hopewell (probably
Richard Hopefield), who claimed to be married to Statia. It seems probable
that Statia was actually Patience. Clarke recovered his property and sold her
to Joseph Hewlett.

Stair Agnew denied the charges against him and benefited from the advice
and legal representation of Ward Chipman, who admitted that his client had
beaten Hopefield, Jr., but claimed it resulted from "disobedient and refractory
and insolent" behaviour and neglect of "duty." Agnew did not dispute that he
prevented "Richard from absenting himself." Agnew justified his actions, however, because Richard was "a Negro Servant, the property of the said Stair ...
bound to serve the said Stair for his the said Richard's life time." Agnew's claims
were damaged by the testimony of other witnesses. In 1801, the York County
Court of General Sessions had indicted him for "Cruel Treatment" of "two
Negro Boys" in his service. At the court, Agnew "publickly pledged" that "he
would manumitt and make free a certain Negro Boy named or called Richard
Hopefield" when he turned 21 years old.

Samuel Denny Street argued that since Hopefield, Sr., was a free man, his
son ought to be free as well. The defence "countered by attempting to show that
Hopefield's parents had never been formally married, so that he had taken the
status of his mother rather than of his [free] father." After a court battle, Hopefield's writ of habeas corpus failed. Also, a civil suit against Agnew for battery
and false imprisonment did not proceed past an early stage. In sum, Hopefield's
case for freedom had failed. As historian David Bell notes, "*Hopefield's* case was
undoubtedly a legal triumph for the slave-owning interests. They had received
a clear legal verdict in favour of the continuance of Negro slavery."

Bell, the best historian on this topic, suggests that the judges were protesting
against the intellectual currents of the time, as illustrated by Nova Scotia's judicial elimination of slavery, the growing agitation against the slave trade, and
the adoption of gradual or immediate emancipation in nearly every northern
state. They believed that a class of gentlemen connected to the Crown should
rule society. From this perspective, ending slavery signalled not progressive
social policy, but rather another step toward a state of anarchy where people
did not accept their God-given places in society. "In a society like that of New
Brunswick," Bell notes, "in which the position of the great was precarious, it
may have been with considerable gratification that three of the judges ensured,

as a matter of law, that the province's Negroes would continue to be very low indeed." Sources: *Richard Hopefield v. Stair Agnew*, 1802/1805, RS 42, Supreme Court Original Jurisdiction Records, PANB; D.G. Bell, "Slavery and the Judges of Loyalist New Brunswick," University of New Brunswick Law Journal, 31 (1982): 9–42 (esp. 24–25, 31); *Saint John Gazette*, June 29, 1792. On Early Saint John, see D.G. Bell, *Early Loyalist Saint John: The Origin of New Brunswick Politics, 1783–1786* (Fredericton: New Ireland Press, 1983); and also David Bell, *Loyalist Rebellion in New Brunswick: A Defining Conflict for Canada's Political Culture* (Halifax: Formac, 2013).

506. STATIA [PATIENCE] (c. 1792, age 30) – Statia and her family attempted to escape from Joseph Clarke. Statia and her family (husband Richard Hopefield – also called Dick Hopewell) had an exceedingly difficult experience after arriving in New Brunswick. In the 1792 runaway advertisement, Joseph Clarke described Statia's family, physical appearance, and personality traits. The advertisement is one of the most important descriptions historians have of a slave family in the Maritimes: "RANAWAY FROM the Subscriber on the night of the 9th instan:, an indented servant Man, named DICK HOPEWELL; about 5 feet 9 inches high – very active and supposed to be near 40 years of age. – Had on when he went off a fearnought grey short coat and trowsers with white metal buttons – a new felt hat, & c. At the same time went off a Negro Woman slave, named STATIA, who he claim'd as a Wife, with two small children – a boy about 5 years old, and a girl about 15 months – she is about 30 years of age, and now pregnant. – Had on when she went off a green duffle petticoat, with a baize short gown of the same colour – she is of the mulatto cast and speaks very fluently. – Whoever will secure said RUN-AWAYS in any goal of this Province, or the Province of Nova-Scotia, so that their master may recover them, shall be entitled to the above reward." Source: *Saint John Gazette*, June 29, 1792.

507. HOPEFIELD JR., RICHARD (c. 1792, age 5) – Approximately 5 years old in 1792, Richard was the son of Statia and Richard Hopefield, Sr. Sources: *Richard Hopefield v. Stair Agnew*, 1802/1805, RS 42, Supreme Court Original Jurisdiction Records, PANB; Bell, "Slavery and the Judges of Loyalist New Brunswick," 9–42 (esp. 24–5, 31); *Saint John Gazette*, June 29, 1792. On Early Saint John, see Bell, *Early Loyalist Saint John* and also Bell, *Loyalist Rebellion in New Brunswick*.

508. UNNAMED GIRL (c. 1792, age 1) – Enslaved to Joseph Clarke, she was the child of Statia and Richard Hopefield, Sr. The family attempted to escape from Joseph Clarke in 1792. Source: *Saint John Gazette*, June 29, 1792.

509. HOPEWELL, AMELIA (c. 1783, age 21) – Enslaved to Lieutenant McDonald, who migrated to the Maritimes after the American Revolution, Amelia was possibly from New York. British officials in New York described her as a "stout wench." Source: Book of Negroes.

510. HUME, BETTY (c. 1787, age 33) – In 1780, John Hume purchased Betty Hume at Carriacou. In 1785, Betty gave birth to her son, described as a mulatto boy. Hume migrated with his slaves to Saint John, New Brunswick, and freed both Betty and her son in 1787. It seems rather likely that Hume fathered the child (or another white man did) since he was mixed race. Source: Smith, "Slave in Canada," 61.

511. UNNAMED SON (c. 1787, age 2) – This unnamed boy was the son of Betty Hume. Source: Smith, "Slave in Canada," 61.

512. HUNTER, JOHN (c. 1784) – John Hunter was probably enslaved to John Stewart in Chedabucto, Nova Scotia. Source: Loyalists from Saint Augustine to Chedabucto, Chipman Papers, Muster Master General's Office, Loyalist Musters, 1776–1785, MG 23, D1, ser. I, vol. 24, LAC.

513. HUNTER, JUBA [or **JUBE**] (c. 1789) – Enslaved to David Hunter, who resided in Windsor, Nova Scotia, Juba (or Jube) was charged with stealing property from Alexander Scott. Source: States, "Presence and Perseverance: Blacks in Hants County," 38–9.

514. HUTCHINGS, SAMUEL (slave/indentured servant? c. 1818) – John Mount placed a brief advertisement in the newspaper claiming that this "Negro Boy" had absconded. Source: *New Brunswick Courier*, September 5, 1818.

515. IRVIN (c. 1802) – Irvin was enslaved to Virginia Loyalist Jacob Ellegood, who mentioned Irvin in his will: "And I give and bequeath unto my said son Samuel Inglis Ellegood my negro boy called Irvin and also one third part of all my negroes." Source: Will of Jacob Ellegood, 1802, York County, PANB.

516. ISAAC (c. 1783, age 17) – Enslaved to Joseph Scribner, who migrated to the Maritimes from New York, Isaac was from Long Island. British officials in New York described him as a "stout boy." Source: Book of Negroes.

517. ISAAC (c. 1784) – Isaac committed assault and battery on the body of his master William Young at Shelburne in 1784. The court determined that he should be publicly whipped with 39 lashes and sentenced him to two months of hard labour. The jail keeper was ordered to whip Isaac at least once per month. Source: General Sessions of Shelburne, Nova Scotia, April 6, 1784, Shelburne Records, MG 4, vol. 141, NSA.

518. ISAAC (slave? c. 1784) – Isaac was possibly an enslaved person who settled at Belle Vue in Beaver Harbour. Although these people might have been nominally free, they were regularly subjected to re-enslavement. Source: Roll of Loyalists Settled at Belle Vue in Beaver Harbour, Chipman Papers, Muster Master General's Office, Loyalist Musters, 1776–1785, MG 23, D1, ser. I, vol. 24, LAC.

519. ISAAC (slave? c. 1784) – Possibly enslaved to Ebenezer Allen, who settled near Halifax, Isaac was the only Black person in Allen's household. Source: Loyalists and Disbanded Troops at Cole Harbour, Chipman Papers, Muster Master General's Office, Loyalist Musters, 1776–1785, MG 23, D1, ser. I, vol. 24, LAC.

520. ISAAC (c. 1784) – John Wentworth sent Isaac and 18 other slaves from Nova Scotia to his "relation" Paul Wentworth in Suriname. Wentworth described these slaves as "American born or well seasoned, and are perfectly stout, healthy, sober, orderly, Industrious, & obedient." Wentworth had the slaves Christened and claimed to be concerned for their welfare. He noted that "Isaac, is a [thorough] good Carpenter & Master Sawyer perfectly capable of overseeing & conducting the rest and strictly honest." Source: John Wentworth to Paul Wentworth or his attorney, February 24, 1784.

521. ISAAC (c. 1786, age 30) – Enslaved to Maryland Loyalist Caleb Jones, Isaac was originally from New York and he lived with Jones's other slaves in New Brunswick. In 1786, Isaac and four other slaves absconded from Caleb Jones. Source: *Royal Gazette* (New Brunswick), July 25, 1786.

522. ISAAC (c. 1791) – Isaac was mentioned as an enslaved man in a letter between Stephen Millidge and Sarah Botsford Millidge. Source: Stephen Millidge to Sarah (Botsford) Millidge, November 6, 1791, W.C. Milner Papers, S11 F1, New Brunswick Museum, cited in States and Smardz Frost, "King's College," section 3, 4n5.

523. IVEY, HILEY (c. 1783, age 12) – Hiley was enslaved to William Wilson, who migrated to the Maritimes from New York with three other slaves, and she was originally from Virginia. British officials described her as a "fine girl." Source: Book of Negroes.

524. IVEY, SAMUEL (c. 1783, age 44) – In 1780 Ivey's owner described his runaway slave as "a carpenter and caulker by trade." By 1783 Ivey was enslaved to James Grayson of England, who migrated to the Maritimes after the American Revolution; Ivey might have been from New York. British officials in New York described Ivey as a "stout fellow." Source: *Royal Gazette* (New York), August 5, 1780; *Royal Gazette* (New York), August 4, 1781; Book of Negroes.

525. JACK (c. 1759) – Jack was enslaved to James Gores, who came from New England to Île Royale. Source: Donovan, "Nominal List of Slaves and Their Owners," 160.

526. JACK (c. 1759) – Jack was enslaved to merchant and politician Malachy Salter, who originally was from Boston; Salter subsequently moved to Halifax and served in the Assembly. In 1759, Salter sent his wife a letter where he commented about his two slaves Hagar and Jack. He seemed impressed with Hagar, noting that she "behaved better than ever." Jack, however, refused to comply with Salter's commands. Salter complained that "Jack is Jack still" and, as a result, he beat Jack almost every day with a whip or stick. He implored his wife to purchase "a negro boy" possibly to replace Jack, who he referred to as an "Idle, deceitfull, villain." Source: Malachy Salter to Mrs. Salter, September 2, 1759, MG 100, vol. 217 no. 27f, NSA.

527. JACK (c. 1783, age 10) – Enslaved to Captain Hicks, who migrated to the Maritimes after the American Revolution with several other slaves, Jack was probably from New York. British officials in New York described him as an "ordinary boy." Source: Book of Negroes.

528. JACK (c. 1783, age 9) – Enslaved to Ensign Carpenter, who migrated to the Maritimes after the American Revolution, Jack was probably from New York. British officials in New York described him as a "likely boy." Source: Book of Negroes.

529. JACK (c. 1783, age 14) – Enslaved to Captain Mills, who migrated to the Maritimes after the American Revolution with another teenage slave, Jack was described by British officials in New York as a "likely boy." Source: Book of Negroes.

530. JACK (c. 1783, age 23) – Enslaved to Joseph Holmes, Jack migrated to the Maritimes from New York along with another male slave and was probably from New Jersey. British officials in New York described him as a "stout B [meaning Black] fellow." Source: Book of Negroes.

531. JACK (c. 1783, age 15) – Enslaved to Francis Wood, who migrated to the Maritimes after the American Revolution with two other slaves, Jack was described by British officials at New York as a "stout lad." Source: Book of Negroes.

532. JACK (c. 1783, age 38) – Enslaved to Nathaniel Dickenson, who migrated to the Maritimes after the American Revolution along with two other slaves, Jack was probably from New Jersey. British officials in New York noted he had been the property of John Day before being sold to Dickinson. These same officials described him as a "stout fellow." Source: Book of Negroes.

533. JACK (c. 1784) – Jack was enslaved to Samuel Acker, who settled at Cheda-bucto. Source: Loyalists from Saint Augustine to Chedabucto, Chipman Papers, Muster Master General's Office, Loyalist Musters, 1776–1785, MG 23, D1, ser. I, vol. 24, LAC.

534. JACK (c. 1789) – Enslaved to Lord Dunmore in Nassau, Jack escaped to Shelburne, Nova Scotia, and ended up in jail. Dunmore appointed George and Robert Ross to send Jack to the Bahamas, which they promised to do as soon as they could "persuade [Jack's] creditors to let him off" for half the fine of £15. Source: Robertson, *King's Bounty*, 95.

535. JACK (c. 1800–1801) – Jack became the centrepiece of the most celebrated slave case in Nova Scotia, *DeLancey v. Woodin*. James DeLancey was one of the more hardened slaveholders in Nova Scotia. According to Joseph Aplin, who was the junior counsel for DeLancey, "Jack, who was legally the slave of Col. DeLancey at New York, accompanied his master to London on the Evacuation of the former Place. From London [he went with] his Master to this Province." It is not clear why Jack stayed with DeLancey when they were in England as he should have been free according to the *Somerset* case of 1772. It is possible Jack did not know about the case or DeLancey prevented him from getting away. In 1800, after years of enslavement, Jack absconded from his owner and went to Halifax. It seems that Jack hoped to enlist in the Royal Nova Scotia Regiment or believed that he would become free simply by escaping to Halifax. After De-Lancey found out that William Woodin had employed Jack, he had his lawyer Thomas Ritchie demand that the slave be returned. Woodin's lawyer, Richard John Uniacke, refused, arguing that there was no statute law related to slavery and so all Blacks in the province were free. At this point, "an action of trover [a claim to obtain damages for the wrongful use of his property] was commenced by Mr. DeLancey against Mr. [Woodin] for the Negro Slave." DeLancey won the case in the Annapolis annual circuit court, but the judgment was arrested. As it turned out, a new trial set for September 1803 did not occur and DeLancey did not "obtain execution of his judgment against Woodin." DeLancey died in May 1804. Although no judgment had been entered regarding DeLancey, many slaveholders took his failure to recover Jack as a sign that the courts would not uphold slaveholding in the province. One important aspect of this case lies in the role that Jack played in freeing himself. By running away, Jack took his own freedom. Of course, the legal system could have returned him to slavery, but thanks to the work of Uniacke and others it did not. But Jack took the original risk of running away and forcing the issue to court. The case of *DeLancey v. Woodin* could not have happened if Jack had not run away and attempted to enlist. Sources: OPINIONS OF SEVERAL GENTLEMEN OF THE LAW, ON THE SUBJECT OF NEGRO SERVITUDE IN THE PROVINCE OF NOVA-SCOTIA (St. John: John Ryan, 1802); Joseph Aplin to James Stewart, November 16, 1803, Brenton Haliburton Fonds, MG 1, Vol. 334, #2, NSA; Cahill, "Slavery and the Judges," 98–104. There was another slave case involving Frederick Williams, who had also been a slaveholder in New York and continued as such in Nova Scotia. His slave had run away and been sheltered in a situation similar to that in the DeLancey case. Unfortu-nately, the decision in this case is not known. However, we do know that Frederick Williams owned slaves as late as 1807 as he was one of the Digby petitioners. Cahill argues that Williams probably would "have been nonsuited" (meaning that the case did not have enough evidence to go forward); see *Williams v. Stayner and Allen*, 1805, RG 39, Box 90, NSA.

536. JACK (c. 1801) – Nova Scotian politician and merchant Benjamin Belcher owned several slaves in Cornwallis, including Jack. Belcher noted: "I give my Negro man named Jack and my Negro boy Samuel and Negro boy James and Negro Girl called Chloe to my son Benjamin and his Heirs." The relationship between Jack, Samuel, James, and Chloe is unclear. Jack might have been the father or another relative or simply fictive kin. In his will, Belcher left strict directions for his heirs about the slaves, noting that he was "for ever charging them my children unto whom I have entrusted these Negro people with never to sell barter or exchange them or any of them under any pretension except it is for whose bad [?] Offences as will render them not safe to be kept in the Family and that to be adjudged of by three Justices of the Peace in said Township and in such case as their order they may be sold and disposed of. And I further request as soon as these young Negroes shall be capable to be taught to read, they shall be learnt the word of God." Source: Will of Benjamin Belcher, 1801, Kings County, NSA.

537. JACK (c. 1801, age 7) – An enslaved boy sold in Yarmouth, Nova Scotia, Jack was mentioned in the bill of sale pertaining to him as "a certain Negro Boy named Jack, about seven years of age, born in my house from a wench and a man, both my sole property." Source: J.R. Campbell, *A History of the County of Yarmouth, Nova Scotia* (Saint John: J & A McMillan, 1876), 145.

538. UNNAMED FATHER OF JACK (c. 1801) – This enslaved man was the father of Jack. Source: Campbell, *History of the County of Yarmouth*, 145.

539. UNNAMED MOTHER OF JACK (c. 1801) – This enslaved woman was the mother of Jack. Source: Campbell, *History of the County of Yarmouth*, 145.

540. JACKSON, LYDIA (c. 1791) – Originally, Lydia settled at Manchester (Guysborough Township) with other free Blacks. As a result of poverty and the desertion of her husband, Jackson indentured herself to a Loyalist for what she thought would be a short time. It turned out that this person had tricked Jackson into signing an indenture that essentially made her a servant for life. This man then sold Jackson as a slave to a Dr. Bulman. As a slave of the doctor, Jackson suffered from the most brutal mistreatment. Bulman regularly beat "her with the tongs, sticks, pieces of rope &c. about the head and face." John Clarkson, a Royal Navy officer and organizer of the Black Loyalist exodus to Sierra Leone in 1792, noted that eventually Jackson escaped to Halifax. According to Clarkson, Jackson's owner planned on "selling her to some planter in the

West Indies to work as a slave." Lydia Jackson's story must be considered in the context of Clarkson's following comment: "I do not know what induced me to mention the above case as I have many others of a similar nature; for example, Scott's case, Mr. Lee, Senr. case, Smith's child, Motley Roads child, Mr. Farish's negro servant, &c." The actual diary entry from Clarkson is worthy of being quoted fully for its details about the challenges free Blacks faced in Nova Scotia:

November 30th – Waited upon Mr. Bulkeley the President of Council who received me with attention and promised to do everything in his power to forward my business and further said that & every other gentleman would and ought to do every thing in their power to assist me, who had upon every occasion conducted myself with so much candour & fairness – Came home, received several visits from people of every description and of whom was a young woman a Black named Lydia Jackson; her case which I have taken from her own mouth I shall relate since it will serve to give some idea of the situation of the Black people in this Province. Mr. Henry Hedley of Manchester finding Lydia Jackson in great distress having been left by her husband, he invited her to come & reside in his house, to live as a companion to his wife, after she had been there for seven days, he required her either to pay him for her board and bind herself to him for seven years; she was unable to pay him and refused to be bound; at length gradually shortening the period by a year at a time, he by dint of fair promises obtained her consent to be indented to him for one year; the writings were in consequence drawn up by a Mr. Harrison of the same place, but taking advantage of her ignorance the term of thirty nine years was specified in the Indenture, instead of the one she had consented to; and to this paper she without the least suspicion made her mark – Henry Hedley told her the next day that she was to serve out the year with Dr. Bulman of Lunenburg and sent her round for this purpose in a Schooner commanded by Alexander Brymer, Dr. Bulman soon after her arrival at Lunenburg informed her to her great astonishment that she had been articled for the term of thirty nine years, and that she had been made over to him for the consideration of £20 which he had paid to Henry Hedley. Dr. Bulman turned out to be a very bad master, frequently beating her with the tongs, sticks, pieces of rope &c. about the head & face, his wife likewise was by no means backward to lend him her assistance on these occasions. For some words she had spoken with the least intention of giving offence Bulman took occasion to knock her down, and though she was then in the last month of pregnancy, in the most inhuman manner, stamped upon her whilst she lay upon the ground; for these and other cruelties she lodged a complaint against him before Mr. Lambert an Attorney at Lunenburg. This gentleman took up her case which was brought into Court but was soon silenced by the overbearing manners & influence of Bulman, who then or soon after expressed his intention of selling her to some Planter in the West Indies to work as a slave. In the meantime he sent her to work upon his farm about three miles from the town, giving authority and sanction to his servants to beat & punish her as they thought fit. After she had continued with Dr. Bulman three years, she made her escape in a wonderful way through the woods & after experiencing innumerable hardships, she reached Halifax, and got a Memorial drawn up and Presented to the Governor, who paid little or no attention to it. At length she applied to the Chief Justice, who promised to enquire into the business and lastly she came to me. I immediately wrote to Dr. Bulman respecting her and consulted a Lawyer on the business who gave it as his opinion that her wages could be recovered for the time she lived under Bulman but the forms of law would most likely prevent its being finally settled, so as to enable her to go with me. Finding there was no chance of the business being settled, while I remained in the Province I advised her to give it up and leave Bulman to his own reflections.

Source: Fergusson, *Clarkson's Mission to America*, 89–90.

541. JACOB (c. 1783, age 17) – Enslaved to John Norris, who migrated to the Maritimes after the American Revolution with a few other slaves, Jacob was described by British officials as a "stout lad." Source: Book of Negroes.

542. JACOB (c. 1783, age 12) – Enslaved to Donn or Dow Van Dyne, who migrated to the Maritimes after the American Revolution with another young slave, Jacob was probably from New York. British officials at New York noted that he was born in Van Dyne's family and described him as a "likely boy." Source: Book of Negroes.

543. JACOB (c. 1783, age 20) – Enslaved to William Wilson, who migrated to the Maritimes from New York with three other slaves. Jacob was from Edisto Island, South Carolina. British officials described him as a "stout fellow." Source: Book of Negroes.

544. JACOB [name changed to **FRANK** by owner] (c. 1777, age 10–11) – This boy was enslaved to Liverpool resident Simeon Perkins, who purchased him for £35. Perkins immediately changed the boy's name from Jacob to Frank. In 1783, Perkins noted that "my Negro Frank, to mow the Island (Bear Island)." Sources: Harold A. Innis, ed., *The Diary of Simeon Perkins*, 1766–1780 (Toronto: The Champlain Society, 1948), 158; Harvey, *Diary of Simeon Perkins*, 1780–1789, 195.

545. JACQUES (c. 1735) – Jacques was an enslaved man in Île Royale. Source: Donovan, "Nominal List of Slaves and Their Owners," 153.

546. JACQUES (c. 1736) – Jacques was enslaved to Louis Jouet. Source: Donovan, "Nominal List of Slaves and Their Owners," 154.

547. JACQUES (c. 1736, age 12) – Enslaved to Jacques LeRay, Jacques was from the West Indies. Source: Donovan, "Nominal List of Slaves and Their Owners," 154.

548. JACQUES (c. 1757) – Enslaved to a ship's captain, who asked a Louisbourg councillor to find a buyer for him, Jacques was eventually purchased by Pierre De La Croix for 800 livres. Source: Donovan, "Slaves and Their Owners in Île Royale," 8–9.

549. JAMES (c. 1783, age 19) – Enslaved to Robert Cook, who migrated to the Maritimes from New York, James was described by British officials as a "stout fellow." Source: Book of Negroes.

550. JAMES (c. 1783, age 13) – Enslaved to James Ettridge, who migrated to the Maritimes after the American Revolution with another slave, James was probably from New York. British officials at New York described him as a "likely boy." Source: Book of Negroes.

551. JAMES (slave? c. 1784) – Possibly enslaved to Theophilis Chamberlain, James lived with one other Black person in Chamberlain's household. Chamberlain had left Connecticut to settle in Nova Scotia. He would be very involved in the settlement of the War of 1812 Black refugees. He encouraged the government to settle the refugees near white farmers in Preston, Nova Scotia, primarily so they could work on local white farms as opposed to their own land. Source: Loyalists and Disbanded Troops at Cole Harbour, Chipman Papers, Muster Master General's Office, Loyalist Musters, 1776–1785, MG 23, D1, ser. I, vol. 24, LAC; Harvey Amani Whitfield, *Blacks on the Border: The Black Refugees in British North America, 1815–1860* (Burlington: University of Vermont Press, 2006).

552. JAMES (c. 1781–1786, age 23 in 1781) – James absconded from his owner, Abel Michener, Esq., twice in a five-year period. Michener described his slave as speaking good English, which means he was probably born in North America. He also commented that James possessed a "lively Countenance." In the first advertisement, Michener promised to forgive James if only his slave would return home, but he made no such offer the second time. Sources: *Nova Scotia Gazette and Weekly Chronicle*, May 22, 1781 and August 22, 1786; Whitfield, *Black Slavery in the Maritimes*, 30.

553. JAMES (c. 1784) – John Wentworth sent James and 18 other slaves from Nova Scotia to his "relation" Paul Wentworth in Suriname. Wentworth described these slaves as, "American born or well seasoned, and are perfectly stout, healthy, sober, orderly, Industrious, & obedient." Wentworth had the slaves Christened and claimed to be concerned for their welfare. He also noted that the male slaves "are expert in boats." Source: John Wentworth to Paul Wentworth or his attorney, February 24, 1784.

554. JAMES (c. 1785) – Samuel Andrews owned James and his family – his wife Bet and children Frank and Judy (or Jude). The entire family absconded from Andrews in 1785: "RUN AWAY from the Subscriber, Four Negroes, A Man, his Wife, and two Children, [named] James, Bet, Frank, and Judy, who all speak good English; the man is a carpenter by trade. WHOEVER apprehends the said negroes, and delivers them to the gaol keeper, or to Capt. John Williams, in Maiden-lane, shall receive EIGHT DOLLARS Reward, or any person that will give information to said Williams, of said negroes, so that he gets hold of them, shall receive a Reward of FIVE DOLLARS from Said Williams. SAMUEL ANDREWS." In 1785, James Singletory (almost certainly the same James) "applied to James McEwen Esq [according to Benjamin Marston, McEwen was a justice of the peace], praying he might be discharged from the service" of Samuel Andrews. Andrews had migrated to Shelburne from St. Augustine and claimed James "as his slave" – producing a pass signed by the Commissary of Claims of Charleston that Andrews had paid £50 for James, his wife, and child. He did not, however, produce a bill of sale. Andrews promised, if given time, to produce a bill of sale proving that the Black family belonged to him. A witness for Andrews, John Fanning, claimed that "Negro James" had always been considered the property of Andrews. The court decided that Andrews had to produce "due attested proof" before the court would send the family back to slavery. Andrews was allowed "Twelve months" to obtain proof of ownership. James, his wife, and child were required to live with Andrews as servants throughout the 12-month period while their owner attempted to find – or more likely to forge – a bill of sale. The court warned Andrews (bound by a £50 payment and his witness John Fanning £25) that the family could not be sold, conveyed out of the province, and should be used as "hired servants." If he could not produce proof, James and his family would be discharged. The court returned James to Andrews's service, even though James had successfully challenged his bondage, and Andrews continued to own slaves throughout the eighteenth century. Nevertheless, the case underlines how one Black family challenged their bondage in Loyalist Nova Scotia. Note: We know that years later, Judy (or Jude) was still enslaved. This is like Lydia Jackson and other cases where Black people in Nova Scotia were told they were servants for a certain number of months or years but ended up servants for life. It seems that some of this family was re-enslaved for a certain amount of time since Judy was still enslaved 15 years later. Sources: Special Sessions at Shelburne, Nova Scotia, Shelburne Records, MG 4, vol. 141, NSA; the original copies of some of these court cases are available at Library and Archives Canada. See also *Nova Scotia Packet and General Advertiser,* October 12, 1785.

555. BET (c. 1785) – The wife of James and mother of Frank and Judy. Samuel Andrews owned Bet and her family (her husband, James, and children, Frank and Judy). The entire family absconded from Andrews in 1785. In the runaway notice, Andrews described the entire family as being able to speak good English. Source: *Nova Scotia Packet and General Advertiser*, October 12, 1785.

556. FRANK (c. 1785) – The son of James and Bet, Samuel Andrews owned Frank and his family (parents James and Bet and sister Judy). In 1785, the entire family absconded from Andrews. Source: *Nova Scotia Packet and General Advertiser*, October 12, 1785.

557. JUDY [or **JUDE**] (c. 1785) – The daughter of Bet and James, Samuel Andrews owned Judy (or Jude) and her family (parents James and Bet and brother Frank). In 1785 the entire family absconded from Andrews. In the runaway notice, Andrews described the entire family as being able to speak good English. In 1800, Samuel Andrews, Jr., reportedly beat a slave named Jude (probably the same Judy) to death. The court acquitted Andrews despite overwhelming medical evidence against him. Sources: *Nova Scotia Packet and General Advertiser*, October 12, 1785; *R. v. Andrews*, May 19, 1801, Shelburne County Special Court of Oyer and Terminer, RG 42, SH vol. 1, file 4, NSA; also see Sharon Robart-Johnson, *Jude and Diana* (Halifax: Fernwood Publishing, 2021).

558. DIANA (c. 1801) – Diana testified at the trial of Samuel Andrews for the murder of her sister Judy or Jude ("sister" could possibly mean a blood relation or fictive kin), where she described the evening prior to her sister's murder and the violence she witnessed upon Jude by Samuel Andrews, Sr., and his sons Samuel, Jr., and John. Sources: *R. v. Andrews*, May 19, 1801, Shelburne County Special Court of Oyer and Terminer, RG 42, SH, vol. 1 files 4.1–4.3, NSA; Robart-Johnson, *Africa's Children*, 29–35; also see Sharon Robart-Johnson, *Jude and Diana* (Halifax: Fernwood Publishing, 2021).

559. JAMES (c. 1785) – Walter Berry owned James, who became involved with other Prince Edward Island slaves in the Jupiter Wise conspiracy. They planned to steal rum, have a party, and escape to Boston. Sources: *King v. Jupiter Wise*, 1786, PAROPEI; Holman, "Slaves and Servants on Prince Edward Island," 100–4; Hornby, *Black Islanders*, 15–19.

560. JAMES (c. 1801) – Nova Scotian politician and merchant Benjamin Belcher owned several slaves in Cornwallis, including James. Belcher noted: "I give my Negro man named Jack and my Negro boy Samuel and Negro boy James and Negro Girl called Chloe to my son Benjamin and his Heirs." The relationship between Jack, Samuel, James, and Chloe is unclear. Jack might have been the father or another relative or simply fictive kin. In his will, Belcher left strict directions for his heirs about the slaves, noting that he was "for ever charging them my children unto whom I have entrusted these Negro people with never to sell barter or exchange them or any of them under any pretension except it is for whose bad [?] Offences as will render them not safe to be kept in the Family and that to be adjudged of by three Justices of the Peace in said Township and in such case as their order they may be sold and disposed of. And I further request as soon as these young Negroes shall be capable to be taught to read, they shall be learnt the word of God." Source: Will of Benjamin Belcher, 1801, Kings County, NSA.

561. JAMES (c. 1787) – The recorder at St. George's Anglican Church in Sydney, Cape Breton, described James as "a Negro, his parents belonging to the 42nd Regt. Baptized 10th May 1787." Source: May 10, 1787, St. George's Sydney, MG 4, no. 147, NSA.

562. MOTHER OF JAMES (c. 1787) – This enslaved woman was the mother of James, who was baptized in Sydney, Cape Breton. Source: May 10, 1787, St. George's Sydney, MG 4, no. 147, NSA.

563. FATHER OF JAMES (c. 1787) – This enslaved man was the father of James, who was baptized in Sydney, Cape Breton. Source: May 10, 1787, St. George's Sydney, MG 4, no. 147, NSA.

564. JAMES (c. 1775) – Enslaved to Joseph Wilson of Falmouth, Nova Scotia, James was left by Wilson to his son. Source: States, "Presence and Perseverance: Blacks in Hants County," 38.

565. JANE (c. 1783, age 17) – Enslaved to Bartholomew Haynes, who migrated to the Maritimes after the American Revolution, Jane was probably from New York. British officials in New York noted that Bartholomew Gidney (from White Plains) had sold Jane to Haynes. These same officials described her as a "fine wench." Source: Book of Negroes.

566. JANE (c. 1793) – Enslaved to Benjamin Belcher in Cornwallis, Nova Scotia, Jane lived with several other slaves and was baptized in 1793. However, she is not mentioned in Belcher's 1801 will like some of the other baptized children, meaning she could have died, escaped, or been sold away. Source: List of Baptisms, June 3, 1793, Cornwallis Township Book, NSA.

567. JANE (c. 1786) – Enslaved to Richard Betts (a Loyalist from New York), Jane was listed in the 1786 inventory of Betts along with three other slaves (and their values). According to the document, Toney, Prince (or Primus), and Jane were listed as worth £35, while Harry commanded the price of £40. The relationship of each slave to the other slaves is unclear – if they were a family or totally unrelated. The total value of Betts's inventory was about £1,053, while the combined value of the slaves was £145. Thus, slaves accounted for 13.77 per cent of the total wealth of his estate. Source: Will of Richard Betts, 1786 Annapolis County, RG 48, NSA.

568. JANE (c. 1787) – Jane was enslaved to tavern keeper Frederick Sinclair. Source: Harris, "Negro Population of the County of Annapolis," 17–18.

569. JANE (c. 1804) – Jane was enslaved to James DeLancey, whose estate valued her at £30. Source: Hanger, "Life of Loyalist Colonel James DeLancey," 52.

570. JANUARY (c. 1784) – John Wentworth sent January and 18 other slaves from Nova Scotia to his "relation" Paul Wentworth in Suriname. Wentworth described these slaves as, "American born or well seasoned, and are perfectly stout, healthy, sober, orderly, Industrious, & obedient." Wentworth had the slaves Christened and claimed to be concerned for their welfare. He also noted "All the men are expert in boats." Source: John Wentworth to Paul Wentworth or his attorney, February 24, 1784.

571. JANUARY, JOHN (c. 1783, age 7) – Enslaved to Ensign Banks, who migrated to the Maritimes from New York, John was possibly from New Jersey. British officials described him as a "small boy." Source: Book of Negroes.

572. JARVIS, ANTHONY (c. 1783) – Enslaved to Daniel Sickles, who migrated to the Maritimes after the American Revolution, Anthony was accompanied by a young free-born 2-year-old girl who was possibly his daughter and was probably from New York. British officials described him as an "ordinary fellow." Source: Book of Negroes.

573. JARVIS, HANNAH (c. 1783, age 26) – Enslaved to Captain Thatcher, who migrated to the Maritimes from New York, Hannah was from New York. Thatcher had purchased her from Stephen Biddle of Staten Island. British officials described her as a "fine wench." Source: Book of Negroes.

574. JASMIN (c. 1738, age 50) – François dit Jasmin (this means he preferred the name Jasmin) was enslaved to Elie and Simone Thesson dit La Floury, who owned an "extensive fishing and mercantile operation." Jasmin was originally from the West Indies and probably worked as a domestic and also "doubtless helped with the farm chores; besides feeding and caring for three cows and two horses, he had to cut hay, churn butter, and attend to numerous other duties associated with a fishing and mercantile property." Source: Donovan, "Slaves in Île Royale," 31.

575. JEAN (c. 1732, age 11) – Enslaved to Michel Daccarette, Jean lived with another young slave named Blaise Simon. Apparently, Daccarette was a cruel master. In one instance, he came home late at night (4 a.m.) and found Blaise asleep in the kitchen. Daccarette proceeded to beat Blaise with his cane. Source: Donovan, "Slaves and Their Owners in Île Royale," 22.

576. JEAN (c. 1753, age 11) – New York Ship Captain James Spellen sold Jean to Île Royale slaveowner Josse Bette. Sources: Donovan, "Slaves and Their Owners in Île Royale," 8; Donovan, "Nominal List of Slaves and Their Owners," 158.

577. JEAN (c. 1783, age 15) – Enslaved to Joseph Marvin, who migrated to the Maritimes from New York after the American Revolution, Jean was possibly from Connecticut. British officials in New York described her as a "stout wench." Source: Book of Negroes.

578. JEAN BAPTISTE (c. 1728, age 10) – Governor St. Ovide owned Jean Baptiste and purchased another young slave one year later. Source: Donovan, "Nominal List of Slaves and Their Owners," 152.

579. JEAN BAPTISTE (c. 1728, age 10) – Enslaved to Jean Baptiste Morel, Jean Baptiste came to Île Royale from the West Indies. Source: Donovan, "Nominal List of Slaves and Their Owners," 152.

580. JEAN BAPTISTE (c. 1741, age 15) – Enslaved to Pierre Martissans, a member of the Superior Council. Source: Donovan, "Nominal List of Slaves and Their Owners," 155.

581. JEANNETON (c. 1739, age 14) – From St. Domingue and enslaved to Pierre Martissans, Jeanneton died at the age of 14. Source: Donovan, "Slaves and Their Owners in Île Royale," 13–14.

582. JEANNETON (c. 1739, age 40) – Jeanneton was enslaved to Jean Martin. Source: Donovan, "Nominal List of Slaves and Their Owners," 155.

583. JEFF (c. 1783, age 9) – Enslaved to John Fox, who migrated to the Maritimes after the American Revolution, British officials in New York noted "[Jeff was] purchased by his [Fox's] brother who gave him to him." They also described Jeff as a "fine boy." Source: Book of Negroes.

584. JEFF (c. 1783, age 12) – Enslaved to Lieutenant Ward [the Book of Negroes says B. Ward, but it might actually be Lieutenant J. Ward], who migrated to the Maritimes from New York, Jeff was probably from New York. British officials described him as a "likely boy." Source: Book of Negroes.

585. JEFFREY (c. 1784) – Jeffrey was enslaved to the Departments of the Army and Navy, which settled at Chedabucto, Nova Scotia. Source: Muster Roll of Settlers at Chedabucto (including Departments of the Army and Navy), Chipman Papers, Muster Master General's Office, Loyalist Musters, 1776–1785, MG 23, D1, ser. I, vol. 24, 1–470, NSA.

586. JEMIMA (c. 1793) – New Brunswick resident John Cock briefly mentioned that he bequeathed his "Negro wench" Jemima to his wife, but also that, if she remarried, Jemima would be given to his son. Source: Will of John Cock, County of Saint John, 1793, PANB.

587. JEN [or **JENNY, JIN,** or **GIN**] (c. 1787, age 18) – In 1783, Thomas Mallard brought Jen to New Brunswick from New York. British officials described her as a "likely mulatto girl." Mallard gave her to James McKown so that he could sell her in Barbados for £56. This unsurprising disposal of a slave to the West Indies ended up in the Supreme Court of New Brunswick because Mallard claimed McKown owed him money from the sale. Source: *Thomas Mallard v. James McKown*, 1788, RS 42, Supreme Court Original Jurisdiction Records, PANB; Book of Negroes.

588. JENNY (c. 1783, age 40) – Enslaved to Richard Carman, who migrated to the Maritimes after the American Revolution with another slave, Jenny was from New York. British officials at New York described her as a "stout wench." Source: Book of Negroes.

589. JENNY (c. 1783, age 40) – Enslaved to Dr. Nathaniel Bullern, who migrated from South Carolina to Nova Scotia with a total of 10 slaves. Bullern's slaves also indicate several different possibilities of family connections and kinship networks. His oldest slaves, Achabee and Catharina, were both 60 at the end of the American Revolution. Jenny and Prince were 40 and 30, respectively. Bullern also owned another male slave in his early 30s and three females ranging in ages 19 to 25. His two youngest slaves were an infant named Sarah and a 6 year old. It is unclear who the parents of these children were, but it is possible that one or both parents were among Bullern's slaves. British officials in New York described Jenny as a "stout wench." Source: Book of Negroes.

590. JENNY (c. 1783, age 12) – Enslaved to Henry Rayden, who migrated to the Maritimes after the American Revolution, Jenny was described by British officials in New York as having been previously been owned by Ethan Sickles and as a "likely girl." Source: Book of Negroes.

591. JEROME (c. 1806) – Jerome was enslaved to Amable Doucet, who bequeathed Jerome to his wife. Source: Stephen A. White, "Doucet, Amable," *Dictionary of Canadian Biography*, vol. 5, http://www.biographi.ca/en/bio/doucet_amable_5E.html.

592. JESSIE (c. 1770) – Martha Pritchard bequeathed Jessie to her daughter and a two-and-a-half-year-old boy named John Patten to her granddaughter. Source: Smith, "Slave in Canada," 14.

593. JIM (c. 1783, age 10) – Enslaved to John McAlpine, who migrated to the Maritimes from New York, Jim was described by British officials as a "stout boy." Source: Book of Negroes.

594. JIM (c. 1783, age 14) – Enslaved to Sam Clarke, who migrated to the Maritimes after the American Revolution, Jim was probably from New York. British officials in New York noted that Jim's owner had a bill of sale from another person and described Jim as a "stout boy." Source: Book of Negroes.

595. JIM (c. 1806) – Enslaved to Joseph Clarke, Jim escaped and found shelter with Samuel Denny Street. Joseph Clarke did everything in his power to maintain slavery in New Brunswick, from filing lawsuits to placing various runaway advertisements in local newspapers. Source: *Joseph Clarke v. Samuel Denny Street*, 1806, RS 42, Supreme Court Original Jurisdiction Records, PANB.

596. JIMMEY (c. 1802) – Jimmey ran away with another slave named Trim from his owner in New Brunswick. The name of the owner is unclear from the advertisement. The advertisement provided a brief description of both men: "ABSCONDED the middle of December last, two able young Negro men belonging to the Subscriber – one named *Trim* and the other *Jimmey*, supposed a Nayo, marked A.R. on the left shoulder, and had a sore on one of his feet near the ancle; both rather of a yellow complexion, and middle sized." Source: *Royal Gazette*, December 15, 1802.

597. JOB (c. 1790, age 4) – Enslaved to Henry Burbidge, who planned to free the boy when he turned 30, Job's father might have been Spence (see entry), but this is unclear. Source: Eaton, *History of Kings County*, 234.

598. JOE (c. 1770) – Joe was enslaved to Joseph Gerrish and was later sold along with two other slaves for £150. Source: Smith, "Slave in Canada," 13; States and Smardz Frost, "Section 5: King's College Students and Slavery Selected Biographies," 9.

599. JOE (c. 1783, age 10) – Enslaved to Gilbert Tippet, who migrated to the Maritimes after the American Revolution with another child slave, Joe was probably from New York. British officials in New York described him as a "stout boy." Source: Book of Negroes.

600. JOE (c. 1783, age 12) – Enslaved to Joseph Forrester, who migrated to the Maritimes after the American Revolution, Joe was probably from New York. British officials at New York noted Joe said Captain Forrester "purchased him." The officials also described him as a "fine boy." Source: Book of Negroes.

601. JOE (c. 1783, age 27) – Enslaved to Caleb Mallory, Joe was described by British officials in New York as a "stout man." Source: Book of Negroes.

602. JOE (c. 1783, age 36) – Joe was enslaved to Reed DeLancey's brigade. DeLancey migrated to the Maritimes from New York with Joe, his wife, and her boy. British officials in New York described him as a "stout man, labourer." Source: Book of Negroes.

603. MARY (c. 1783, age 26) – Wife of Joe, Mary was also enslaved to Reed DeLancey's brigade. She came to the Maritimes with her husband and a boy, and British officials in New York described her as a "stout wench." Source: Book of Negroes.

604. UNNAMED SON OF JOE AND MARY (c. 1783) – This child was the son of Joe and Mary. Source: Book of Negroes.

605. JOE (slave? c. 1784) – Possibly an enslaved person, who settled at Belle Vue in Beaver Harbour, Joe might have been nominally free but may have been subjected to re-enslavement – as were many Blacks in the Maritimes. Source: Roll of Loyalists Settled at Belle Vue in Beaver Harbour, Chipman Papers, Muster Master General's Office, Loyalist Musters, 1776–1785, MG 23, D1, ser. I, vol. 24, LAC.

606. JOE (slave? c. 1784) – Joe was possibly enslaved to Lieutenant Cornwall, who migrated to Country Harbour with other southern Loyalists. The majority of these Loyalists and their slaves were from North Carolina, South Carolina, and Georgia. They had settled briefly in East Florida before moving to Nova Scotia. Black people at Country Harbour were either slaves or "quasi-free" and subject to re-enslavement. Abolitionist Thomas Clarkson explained the phenomenon of re-enslavement: "It was not long till these loyalists, many of whom had been educated with all the ideas of the justice of slavery, the inferiority of negroes, and the superiority of white men, that are universal in the southern provinces of America, began to harass and oppress the industrious black settlers, and even wantonly to deprive them of the fruits of their labour, expelling them from the lands they had cleared." Clarkson continued by noting that whites reduced "again to slavery those negroes who had so honourably obtained their freedom. They hired them as servants, and, at the end of the stipulated time, refused payment of their wages, insisting that they were slaves: in some instances they destroyed their tickets of freedom, and then enslaved the negroes for want of them; in several instances, the unfortunate Africans were taken onboard vessels, carried to the West Indies, and there sold for the benefit of their plunderers." At Country Harbour, Black people were listed on the musters as the "Servants" of a white Loyalist, which meant it was very easy for them to be re-enslaved if they were not already enslaved. Sources: Clarkson, "Some Account of the New Colony at Sierra Leone," 229–30; Settlers at Country Harbour, Chipman Papers, Muster Master General's Office, Loyalist Musters, 1776–1785, MG 23, D1, ser. I, vol. 24, LAC. Note: Ellen Wilson believed that the information Clarkson used came from Thomas Peters; see Wilson, *Loyal Blacks*, 181.

607. JOE (c. 1786) – The "property of Robert Sommerville," Joe was "convicted on Oath, of stealing Sundry Articles" from his owner. The court sentenced him to 39 lashes. Source: September 15, 1785, Special Session, Shelburne, RG 50, #8.4, NSA.

608. JOE (c. 1785) – Enslaved to George Burns of Prince Edward Island, Joe lived with Jupiter Wise (see entry). Sources: *King v. Jupiter Wise*, 1786, PAROPEI; Holman, "Slaves and Servants on Prince Edward Island," 100–4; Hornby, *Black Islanders*, 15–19.

609. JOE (c. 1798) – George Dixon purchased Joe, who had been in trouble with the local authorities in New Brunswick but had received a pardon from the governor. Joe escaped from Dixon and was "harboured" by one Abraham Gunter, who took Joe to Nova Scotia. Dixon sued Gunter for £35. Supreme Court Justice Joshua Upham ordered "that the said Abraham Gunter be held to Bail in the Sum of Thirty Five Pounds current money of this Province." The court accepted the enslavement of Joe. The issue for Upham was not whether Joe was a slave, but whether Gunter had stolen the property of Dixon. Source: *G. Dixon v. A. Gunter*, 1798, RS 42, Supreme Court Original Jurisdiction Records, PANB.

610. JOHN (slave? c. 1769) – Described as "a Negro servant," John was baptized by Reverend Seccombe. Given the year, it is extremely unlikely that John was simply a servant. Source: Smith, "Slave in Canada," 85.

611. JOHN (c. 1780) – John was enslaved to Colonel Henry Denson, whose estate sold him for £60. Source: Smith, "Slave in Canada," 15–16.

612. JOHN (c. 1783, age 26) – Enslaved to Joseph Montgomery, who migrated to the Maritimes after the American Revolution, John was probably from North

Carolina. British officials in New York described him as an "ordinary fellow."
Source: Book of Negroes.

613. JOHN (slave? c. 1784) – Possibly enslaved to Theophilis Chamberlain, John lived with one other Black person in Chamberlain's household. Chamberlain had left Connecticut to settle in Nova Scotia and was involved in the settlement of the War of 1812 Black refugees. He encouraged the government to settle the refugees near white farmers in Preston, Nova Scotia, primarily so they could work on local white farms as opposed to their own land. Source: Loyalists and Disbanded Troops at Cole Harbour, Chipman Papers, Muster Master General's Office, Loyalist Musters, 1776–1785, MG 23, D1, ser. I, vol. 24, LAC; Whitfield, *Blacks on the Border*.

614. JOHN (c. 1784) – John Wentworth sent John and 18 other slaves from Nova Scotia to his "relation" Paul Wentworth in Suriname. Wentworth described these slaves as, "American born or well seasoned, and are perfectly stout, healthy, sober, orderly, Industrious, & obedient." Wentworth had the slaves Christened and claimed to be concerned for their welfare. He noted that "John [is] also a good axe man." Source: John Wentworth to Paul Wentworth or his attorney, February 24, 1784.

615. JOHN (c. 1802) – John was enslaved to Virginia Loyalist Jacob Ellegood, who owned several slaves. Ellegood served in the New Brunswick legislative assembly and also owned a large farm. He was the brother-in-law of John Saunders, who served as chief justice of the New Brunswick Supreme Court (and also from Virginia). Source: Will of Jacob Ellegood, 1802, PANB.

616. JOHN (slave? c. 1788) – Possibly an enslaved person, John was baptized along with several other Black people in New Brunswick. Source: Early Parish Records, New Brunswick, September 14, 1788, possibly PANB.

617. JOHN (c. 1791) – John was possibly an enslaved child who was baptized in New Brunswick. A notation described him as "John black Servant child of Mr. John [Simpson?]." Source: April 26, 1791; Parish of Maugerville Records, FC LCR N4C3R4, PANB.

618. JOHNSTON, CATO (slave? c. 1784) – Possibly an enslaved person, who settled at Belle Vue in Beaver Harbour, Cato may have been nominally free but he might have been subjected to re-enslavement – as were many Blacks in the Maritimes. Source: Roll of Loyalists Settled at Belle Vue in Beaver Harbour, Chipman Papers, Muster Master General's Office, Loyalist Musters, 1776–1785, MG 23, D1, ser. I, vol. 24, LAC.

619. JOHNSTON, JAMES (slave? c. 1784) – Possibly an enslaved person, who settled at Belle Vue in Beaver Harbour, James may have been nominally free but he might have been subjected to re-enslavement – as were many Blacks in the Maritimes. Source: Roll of Loyalists Settled at Vue in Beaver Harbour, Chipman Papers, Muster Master General's Office, Loyalist Musters, 1776–1785, MG 23, D1, ser. I, vol. 24, LAC.

620. JOHNSTON, LUCY (slave? c. 1784) – Possibly an enslaved person, who settled at Belle Vue in Beaver Harbour, Lucy may have been nominally free but she might have been subjected to re-enslavement – as were many Blacks in the Maritimes. Source: Roll of Loyalists Settled at Belle Vue in Beaver Harbour, Chipman Papers, Muster Master General's Office, Loyalist Musters, 1776–1785, MG 23, D1, ser. I, vol. 24, LAC.

621. JOLLY, GEORGE (slave? c. 1800) – George Jolly worked as a skilled seaman and his master, James Cox, hired him out to one Captain Mann for a voyage to Newfoundland. Mann paid $14.00 a month for his services. This is possibly the same George that was owned by Richard Jenkins (see entry for George). Source: Robertson, *King's Bounty*, 93.

622. JONES, ANTHONY (c. 1783, age 40) – Enslaved to Mary Rinn, who migrated to the Maritimes from New York with seven other slaves, Anthony had been previously owned by Marianna Jones who gave four slaves to Mary Rinn. British officials described him as a "stout fellow." Source: Book of Negroes.

623. JOSEPH (c. 1745) – Joseph was enslaved to the Connecticut Regiment during the siege and takeover of Louisbourg. Source: Donovan, "Nominal List of Slaves and Their Owners," 156.

624. JOSEPH (c. 1783, age 30) – Enslaved to John Moore, who migrated to the Maritimes after the American Revolution, Joseph was possibly from North Carolina. British officials in New York described him as an "ordinary fellow." Source: Book of Negroes.

625. JOSHUA (c. 1783, age 22) – Enslaved to John Demill's father-in-law, who migrated to the Maritimes after the American Revolution, Joshua was from New York. British officials in New York noted he was a "Slave to Doctor Smith of Long Island" and described him as a "stout fellow." Source: Book of Negroes.

626. JOSSELIN, PIERRE (c. 1733, age 25) – Enslaved to carpenter Joseph Dugas, Pierre probably worked as a domestic for his owner's family – a family that included nine children. Pierre would have been around other Black slaves as six out of ten households on the Dugas's block had slaves. He died at age 25 during a smallpox outbreak. Source: Donovan, "Slaves and Their Owners in Île Royale, 1713–1760," 16.

627. JUBA (c. 1780) – Enslaved to Colonel Henry Denson, Juba was sold by Denson's estate for £30 – a substantially lower sum than Denson's other two slaves were sold (Spruce for £75 and John for £60). Source: Smith, "Slave in Canada," 16.

628. JUBA (c. 1784) – Juba was probably enslaved to well-known Loyalist Edward Winslow in the Maritimes along with two other men. Source: Accounts of Edward Winslow, 1783–84, June 17, 1784, The Winslow Papers (online), https://www.lib.unb.ca /winslow/fullrecord.cgi?id=500&level=2&BACKSTR=fields=Title%2Ccreator_name%2CSubject %2CSource%2CETC_Sequence&order_by=Identifier&level=2&Creator_name=&Title=&Subject =Caesar&Source=&Keyword=.

629. JUDE (c. 1783, age 14) – Enslaved to Donn or Dow Van Dyne, who migrated to the Maritimes after the American Revolution with another young slave, Jude was probably from New York. British officials at New York noted that she was born in Van Dyne's family and described her as a "short wench." Source: Book of Negroes.

630. JUDE (c. 1783, age 9) – Enslaved to Francis Wood, who migrated to the Maritimes after the American Revolution with other slaves, Jude was described by British officials in New York as a "fine girl." Source: Book of Negroes.

631. JUDGE (slave? c. 1784) – Judge was possibly an enslaved person settled at Belle Vue in Beaver Harbour who might have been nominally free. But he might have been subjected to re-enslavement – as were many Blacks in the Maritimes. Source: Roll of Loyalists Settled at Belle Vue in Beaver Harbour, Chipman Papers, Muster Master General's Office, Loyalist Musters, 1776–1785, MG 23, D1, ser. I, vol. 24, LAC.

632. JUDITH (c. 1783, age 40) – Enslaved to Mrs. Van Horn, who migrated to the Maritimes after the American Revolution with a few other slaves, Judith was probably from New Jersey. British officials at New York described her as an "ordinary wench." Source: Book of Negroes.

633. JULES LOUIS (c. 1755, age 12) – Jules Louis was enslaved to Mr. de Ruis. Source: Donovan, "Nominal List of Slaves and Their Owners," 159.

634. JUNE, ZABUD (c. 1746) – Zabud was from New England and served as an enslaved man under the command of Nathan Whiting. Source: Donovan, "Nominal List of Slaves and Their Owners," 156.

635. JUPITER (c. 1780s/1790s) – Folklorist Clara Dennis interviewed the grandson of Jupiter and Venus, who "were brought to Nova Scotia as slaves." According to the grandson (an elderly man by the 1930s), Jupiter liked Nova

Scotia better than the South because there's "better doin's here." After becoming free, Jupiter built a house through hard work. Source: Clara Dennis, *Down in Nova Scotia: My Own, My Native Land* (Toronto: Ryerson Press, 1934), 355–6.

636. VENUS (c. 1780s/1790s) – The wife of Jupiter, whom her grandson described as a "smart woman," Venus was a skilled knitter. Source: Clara Dennis, *Down in Nova Scotia*, 355–6.

637. MOSES (c. 1780s/1790s) – Possibly an enslaved man who befriended Jupiter when he was a boy, Moses and his residence at Birchtown were described by Clara Dennis in a way that suggested that Moses had actually been free in Nova Scotia and enslaved in the United States. But it is possible he remained enslaved in Nova Scotia after the American Revolution and became free after a few years of living in Nova Scotia. Source: Dennis, *Down in Nova Scotia*, 1.

638. JUPITER (c. 1783–84, age 33) – Jupiter was enslaved to Dr. Nathaniel Bullern, who migrated from South Carolina to Nova Scotia with a total of 10 slaves. Bullen's slaves also indicate several different possibilities of family connections and kinship networks. His oldest slaves, Achabee and Catharina, were both 60 at the end of the American Revolution. Jenny and Prince were 40 and 30, respectively. Bullern also owned another male slave in his early 30s and three females ranging in ages 19 to 25. His two youngest slaves were an infant named Sarah and a 6 year old. It is unclear who the parents of these children were, but it is possible that one or both parents were among Bullern's slaves. In 1784, Bullern placed a runaway advertisement in the local paper complaining that Jupiter had escaped with another one of his servant/slaves named Clarinda. In the advertisement, Bullern lists one of them as an indented servant and the other a slave. It is not clear whether Jupiter or Clarinda had become indentured as opposed to enslaved, but this might have been a difference of degree rather than kind as they both absconded from Bullern. Sources: Book of Negroes; *Nova Scotia Gazette and Weekly Chronicle*, September 21, 1784.

639. KATE (c. 1783, age 5) – Enslaved to Lieutenant DeVeber, who migrated to the Maritimes after the American Revolution, Kate was probably from New York. British officials in New York described her as a "likely child." It is possible that Kate is the same person mentioned in DeVeber's 1827 will when he refers to Catherine. Source: Book of Negroes.

640. KATE (c. 1789) – Enslaved to Lord Dunmore in Nassau, Kate escaped to Shelburne, Nova Scotia. Dunmore appointed George and Robert Ross of Shelburne to capture Kate. These men assured Dunmore they would find her and send her back to the Bahamas. Source: Robertson, *King's Bounty*, 95.

641. KATE (c. 1802) – Enslaved to Dr. Bond, Kate married Manuel, who had been brought to the Maritimes by his owner. Source: Smith, "Slave in Canada," 64.

642. JARVIS, MANUEL (c. early 1800s) – Originally from the West Indies, Manuel was enslaved to Dr. Bond who had purchased him from Lewis Blanchard. He married Kate and they lived in Yarmouth, Nova Scotia. Source: Smith, "Slave in Canada," 64.

643. HESTER (c. 1802) – The infant daughter of Kate and Manuel Jarvis, Hester was enslaved to the daughter of Dr. Bond in Yarmouth, who named Hester after Lady Hester Stanhope, the heroine of the romantic adventures that Bond's daughter had just finished reading. Sources: Smith, "Slave in Canada," 82; Robart-Johnson, *Africa's Children*, 48–9.

644. KATTY (slave? c. 1784) – Probably enslaved to Joseph Russell, who planned to settle near Halifax, Katty and three other Black people lived in Russell's household. Source: Loyalists and Disbanded Troops at Cole Harbour, Chipman Papers, Muster Master General's Office, Loyalist Musters, 1776–1785, MG 23, D1, ser. I, vol. 24, LAC.

645. KATY (c. 1783, age 6) – Katy was enslaved to Dr. Nathaniel Bullern, who migrated from South Carolina to Nova Scotia with a total of 10 slaves. Bullern's slaves also indicate several different possibilities of family connections and kinship networks. His oldest slaves, Achabee and Catharina, were both 60 at the end of the American Revolution. Jenny and Prince were 40 and 30, respectively. Bullern also owned another male slave in his early 30s and three females ranging in ages 19 to 25. His two youngest slaves were an infant named Sarah and a 6 year old. It is unclear who the parents of these children were, but it is possible that one or both parents were among Bullern's slaves. British officials in New York described Katy as a "fine girl." Source: Book of Negroes.

646. KETCHIM, PHILLIS (c. 1783, age 44) – Enslaved to John Ketchim, who was involved in the West Indian slave trade, Phillis arrived in the Maritimes from New York as Ketchim's only slave. She was probably from Connecticut, and British officials described her as old and worn. Source: Book of Negroes.

647. KETCH (slave? c. 1784) – Ketch was possibly enslaved to Captain Daniel McNeill (also spelled MacNeil and McNeil), who migrated to Country Harbour with other southern Loyalists. The majority of these Loyalists and their slaves were from North Carolina, South Carolina, and Georgia. They had settled briefly in East Florida before moving to Nova Scotia. Black people at Country Harbour were either slaves or "quasi-free" and subject to re-enslavement. Abolitionist Thomas Clarkson explained the phenomenon of re-enslavement:

"It was not long till these loyalists, many of whom had been educated with all the ideas of the justice of slavery, the inferiority of negroes, and the superiority of white men, that are universal in the southern provinces of America, began to harass and oppress the industrious black settlers, and even wantonly to deprive them of the fruits of their labour, expelling them from the lands they had cleared." Clarkson continued by noting that whites reduced "again to slavery those negroes who had so honourably obtained their freedom. They hired them as servants, and, at the end of the stipulated time, refused payment of their wages, insisting that they were slaves: in some instances they destroyed their tickets of freedom, and then enslaved the negroes for want of them; in several instances, the unfortunate Africans were taken onboard vessels, carried to the West Indies, and there sold for the benefit of their plunderers." At Country Harbour, Black people were listed on the musters as the "Servants" of a white Loyalist, which meant it was very easy for them to be re-enslaved if they were not already enslaved. Sources: Clarkson, "Some Account of the New Colony at Sierra Leone," 229–30; Settlers at Country Harbour, Chipman Papers, Muster Master General's Office, Loyalist Musters, 1776–1785, MG 23, D1, ser. I, vol. 24, LAC. Note: Ellen Wilson believed that the information Clarkson used came from Thomas Peters; see Wilson, *Loyal Blacks*, 181.

648. KEZIAH (c. 1787, age 20) – In 1787, Keziah (also spelled Kezzia) absconded from her owner Thomas Bean in New Brunswick. In his description of Keziah, Bean noted that she stood "about five feet high, has the marks of a cut and a burn, I believe, on her right cheek, near her mouth." This description of scarification on her face indicates that Keziah might have been born in Africa. According to the Book of Negroes, Bean had purchased her from another owner before they left New York for the Maritimes. In 1783, British officials described her as a "likely wench." Source: Book of Negroes; *Royal Gazette*, August 21, 1787.

649. KITTY (c. 1784) – Enslaved to Robert Mills, Kitty was described as "his property." Source: Muster Roll of Settlers at Chedabucto (including Departments of the Army and Navy), Chipman Papers, Muster Master General's Office, Loyalist Musters, 1776–1785, MG 23, D1, ser. I, vol. 24, LAC.

650. KNAPP, DINAH (c. 1783, age 29) – Enslaved to Captain Knapp, who migrated to the Maritimes after the American Revolution, Dinah was probably from New York. The two slave children belonging to Captain Knapp were probably Dinah's children. British officials at New York described her as a "stout wench." Source: Book of Negroes.

651. KNAPP, ALICE (c. 1783, age 6) – The daughter of Dinah, Alice was an enslaved child to Captain Knapp and migrated to the Maritimes with her mother and brother. Source: Book of Negroes.

652. KNAPP, JOB (c. 1783, age 1) – The son of Dinah, Job was enslaved to Captain Knapp and migrated to the Maritimes with his mother and sister. Source: Book of Negroes.

653. LAFFERTS, GILBERT (c. 1783, age 21) – Enslaved to James Henderson, who migrated to the Maritimes from New York, Gilbert was probably from North Carolina. British officials noted that he was "Henderson's possession, proved to be the property of Mr. James Henderson, Waggon Master & Bill of Sale produced." They also described him as a "likely lad." Source: Book of Negroes.

654. LAURENT (c. 1742) – Laurent was enslaved to Michel Rodrigue. Source: Donovan, "Nominal List of Slaves and Their Owners," 155.

655. LAURENT (c. 1744, age 15) – Enslaved to Leon Fautoux, Laurent was from the West Indies. Source: Donovan, "Nominal List of Slaves and Their Owners," 155.

656. LA VIELLE, JEAN (c. 1749) – Jean was enslaved to the Brothers of Charity in Louisbourg. Source: Donovan, "Nominal List of Slaves and Their Owners," 155.

657. LAWRENCE, LOUISE (c. 1745) – Enslaved to Laurent Meyracq, Louise came from New England. Source: Donovan, "Nominal List of Slaves and Their Owners," 156.

658. LAWRENCE, PETER (c. 1792) – In 1792, Peter Lawrence ran away from his owner along with another slave named Joe Odel. Their owners placed the following runaway advertisement in the local paper: "RUN AWAY, Joseph Odel and Peter Lawrence (Negroes) from their Masters, and left Digby last evening, the first mentioned is about Twenty four year of Age, five feet six Inches high, had on a light brown coat, red waistcoat and thickset breeches, took other cloaths with him, he is a likely young Fellow with remarkable white Teeth. – The other is about five Feet eight Inches high, very Black, had on lightesh coloured clothes. – Whoever will secure said Negroes so that their Masters may have them again, shall receive TEN DOLLARS Reward, and all reasonable Charges paid." Source: *Royal Gazette* (Nova Scotia), July 10, 1792.

659. LE NÈGRE (c. 1755) – This person was enslaved to a man who lived at Lake Catalogne. Source: Donovan, "Nominal List of Slaves and Their Owners," 159.

660. LEN (c. 1806/1820) – Enslaved to James Peters in New Brunswick, who planned to manumit Len on January 1, 1807, Len served the Peters family along with a female slave named Caro (Cairo). Source: Will of James Peters, Queens County, 1806/1820, PANB.

661. LETISHA (c. 1786) – Thomas Cornwell sold Letisha to Isaac and David Bonnell (or Bonnett) in Annapolis, Nova Scotia. She might have been the mother of Bonnell's three male slaves who were born in the 1790s (see entries for George, Tom, and Bob). Source: Harris, "Negro Population of the County of Annapolis," 17.

662. LETITIA (c. 1783, age 25) – Enslaved to Elias Bolner, who migrated to the Maritimes after the American Revolution, Letitia was described by British officials in New York as a "squat stout wench." Source: Book of Negroes.

663. LETITIA (c. 1783, age 16) – Enslaved to Benjamin Lester, who migrated to the Maritimes with four other slaves, Letitia was from New York. British officials in New York described her as a "stout wench." Source: Book of Negroes.

664. LETTIA (c. 1783, age 5) – Enslaved to Patrick Wall, who migrated to the Maritimes after the American Revolution with other slaves, Lettia was from Massachusetts. British officials in New York described her as a "fine child." Source: Book of Negroes.

665. LEWES (slave? c. 1784) – Lewes (Lewis?) was possibly enslaved to Colonel Hamilton, who migrated to Country Harbour with other southern Loyalists. The majority of these Loyalists and their slaves were from North Carolina, South Carolina, and Georgia. They had settled briefly in East Florida before moving to Nova Scotia. Black people at Country Harbour were either slaves or "quasi-free" and subject to re-enslavement. Abolitionist Thomas Clarkson explained the phenomenon of re-enslavement: "It was not long till these loyalists, many of whom had been educated with all the ideas of the justice of slavery, the inferiority of negroes, and the superiority of white men, that are universal in the southern provinces of America, began to harass and oppress the industrious black settlers, and even wantonly to deprive them of the fruits of their labour, expelling them from the lands they had cleared." Clarkson continued by noting that whites reduced "again to slavery those negroes who had so honourably obtained their freedom. They hired them as servants, and, at the end of the stipulated time, refused payment of their wages, insisting that they were slaves: in some instances they destroyed their tickets of freedom, and then enslaved the negroes for want of them; in several instances, the unfortunate Africans were taken onboard vessels, carried to the West Indies, and there sold for the benefit of their plunderers." At Country Harbour, Black people were listed on the musters as the "Servants" of a white Loyalist, which meant it was very easy for them to be re-enslaved if they were not already enslaved. Sources: Clarkson, "Some Account of the New Colony at Sierra Leone," 229–30; Settlers at Country Harbour, Chipman Papers, Muster Master General's Office, Loyalist Musters, 1776–1785, MG 23, D1, ser. I, vol.

24, LAC. Note: Ellen Wilson believed that the information Clarkson used came from Thomas Peters; see Wilson, *Loyal Blacks*, 181.

666. LEWIS (c. 1783, age 45) – Enslaved to Benjamin Lester, who went to the Maritimes with four other slaves, Lewis was from New York. Given the ages of Lewis and the other slaves, it is possible they were a family, but the mother seems to be missing from the shipping records. British officials in New York described Lewis as a "stout fellow." Source: Book of Negroes.

667. LIBERTY (c. 1783, age 25) – Enslaved to Captain Dunbar, who migrated to the Maritimes from New York after the American Revolution, British officials in New York noted that Liberty "acknowledges to have been purchased by the Capt. At the West Indies 17 years ago." These same officials described him as a "stout fellow." Source: Book of Negroes.

668. LIBERTY (c. 1784) – Liberty was enslaved to Loyalist James Lysle (probably Lyle) in Nova Scotia along with Sarah and Pegg, a mother and daughter, whose relationship to Liberty is unclear. Liberty was possibly from Savannah, Georgia. Source: Loyalists from Saint Augustine bound to Chedabucto, July 1784, Chipman Papers, Muster Master General's Office, Loyalist Musters, 1776–1785, MG 23, D1, ser. I, vol. 24, LAC; Harriet Cunningham Hart, *History of the County of Guysborough, Nova Scotia* (1877; repr. Guysborough: Guysborough Historical Society, 2016), 250–2.

669. LIDGE (c. 1786–1816, age 4 in 1786) – Maryland Loyalist Caleb Jones brought Lidge to New Brunswick as a child after the American Revolution. In 1786, several of Jones's adult slaves ran away and took Lidge with them. In a runaway notice, Jones commented "NANCY about 24 years old, who took with her a Negro child, about four years old called LIDGE." It is unclear if Nancy was Lidge's mother or some other type of relation. In 1816, Lidge attempted to escape from Jones again. The runaway advertisement is telling: "On the night of the 15th June, a Negro Slave, called LIDGE, under five feet high, broad face and very large lips; brought him from Maryland with my family; – he took with him a large CANOE with a Lathe across her; tared on the outside of the head with raw Tar, which looks red – he was seen going down the River[.] Any person that will apprehend him and get the canoe, shall receive the above reward." Source: *Royal Gazette* (New Brunswick), July 25, 1786; *Royal Gazette* (New Brunswick), July 9, 1816.

670. LILLY (c. 1783, age 12) – Enslaved to James Fraser or Frazer, who migrated to the Maritimes from New York with one other slave, Lilly was probably from South Carolina. British officials described her as a "fine girl." Source: Book of Negroes.

671. LILLY (c. 1783, age 30) – Enslaved to William Wilbank, who migrated to the Maritimes after the American Revolution, Lilly brought her daughter (the placement and wording in the Book of Negroes indicates that Lilly was Leah's mother). British officials in New York described her as a "stout wench." Source: Book of Negroes.

672. LEAH (c. 1783, age 4) – Enslaved to William Wilbank, who went to the Maritimes also with her mother, Leah was described by British officials in New York as a "fine child." Source: Book of Negroes.

673. LOIS (c. 1806) – Lois was an enslaved "mulatto" child of Mrs. Tritton, who had her baptized (possibly Lois Tritton – see entry). Source: List of Baptisms, May 1, 1806, Cornwallis Township Book, NSA.

674. LONDON (c. 1787, age 18) – London was an enslaved man of Connecticut Loyalist Joseph Clarke in New Brunswick. London attempted to escape multiple times. In 1785, Miles Urion (or Union) sheltered London, refused to return him to Clarke, and then took him to Digby, Nova Scotia. Clarke's legal action against Urion was trover and conversion, which meant that Clarke wanted to recover the value of London, whom Urion had converted to his own use. He successfully recovered London, who again ran away in 1787. Source: *Joseph Clarke v. Miles Urion*, 1786, RS 42, Supreme Court Original Jurisdiction Records, PANB; for more context on Saint John, see Bell, *Early Loyalist Saint John,* and *Royal Gazette* (New Brunswick), August 17, 1787.

675. LONDON (c. 1783, age 68) – Enslaved to Thomas Bosworth, who migrated to the Maritimes after the American Revolution, London might have been from New York but given his age it seems possible that he came from Africa. British officials at New York described him as a cooper and "worn out." Source: Book of Negroes.

676. LONGFORD (slave? c. 1752) – Longford was aboard a vessel that left coastal New Hampshire for Louisbourg. It seems likely that he remained enslaved, but some Black sailors enjoyed a modicum of freedom during work on the high seas. Source: Donovan, "Slaves and Their Owners in Île Royale, 1713–1760," 9.

677. LOOSELY, JACK (c. 1783, age 28) – Jack was enslaved to Charles Loosely, who migrated to the Maritimes from New York along with a teenager indentured to Loosely. Jack was described by British officials as a "stout fellow." Source: Book of Negroes.

678. LOUIS (c. 1752) – Louis was enslaved to an unknown person living in Louisbourg. Source: Donovan, "Nominal List of Slaves and Their Owners," 157.

679. LOUISA (c. 1767) – Halifax merchant Charles Proctor sold Louisa, a mixed-race slave ("Mulotta"), to Mary Wood for £15. Source: Smith, "Slave in Canada," 14–15.

680. LOUISE (c. 1755, age 20) – Louise was enslaved to Louis La Groix, who also had another slave named Cezar (see entry). Their owner had long been involved in the trade between the West Indies and Louisbourg. Louise died at the age of 20. Source: Donovan, "Slaves in Île Royale," 35.

681. LUCIA (slave? c. 1762) – One of two young Black girls who were baptized at St. Paul's Church in Halifax, it is likely that both Lucia and the other girl were enslaved. Source: Smith, "Slave in Canada," 85.

682. LUCY (c. 1783, age 16) – Enslaved to Albert Vanshant, who migrated to the Maritimes from New York, Lucy was described by British officials as a "stout wench, mulatto." Source: Book of Negroes.

683. LUCY (slave? c. 1784) – Lucy was possibly enslaved to Captain Daniel McNeill (also spelled MacNeil and McNeil), who migrated to Country Harbour with other southern Loyalists. The majority of these Loyalists and their slaves were from North Carolina, South Carolina, and Georgia. They had settled briefly in East Florida before moving to Nova Scotia. Black people at Country Harbour were either slaves or "quasi-free" and subject to re-enslavement. Abolitionist Thomas Clarkson explained the phenomenon of re-enslavement: "It was not long till these loyalists, many of whom had been educated with all the ideas of the justice of slavery, the inferiority of negroes, and the superiority of white men, that are universal in the southern provinces of America, began to harass and oppress the industrious black settlers, and even wantonly to deprive them of the fruits of their labour, expelling them from the lands they had cleared." Clarkson continued by noting that whites reduced "again to slavery those negroes who had so honourably obtained their freedom. They hired them as servants, and, at the end of the stipulated time, refused payment of their wages, insisting that they were slaves: in some instances they destroyed their tickets of freedom, and then enslaved the negroes for want of them; in several instances, the unfortunate Africans were taken onboard vessels, carried to the West Indies, and there sold for the benefit of their plunderers." At Country Harbour, Black people were listed on the musters as the "Servants" of a white Loyalist, which meant it was very easy for them to be re-enslaved if they were not already enslaved. Sources: Clarkson, "Some Account of the New Colony at Sierra Leone," 229–30; Settlers at Country Harbour, Chipman Papers, Muster Master General's Office, Loyalist Musters, 1776–1785, MG 23, D1, ser. I, vol. 24, LAC. Note: Ellen Wilson believed that the information Clarkson used came from Thomas Peters; see Wilson, *Loyal Blacks*, 181.

684. LUCY (ca. 1780s/1790s) – An enslaved woman who was traded between Joseph Wesley and William Taylor. The transcribed document on the website blackloyalist.com is not clear about her owner. The document reads "Received of Joseph Wesley a Negro Slave named Lucy in full payment of his note of hand with interest amount of seventy pounds sterling. And I do hereby promise to the said Joseph Wesley that I will return him the above mentioned Negro slave Lucy except death desertion or any other unforeseen accident prevent it. If he pays to me the above mentioned sum of seventy pounds sterling within the term of six months from this date whereof witness my hand. William Taylor." Source: https://blackloyalist.com/cdc/documents /official/joseph_wesley_lucy.htm.

685. LUCY (c. 1797) – Lucy was enslaved to Munson Jarvis, who sold her and a man named Abraham to Abraham de Peyster in Saint John, New Brunswick. Source: David Russell Jack, "General John Watts de Peyster," *Acadiensis* 7, no. 3 (July 1907): 290.

686. LUDLOW, EDWARD (slave? c. 1788) – Edward was possibly an enslaved person who was baptized along with several other Black people in New Brunswick. Source: Early Parish Records, New Brunswick, September 14, 1788, possibly PANB.

687. LUKE (c. 1792, age 11) – Thomas Chandler sold Luke to Charles Dixon. Source: Luke, Bill of Sale, January 27, 1792; the archive is unclear because it lacks a stamp.

688. LUTHER, ISAAC (c. 1791, age 20) – Isaac was probably enslaved to Peter Parker of the ship *Friends Adventure*. The master of the ship asked that Isaac be apprehended and delivered to either Shelburne merchants Charles Hill or Richard Townshend (or Townsend). The runaway advertisement described Isaac as "part of the Mulatto breed" and mentioned that Isaac spoke good English and took several clothing items with him. Source: *Royal Gazette*, July 12, 1791.

689. LYDDY (slave? c. 1784) – Lyddy was possibly enslaved to George Westphal, who planned to settle near Halifax. Westphal had six Black people living in his household. Source: Loyalists and Disbanded Troops at Cole Harbour, Chipman Papers, Muster Master General's Office, Loyalist Musters, 1776–1785, MG 23, D1, ser. I, vol. 24, LAC.

690. LYDIA (slave? c. 1788) – Possibly enslaved to Colonel Ludlow of New Brunswick. Source: Smith, "Slave in Canada," 86.

691. LYMAS (c. 1784) – John Wentworth sent Lymas and 18 other slaves from Nova Scotia to his "relation" Paul Wentworth in Suriname. Wentworth described these slaves as, "American born or well seasoned, and are perfectly stout, healthy, sober, orderly, Industrious, & obedient." Wentworth had the slaves Christened and claimed to be concerned for their welfare. He noted that "Lymas is a rough carpenter & Sawyer." Source: John Wentworth to Paul Wentworth or his attorney, February 24, 1784.

692. LYNCH, TINNIA (c. 1783, age 25) – Tinnia was enslaved to Peter Lynch, who migrated to the Maritimes from New York with her child Sally and another slave named Joseph Skinner. Tinnia was probably from New Jersey as her first owner, Thomas Skinner, was from Amboy. British officials described her as a "stout wench." Source: Book of Negroes.

693. LYNCH, SALLY (c. 1783, age 6) – Probably the daughter of Tinnia and enslaved to Peter Lynch, Sally was described by British officials as a "fine girl." Source: Book of Negroes.

694. MADELAINE (c. 1749) – Madelaine was enslaved to the Brothers of Charity in Louisbourg. Source: Donovan, "Nominal List of Slaves and Their Owners," 155.

695. MALFICH (c. 1736) – Malfich was enslaved to Bertrand Larreguy. Source: Donovan, "Nominal List of Slaves and Their Owners," 158.

696. MANUEL (c. 1786) – Enslaved to Delaware Loyalist Thomas Robinson, Manuel was given by Robinson to a relative in his will originally filed in Shelburne, Nova Scotia. Source: Will of Thomas Robinson, Shelburne County, 1786/1787, NSA.

697. MARCH (c. 1784) – Enslaved to Georgia Loyalist John Todd at Chedabucto, Nova Scotia, along with several other slaves, March and the other slaves were probably from Georgia, South Carolina, East Florida, or another southern state. Source: Loyalists from Saint Augustine bound to Chedabucto, July 1784, Chipman Papers, Muster Master General's Office, Loyalist Musters, 1776–1785, MG 23, D1, ser. I, vol. 24, LAC.

698. MARCH (c. 1783) – March was enslaved to Ranald MacKinnon, who migrated from Scotland to the Maritimes. Eventually, MacKinnon settled at Argyle on the south shore of Nova Scotia during the mid-1760s. MacKinnon's nephew John wrote a letter from London, which stated "I have sent you March, who is a black boy and who it cost me some pains to procure for you." Source: Robart-Johnson, *Africa's Children*, 37.

699. MARGUERITE (c. 1738) – Marguerite was enslaved to Madame De la Valliere. Sources: Donovan, "Female Slaves as Sexual Victims in Île Royale," 149; Donovan, "Nominal List of Slaves and Their Owners," 158.

700. JOSEPH (c. 1739) – Joseph was a child of Marguerite. Sources: Donovan, "Female Slaves as Sexual Victims in Île Royale," 149; Donovan, "Nominal List of Slaves and Their Owners," 158.

701. ANGELIQUE (c. 1743) – Angelique was a child of Marguerite. Sources: Donovan, "Female Slaves as Sexual Victims in Île Royale," 149; Donovan, "Nominal List of Slaves and Their Owners," 158.

702. MARIA (c. 1783, age 21) – Enslaved to Captain Campbell, who migrated to the Maritimes from New York, Maria was accompanied by her child and was from New Jersey. British officials described her as a "stout wench." They also noted that she had previously been a slave "to Mr. McRae, Hatter, New Jersey, who sold her to Mr. Burton, New York, & has since been purchased as she says by Capt. Campbell." Source: Book of Negroes.

703. MINGO (c. 1783, document unclear on age) – Mingo was the son of Maria and enslaved to Captain Campbell, who migrated to the Maritimes. Source: Book of Negroes.

704. MARIA (slave? c. 1788) – Maria was possibly enslaved to Colonel Ludlow of New Brunswick. Source: Smith, "Slave in Canada," 86.

705. MARIANNA (c. 1783, age 29) – Enslaved to Courtney Taylor, who migrated to the Maritimes from New York with one other slave. British officials in New York described Marianna as a "stout wench." Source: Book of Negroes.

706. MARIANNE (c. 1787) – Enslaved to Margret Murray of Halifax, Marianne lived with two other slaves, including a child named Brutus. Murray freed the two adult slaves, Flora and Marianne, in her will. Source: Will of Margaret Murray, 1787, Halifax County, NSA; Smith, "Slave in Canada," 91.

707. MARIE (c. 1754) – Marie was enslaved to the Villejoint family. Source: Donovan, "Nominal List of Slaves and Their Owners," 159.

708. MARIE (c. 1749) – Marie was enslaved to Philippe Beaubassin. Source: Donovan, "Nominal List of Slaves and Their Owners," 157.

709. MARIE (c. 1743) – Marie was an enslaved woman who gave birth to twins. Source: Donovan, "Female Slaves as Sexual Victims in Île Royale," 149.

710. MADELINE (c. 1743) – Madeline was the infant daughter of Marie. Source: Donovan, "Female Slaves as Sexual Victims in Île Royale," 149.

711. GENEVIEVE (c. 1743) – Genevieve was the infant daughter of Marie. Source: Donovan, "Female Slaves as Sexual Victims in Île Royale," 149.

712. MARIE (c. 1743) – Enslaved to the powerful merchant Jean Pere, Marie was probably sexually abused by him. Source: Donovan, "Female Slaves as Sexual Victims in Île Royale," 153–6.

713. MADELAINE (c. 1743) – Madelaine was the daughter of Marie and enslaved to powerful merchant Jean Pere. Source: Donovan, "Female Slaves as Sexual Victims in Île Royale," 153.

714. MARIE (c. 1756) – Marie was an enslaved woman who gave birth to Victor. Source: Donovan, "Female Slaves as Sexual Victims in Île Royale," 150.

715. VICTOR (c. 1756) – Victor was the infant son of Marie. Source: Donovan, "Female Slaves as Sexual Victims in Île Royale," 150.

716. MARIE ANNE (c. 1753) – Marie Anne was enslaved and gave birth to a son. Source: Donovan, "Female Slaves as Sexual Victims in Île Royale," 150.

717. JOSEPH (c. 1753) – Joseph was the infant son of Marie Anne. Source: Donovan, "Female Slaves as Sexual Victims in Île Royale," 150.

718. MARIE ANNE (c. 1754) – Marie Anne was enslaved to Jean B. D. Estimanville. Source: Donovan, "Nominal List of Slaves and Their Owners," 159.

719. MARIE ANNE (c. 1753) – Enslaved to M. Des Noyes, Marie Anne had a young child named Joseph. Source: Donovan, "Nominal List of Slaves and Their Owners," 157.

720. JOSEPH (c. 1753) – Joseph was the infant son of Marie Anne. Source: Donovan, "Nominal List of Slaves and Their Owners," 157.

721. MARIE CLEMENCE (c. 1754) – Marie Clemence was enslaved to Antoine Rodrigue. Source: Donovan, "Nominal List of Slaves and Their Owners," 159.

722. MARIE FLORE (c. 1741, age 1) – Originally from Martinique, ship's Captain Jean Boullot brought Marie Flore to Île Royale. Boullot traded various goods (including slaves) between Martinique and Île Royale. Marie grew up in the Boullot household and served as a nanny and servant. Historian Ken Donovan notes that Marie "was likely Boullot's daughter. Describing her in 1762, Boullot noted that 'he kept a creole from Martinique at his home for approximately 20 years.'" She had a son named Denis. Sources: Donovan, "Slaves in Île Royale," 35; Donovan, "Female Slaves as Sexual Victims in Île Royale," 150.

723. DENIS (c. 1758) – Denis was the infant son of Marie Flore. Source: Donovan, "Female Slaves as Sexual Victims in Île Royale," 150.

724. MARIE LOUISE (c. 1736) – Originally from Africa, Marie Louise had the misfortune of becoming the slave of merchant Louis Jouet. She served him for many years, giving birth to seven "illegitimate" slave children. In 1754, she married a poor white man named Louis Coustard. Marie Louise bore him two children who were free since Coustard was white. Sources: Donovan, "Nominal List of Slaves and Their Owners," 154; Donovan, "Female Slaves as Sexual Victims in Île Royale," 149; Donovan, "Slaves and Their Owners in Île Royale," 30.

725. JEAN BAPTISTE (c. 1736) – Jean Baptiste was the enslaved son of Marie Louise and probably her owner Louis Jouet. Sources: Donovan, "Nominal List of Slaves and Their Owners," 154; Donovan, "Female Slaves as Sexual Victims in Île Royale," 149.

726. ISABELLE (c. 1737) – Isabelle was the enslaved daughter of Marie Louise and probably her owner Louis Jouet. Sources: Donovan, "Nominal List of Slaves and Their Owners," 154; Donovan, "Female Slaves as Sexual Victims in Île Royale," 149.

727. JACQUES (c. 1739) – Jacques was the enslaved son of Marie Louise and probably her owner Louis Jouet. Source: Donovan, "Nominal List of Slaves and Their Owners," 154; Donovan, "Female Slaves as Sexual Victims in Île Royale," 149.

728. MARIE JEANNE (c. 1742) – Marie Jeanne was the enslaved daughter of Marie Louise and probably her owner Louis Jouet. Source: Donovan, "Nominal List of Slaves and Their Owners," 154; Donovan, "Female Slaves as Sexual Victims in Île Royale," 149.

729. CATHERINE (c. 1743) – Catherine was the enslaved daughter of Marie Louise and probably her owner Louis Jouet. Sources: Donovan, "Nominal List of Slaves and Their Owners," 154; Donovan, "Female Slaves as Sexual Victims in Île Royale," 149.

730. JEAN PIERRE (c. 1749) – Jean Pierre was the enslaved son of Marie Louise and probably her owner Louis Jouet. Sources: Donovan, "Nominal List of Slaves and Their Owners," 154; Donovan, "Female Slaves as Sexual Victims in Île Royale," 149.

731. JEAN CHARLES (c. 1753) – Jean Charles was the enslaved son of Marie Louise and probably her owner Louis Jouet. Sources: Donovan, "Nominal List of Slaves and Their Owners," 154; Donovan, "Female Slaves as Sexual Victims in Île Royale," 149.

732. MARIE THÉRÈSE (c. 1730, age 15) – Enslaved to Charles J. Dailleboust, Marie Thérèse had three children between 1734 and 1738. Source: Donovan, "Nominal List of Slaves and Their Owners," 152.

733. MARIE FRANÇOISE (c. 1734) – Marie Françoise was the daughter of Marie Thérèse. Source: Donovan, "Nominal List of Slaves and Their Owners," 152.

734. MARIE ANGELIQUE (c. 1738) – Marie Angelique was the daughter of Marie Thérèse. Source: Donovan, "Nominal List of Slaves and Their Owners," 152.

735. CLAUDE (c. 1738) – Claude was the son of Marie Thérèse. Source: Donovan, "Nominal List of Slaves and Their Owners," 152.

736. MARGARET (c. 1783, age 15) – Enslaved to James Irwin, who migrated to the Maritimes after the American Revolution, Margaret was probably from New York. British officials in New York described her as a "fine wench." Source: Book of Negroes.

737. MARGARET (c. 1783, age 19) – Enslaved to Timothy Clows (or Clowes), who migrated to the Maritimes from New York, Margaret was accompanied by her daughter and was probably from New York. British officials described her as a "stout wench with a girl 3 years old." Source: Book of Negroes.

738. UNNAMED DAUGHTER (c. 1783, age 3) – She was enslaved to Timothy Clows, who migrated to the Maritimes, and she came with her mother, Margaret. Source: Book of Negroes.

739. MARGARET (c. 1790) – Margaret was an enslaved female who was baptized in Annapolis, Nova Scotia, in 1790. The recorder noted that she and two other slaves belonged to John Polhemus. It is unclear if she is included in the 1807 Digby slaveholder petition, where Polhemus noted he owned 10 slaves. Source: Register of Baptisms, February 1790, St. Luke's Anglican Church, Annapolis Royal, Annapolis County.

740. MARSHALL, GEORGE (c. 1770) – George Marshall was enslaved to Joseph Gerrish and was later sold along with two other slaves for £150. Source: Smith, "Slave in Canada," 13; States and Smardz Frost, "Section 5: King's College Students and Slavery Selected Biographies," 9.

741. MARTIN (c. 1786) – Enslaved to Matthew Harris, Martin was described as a "mulatto." Apparently, the Reverend James McGregor, an anti-slavery devotee, encouraged Harris to free Martin "on condition of a certain term of good service." Harris had previously owned 12-year-old Abram in 1779, whom he had sold away. Source: Smith, "Slave in Canada," 57.

742. MARTIN, PHEBE (c. 1786) – Enslaved to Rebel William Martin, Phebe Martin ran away during the war to Ninety-Six, South Carolina, and gained her freedom. After a short time in St. Augustine, she removed to Nova Scotia and also "lived with [Captain?] Hamilton." She claimed that she "was never [Hamilton's] slave, or ever received any Wages from him." Molly Sinclair had been born in Charleston and lived with her master, James Sinclair, for most of her life. During the Revolution, she "was taken, with the other Plantation Negros" to Charleston. She went to St. Augustine before settling in Country Harbour with Colonel Hamilton. Although these Black Loyalists were free subjects of His Majesty, they found that freedom in the Maritime colonies could be fleeting at best. Moses Reed and Jameson Davis were "two years in the Service of Colonel Hamilton" and "received no wages." After two years of being re-enslaved, these captive labourers resorted to escaping from their would-be master by travelling to distant Halifax where they hoped to be safe. At this point Hamilton, along with Captain Daniel McNeil, organized what can only be termed a slave patrol, which attempted to recapture the escaped labourers. The slave catchers found the four runaways, put them in irons, and locked them in a ship's hold, but not before they beat Jameson Davis with a "Cudgell." Molly Sinclair recalled "she was Chained to Moses Reed when put on the vessell." The re-enslaved men and women were taken to Shelburne, but before they could be shipped away local officials got word of their condition and ordered McNeil to bring them ashore for an inquiry and court investigation. McNeil claimed that he had been told to take the re-enslaved Black Loyalists to Shelburne and give them to a Mr. Dean, who "was to give him a Receipt for them, and, as he understood, was to carry them to the Bahamas." After hearing the testimony of the four men and women along with McNeil's statement, the Shelburne court considered whether the Blacks were the rightful property of Hamilton (there was no evidence such as a bill of sale) or should go free. The majority of the court, five in favour of freeing them and two against, decided that "the aforesaid Negros" would be allowed to "go where they pleased." Source: Special Sessions at Shelburne, August 5, 1786, Shelburne Records, MG 4, vol. 141, NSA; Settlers at Country Harbour, Chipman Papers, Muster Master General's Office, Loyalist Musters, 1776–1785, MG 23, D1, ser. I, vol. 24, LAC; Troxler, "Hidden from History." See also Troxler, "Southern Loyalists' Claim on East Florida," 582–90; Troxler, "Loyalist Refugees and the British Evacuation of East Florida," 1–28; Troxler, "Migration of Carolina and Georgia Loyalists to Nova Scotia and New Brunswick." There were two Hamilton's, one a captain and the other a colonel.

743. MARY (c. 1783, age 14) – Enslaved to Dr. Henry Mallow, who migrated to the Maritimes after the American Revolution, British officials at New York described Mary as a "stout wench." Source: Book of Negroes.

744. MARY (c. 1783, age 36) – Enslaved to John Van Winkle, who migrated to the Maritimes from New York after the American Revolution, Mary was accompanied by her two children and was probably from New Jersey. British officials described her as a "stout wench." Source: Book of Negroes.

745. SALLY (c. 1783, age 6 months) – Sally was a child of Mary and enslaved to John Van Winkle. Source: Book of Negroes.

746. JACKEY (c. 1783, age 3) – Jackey was a child of Mary and enslaved to John Van Winkle. Source: Book of Negroes.

747. MARY (c. 1783, age 20) – Enslaved to John Polhemus, who migrated to the Maritimes after the American Revolution, Mary had with her an infant daughter named Dinah and was probably from New York. British officials at New York described her as a "likely wench." It is possible that Mary and her daughter are listed among the 10 adult slaves of Polhemus in the 1807 Digby petition, but this is unclear. Source: Book of Negroes.

748. DINAH (c. 1783, age 6 months) – Dinah was the daughter of Mary and also enslaved to John Polhemus. Source: Book of Negroes.

749. MARY (c. 1783, age 41) – Enslaved to Ensign Cheace or Chase, who migrated to the Maritimes after the American Revolution, Mary was probably from New York. British officials in New York described her as an "ordinary wench." Source: Book of Negroes.

750. MARY (slave? c. 1801) – According to William Bailey, Mary was "bound to serve the said William as a Servant for her life time by her free consent." In 1801, at the New Brunswick Supreme Court, Mary and her husband, Isaac York, claimed that Bailey had wrongfully imprisoned Mary for 10 days after she was no longer his slave. Bailey, through his attorney, denied any wrongdoing. Source: *Isaac York v. William Bailey*, 1801, RG 42 Supreme Court Jurisdiction Records, PANB.

751. MARY ANNE (c. 1783, age 43) – Enslaved to Bartholomew Coxeter, who migrated to the Maritimes after the American Revolution, Mary Anne was accompanied by her 12-year-old daughter, Rebecca, and was probably from New York. British officials in New York described her as a "stout wench." Source: Book of Negroes.

752. REBECCA (c. 1783, age 12) – The daughter of Mary Anne and enslaved to Bartholomew Coxeter, who migrated to the Maritimes after the American

Revolution, British officials in New York described Rebecca as a "likely girl."
Source: Book of Negroes.

753. MARY JANE (c. 1828, age 13) – Mary Jane was enslaved to the Ormsby family of Prince Edward Island. In the Montserrat slave registry of 1828, a notation was made that listed four slaves of the Ormsby household who were living in Prince Edward Island: "I Matthew William Blake (for Catharine Ormsby) do swear that the Return now by me delivered to be registered contains to the best of my knowledge and belief a true faithful and accurate account and description of all the Slaves belonging to Catharine Ormsby and being within this Island (Save and Except the following Slaves of the Names as follows Charles Male Black Twenty Years, Mary Jane Female Black Thirteen Years, Fanny Female Coloured Eleven Years, Edward Male Black Eight Years, residing with Mr. Ormsby at Prince Edward Island)." Source: December 13, 1828, Montserrat Slave Register, TNA. The author thanks Mr. Neil How of the Montserrat National Trust, Montserrat, West Indies, for sharing this document.

754. MASO (c. 1784, age 9) – Maso was enslaved to John Grant. Originally from Scotland, after serving the British army near Ticonderoga during the Seven Years War Grant settled in Queens County, Long Island. After the American Revolution, he settled in Nova Scotia with a large family and nine slaves. These enslaved people might have been a family unit. Sources: Cottreau-Robins, "Landscape of Slavery in Loyalist Era Nova Scotia," 131–2; also Smith, "Slave in Canada," 93–4.

755. MATTHEW (c. 1784) – In 1784, John Wentworth sent 19 slaves to Suriname from Halifax. He kept two slaves with him: Matthew and Susannah. Source: John Wentworth to Paul Wentworth or his attorney, February 24, 1784.

756. MELINDA (c. 1783, age 11) – Enslaved to Major Menzies, who migrated to the Maritimes from New York with another young slave, British officials noted that Melinda had been "Born & bred in the Major's family." These officials described her as a "likely girl." Source: Book of Negroes.

757. MERCURY (c. 1783, age 20) – Enslaved to Dr. Wright of Halifax, who migrated to the Maritimes after the American Revolution, it is possible that Mercury was from Nova Scotia, but this is unclear. British officials in New York described him as a "likely lad." Source: Book of Negroes.

758. MERRIT, ISRAEL (c. 1783, age 25) – Enslaved to Captain Kipp, who migrated to the Maritimes after the American Revolution, Israel was probably from New York. The British official at New York described him as a "stout fellow." Source: Book of Negroes.

759. MICHAEL (slave? c. 1784) – Michael was possibly enslaved to John Legett, who migrated to Country Harbour with other southern Loyalists (consisting of various regiments such as the Royal North Carolina Regiment and the King's Carolina Rangers). The majority of these Loyalists and their slaves were from North Carolina, South Carolina, and Georgia. They had settled briefly in East Florida before moving to Nova Scotia. According to historian Carole Watterson Troxler, Legett had seven "servants" who were probably enslaved. A muster roll shows that Michael and Phillis remained in Country Harbour in June 1784 while the other five "servants" were likely in Halifax. In 1797, Michael and Phillis appear in the record of the birth of their daughter, Dinah. Black people at Country Harbour were either slaves or "quasi-free" and subject to re-enslavement. Abolitionist Thomas Clarkson explained the phenomenon of re-enslavement: "It was not long till these loyalists, many of whom had been educated with all the ideas of the justice of slavery, the inferiority of negroes, and the superiority of white men, that are universal in the southern provinces of America, began to harass and oppress the industrious black settlers, and even wantonly to deprive them of the fruits of their labour, expelling them from the lands they had cleared." Clarkson continued by noting that whites reduced "again to slavery those negroes who had so honourably obtained their freedom. They hired them as servants, and, at the end of the stipulated time, refused payment of their wages, insisting that they were slaves: in some instances they destroyed their tickets of freedom, and then enslaved the negroes for want of them; in several instances, the unfortunate Africans were taken onboard vessels, carried to the West Indies, and there sold for the benefit of their plunderers." At Country Harbour, Black people were listed on the musters as the "Servants" of a white Loyalist, which meant it was very easy for them to be re-enslaved if they were not already enslaved. Sources: Carole Watterson Troxler, "'The Great Man of the Settlement': North Carolina's John Legett at Country Harbour, Nova Scotia, 1783–1812," *North Carolina History Review* 67, no. 3 (July 1990), 285–314; Clarkson, "Some Account of the New Colony at Sierra Leone," 229–30; Settlers at Country Harbour, Chipman Papers, Muster Master General's Office, Loyalist Musters, 1776–1785, MG 23, D1, ser. I, vol. 24, LAC. Note: Ellen Wilson believed that the information Clarkson used came from Thomas Peters; see Wilson, *Loyal Blacks*, 181.

760. PHILLIS (slave? c. 1784) – Phillis was possibly enslaved to Captain John Legett, who along with other southern Loyalists (consisting of various regiments such as the Royal North Carolina Regiment and the King's Carolina Rangers) settled at Country Harbour, Nova Scotia. The majority of these settlers and their slaves were from North Carolina, South Carolina, and Georgia. They had settled briefly in East Florida before moving to Nova Scotia. In a letter to Colonel Edward Winslow discussing these southern settlers, William Shaw expressed surprise that some of the Blacks with these southern settlers were not slaves; but his wording, as historian Carole Watterson Troxler notes, meant that some were "indeed slaves." In fact, as she points out, Blacks at Country Harbour were denied any land grants, and those who were not slaves were "quasi-free." A muster roll shows that Michael and Phillis remained in Country Harbour in June 1784 while Legett's five other slaves were likely in Halifax. In an article, abolitionist Thomas Clarkson described what some white Loyalists did to supposedly free Black Loyalists: "It was not long till these loyalists, many of whom had been educated with all the ideas of the justice of slavery, the inferiority of negroes, and the superiority of white men, that are universal in the southern provinces of America, began to harass and oppress the industrious black settlers, and even wantonly to deprive them of the fruits of their labour, expelling them from the lands they had cleared." Clarkson continued by noting that whites reduced "again to slavery those negroes who had so honourably obtained their freedom. They hired them as servants, and, at the end of the stipulated time, refused payment of their wages, insisting that they were slaves: in some instances they destroyed their tickets of freedom, and then enslaved the negroes for want of them; in several instances, the unfortunate Africans were taken onboard vessels, carried to the West Indies, and there sold for the benefit of their plunderers." In the case of Black people at Country Harbour, they were listed on the musters as the "Servants" of a white Loyalist, which meant it was very easy for them to be re-enslaved if they were not already enslaved. Sources: Troxler, "John Legett at Country Harbour," 310; Clarkson, "Some Account of the New Colony at Sierra Leone," 229–30; Settlers at Country Harbour, Chipman Papers, Muster Master General's Office, Loyalist Musters, 1776–1785, MG 23, D1, ser. I, vol. 24, LAC. Note: Ellen Wilson believed that the information Clarkson used came from Thomas Peters; see Wilson, *Loyal Blacks*, 181.

761. DINAH (slave? c. 1797) – Daughter of Michael and Phillis, it is unknown if Dinah was ever enslaved. She married Jacob Syms, and, after his death, she regularly fished, did housework for others, and boated 100 miles to Halifax to purchase flour with money she made from knitting. Source: Troxler, "John Legett at Country Harbour," 310–11.

762. MILLER, JOE (c. 1783, age 12) – Enslaved to Moses Miller, who migrated to the Maritimes after the American Revolution, Joe was probably from New York. British officials at New York described him as a "likely boy." Source: Book of Negroes.

763. MIMA (c. 1783, age 26) – Enslaved to John Cook, who migrated to the Maritimes after the American Revolution, British officials at New York noted her owner had purchased Mima 13 years earlier and described her as a "stout wench." Source: Book of Negroes.

764. MINGO (c. 1785) – Enslaved to Captain Callbeck, Mingo was involved in the Jupiter Wise conspiracy to steal rum, have a party, and escape to Boston. He told the other conspirators that his master had "just been beating him" and he wanted to run away (see Jupiter Wise). Sources: *King v. Jupiter Wise*, 1786, PAROPEI; Holman, "Slaves and Servants on Prince Edward Island," 100–4; Hornby, *Black Islanders*, 15–19.

765. MINTUR (c. 1779) – In 1779 Joseph Northup sold Mintur to John Palmer for £100, which was an exceedingly high price and indicates the value that both men placed on him. According to the Nova Scotia Archives virtual exhibit on slavery, Mintur eventually gained his freedom, married, and had a son named Freeman. Source: Bill of Sale, 1779, MG 100, vol. 14, #113, NSA; https://novascotia.ca/archives /africanns/archives.asp?ID=13.

766. MOLL (c. 1751) – Enslaved to Louisbourg merchant Pierre Augruax, who decided to free Moll after he died, Moll came to Île Royale from New England. Source: Donovan, "Slaves and Their Owners in Île Royale," 23.

767. MOLLY (slave? c. 1784) – Molly was possibly enslaved to Lieutenant Cameron, who migrated to Country Harbour with other southern Loyalists. The majority of these Loyalists and their slaves were from North Carolina, South Carolina, and Georgia. They had settled briefly in East Florida before moving to Nova Scotia. Black people at Country Harbour were either slaves or "quasi-free" and subject to re-enslavement. Abolitionist Thomas Clarkson explained the phenomenon of re-enslavement: "It was not long till these loyalists, many of whom had been educated with all the ideas of the justice of slavery, the inferiority of negroes, and the superiority of white men, that are universal in the southern provinces of America, began to harass and oppress the industrious black settlers, and even wantonly to deprive them of the fruits of their labour, expelling them from the lands they had cleared." Clarkson continued by noting that whites reduced "again to slavery those negroes who had so honourably obtained their freedom. They hired them as servants, and, at the end of the stipulated time, refused payment of their wages, insisting that they were slaves: in some instances they destroyed their tickets of freedom, and then enslaved the negroes for want of them; in several instances, the unfortunate Africans were taken onboard vessels, carried to the West Indies, and there sold for the benefit of their plunderers." At Country Harbour, Black people were listed on the musters as the "Servants" of a white Loyalist, which meant it was very easy for them to be re-enslaved if they were not already enslaved. Sources: Clarkson, "Some Account of the New Colony at Sierra Leone," 229–30; Settlers at Country Harbour, Chipman Papers, Muster Master General's Office, Loyalist Musters, 1776–1785, MG 23, D1, ser. I, vol. 24, LAC. Note: Ellen Wilson believed that the information Clarkson used came from Thomas Peters; see Wilson, *Loyal Blacks*, 181.

768. MOORE, JOSHUA (c. 1786, age 20) – Joshua was enslaved to Frederick William Hecht, who manumitted him a few years after Hecht migrated to New Brunswick. Joshua was born in New York City in 1766 and Hecht described him as a "Molatto Man." Source: Manumission of Joshua Moore, Registered City of Saint John, December 21, 1786, 145. This document is probably from either the New Brunswick Museum or Provincial Archives of New Brunswick. The author has two photocopies of this document, but not the identifying repository.

769. MOORE, NED (c. 1783, age 45) – Enslaved to Gabriel Purdy, who migrated to the Maritimes with several other slaves, Ned was accompanied by his wife, Belinda, and child called "Ned the Younger." British officials in New York described him as a "stout fellow." In his will, Purdy gave his slaves to his son. Source: Book of Negroes; Harris, "Negro Population of the County of Annapolis," 16.

770. BELINDA (c. 1783, age 43) – Belinda was the wife of Ned and enslaved to Gabriel Purdy, who migrated to the Maritimes, and she was accompanied by her husband and son (Ned the Younger). British officials in New York described her as a "stout wench." In his will Purdy gave his slaves to his son. Source: Book of Negroes; Harris, "Negro Population of the County of Annapolis," 16.

771. HESTER (c. 1798) – Enslaved to New York Loyalist Gabriel Purdy, Hester was the daughter of Ned and Belinda. She also lived with Ned the Younger (probably her brother). She was baptized in 1788 at Annapolis. Source: Harris, "Negro Population of the County of Annapolis," 16; Register of Baptisms, September 1788, St. Luke's Anglican Church, Annapolis Royal, Annapolis County, MG 4, vol. 4, NSA.

772. NED THE YOUNGER (c. 1783, age 3) – Enslaved to Gabriel Purdy, Ned the Younger was the son of Ned and Belinda. The Book of Negroes simply notes that Belinda had a 3-year-old son. In the Maritimes, he lived with three other slaves including Hester – possibly his sister. Source: Book of Negroes; Harris, "Negro Population of the County of Annapolis," 16.

773. MORRIS, CHARITY (c. 1783–1784, age 28) – According to the Book of Negroes, Charity was born free and lived with Jonathan Mills on Long Island until she reached adulthood (18). When she left New York, she had three children; but by the time of her attempted escape in May 1784, she seems to only have had her oldest child. Like her husband, Edward Morris, she seems to have been either re-enslaved or forced into indentured servitude. The 1784 runaway advertisement noted that she was "a half bred Indian of the tribe on Long Island, province of New York, and a small boy about eleven years of age, son of the said wench by an Indian father." Sources: *Royal Saint John's Gazette* (Saint

John), May 13, 1784; Book of Negroes. See the entry for Andrew Bush for a lengthy description of this runaway advertisement.

774. MORRIS, EDWARD [or **NED**] (c. 1783–1784, age 36) – According to the Book of Negroes, Gideon Wakeman owned Edward in Fairfield, Connecticut, but he escaped to British lines in 1777. Although technically free after the American Revolution, he came to New Brunswick in "possession" of one Thomas Rodgers (meaning Rodgers was supposed to hire him and pay him wages). Between the time he arrived in New Brunswick and May 1784, Rodgers seems to have re-enslaved or forced Edward into indentured servitude. As a result, he ran away with several other Black people who were working for Rodgers, including his wife, Charity. According to a 1784 runaway advertisement, Edward "is a celebrated methodist preacher among the negroes." Strangely, the Book of Negroes describes him as stout, but the runaway notice describes him as elderly. Source: *Royal Saint John's Gazette* (Saint John), May 13, 1784; Book of Negroes.

775. MORRIS, EDWARD (c. 1783, age 5) – Edward was the son of Charity Morris, and it is unclear what happened to him – if he was re-enslaved and sold away or died. Source: *Royal Saint John's Gazette* (Saint John), May 13, 1784; Book of Negroes.

776. MORRIS, ISAAC (c. 1783–1784, age 10 or 11) – Charity Morris was Isaac's mother, and his father was possibly Indigenous, while Edward Morris might have been his adoptive father. His parents brought him with them on their escape attempt. Source: *Royal Saint John's Gazette* (Saint John), May 13, 1784; Book of Negroes.

777. MORRIS, MARY ANN (c. 1783–1784, age 3) – The daughter of Charity Morris, the Book of Negroes described Mary Ann as a "fine girl." It is unclear what happened to her – if she was re-enslaved and sold away or died. Source: *Royal Saint John's Gazette* (Saint John), May 13, 1784; Book of Negroes.

778. MOSES (c. 1786) – Described as "belonging to Mr. Gersham Hillyard" of Saint John, New Brunswick, Moses took some goods from his owner's store and neighbours chased him down to the wharf where he jumped into the water and died. Source: *Royal Gazette* (New Brunswick), June 13, 1786.

779. MOSES, AESOP (c. ?) – Aesop was enslaved to Frederick Devoue. Source: Harris, "Negro Population of the County of Annapolis," 10.

780. MOSES, ZIP (ca 1780s/1790s) – Enslaved to Frederick Devoue, Zip might have been the same person listed as Aesop Moses or he might have been listed on the 1807 Digby slave petition as an adult male slave of Frederick Devoue. T.W Smith uses the example of Zip Moses to say that not all slaves wanted freedom.

Devoue's granddaughters claimed to Smith that Moses was treated well. This almost certainly says more about how some white people wanted to remember slavery as opposed to how enslaved people actually felt about it. Source: Smith, "Slave in Canada," 89.

781. MOTHER OF ANTOINE (c. 1745) – This enslaved woman gave birth to an infant son named Antoine. Source: Donovan, "Female Slaves as Sexual Victims in Île Royale," 149.

782. ANTOINE (c. 1745) – Antoine was the son of an enslaved mother. Source: Donovan, "Female Slaves as Sexual Victims in Île Royale," 149.

783. MOTHER OF ESTIENNE (c. ?) – This enslaved woman gave birth to a female child named Estienne. Source: Donovan, "Female Slaves as Sexual Victims in Île Royale," 149.

784. ESTIENNE (c. ?) – Estienne was the infant of an enslaved mother. Source: Donovan, "Female Slaves as Sexual Victims in Île Royale," 149.

785. MOTHER OF GENEVIEVE (c. ?) – This enslaved woman gave birth to a female child named Genevieve. Source: Donovan, "Female Slaves as Sexual Victims in Île Royale," 149.

786. GENEVIEVE (c. ?) – Genevieve was the infant of an enslaved mother. Source: Donovan, "Female Slaves as Sexual Victims in Île Royale," 149.

787. MOTHER OF JULE LOUIS (c. ?) – This enslaved woman gave birth to a daughter named Jule Louis. Source: Donovan, "Female Slaves as Sexual Victims in Île Royale," 149.

788. JULE LOUIS (c. ?) – Jule Louis was the infant of an enslaved mother. Source: Donovan, "Female Slaves as Sexual Victims in Île Royale," 149.

789. MOTHER OF MAGDELEINE (c. ?) – This enslaved woman gave birth to a female child named Magdeleine. Source: Donovan, "Female Slaves as Sexual Victims in Île Royale," 149.

790. MAGDELEINE (c. ?) – Magdeleine was the infant of an enslaved mother. Source: Donovan, "Female Slaves as Sexual Victims in Île Royale," 149.

791. MOTHER OF MARGUERITE (c. ?) – This enslaved woman gave birth to a female child named Marguerite. Source: Donovan, "Female Slaves as Sexual Victims in Île Royale," 149.

792. MARGUERITE (c. ?) – Marguerite was the infant of an enslaved mother. Source: Donovan, "Female Slaves as Sexual Victims in Île Royale," 149.

793. MOTHER OF MARIE (c. ?) – This enslaved person gave birth to a daughter named Marie. Source: Donovan, "Female Slaves as Sexual Victims in Île Royale," 149.

794. MARIE (c. ?) – Marie was the infant of an enslaved mother. Source: Donovan, "Female Slaves as Sexual Victims in Île Royale," 149.

795. MOTHER OF MARIE ANNE (c. ?) – This enslaved person gave birth to a daughter named Marie Anne. Source: Donovan, "Female Slaves as Sexual Victims in Île Royale," 149.

796. MARIE ANNE (c. ?) – Marie Anne was the infant of an enslaved mother. Source: Donovan, "Female Slaves as Sexual Victims in Île Royale," 149.

797. MOTHER OF MARIE CLEMENCE (c. ?) – This enslaved woman gave birth to a daughter named Marie Clemence. Source: Donovan, "Female Slaves as Sexual Victims in Île Royale," 149.

798. MARIE CLEMENCE (c. ?) – Marie Clemence was the infant of an enslaved mother. Source: Donovan, "Female Slaves as Sexual Victims in Île Royale," 149.

799. MOTHER OF MARIE HECTOR (c. ?) – This enslaved woman gave birth to a daughter named Marie Hector. Source: Donovan, "Female Slaves as Sexual Victims in Île Royale," 149.

800. MARIE HECTOR (c. ?) – Marie Hector was the infant of an enslaved woman. Source: Donovan, "Female Slaves as Sexual Victims in Île Royale," 149.

801. MOTHER OF MARIE MARGUERITE (c. ?) – This enslaved woman gave birth to a daughter named Marie Marguerite. Source: Donovan, "Female Slaves as Sexual Victims in Île Royale," 149.

802. MARIE MARGUERITE (c. ?) – Marie Marguerite was the infant of an enslaved mother. Source: Donovan, "Female Slaves as Sexual Victims in Île Royale," 149.

803. MOTHER OF PIERRE (c. ?) – This enslaved woman gave birth to a son named Pierre. Source: Donovan, "Female Slaves as Sexual Victims in Île Royale," 149.

804. PIERRE (c. ?) – Pierre was the infant of an enslaved mother. Source: Donovan, "Female Slaves as Sexual Victims in Île Royale," 149.

805. MOTHER OF PIERRE JOSEPH (c. ?) – This enslaved woman gave birth to a male child named Pierre Joseph. Source: Donovan, "Female Slaves as Sexual Victims in Île Royale," 149.

806. PIERRE JOSEPH (c. ?) – Pierre Joseph was the infant of an enslaved mother. Source: Donovan, "Female Slaves as Sexual Victims in Île Royale," 149.

807. MOTHER OF VICTOR (c. ?) – This enslaved woman gave birth to boy named Victor. Source: Donovan, "Female Slaves as Sexual Victims in Île Royale," 149.

808. VICTOR (c. ?) – Victor was the infant of an enslaved mother. Source: Donovan, "Female Slaves as Sexual Victims in Île Royale," 149.

809. MOTHER OF VICTORIE (c. ?) – This enslaved woman gave birth to a female child named Victorie. Source: Donovan, "Female Slaves as Sexual Victims in Île Royale," 149.

810. VICTORIE (c. ?) – Victorie was the infant of an enslaved mother. Source: Donovan, "Female Slaves as Sexual Victims in Île Royale," 149.

811. MUNGO (c. 1780, age 14) – Mungo was enslaved to Benjamin DeWolfe, who was possibly a member of a slave-trading family from Rhode Island. Mungo attempted to escape from DeWolfe, who placed an advertisement in the local newspaper describing Mungo as "well built" Sources: States, "Presence and Perseverance: Blacks in Hants County," 37; Smith, "Slave in Canada," 12.

812. NAN (c. 1783, age 7) – Nan was enslaved to Samuel Davenport, who migrated to the Maritimes after the American Revolution with another enslaved child. Nan was from New York, and British officials at New York described her as a "fine girl." Source: Book of Negroes.

813. NANCE (c. 1784, age 28 or 29) – Nance was enslaved to John Grant, who was originally from Scotland. After serving the British army near Ticonderoga during the Seven Years War, Grant settled in Queens County, Long Island. After the American Revolution, he settled in Nova Scotia with a large family and nine slaves. These enslaved people might have been a family unit. Source: Cottreau-Robins, "Landscape of Slavery in Loyalist Era Nova Scotia," 131–2; also Smith, "Slave in Canada," 93–4.

814. NANCE (c. 1804) – Nance was enslaved to James DeLancey in Annapolis, Nova Scotia, and in his estate inventory she was described as "at present disordered and infirm mind, of no value." Source: Hanger, "Life of Loyalist Colonel James DeLancey," 52–3.

815. NANCY (c. 1783) – Alexander Campbell, a South Carolina Loyalist captain, sold Nancy to Thomas Green for £40. Nancy went before the local justice of the peace and "freely acknowledged herself a slave and the property of the within named Captain Alexander Campbell." She would later be sold again along with her son Tom. Source: Smith, "Slave in Canada," 50–1.

816. TOM (c. 1784) – Tom was the son of Nancy. Source: Smith, "Slave in Canada," 51.

817. NANCY (c. 1783, age 40) – Enslaved to John Boggs, who migrated to the Maritimes after the American Revolution, Nancy brought her mentally challenged son with her. Nancy was from North Carolina, and British officials in New York noted she "says she is his [Boggs's] property having purchased her 11 years ago." They also described her as a "stout wench." Source: Book of Negroes.

818. DAVID (c. 1783, age 7) – The son of Nancy and enslaved to John Boggs, British officials described David as mentally challenged and born "in the family of John Boggs." Source: Book of Negroes.

819. NANCY (c. 1783, age 25) – Nancy was an enslaved woman of Dr. Nathaniel Bullern, who migrated from South Carolina to Nova Scotia with a total of 10 slaves. Bullern's slaves also indicate several different possibilities of family connections and kinship networks. His oldest slaves, Achabee and Catharina, were both 60 at the end of the American Revolution. Jenny and Prince were 40 and 30, respectively. Bullern also owned another male slave in his early 30s and three females ranging in ages 19 to 25. His two youngest slaves were an infant named Sarah and a 6 year old. It is unclear who the parents of these children were, but it is possible that one or both parents were among Bullern's slaves. British officials in New York described Nancy as a "stout wench." Source: Book of Negroes.

820. SARAH (c. 1783, age 6 months) – Possibly the daughter of Nancy and also enslaved to Dr. Nathaniel Bullern, British officials in New York described Sarah as an "infant." Source: Book of Negroes.

821. NANCY (c. 1783, age 11) – Nancy was enslaved to Gilbert Tippet, who migrated to the Maritimes after the American Revolution with another child slave. British officials in New York described her as "incurably lame." Source: Book of Negroes.

822. NANCY (c. 1786, age 24) – The slave of Maryland Loyalist Caleb Jones, in 1786 Nancy attempted to escape along with four other slaves. According to Jones, she "took with her a Negro child, about four years old called LIDGE."

Jones recaptured some of the slaves, including Nancy, because she would later be part of one of the most important legal cases about slavery in New Brunswick history. In 1800, the issue of the status of a slave woman was brought before the court in the cases *R. v. Jones* and *R. v. Agnew*. The first case involved a woman named "Ann otherwise called Nancy" whom Jones had brought from Maryland in 1785. The second case involved one of Virginian Loyalist Stair Agnew's female slaves. Both cases began at the same time, but once a decision was rendered in *R. v. Jones* the other case did not proceed. The slave woman in *R. v. Jones* is probably the same Nancy as the one on the 1786 runaway notice. In the summer of 1799, a writ of habeas corpus was "brought by a Negro woman claimed as a Slave by Captain Jones of Fredericton, in order to procure her liberation." During the trial, the "question of Slavery upon general principles was discussed at great length." After hearing the testimony, the court remained divided and did not reach a judgment. As a result, Caleb Jones retained Nancy. The 1800 non-decision is noteworthy because all of the judges either owned slaves in New Brunswick or had possessed them in the United States. Sources: *Royal Gazette* (New Brunswick), July 25, 1786; *Royal Gazette* (New Brunswick), February 18, 1800; Bell, "Judges of Loyalist New Brunswick," 9–42; W.A. Spray, "Jones, Caleb," *Dictionary of Canadian Biography*, http://www.biographi.ca/en/bio/jones_caleb_5E.html.

823. NANCY (c. 1787) – Enslaved to the Walker family, Nancy lived with another slave named Nancy. She was baptized at Wilmot, Nova Scotia. Source: List of Baptisms, September 3, 1787, Cornwallis Township Book, NSA.

824. NANCY (c. 1789) – Enslaved to Captain William Booth, Nancy was probably from Grenada where Booth's brother-in-law was a planter and merchant. She lived with another slave in Shelburne named Betty Anna (see entry) who was sent to Grenada. Nancy remained with Booth in Shelburne. In his memorandum book and diary, Booth complained that Nancy had once attempted to prevent Betty Anna from eating her dinner and noted "Nancy has behaved very disrespectful for some time pass'd." Source: Booth, *Remarks and Rough Memorandums*, 85, vi–vii.

825. NANCY (c. 1809) – D. Brown offered Nancy for sale without listing any of her work capabilities or age. It is possible that she is the same Nancy that attempted to escape from Caleb Jones and played an important role in the 1800 New Brunswick slave case, but it would be difficult to prove conclusively unless a new document is unearthed. Source: *Royal Gazette* (New Brunswick), October 16, 1809.

826. NANNY [or **NANCY**] (slave? c. 1784) – Nanny was possibly enslaved to Joseph Russell, who planned to settle near Halifax. Russell had three other Black people in his household. Source: Loyalists and Disbanded Troops at Cole Harbour,

Chipman Papers, Muster Master General's Office, Loyalist Musters, 1776–1785, MG 23, D1, ser. I, vol. 24, LAC.

827. NANON, ANNE HONICHE (c. 1758, age 24) – Originally from Africa, Anne worked in the household of Nicholas Larcher, a wealthy member of the Superior Council. Anne probably controlled "Larcher's household affairs" and worked as a cook. Anne was baptized when she went to France with her owner. Source: Donovan, "Slaves in Île Royale," 33.

828. NARCISSE, JEAN (c. 1754) – The slave of commissaire-ardonnateur Jacques Prevost and his large family, Jean lived with three other slaves. Source: Donovan, "Slaves and Their Owners in Île Royale," 11.

829. NATHANIEL (slave? c. 1788) – Nathaniel was possibly an enslaved person who was baptized along with several other Black people in New Brunswick. Source: Early Parish Records, New Brunswick, September 14, 1788, possibly PANB, but this repository did not stamp this document so it is unclear if it is from PANB, NBM, or the UNB Loyalist Collection.

830. NATT (slave? c. 1784) – Natt was possibly an enslaved person who settled at Belle Vue in Beaver Harbour. Although these people might have been nominally free, they were regularly subjected to re-enslavement. Source: Roll of Loyalists Settled at Belle Vue in Beaver Harbour, Chipman Papers, Muster Master General's Office, Loyalist Musters, 1776–1785, MG 23, D1, ser. I, vol. 24, LAC.

831. NED (c. 1783, age 40) – Enslaved to Richard Carman, who migrated to the Maritimes after the American Revolution with another slave, Ned was from New York. British officials at New York described him as a "stout fellow." Source: Book of Negroes.

832. NED (c. 1784, age 20) – Enslaved to Major John Van Dyke, who migrated to the Maritimes from New York, Ned was probably from New Jersey. British officials described him as a "stout fellow." Source: Book of Negroes.

833. NED (slave? c. 1784) – Ned was possibly enslaved to Lieutenant Boisseau, who migrated to Country Harbour with other southern Loyalists. The majority of these Loyalists and their slaves were from North Carolina, South Carolina, and Georgia. They had settled briefly in East Florida before moving to Nova Scotia. Black people at Country Harbour were either slaves or "quasi-free" and subject to re-enslavement. Abolitionist Thomas Clarkson explained the phenomenon of re-enslavement: "It was not long till these loyalists, many of whom had been educated with all the ideas of the justice of slavery, the inferiority of negroes, and the superiority of white men, that are universal in the southern provinces of America, began to harass and oppress the industrious black settlers, and even wantonly to deprive them of the fruits of their labour, expelling them from the lands they had cleared." Clarkson continued by noting that whites reduced "again to slavery those negroes who had so honourably obtained their freedom. They hired them as servants, and, at the end of the stipulated time, refused payment of their wages, insisting that they were slaves: in some instances they destroyed their tickets of freedom, and then enslaved the negroes for want of them; in several instances, the unfortunate Africans were taken onboard vessels, carried to the West Indies, and there sold for the benefit of their plunderers." At Country Harbour, Black people were listed on the musters as the "Servants" of a white Loyalist, which meant it was very easy for them to be re-enslaved if they were not already enslaved. Sources: Clarkson, "Some Account of the New Colony at Sierra Leone," 229–30; Settlers at Country Harbour, Chipman Papers, Muster Master General's Office, Loyalist Musters, 1776–1785, MG 23, D1, ser. I, vol. 24, LAC. Note: Ellen Wilson believed that the information Clarkson used came from Thomas Peters; see Wilson, *Loyal Blacks*, 181.

834. NED (slave/indentured? c. 1790) – This "boy" is mentioned in Simeon Perkins's diary as "Mr. Parkers Black boy Ned." Source: Fergusson, *Diary of Simeon Perkins, 1790–1796*, 29.

835. NEGRESSE (c. 1750s) – The enslaved property of Pierre Boullot, this woman lived with another slave named Marie Flore, Marie's child, and another slave only known as Carib. Source: Donovan, "Slaves in Île Royale," 35.

836. NEGRO DRUMMER (c. 1745) – From New England, this enslaved man served as a drummer under the command of Samuel Rhodes during the 1745 Siege of Louisbourg. Source: Donovan, "Nominal List of Slaves and Their Owners," 156.

837. NEGRO TOM (c. 1747) – Negro Tom hired out some of his time and received a wage at Louisbourg. Originally from New England, it seems very likely that he remained enslaved (there were a small number of free Blacks in 1747 throughout North America) and had to give part of his wages to his owner. Source: Donovan, "Nominal List of Slaves and Their Owners," 157.

838. NEGRO WILL (c. 1747) – Negro Will hired out some of his time and received a wage at Louisbourg. Originally from New England, it seems very likely that he remained enslaved (there were a small number of free Blacks in 1747 throughout North America) and had to give part of his wages to his owner. Source: Donovan, "Nominal List of Slaves and Their Owners," 157.

839. NELLY (c. 1783, age 18) – Enslaved to Major Coffin, who migrated to the Maritimes after the American Revolution with also a young male slave, Nelly was from South Carolina. British officials in New York noted that Nelly became the property of Major Coffin "by the marriage to Mrs. Coffin," who was from South Carolina. These same officials described her as a "likely wench." Source: Book of Negroes.

840. NELLY (slave? c. 1784) – Nelly was possibly enslaved to Lieutenant Boisseau, who migrated to Country Harbour with other southern Loyalists. The majority of these Loyalists and their slaves were from North Carolina, South Carolina, and Georgia. They had settled briefly in East Florida before moving to Nova Scotia. Black people at Country Harbour were either slaves or "quasi-free" and subject to re-enslavement. Abolitionist Thomas Clarkson explained the phenomenon of re-enslavement: "It was not long till these loyalists, many of whom had been educated with all the ideas of the justice of slavery, the inferiority of negroes, and the superiority of white men, that are universal in the southern provinces of America, began to harass and oppress the industrious black settlers, and even wantonly to deprive them of the fruits of their labour, expelling them from the lands they had cleared." Clarkson continued by noting that whites reduced "again to slavery those negroes who had so honourably obtained their freedom. They hired them as servants, and, at the end of the stipulated time, refused payment of their wages, insisting that they were slaves: in some instances they destroyed their tickets of freedom, and then enslaved the negroes for want of them; in several instances, the unfortunate Africans were taken onboard vessels, carried to the West Indies, and there sold for the benefit of their plunderers." At Country Harbour, Black people were listed on the musters as the "Servants" of a white Loyalist, which meant it was very easy for them to be re-enslaved if they were not already enslaved. Sources: Clarkson, "Some Account of the New Colony at Sierra Leone," 229–30; Settlers at Country Harbour, Chipman Papers, Muster Master General's Office, Loyalist Musters, 1776–1785, MG 23, D1, ser. I, vol. 24, LAC. Note: Ellen Wilson believed that the information Clarkson used came from Thomas Peters; see Wilson, *Loyal Blacks*, 181.

841. NELLY (c. 1796) – Nelly was enslaved to Isaac Hatfield, but died of pleurisy. Source: Death records, February 14, 1796, Records of the Anglican Church, Digby Township Book, MG 4, vol. 23, item 3, NSA.

842. NELLY (c. 1807, age 25) – The Allison family sold Nelly to Wolfville resident Simon Fitch. Source: Sale of Nelly, William Cochrane Milner Fonds, S 13, F 142, NBM.

843. NERO (c. 1783, age 15) – Enslaved to Captain Palmer, who migrated to the Maritimes after the American Revolution, Nero was from New York. British officials in New York described him as an "ordinary fellow." Source: Book of Negroes.

844. NERO (slave? c. 1784) – Nero was possibly enslaved to Ensign Douglass, who migrated to Country Harbour with other southern Loyalists. The majority of these Loyalists and their slaves were from North Carolina, South Carolina, and Georgia. They had settled briefly in East Florida before moving to Nova Scotia. Black people at Country Harbour were either slaves or "quasi-free" and subject to re-enslavement. Abolitionist Thomas Clarkson explained the phenomenon of re-enslavement: "It was not long till these loyalists, many of whom had been educated with all the ideas of the justice of slavery, the inferiority of negroes, and the superiority of white men, that are universal in the southern provinces of America, began to harass and oppress the industrious black settlers, and even wantonly to deprive them of the fruits of their labour, expelling them from the lands they had cleared." Clarkson continued by noting that whites reduced "again to slavery those negroes who had so honourably obtained their freedom. They hired them as servants, and, at the end of the stipulated time, refused payment of their wages, insisting that they were slaves: in some instances they destroyed their tickets of freedom, and then enslaved the negroes for want of them; in several instances, the unfortunate Africans were taken onboard vessels, carried to the West Indies, and there sold for the benefit of their plunderers." At Country Harbour, Black people were listed on the musters as the "Servants" of a white Loyalist, which meant it was very easy for them to be re-enslaved if they were not already enslaved. Sources: Clarkson, "Some Account of the New Colony at Sierra Leone," 229–30; Settlers at Country Harbour, Chipman Papers, Muster Master General's Office, Loyalist Musters, 1776–1785, MG 23, D1, ser. I, vol. 24, LAC. Note: Ellen Wilson believed that the information Clarkson used came from Thomas Peters; see Wilson, *Loyal Blacks*, 181.

845. NERO (c. 1797) – Nero ran away from his owner Titus Knapp, who owned several slaves and described Nero as 27 years old and around five foot seven inches. The advertisement said little other than Nero ran away from Knapp's property in Westmoreland. Source: *Saint John Gazette*, May 5, 1797.

846. ODEL, JOSEPH [or **JOE**] (c. 1783–1792, age 14 in 1783) – In 1783, Daniel Odel (or Odell) brought his slave Joe to Annapolis Royal from New York as part of the Loyalist influx after the American Revolution. British officials in New York described him as a "fine boy." Joe remained enslaved for another nine years before he ran away from his owner with another slave (Peter Lawrence). Daniel Odel and Phillip Earl (Lawrence's owner) placed the following advertisement in a local newspaper: "RUN AWAY, Joseph Odel and Peter Lawrence (Negroes) from their Masters, and left Digby last evening, the first mentioned is about Twenty four year of Age, five feet six Inches high, had on a light brown coat, red waistcoat and thickset breeches, took other cloaths with him, he is a likely young Fellow with remarkable white Teeth. – The other is about five Feet eight Inches high, very Black, had on lightesh coloured clothes. – Whoever will secure said Negroes so that their Masters may have them again, shall receive TEN DOLLARS Reward, and all reasonable." Source: *Royal Gazette*, July 10, 1792.

847. OLD ANDY (c. ?) – Old Andy was enslaved to J.F.W. DesBarres in Hants County, Nova Scotia. Source: States, "Presence and Perseverance: Blacks in Hants County," 40.

848. ORANGE (c. 1752) – Enslaved to Thomas Thomas, Orange was brought to Halifax from New York. Orange might have been born in New York or possibly Africa. Source: Smith, "Slave in Canada," 9.

849. PARKIN, VIOLET (c. 1783, age 27) – Enslaved to Mr. Parkin, who migrated to the Maritimes from New York, Violet brought her infant. British officials in New York described her as an "ordinary wench." Source: Book of Negroes.

850. DICK (c. 1783, age 6 months) – Dick was the child of Violet. Source: Book of Negroes.

851. PATTEN, JOHN (c. 1770, age 2 ½) – John was enslaved to Mrs. Pritchard, who gave the child to her granddaughter. This granddaughter would later marry Richard John Uniacke, who fought against slavery in Nova Scotia. Source: Smith, "Slave in Canada," 14.

852. PATTY (slave? c. 1784) – Patty was possibly enslaved to Ensign Waldron, who migrated to Country Harbour with other southern Loyalists. The majority of these Loyalists and their slaves were from North Carolina, South Carolina, and Georgia. They had settled briefly in East Florida before moving to Nova Scotia. Black people at Country Harbour were either slaves or "quasi-free" and subject to re-enslavement. Abolitionist Thomas Clarkson explained the phenomenon of re-enslavement: "It was not long till these loyalists, many of whom had been educated with all the ideas of the justice of slavery, the inferiority of negroes, and the superiority of white men, that are universal in the southern provinces of America, began to harass and oppress the industrious black settlers, and even wantonly to deprive them of the fruits of their labour, expelling them from the lands they had cleared." Clarkson continued by noting that whites reduced "again to slavery those negroes who had so honourably obtained their freedom. They hired them as servants, and, at the end of the stipulated time, refused payment of their wages, insisting that they were slaves: in some instances they destroyed their tickets of freedom, and then enslaved the negroes for want of them; in several instances, the unfortunate Africans were taken onboard vessels, carried to the West Indies, and there sold for the benefit of their plunderers." At Country Harbour, Black people were listed on the musters as the "Servants" of a white Loyalist, which meant it was very easy for them to be re-enslaved if they were not already enslaved. Sources: Clarkson, "Some Account of the New Colony at Sierra Leone," 229–30; Settlers at Country Harbour, Chipman Papers, Muster Master General's Office, Loyalist Musters, 1776–1785, MG 23, D1, ser. I, vol. 24, LAC. Note: Ellen Wilson believed that the information Clarkson used came from Thomas Peters' petition; see Wilson, *Loyal Blacks*, 181.

853. PEG (c. 1783, age 22) – Enslaved to Samuel Dickenson, who went to the Maritimes after the American Revolution, Peg was from New York. British officials in New York described her as a "stout wench." Source: Book of Negroes.

854. PEG (c. 1783, age 16) – Enslaved to George McCall, who migrated to the Maritimes from New York after the American Revolution, Peg was possibly from Massachusetts. British officials described her as a "stout girl, lame of one leg." Source: Book of Negroes.

855. PEG (c. 1785) – Peg was an enslaved woman of Prince Edward Island Governor Walter Patterson. During the Jupiter Wise conspiracy (see Jupiter Wise entry), Peg was not told of the other slaves' plan because they did not trust her. Sources: *King v. Jupiter Wise*, 1786, PAROPEI; Henry Holman, "Slaves and Servants on Prince Edward Island," 100–4; Hornby, Black Islanders, 15–19.

856. PEG (c. 1804) – Peg was enslaved to James DeLancey, whose estate valued her at £40. Source: Hanger, "Life of Loyalist Colonel James DeLancey," 52–3.

857. PERCILLA (c. 1804, age 8) – The estate of Robert Dickson sold Percilla to one William Robertson. It is clear that Dickson's executors had absolutely no issue with selling an 8-year-old child. Source: Sale of a Slave, MG 100, vol. 103, #F3a, NSA.

858. PERO (c. 1786) – In 1786, Pero and Tom were re-enslaved. Joseph Robins claimed that he had purchased both men for £29 sterling. Patrick Licet said he had observed Joseph Robins purchase Pero for a horse and eight guineas. The second witness claimed he had hired Pero from Robins and "always understood the said Negro to be the Property of Joseph Robins." This same witness, James Stone, claimed that he had heard Pero admit to being the slave of Robins. During his examination, Pero stated that he had gone to St. Augustine with James Stone, instead of returning to his rebel master. But he denied being the property of Stone. Tom commented that he had belonged to Philip Caine in "Carolina" and had run away to Charleston, where he worked in the wood yard. Tom accompanied Joseph Robins to St. Augustine. Afterwards, he recalled being sold for a horse, but firmly denied being owned by Robins. The court ordered Joseph

Robins to "take Possession" of Tom and Pero but required that he not sell them out of the province for 12 months. The continued enslavement or re-enslavement of these Blacks is instructive for several reasons. Tom and Pero both realized that they could assert their freedom in court. Although they lost, they either told the truth or were smart enough to construct a narrative that aligned with the history of most free Blacks in the region – that is, running away from a rebel owner and performing loyal services to His Majesty before migrating to St. Augustine and finally Nova Scotia. These slaves realized that the legalities of slavery and freedom were shifting and unclear. They attempted to use the confusion to gain their freedom. Source: General Sessions at Shelburne, Nova Scotia, April 10, 1786, Shelburne Records, MG 4, vol. 141, NSA.

859. PETER (c. 1745) – Peter was enslaved to Robert Glovers during the 1745 siege of Louisbourg. Source: Donovan, "Nominal List of Slaves and Their Owners," 156.

860. PETER (c. 1783, age 19) – Enslaved to Gabriel Purdy, who migrated to the Maritimes after the American Revolution with other slaves, Peter was probably from New York. British officials in New York described him as a "stout fellow." Source: Book of Negroes.

861. PETER (c. 1783, age 17) – Peter escaped from his owner in 1783, shortly after the influx of Loyalists to Nova Scotia. He came from Africa, as indicated by his owner's description of his speech patterns and "Country marks" (ritual scarification among African ethnic groups). His master, Hugh Kirkham, lived in South Carolina before the American Revolution. According to Kirkham, Peter "[had] been used to the carpenter's business." Source: *Nova Scotia Gazette and Weekly Chronicle*, May 20, 1783.

862. PETER (c. 1784) – James Selkring listed "A Negroe Man Slave, Peter" in his estate inventory at Shelburne. Selkring valued Peter at £25. Source: Will of James Selkring, 1784, Estate Papers and Wills, Shelburne County, 1784–1790, NSA.

863. PETER (c. 1785) – Enslaved to Prince Edward Island's chief justice, Peter was part of Jupiter Wise's conspiracy to steal rum, have a party, then escape to Boston on Governor Patterson's sloop. Sources: *King v. Jupiter Wise*, 1786, PAROPEI; Holman, "Slaves and Servants on Prince Edward Island," 100–4; Hornby, *Black Islanders*, 15–19.

864. PETER (c. 1804) – Peter was enslaved to James Law and later sold to Titus Knapp. Unfortunately, the boy was sold again six years later to Isaac Hewson. He stayed with Hewson "until after the emancipation of slaves." Source: Smith, "Slave in Canada," 67.

865. PHEBE (c. 1780) – Enslaved to Colonel Henry Denson in Hants County, Nova Scotia, Phebe lived with four other slaves. Source: States, "Presence and Perseverance: Blacks in Hants County," 39.

866. PHEBE (c. 1783, age 21) – Phebe was enslaved to Major Coffin, who was part of Edmund Fanning's King's American Regiment. Coffin purchased her from a Mr. Greentree. Phebe went to the Maritimes from New York along with Coffin's two other slaves. British officials in New York described her as a "stout wench." Source: Book of Negroes.

867. PHEBE (c. 1791, age 22) – Miscegenation and forced sexual relations between masters and slaves occurred frequently. Terms such as "mulatto" and "molatta" in slave advertisements, bills of sale, and other documents indicate the presence of interracial sex and mixed ancestry. If there is no evidence supporting "mutually tender feelings," then these sexual encounters must be viewed as fundamentally violent, exploitative, and oppressive. This should not blind us to the variety of sexual encounters between Blacks and whites. The study of "sex and love across racial boundaries in North America" reveals a wide range of encounters, including violent sexual exploitation and "devoted relationships." Words such as miscegenation, interracial encounters, and racial mixture have various contextual meanings. In the Maritime colonies, as in New England, white men could be taken to court for the crime of raping Black women. This did not necessarily mean a likelihood of conviction, but in some cases they did at least have to face the court system.

Phebe provides another powerful example of the trials that Black female slaves faced. In the late 1780s, Phebe became the property of Benjamin Douglass. During her time with Douglass, Phebe became involved in a relationship with her owner. According to one witness, "Douglass was the Father off [*sic*] several children she was Delivered of while being in his service." Phebe and Douglass slept in the same room together, where there was only one bed. However, Douglass "drove her out of bed too Early in the morning." Forcing her out of the bedroom might have two meanings. Douglass did so because he did not want their relationship to be known or he sent her to work at an extraordinarily early hour. At the same time that Douglass had been sleeping with Phebe, he "was connected with other women." Douglass's liaisons with the other women apparently upset Phebe who came "home crying [and] said that she had caught Mr. Douglass in bed with Charlotte [and] she thought that Mr. Douglass had used her ill." Angered by finding Douglass engaged in sex with another woman, Phebe seemed surprised that "he had kept her [and] she did not think that he would have done so." Phebe admitted to being Douglass's slave and also said she was willing to remain in his service if freed and paid a small wage. Phebe saw herself as more than an unwilling sexual partner with Douglass, as indicated by her surprise that he had "kept her." At the same time, his willingness to drive her out of bed early in the morning probably indicates the shame he felt in sharing the same bed as her. The encounter between Benjamin Douglass and Phebe demonstrates the oppression that Black women endured as slaves of sexually predatory masters. Source: *Douglass v. MacNeill*, 1791, Halifax, vol. 62, no. 62, RG 39 C, NSA. See also Martha Hodes, ed., *Sex, Love, Race: Crossing Boundaries in North American History* (New York: New York University Press, 1999), 1–2; Catherine Adams and Elizabeth H. Pleck, *Love of Freedom: Black Women in Colonial and Revolutionary New England* (New York: Oxford University Press, 2009); and Brenda Stevenson, "What's Love Got to Do with It? Concubinage and Enslaved Black Women and Girls in the Antebellum South," *Journal of African American History* 98 (Winter 2013): 99–125.

868. PHEMY (c. 1790s) – Enslaved to Isaac Ketchum, family traditions describe Phemy as the loyal best friend of her mistress. Source: Smith, "Slave in Canada," 83–84.

869. PHILIP (c. 1786) – Philip (a blacksmith) was enslaved to Delaware Loyalist Thomas Robinson, who gave him to his brother in a will filed in Shelburne, Nova Scotia. Source: Will of Thomas Robinson, Shelburne County, 1786/1787, NSA.

870. PHILIP, JAMES (c. 1783, age 40) – James was enslaved to Captain Symon, who migrated to the Maritimes after the American Revolution. British officials in New York described James as a "stout fellow." Source: Book of Negroes.

871. PHILIPPE (c. 1753) – Philippe was enslaved to Charles Le Coutre. Source: Donovan, "Nominal List of Slaves and Their Owners," 159.

872. PHILIPS, ANTHONY (c. 1783, age 23) – Enslaved to Captain Philips, British officials described Anthony as "stout." Source: Book of Negroes.

873. PHILLIS (c. 1783, age 15) – Enslaved to Captain Longstreet, Phillis migrated to the Maritimes from New York with one other slave. Phillis was probably from New Jersey, and British officials described her as a "likely wench." Source: Book of Negroes.

874. PHILLIS (c. 1783, age 14) – Enslaved to Charles Hale, who went to the Maritimes after the American Revolution, British officials in New York described Phillis as a "stout wench." Source: Book of Negroes.

875. PHILLIS (c. 1783, age 6) – Enslaved to Captain Hicks, who migrated to the Maritimes after the American Revolution with several other slaves, Phillis was possibly from New York or Pennsylvania. She might have been the child of Elizabeth (see entry). British officials in New York described her as a "likely child." Source: Book of Negroes.

876. PHILLIS (c. 1785, age 30) – Phillis was enslaved to Mr. Denoon in Halifax, who described her in unflattering physical terms by noting a wart on her nose and stye on her eye. Source: *Nova Scotia Gazette*, October 18, 1785.

877. PHILLIS (c. 1788) – Thomas Leonard noted in his will that he had freed Phillis and her unnamed child and wanted his executors to give them the sum of £50 over a set period of time: "I Give and Bequeath to my former Negro Woman Phillis [?] I have given her freedom with her Child. Fifty Pounds Nova Scotia Currency to be paid her as follows. Viz. Ten Pounds in three months after my decease and ten pounds a year for four years after making the Said fifty Pounds." Source: Thomas Leonard, 1788, Kings County, RG 48, Probate Records, NSA.

878. UNNAMED CHILD OF PHILLIS (c. 1788) – In his will, Thomas Leonard noted that he had freed Phillis and her unnamed child and wanted the executors of the will to give them the sum of £50 over a set period of time. Source: Thomas Leonard, 1788, Kings County, RG 48, Probate Records, NSA.

879. PHILLIS (c. 1795) – New York Loyalist Samuel Hallett mentioned Phillis in his will, leaving her to his wife in New Brunswick. Source: Will of Samuel Hallett, Saint John County, 1795, PANB.

880. PHOEBE (c. 1800) – Enslaved to Edward Barron in Cumberland County, Nova Scotia, Barron freed Phoebe in his will and offered freedom to her son and unborn child. Barron also gave Phoebe two cows and six ewes. Source: Raylene Fairfax, "Blacks in Cumberland County, 1600–1920" (unpublished manuscript, 1984), Mount Allison University Archives.

881. HUGH (c. 1800) – Hugh was Phoebe's son, and he was likely freed at age 21. Source: Fairfax, "Blacks in Cumberland County."

882. PHYLLIS (c. 1790s–1800s) – Phyllis was enslaved to Judge DeWolfe. Source: Eaton, *History of Kings County*, 493.

883. PIERRE (c. 1751) – Pierre was enslaved to an unknown master. Source: Donovan, "Nominal List of Slaves and Their Owners," 159.

884. PIERRE (c. 1754) – Enslaved to commissaire-ordonnateur Jacques Prevost, Pierre lived with three other slaves. Source: Donovan, "Nominal List of Slaves and Their Owners," 157.

885. PLATO (c. 1783, age 20) – Enslaved to John Marshall, who migrated to the Maritimes after the American Revolution, Plato was possibly from New York. British officials in New York described him as a "stout fellow." Source: Book of Negroes.

886. PLATO (c. 1783, age 18) – Enslaved to Captain Barbaree/Barbarie, Plato was possibly from New Jersey and went to the Maritimes from New York with one other slave. British officials described him as a "likely boy" and "born in the Captain's family." Source: Book of Negroes.

887. PLATT, PLENTY (c. 1784) – Plenty was enslaved to the Departments of the Army and Navy, which settled at Chedabucto, Nova Scotia. Source: Muster Roll of Settlers at Chedabucto (including Departments of the Army and Navy), Chipman Papers, Muster Master General's Office, Loyalist Musters, 1776–1785, MG 23, D1, ser. I, vol. 24, LAC.

888. PLEASANT (ca 1802) – Pleasant was enslaved to Virginia Loyalist Jacob Ellegood. In his will, Ellegood wrote "I give to my said son John Saunders Ellegood my mulatto wench called Pleasant and her three children James, Sally, and William." Ellegood served in the New Brunswick legislative assembly and also owned a large farm. He was the brother-in law of John Saunders, who served as chief justice of the New Brunswick Supreme Court (and was also from Virginia). Source: Will of Jacob Ellegood, York County, 1802, PANB.

889. JAMES (c. 1802) – James was a son of Pleasant and enslaved to Virginia Loyalist Jacob Ellegood. Source: Will of Jacob Ellegood, York County, 1802, PANB.

890. SALLY (c. 1802) – Sally was a daughter of Pleasant and enslaved to Virginia Loyalist Jacob Ellegood. Source: Will of Jacob Ellegood, York County, 1802, PANB.

891. WILLIAM (c. 1802) – William was a son of Pleasant and enslaved to Virginia Loyalist Jacob Ellegood. Source: Will of Jacob Ellegood, York County, 1802, PANB.

892. PLUMB, CHARLOTTE (c. 1783) – Enslaved to Thomas Plumb, her mulatto father, Charlotte went to the Maritimes from New York with him. Thomas was born free in Virginia and worked as a carpenter. British officials described Charlotte as a "fine girl." Sometimes Black or mixed-race fathers owned their children to keep their families together. Thomas possibly purchased Charlotte from her owner to protect her. Source: Book of Negroes; David L. Lightner and Alexander M. Ragan, "Were African American Slaveholders Benevolent or Exploitative? A Quantitative Approach," Journal of Southern History 71, no. 3 (August 2005): 535–58.

893. POLHEMUS, JOSEPH (c. 1796) – Enslaved to John Polhemus, Joseph was baptized in Clements, Nova Scotia. It is possible that he was included by

Polhemus in his listing of 10 slaves in the 1807 Digby slaveholder petition (the same is true for his children), but we cannot be sure because the petition did not list the names of individual slaves. It simply listed the number of slaves in each individual slaveholder's household. Source: List of Baptisms, February 14, 1796, Records of the Anglican Church, Digby Township Book, NSA.

894. CAESAR (c. 1796) – Caesar was the son of Joseph and enslaved to John Polhemus. Source: List of Baptisms, February 14, 1796, Records of the Anglican Church, Digby Township Book, NSA.

895. SYLVIA (c. 1801) – Sylvia was the daughter of Joseph and enslaved to John Polhemus. Source: List of Baptisms, June 28, 1801, Records of the Anglican Church, Digby Township Book, NSA.

896. POLHEMUS, SAMUEL (c. 1796) – Samuel was enslaved to John Polhemus. Source: List of Baptisms, February 14, 1796, Records of the Anglican Church, Digby Township Book, NSA.

897. POLIDOR (c. 1753) – Polidor was enslaved to M. Pascault. Source: Donovan, "Nominal List of Slaves and Their Owners," 158.

898. POLL (c. 1783, age 16) – Poll was an enslaved person of William Summers, who migrated to the Maritimes from New York after the American Revolution. Poll was from Massachusetts, and British officials described her as a "stout girl." Source: Book of Negroes.

899. POLL (c. 1791, age 17) – Poll escaped from her owner Alexander Morton in 1791. The runaway advertisement did not give many details about Poll's life or personality other than to say she had survived smallpox. Source: *Saint John Gazette*, September 30, 1791.

900. POLLY/POLLEY [alias **MARY MOORE?**] (c. 1780s/1790s) – Enslaved to PEI Lieutenant Governor Edmund Fanning, Polly might have married Dimbo Suckles, but this is unclear. Source: Hornby, *Black Islanders*, 31.

901. POMP (c. 1786) – Enslaved to Mr. Chandler in Annapolis, Nova Scotia, Pomp was baptized in the spring of 1786. Source: Register of Baptisms, May 1786, St. Luke's Anglican Church, Annapolis Royal, Annapolis County, NSA.

902. POMP (c. 1787) – Pomp was enslaved to John Huston of Cornwallis, who bequeathed Pomp to his wife. Source: Smith, "Slave in Canada," 16.

903. POMPÉE (c. 1732, age 12) – Pompée was enslaved to Councillor Joseph Lartigue, who was involved in the fishing business and trade. In 1732, Pompée died during a smallpox epidemic; he was baptized during his illness. Source: Donovan, "Slaves and Their Owners in Île Royale," 13.

904. POMPEY (c. 1781) – Enslaved to Colonel Henry Denson in Hants County, Nova Scotia, Pompey lived with four other slaves. Source: States, "Presence and Perseverance: Blacks in Hants County," 39.

905. POMPEY (c. 1783, age 32) – Enslaved to Jonathan Clawson, who migrated to the Maritimes with his family, Pompey was from New Jersey. British officials in New York described him as a "stout fellow." Source: Book of Negroes.

906. WIFE OF POMPEY (c. 1783) – Pompey's wife was enslaved to Jonathan Clawson, who migrated to the Maritimes with her husband and children. Source: Book of Negroes.

907. CHILD OF POMPEY (c. 1783) – Pompey's child was enslaved to Jonathan Clawson, who migrated to the Maritimes with his or her family. Source: Book of Negroes.

908. CHILD OF POMPEY (c. 1783) – Pompey's child was enslaved to Jonathan Clawson, who migrated to the Maritimes with his or her family. Source: Book of Negroes.

909. POMPEY (c. 1783/1784) – Pompey was enslaved to Captain Isaac Young in Digby, Nova Scotia. Young's slaves were from New York. Source: Smith, "Slave in Canada," 25.

910. POMPEY (c. 1784) – Enslaved to Balthazar (Bethaser) Creamer, who settled outside of Halifax, Pompey lived with three other slaves. But he was not in Creamer's 1796 will, which meant he either died, absconded, or Creamer sold him away. Source: Loyalists and Disbanded Troops at Cole Harbour, Chipman Papers, Muster Master General's Office, Loyalist Musters, 1776–1785, MG 23, D1, ser. I, vol. 24, LAC.

911. POMPEY (c. 1786, age 21) – In 1786, John Whitlock placed an advertisement for his runaway slave named Pompey in which he described Pompey as "stout well made" and about 21 years old. In running away, Pompey took an astonishing amount of clothing with him. Source: Royal Gazette, May 16, 1786.

912. POMPY (c. 1784, age 22) – Pompy was enslaved to John Grant. Originally from Scotland, after serving the British army near Ticonderoga during the Seven Years War, Grant settled in Queens County, Long Island. After the American Revolution, he settled in Nova Scotia with a large family and nine slaves. These enslaved people might have been a family unit. Source: Cottreau-Robins, "Landscape of Slavery in Loyalist Era Nova Scotia," 131–2; also Smith, "Slave in Canada," 93–4.

913. PORTER, BON (c. 1780, age 30) – Porter was enslaved to one [Mr.?] Richardson in Halifax, Nova Scotia. In 1780, he and Silas Ruen absconded from Richardson who put a runaway advertisement in the *Nova Scotia Gazette*. Richardson described Porter as "lame in one Foot, and limps much in his Walk" and offered a reward of four guineas for both men. Source: Charmaine Nelson, "Slavery and McGill University: Bicentenary Recommendations," Black Canadian Studies, McGill University, https://www.blackcanadianstudies.com/Recommendations_and_Report.pdf, 26–27.

914. POSTELL, MARY (c. 1791) – The most famous or infamous case of re-enslavement in the Maritimes is that of Mary Postell and her children. Unlike most aspects of the history of Maritime slavery, this particular incident has received sustained attention. Sylvia Hamilton memorialized Postell in a poem entitled "Potato Lady," while Carole Watterson Troxler has published an excellent essay about her sad life. The case is rare in that there is clear documentation that demonstrates re-enslavement and cruelty, but it also illustrates the ways in which Black people attempted to negotiate their way out of bondage. The story highlights the evil treatment of a mother and her brutally imposed separation from her children.

In 1791, Mary Postell went to the court and "Complained against Jesse Gray, of Argyle, for taking away her children." The indictment against Jesse Gray included the details of his re-enslavement and treatment of Mary Postell and her children, including that in 1785 Jesse Gray had violated the King's peace by enslaving Mary Postell and her two children, Flora and Nelly (also Nell), in St. Augustine and Shelburne. Gray, the indictment continued, through a combination of "grievous threatenings and other enormous abuses [did] compel terrify and oblige [the three] to serve, Work, and Labour" for his profit. Gray forced Mary Postell and her children into "the Hold of the said Ship or Vessel called the *Spring* Transport upon the High Seas for a long space of Time," and after 25 days they landed at Shelburne. For the next two years, Gray forced Mary Postell and her children to "Work and Labour … as the Slave and Slaves of him." The court papers also importantly noted that Gray had set an "Evil Example of all others offending in the like kind." After exploiting Postell and her children, Gray decided to sell her to William Mangham for "One Hundred Bushels of Potatoes." In 1790, Gray sold Flora Postell to John Henderson for £5. Henderson then took the child, around 9 or 10 years old, to North Carolina.

The case hinged on the testimony given by Mary Postell, Jesse Gray, and others. Mary Postell told the court that she had been born in South Carolina and was the "property of a certain Elijah Postell." After Elijah Postell's death, she became the slave of his son, who served in the Continental Army during the war. She "joined" His Majesty's forces near Charleston and evacuated to St. Augustine and eventually reached Shelburne with Jesse Gray who promised to "use her well." Postell said that Gray sold her to William Mangham and also sold her oldest child to John Henderson, who took her out of the province. Postell stated that Gray "has no right whatever to her or her Children and that she is afraid that said Jesse Gray or William Mangham will seize her and Child and carry them away." In support of Postell, Scipio and Dinah Wearing testified that Mr. Postell had owned Mary. Dinah claimed that Postell had run away from her owner and came into British lines. Scipio stated that Postell had been employed in public works for the British. Significantly, Dinah further pointed out that she had never known anyone else to own Mary Postell aside from the Postell family.

In his defence, Jesse Gray claimed that he had originally purchased Mary and her child Flora from Joseph Rea (or Wray) of Virginia in St. Augustine in 1783. Gray claimed that he then sold Mary and Flora to his brother Samuel Gray. Allegedly, Mary and Flora lived with Samuel for about two years during which time Mary gave birth to her younger daughter Nell. At this point, Gray purchased Mary and her children from his brother and migrated to Shelburne. Gray also stated that he sold Mary to William Mangham and her daughter Flora to John Henderson. But he kept Nell at his house. Gray obtained the support of a few witnesses. Not surprisingly, William Mangham stated that he had purchased Mary in 1787 for the hundred bushels of potatoes. He also mentioned knowing that Jesse Gray had a bill of sale from Samuel Gray. Gray also called Margaret Harris who lived in East Florida. She claimed that Mary Postell wanted Harris's husband to purchase Mary and her daughter Flora.

The court decided that the defendant was not guilty. Gray had been originally charged with a misdemeanor, that he was not the owner of Mary Postell and her children. Simply stated, Postell did not prove that she had been a free person. The decision to return Mary Postell to slavery underlined the presumption that a Black person was a slave unless proven otherwise. That Postell was re-enslaved, however, should not obscure for historians the way she pressed her claim as far as possible. In the years after the Postell decision, Nova Scotia judges reversed the course set by the Postell case. Instead of forcing alleged slaves to prove they were free, slaveowners had to prove they had the legal right to hold slaves – which, for many, turned out to be difficult or impossible. After the Mary Postell case, Black people continued to appear in the local courts but in much lesser numbers than during the 1780s and early 1790s. The reason for this is twofold. First, some people of African descent left for Sierra Leone or migrated away from the Shelburne/Birchtown area. Second, by the mid-1790s,

Shelburne had been practically deserted and some of the out-migrants were slaveholders. Sources: *R. v. Gray*, April to November 1791, Shelburne County Court of General Sessions of the Peace, RG 60, vol. 1, #49.4, NSA; Affadavit of Mary Postell [no date]; General Sessions at Shelburne, Nova Scotia, July 8, 1791, Shelburne Records, MG 4, vol. 141, NSA; Carole Watterson Troxler, "Re-enslavement of Black Loyalists: Mary Postell in South Carolina, East Florida, and Nova Scotia," *Acadiensis* 37 (Summer/Fall 2008): 70–85.

915. FLORA (c. 1791) – Flora is the older daughter of Mary Postell, who was sold to a man who took her to North Carolina (see entry for Mary Postell). Sources: *R. v. Gray*, April to November 1791, Shelburne County Court of General Sessions of the Peace, RG 60, vol. 1, #49.4, NSA; Affadavit of Mary Postell [no date], NSA; General Sessions at Shelburne, Nova Scotia, July 8, 1791, Shelburne Records, MG 4, vol. 141, NSA; Troxler, "Re-enslavement of Black Loyalists," 70–85.

916. NELL (c. 1791) – Nell was the younger daughter of Mary Postell, who Jesse Gray took away from her mother (see entry for Mary Postell). Sources: *R. v. Gray*, April to November 1791, Shelburne County Court of General Sessions of the Peace, RG 60, vol. 1, #49.4, NSA; Affadavit of Mary Postell [no date], NSA; General Sessions at Shelburne, Nova Scotia, July 8, 1791, Shelburne Records, MG 4, vol. 141, NSA; Troxler, "Re-enslavement of Black Loyalists," 70–85.

917. PRIME (c. 1784) – Prime was an enslaved person to Georgia Loyalist John Todd, who settled at Chedabucto, Nova Scotia, along with several other slaves. These slaves were probably from Georgia, South Carolina, East Florida, or another southern state. Source: Loyalists from Saint Augustine bound to Chedabucto, July 1784, Chipman Papers, Muster Master General's Office, Loyalist Musters, 1776–1785, MG 23, D1, ser. I, vol. 24, LAC.

918. PRIMOS, JOHN (c. 1758) – An enslaved man from Portsmouth, New Hampshire, John spent some time in Île Royale. Source: Donovan, "Nominal List of Slaves and Their Owners," 160.

919. PRIMUS (c. 1783, age 19) – Enslaved to George Thomas, Primus went to the Maritimes from New York along with a female slave. Primus was from South Carolina, and British officials described him as a "stout fellow." Source: Book of Negroes.

920. PRIMUS (c. 1783, age 11) – Enslaved to Major Menzies, Primus went to the Maritimes from New York with another young slave. British officials noted that he had been "Born & bred in the Major's family." These officials described him as a "likely boy." Source: Book of Negroes.

921. PRINCE (c. 1773) – Prince was enslaved to Joseph Pierpont, who wanted to sell him in a private sale. Source: Smith, "Slave in Canada," 10.

922. PRINCE (c. 1783, age 30) – Prince was enslaved to Dr. Nathaniel Bullern, who migrated from South Carolina to Nova Scotia with a total of 10 slaves. Bullern's slaves also indicate several different possibilities of family connections and kinship networks. His oldest slaves, Achabee and Catharina, were both 60 at the end of the American Revolution. Jenny and Prince were 40 and 30, respectively. Bullern also owned another male slave in his early 30s and three females ranging in ages 19 to 25. His two youngest slaves were an infant named Sarah and a 6 year old. It is unclear who the parents of these children were, but it is possible that one or both parents were among Bullern's slaves. British Officials in New York described Prince as a "stout fellow." Source: Book of Negroes.

923. PRINCE (c. 1783, age 22) – Enslaved to Chaplain Brown, who migrated to the Maritimes after the American Revolution, British officials in New York described Prince as a "stout fellow." Source: Book of Negroes.

924. PRINCE (c. 1783, age 19) – Enslaved to Richard Ruggles, Prince migrated to the Maritimes from New York though he was originally from Massachusetts. British officials described him as "stout." Source: Book of Negroes.

925. PRINCE (c. 1783, age 11) – Enslaved to Dr. McIntyre (of the General Hospital), who migrated to the Maritimes after the American Revolution, Prince might have been from Massachusetts, but it is unclear. McIntyre seems to have left Boston in 1776 but returned to New York with his regiment later in the war before coming to Nova Scotia in 1783. British officials in New York described Prince as a "likely boy." Source: Book of Negroes.

926. PRINCE (slave? c. 1784) – Prince was possibly enslaved to Ensign Douglass, who along with other southern Loyalists (consisting of various regiments such as the Royal North Carolina Regiment and the King's Carolina Rangers) settled at Country Harbour, Nova Scotia. The majority of these settlers and their slaves were from North Carolina, South Carolina, and Georgia. They had settled briefly in East Florida before moving to Nova Scotia. In a letter to Colonel Edward Winslow discussing these southern settlers, William Shaw expressed surprise that some of the Blacks with these southern settlers were not slaves; but, as historian Carole Watterson Troxler notes, this meant that some were "indeed slaves." In fact, as she points out, Blacks at Country Harbour were denied any land grants and those who were not slaves were "quasi-free." In an article, abolitionist Thomas Clarkson described what some white Loyalists did to supposedly free Black Loyalists: "It was not long till these loyalists, many of whom had been educated with all the ideas of the justice of slavery, the inferiority of negroes, and the superiority of white men, that are universal in the southern provinces of America, began to harass and oppress the industrious black settlers, and even wantonly to deprive them of the fruits of their labour, expelling them from the lands they had cleared." Clarkson continued by noting that whites reduced "again to slavery those negroes who had so honourably obtained their freedom. They hired them as servants, and, at the end of the stipulated time, refused payment of their wages, insisting that they were slaves: in some instances they destroyed their tickets of freedom, and then enslaved the negroes for want of them; in several instances, the unfortunate Africans were taken onboard vessels, carried to the West Indies, and there sold for the benefit of their plunderers." In the case of Black people at Country Harbour, they were listed on the musters as the "Servants" of a white Loyalist, which meant it was very easy for them to be re-enslaved if they were not already enslaved. Sources: Troxler, "John Legett at Country Harbour," 310; Clarkson, "Some Account of the New Colony at Sierra Leone," 229–30; Settlers at Country Harbour, Chipman Papers, Muster Master General's Office, Loyalist Musters, 1776–1785, MG 23, D1, ser. I, vol. 24, LAC. Note: Ellen Wilson believed that the information Clarkson used came from Thomas Peters' petition; see Wilson, *Loyal Blacks*, 181.

927. PRINCE [or **PRIMUS**] (c. 1786) – Prince was enslaved to Annapolis County resident Richard Betts, a Loyalist from New York. Richard Betts's 1786 inventory listed four slaves and their values. According to the document, Toney, Prince (or Primus), and Jane were listed as worth £35, while Harry commanded the price of £40. The relationship of each slave to the other slaves is unclear – if they were a family or totally unrelated. The total value of Betts's inventory was about £1,053, while the combined value of the slaves was £145. Thus, slaves accounted for 13.77 per cent of the total wealth of his estate. Source: Will of Richard Betts, 1786 Annapolis County, RG 48, NSA.

928. PRINCE (c. 1792) – Enslaved to John Agnew, in 1792 Prince attempted to escape from his owner. It is likely that Prince had been previously owned by Benjamin Davis, who placed a runaway advertisement for him in 1788. Davis's advertisement highlighted that Prince was "a stout well-made fellow, about five feet eight inches high, has a sour down look." Agnew also noted "He is artful, has a gloomy and malevolent look – is a daring liar, and has attempted twice before this to RUN-AWAY." Source: *Royal Gazette*, June 17, 1788; *Saint John Gazette*, June 29, 1792.

929. PRINCE (c. 1801) – Prince was enslaved to Nova Scotia politician and merchant Benjamin Belcher, who noted "I give and bequeath my Negro Boy called Prince to my son Stephen Belcher during his life." In his will, Belcher left strict directions for his heirs about the slaves, noting that he was "forever charging them my children unto whom I have entrusted these Negro people with never to sell barter or exchange them or any of them under any pretension except it is for whose bad [?] Offences as will render them not safe to be kept in the Family and that to be adjudged of by three Justices of the Peace in said Township and in such case as their order they may be sold and disposed of. And I further request as soon as these young Negroes shall be capable to be taught to read, they shall be learnt the word of God." Source: Will of Benjamin Belcher, 1801, Kings County, NSA.

930. PRINCE (slave? c. 1794/1802) – Possibly enslaved to Frederick Williams. British officials described Prince as a "Stout Fellow." The grand jury in Annapolis County heard a complaint about Mrs. Nelly Hewitt made by Prince "a Negro lately the Property of Frederick Williams for Enticing Sd. Negro to feloniously Defraud his Sd. Master of his property." But the grand jury voted "No Bill." Frederick Williams owned several slaves (and signed the 1807 Digby slaveholder petition). In 1802, Prince escaped from Frederick Williams and worked for John Allen and John Stayner. Williams attempted to regain control of Prince, but Allen and Stayner refused to recognize Williams's claim to own Prince. Williams said that his father originally owned Prince in Westchester, New York, before the American Revolution. Williams brought Prince to the Annapolis region of Nova Scotia where he worked for Williams, but also seems to have been hired out to Jonathan Morehouse. The court did not enter a judgment on this case. Source: Book of Negroes; Grand Jury, Country of Annapolis, April/November 1794, NSA. Cahill argues that Williams probably would "have been nonsuited." See *Williams v. Stayner and Allen*, 1805, RG 39, Box 90, NSA and Cahill, "Slavery and the Judges," 116–17.

931. PRINCE HUGHGINE (c. 1758) – Enslaved to Nathaniel McFervey, Prince was from New England. Source: Donovan, "Nominal List of Slaves and Their Owners," 160.

932. PRISCILLA (c. 1783, age 32) – Enslaved to John Ryerson, who migrated to the Maritimes after the American Revolution with a child named Sam who was probably Priscilla's son, she was likely from New Jersey. Ryerson's other slave, Tom, might have been the father of Priscilla's son. British officials at New York described her as a "stout wench." Source: Book of Negroes.

933. SAM (c. 1783, age 2, described as an infant) – Sam was probably the child of Priscilla and enslaved to John Ryerson. Source: Book of Negroes.

934. PRISCILLA (c. 1784) – John Wentworth sent Priscilla and 18 other slaves from Nova Scotia to his "relation" Paul Wentworth in Suriname. Wentworth described these slaves as "American born or well-seasoned, and are perfectly stout, healthy, sober, orderly, Industrious, & obedient."

Wentworth had the slaves Christened and claimed to be concerned for their welfare. He also claimed that the female slaves "promise well to increase their numbers." Source: John Wentworth to Paul Wentworth or his attorney, February 24, 1784.

935. PRISCILLA (c. 1786) – Delaware Loyalist Thomas Robinson owned at least four slaves. After the war, he settled in Shelburne, Nova Scotia, and, in his will, he gave Priscilla and her daughter Sally to his daughter. Source: Will of Thomas Robinson, Shelburne County, 1786/1787, NSA.

936. SALLY (c. 1786) – Sally was the daughter of Priscilla. Source: Will of Thomas Robinson, Shelburne County, 1786/1787, NSA.

937. PURDIE [PURDY], LYDIA (c. 1783, age 15) – Enslaved to Gabriel Purdy, who migrated to the Maritimes after the American Revolution, Lydia was probably from New York. The British official at New York described her as a "stout wench." Source: Book of Negroes.

938. QUACO (c. 1783, age 22) – Enslaved to Thomas Bannister, who migrated to the Maritimes after the American Revolution, Quaco was probably from Rhode Island and possibly originated in Africa. British officials in New York described him as a "stout fellow." Source: Book of Negroes.

939. QUAKO (c. 1784) – John Wentworth sent Quako and 18 other slaves from Nova Scotia to his "relation" Paul Wentworth in Suriname. Wentworth described these slaves as "American born or well-seasoned, and are perfectly stout, healthy, sober, orderly, Industrious, & obedient." Wentworth had the slaves Christened and claimed to be concerned for their welfare. He noted "Quako is a field Negro, has met an Accident in his arm, which will require some Indulgence." Source: John Wentworth to Paul Wentworth or his attorney, February 24, 1784.

940. QUASH (c. 1747) – This man was able to hire out some of his time and receive a wage at Louisbourg. Originally from New England, it seems likely that Quash was still enslaved (there were a very small number of free Blacks in 1747) and had to give part of his wages to his owner. Source: Donovan, "Nominal List of Slaves and Their Owners," 157.

941. QUINE (c. 1769) – In Hants County, Nova Scotia, the local court convicted Quine and another Black woman named Flora of stealing items from John Cunningham and sentenced both women to 25 lashes. Source: States, "Presence and Perseverance: Blacks in Hants County," 41.

942. RACHEL (c. 1783, age 28) – Enslaved to Isaac Enslow, Rachel went to the Maritimes from New York with one other slave who was probably her son. British officials described her as a "stout wench." Source: Book of Negroes.

943. DAVID (c. 1783, age 8) – David was probably the son of Rachel and enslaved to Isaac Enslow. Source: Book of Negroes.

944. RACHEL (c. 1783, age 32) – Enslaved to Lieutenant McLeod, who migrated to the Maritimes after the American Revolution with another slave, Rachel was described by British officials at New York as an "ordinary wench." Source: Book of Negroes.

945. RACHEL (c. 1784) – John Wentworth sent Rachel and 18 other slaves from Nova Scotia to his "relation" Paul Wentworth in Suriname. Wentworth described these slaves as "American born or well-seasoned, and are perfectly stout, healthy, sober, orderly, Industrious, & obedient." Wentworth had the slaves Christened and claimed to be concerned for their welfare. He also claimed that the female slaves "promise well to increase their numbers." Source: John Wentworth to Paul Wentworth or his attorney, February 24, 1784.

946. RACHEL (c. 1783) – Rachel was enslaved to William Hubbard, who died in the summer of 1783. Source: Smith, "Slave in Canada," 86.

947. RANGER, JOHN (c. 1783, age 24) – Enslaved to James Wright, who migrated to the Maritimes after the American Revolution, British officials in New York described John as a "stout fellow." Source: Book of Negroes.

948. RANSOM, WILLIAM (slave? c. 1784) – William was possibly enslaved to Captain George Dawkins, who, along with other southern Loyalists (consisting of various regiments such as the Royal North Carolina Regiment and the King's Carolina Rangers), settled at Country Harbour, Nova Scotia. The majority of these settlers and their slaves were from North Carolina, South Carolina, and Georgia. They had settled briefly in East Florida before moving to Nova Scotia. In a letter to Colonel Edward Winslow discussing these southern settlers, William Shaw expressed surprise that some of the Blacks with these southern settlers were not slaves; but his wording, as historian Carole Watterson Troxler notes, meant that some were "indeed slaves." In fact, as she points out, Blacks at Country Harbour were denied any land grants and those who were not slaves were "quasi-free." In an article, abolitionist Thomas Clarkson described what some white Loyalists did to supposedly free Black Loyalists: "It was not long till these loyalists, many of whom had been educated with all the ideas of the justice of slavery, the inferiority of negroes, and the superiority of white men, that are universal in the southern provinces of America, began to harass and oppress the industrious black settlers, and even wantonly to deprive them of the fruits of their labour, expelling them from the lands they had cleared." Clarkson continued by noting that whites reduced "again to slavery those negroes who had so honourably obtained their freedom. They hired them as servants, and, at the end of the stipulated time, refused payment of their wages, insisting that they were slaves: in some instances they destroyed their tickets of freedom, and then enslaved the negroes for want of them; in several instances, the unfortunate Africans were taken onboard vessels, carried to the West Indies, and there sold for the benefit of their plunderers." In the case of Black people at Country Harbour, they were listed on the musters as the "Servants" of a white Loyalist, which meant it was very easy for them to be re-enslaved if they were not already enslaved. Sources: Troxler, "John Legett at Country Harbour," 310; Clarkson, "Some Account of the New Colony at Sierra Leone," 229–30; Settlers at Country Harbour, Chipman Papers, Muster Master General's Office, Loyalist Musters, 1776–1785, MG 23, D1, ser. I, vol. 24, LAC. Note: Ellen Wilson believed that the information Clarkson used came from Thomas Peters' petition; see Wilson, *Loyal Blacks*, 181.

949. RANTY (slave? c. 1784) – Ranty was possibly enslaved to Ensign Hamilton, who, along with other southern Loyalists (consisting of various regiments such as the Royal North Carolina Regiment and the King's Carolina Rangers), settled at Country Harbour, Nova Scotia. The majority of these settlers and their slaves were from North Carolina, South Carolina, and Georgia. They had settled briefly in East Florida before moving to Nova Scotia. In a letter to Colonel Edward Winslow discussing these southern settlers, William Shaw expressed surprise that some of the Blacks with these southern settlers were not slaves; but his wording, as historian Carole Watterson Troxler notes, meant that some were "indeed slaves." In fact, as she points out, Blacks at Country Harbour were denied any land grants and those who were not slaves were "quasi-free." In an article, abolitionist Thomas Clarkson described what some white Loyalists did to supposedly free Black Loyalists: "It was not long till these loyalists, many of whom had been educated with all the ideas of the justice of slavery, the inferiority of negroes, and the superiority of white men, that are universal in the southern provinces of America, began to harass and oppress the industrious black settlers, and even wantonly to deprive them of the fruits of their labour, expelling them from the lands they had cleared." Clarkson continued by noting that whites reduced "again to slavery those negroes who had so honourably obtained their freedom. They hired them as servants, and, at the end of the stipulated time, refused payment of their wages, insisting that they were slaves: in some instances they destroyed their tickets of freedom, and then enslaved the negroes for want of them; in several instances, the unfortunate Africans were taken onboard vessels, carried to the West Indies, and there sold for the benefit of their plunderers." In the case of Black people at Country Harbour, they were listed on the musters as the "Servants" of a white Loyalist, which meant it was very easy for them to be re-enslaved if they were not already enslaved. Sources: Troxler, "John Legett at Country Harbour," 310; Clarkson, "Some Account of the New Colony at Sierra Leone," 229–30; Settlers at Country Harbour, Chipman Papers, Muster Master General's Office, Loyalist Musters, 1776–1785, MG 23, D1, ser. I, vol. 24, LAC. Note: Ellen Wilson believed that the information Clarkson used came from Thomas Peters' petition; see Wilson, *Loyal Blacks*, 181.

950. REED, ELIZABETH (c. 1779) – This enslaved woman testified on behalf of Elizabeth Watson, who unsuccessfully challenged her enslavement in a Halifax court. Sources: *Woodin v. Watson*, RG 37, 22/45, NSA; Franco Paz, "On the Edge of Freedom: The Re-enslavement of Elizabeth Watson," (MA Thesis, University of Vermont, 2018).

951. REED, MOSES (c. 1786) – Enslaved to Peter Green during the American Revolution, Moses and other slaves worked on Green's farm in Bute County, North Carolina. During the Loyalist occupation of Charleston, Moses Reed, Jameson Davis, and an elderly slave "ran away from Mr. Green, who was a Rebell." The older man died, but Davis and Reed both made it to Charleston, where they worked for the British. After the evacuation of Charleston, they accompanied other Southern Loyalists to St. Augustine, before eventually settling in Country Harbour, Nova Scotia, as free labourers for Colonel (or Captain) Hamilton. Molly Sinclair had been born in Charleston and lived with her master, James Sinclair, for most of her life. During the Revolution, she "was taken, with the other Plantation Negros" to Charleston. She migrated to St. Augustine before settling in Country Harbour with Colonel Hamilton. Her fellow servant, Phebe Martin, was the slave of Rebel William Martin. During the war, she ran away to Ninety-Six, South Carolina, and gained her freedom. After a short time in St. Augustine, she removed to Nova Scotia and also "lived with [Colonel?] Hamilton." Although these Black Loyalists were free subjects of His Majesty, they found that freedom in the Maritime colonies could be fleeting at best. Moses Reed and Jameson Davis were "two years in the Service of Colonel Hamilton" and "received no wages." Phebe Martin claimed that she "was never [Hamilton's] slave, or ever received any Wages from him." After two years of being re-enslaved, these captive labourers resorted to escaping from their would-be master by travelling to distant Halifax where they hoped to be safe. At this point Hamilton, along with Captain Daniel McNeil, organized what can only be termed a slave patrol, which attempted to recapture the escaped labourers. The slave catchers found the four runaways, put them in irons, and locked them in a ship's hold, but not before they beat Jameson Davis with a "Cudgell." Molly Sinclair recalled "she was Chained to Moses Reed when put on the vessell." The re-enslaved men and women were taken to Shelburne, but before they could be shipped away local officials got word of their condition and ordered McNeil to bring them ashore for an enquiry and court investigation. McNeil claimed that he had been told to take the re-enslaved Black Loyalists to Shelburne and give them to a Mr. Dean, who "was to give him a Receipt for them, and, as he understood, was to carry them to the Bahamas." After hearing the testimony of the four men and women along with McNeil's statement, the Shelburne court considered whether the Blacks were the rightful property of Hamilton (there was no evidence such as a bill of sale) or should go free. The majority of the court, five in favour of freeing them and two against, decided that "the aforesaid Negros" would be allowed to "go where they pleased." Source: Special Sessions at Shelburne, August 5, 1786, Shelburne Records, MG 4, vol. 141, NSA; Troxler, "Hidden from History." See also Troxler, "Southern Loyalists' Claim on East Florida," 582–90; Troxler, "Loyalist Refugees and the British Evacuation of East Florida," 1–28; and Troxler, "Migration of Carolina and Georgia Loyalists to Nova Scotia and New Brunswick." There were two Hamiltons – one a captain and the other a colonel.

952. RHYNO, DINAH (c. 1786) – Dinah was enslaved to Matthew Harris, who had previously owned 12-year-old Abram in 1779 but had later sold him away. Rhyno eventually obtained her freedom and married a Black Loyalist named George Mingo. Source: Smith, "Slave in Canada," 57.

953. RICHARD, ROSE (c. 1783, age 20) – Enslaved to Thomas Richard, who migrated to the Maritimes after the American Revolution, Rose was from Philadelphia. British officials at New York described her as a "healthy young woman." Source: Book of Negroes.

954. RICHARD (slave? c. 1784) – Richard was possibly enslaved to Captain Daniel McNeil (also spelled MacNeill), who, along with other southern Loyalists (consisting of various regiments such as the Royal North Carolina Regiment and the King's Carolina Rangers), settled at Country Harbour, Nova Scotia. The majority of these settlers and their slaves were from North Carolina, South Carolina, and Georgia. They had settled briefly in East Florida before moving to Nova Scotia. In a letter to Colonel Edward Winslow discussing these southern settlers, William Shaw expressed surprise that some of the Blacks with these southern settlers were not slaves; but his wording, as historian Carole Watterson Troxler notes, meant that some were "indeed slaves." In fact, as she points out, Blacks at Country Harbour were denied any land grants and those who were not slaves were "quasi-free." In an article, abolitionist Thomas Clarkson described what some white Loyalists did to supposedly free Black Loyalists: "It was not long till these loyalists, many of whom had been educated with all the ideas of the justice of slavery, the inferiority of negroes, and the superiority of white men, that are universal in the southern provinces of America, began to harass and oppress the industrious black settlers, and even wantonly to deprive them of the fruits of their labour, expelling them from the lands they had cleared." Clarkson continued by noting that whites reduced "again to slavery those negroes who had so honourably obtained their freedom. They hired them as servants, and, at the end of the stipulated time, refused payment of their wages, insisting that they were slaves: in some instances they destroyed their tickets of freedom, and then enslaved the negroes for want of them; in several instances, the unfortunate Africans were taken onboard vessels, carried to the West Indies, and there sold for the benefit of their plunderers." In the case of Black people at Country Harbour, they were listed on the musters as the "Servants" of a white Loyalist, which meant it was very easy for them to be re-enslaved if they were not already enslaved. Sources: Troxler, "John Legett at Country Harbour," 310; Clarkson, "Some Account of the New Colony at Sierra Leone," 229–30; Settlers at Country Harbour, Chipman Papers, Muster Master General's Office, Loyalist Musters, 1776–1785, MG 23, D1, ser. I, vol. 24, LAC. Note: Ellen Wilson believed that the information Clarkson used came from Thomas Peters' petition; see Wilson, *Loyal Blacks*, 181.

955. RICHARD (c. 1791) – Enslaved to David Hurd in Shelburne, Richard escaped from Hurd and worked for William Hill. Source: Marion Robertson, *King's Bounty*, 94–5.

956. RINN, BILLY (c. 1783, age 40) – Enslaved to Mary Rinn, Billy went to the Maritimes from New York with seven other slaves. British officials described him as an "ordinary fellow." Source: Book of Negroes.

957. RINN, CARSY (c. 1783, age 28) – Enslaved to Mary Rinn, Carsy went to the Maritimes from New York with seven other slaves. British officials described her as an "ordinary wench." Source: Book of Negroes.

958. RINN, CHARLES (c. 1783, age 32) – Enslaved to Mary Rinn, Charles went to the Maritimes from New York with seven other slaves. British officials described him as "tall and stout." Source: Book of Negroes.

959. RINN, PHILLIS (c. 1783, age 32) – Enslaved to Mary Rinn, Phillis went to the Maritimes from New York with seven other slaves. British officials described her as "stout & short." Source: Book of Negroes.

960. ROADS, MOTLEY (c. 1791) – According to John Clarkson, Motley was a re-enslaved child. After telling Lydia Jackson's story (who was re-enslaved and almost sold to the West Indies), Clarkson commented: "I do not know what induced me to mention the above case as I have many others of a similar nature; for example, Scott's case, Mr. Lee, Senr. Case, Smith's child, Motley Roads child, Mr. Farish's negro servant, &c." Source: Fergusson, *Clarkson's Mission to America*, 90.

961. ROBERT (c. 1783, age 30) – Enslaved to Lawrence Van Buskirk, who migrated to the Maritimes from New York with one other slave, Robert was probably from New York. British officials described him as a "stout fellow." Source: Book of Negroes.

962. ROBERT (slave? c. 1784) – Robert was possibly enslaved to Captain Daniel McNeil (also spelled MacNeill) who, along with other southern Loyalists (consisting of various regiments such as the Royal North Carolina Regiment and the King's Carolina Rangers), settled at Country Harbour, Nova Scotia. The majority of these settlers and their slaves were from North Carolina, South Carolina, and Georgia. They had settled briefly in East Florida before moving to Nova Scotia. In a letter to Colonel Edward Winslow discussing these southern settlers, William Shaw expressed surprise that some of the Blacks with these southern settlers were not slaves; but his wording, as historian Carole Watterson Troxler notes, meant that some were "indeed slaves." In fact, as she points out, Blacks at Country Harbour were denied any land grants and those who were not slaves were "quasi-free." In an article, abolitionist Thomas Clarkson described what some white Loyalists did to supposedly free Black Loyalists: "It was not long till these loyalists, many of whom had been educated with all the ideas of the justice of slavery, the inferiority of negroes, and the superiority of white men, that are universal in the southern provinces of America, began to harass and oppress the industrious black settlers, and even wantonly to deprive them of the fruits of their labour, expelling them from the lands they had cleared." Clarkson continued by noting that whites reduced "again to slavery those negroes who had so honourably obtained their freedom. They hired them as servants, and, at the end of the stipulated time, refused payment of their wages, insisting that they were slaves: in some instances they destroyed their tickets of freedom, and then enslaved the negroes for want of them; in several instances, the unfortunate Africans were taken onboard vessels, carried to the West Indies, and there sold for the benefit of their plunderers." In the case of Black people at Country Harbour, they were listed on the musters as the "Servants" of a white Loyalist, which meant it was very easy for them to be re-enslaved if they were not already enslaved. Sources: Troxler, "John Legett at Country Harbour," 310; Clarkson, "Some Account of the New Colony at Sierra Leone," 229–30; Settlers at Country Harbour, Chipman Papers, Muster Master General's Office, Loyalist Musters, 1776–1785, MG 23, D1, ser. I, vol. 24, LAC. Note: Ellen Wilson believed that the information Clarkson used came from Thomas Peters' petition; see Wilson, *Loyal Blacks*, 181.

963. ROBERT (slave? c. 1800) – In 1800 Charles Harrison left £10 to his "old Servant Negroe" Robert. Harrison lived on a farm in New Brunswick. Source: Will of Charles Harrison, 1800, Sunbury County, PANB.

964. ROBERT (c. 1804, age 12) – Robert was enslaved to Reverend James Scovil. In his will, Scovil promised his slaves Robert and Sampson (see entry) their freedom when they turned 26. Source: Will of James Scovil, Kings County, PANB.

965. ROGER (c. 1789) – Enslaved to Lord Dunmore in Nassau, Roger escaped to Shelburne, Nova Scotia. He seems to have been apprehended by George and Robert Ross, who Dunmore appointed to send Roger back to the Bahamas. Source: Robertson, *King's Bounty*, 95.

966. ROSALIE (c. 1736, age 14) – Enslaved to Andre Carrerot, Rosalie worked as a domestic and helped out with Carrerot's large family. Source: Donovan, "Slaves in Île Royale, 1713–1758," 31.

967. ROSE (c. 1783, age 14) – Enslaved to Captain Mills, who migrated to the Maritimes after the American Revolution with another teenage slave, Rose was described by British officials in New York as a "likely wench." Source: Book of Negroes.

968. ROSE (c. 1783) – Rose was enslaved, along with her 4-month-old son, to Enoch Plummer of the 69th Regiment of Foot. Plummer freed Rose's 4-month-old son in consideration of her faithful service. The document does not seem to free Rose. Plummer described Rose as a "Negro Woman Slave" while styling her son James as "mulatto." It seems likely that Plummer was the father. Source: Commissioner of Public Records, RG 1, vol. 170, p. 350, Nova Scotia Archives, https://novascotia.ca/archives/africanns/archives.asp?ID=27.

969. JAMES (c. 1783) – James was the child of Rose. Source: Commissioner of Public Records, RG 1, vol. 170, p. 350, Nova Scotia Archives, https://novascotia.ca/archives/africanns/archives.asp?ID=27.

970. ROSE (age 19, c. 1780s) – Rose was enslaved to Stephen Millidge of Sackville, New Brunswick. Source: States and Smardz Frost, "King's College," section 3, p. 4.

971. ROSE (c. 1788) – Rose was enslaved to Ann Cosby at Annapolis Royal in Nova Scotia. Cosby owned three slaves and freed all of them in her 1788 will, which read in part: "I do also give and devise unto my black Woman named Rose, a Molotto Girl named Agatha, and my black Man named John Bulkley … their full Freedom." Source: Will of Ann Cosby, 1788, Annapolis County, file C 11, NSA.

972. ROSE (c. 1790) – Enslaved to John Polhemus, Rose was baptized in 1790 and described as "belonging to Capt. Polhemus." It is possible that Rose was included by Polhemus in his listing of 10 slaves in the 1807 Digby slaveholder petition, but we cannot be sure because the petition did not list the names of individual slaves. Source: Register of Baptisms, February 1790, St. Luke's Anglican Church, Annapolis Royal, Annapolis County, NSA.

973. ROSE [also called **POL. WELCH**] (c. 1793) – Rose was the "Servant or Slave to Benjah Collins, Esq." The court in Liverpool charged her with the murder of her daughter, but she was found not guilty. Source: Fergusson, *Diary of Simeon Perkins, 1790–1796,* 237.

974. ROSE, MARIE MARGUERITE (c. 1736, age 19) – Originally from Africa, Marie Marguerite was enslaved to an officer named Jean Loppinot. She would remain the domestic slave of this family until 1755. During that time, she took care of Loppinot's 12 children. In 1738, Marie Marguerite had her own son named Jean Francois, but he died at the age of 13. In 1755 she gained her freedom and married Jean Baptiste, a Mi'kmaq man described in the record as an "Indian." With her freedom, Marie Marguerite and her husband opened a tavern, but she died in 1757 only two years after obtaining her freedom. As historian Ken Donovan notes, the inventory of her estate shows that she had a wide variety of skills and tastes. She possessed a cookbook, an extensive clothing wardrobe, and various items indicating that Marie was also a seamstress. Marie also seems to have kept a valuable garden before her death. What we have here is the remarkable but incredibly fragmented history of a woman who went from Africa to the northern French Atlantic world. She suffered from nearly two decades of enslavement in Île Royale, but eventually became free and married into the local Indigenous community. Source: Donovan, "Slaves in Île Royale," 33–4.

975. JEAN FRANÇOIS (c. 1738) – Jean François was the son of Marie Marguerite Rose. Source: Donovan, "Female Slaves as Sexual Victims in Île Royale," 149.

976. ROSE (c. 1755) – Rose was enslaved to a Madame Rodrigue. Source: Donovan, "Nominal List of Slaves and Their Owners," 159.

977. RUBEN (c. 1745) – Ruben was enslaved to Daniel Bacon at Louisbourg. Source: Donovan, "Nominal List of Slaves and Their Owners," 156.

978. RUBIN (c. 1746) – Enslaved to Captain Hufton, Rubin was from New England. Source: Donovan, "Nominal List of Slaves and Their Owners," 157.

979. RUEN, SILAS (c. 1780, age 18) – Ruen was enslaved to one [Mr.?] Richardson in Halifax, Nova Scotia. In 1780, he and Bon Porter absconded from Richardson who put a runaway advertisement in the *Nova Scotia Gazette.*

Richardson described Ruen as "a thin made Negroe, about Eighteen Years of Age, has a sauntering Walk, and a sullen look." Richardson offered a reward of four guineas for both men. Source: Nelson, "Slavery and McGill University," 26–27.

980. RUGGLES, HESTER (c. 1783, age 7) – Enslaved to General Timothy Ruggles, Hester went to the Maritimes with another child slave. Hester was from Massachusetts, and British officials described her as a "fine wench." Source: Book of Negroes.

981. RUGGLES, JEFFERY (c. 1783, age 6) – Enslaved to General Timothy Ruggles, Jeffery migrated to the Maritimes with another child slave. Jeffery was from Massachusetts, and British officials described him as a "fine boy." Source: Book of Negroes.

982. RUMFORD (c. 1760) – Enslaved to Nathaniel Patten, Rumford was from Boston. Source: Donovan, "Nominal List of Slaves and Their Owners," 160.

983. SALLY (c. 1783, age 10) – Enslaved to Captain Raymond, Sally went to the Maritimes from New York. British officials described her as an "ordinary wench." Source: Book of Negroes.

984. SALLY (c. 1783, age 40) – Sally was enslaved to Mr. Elliot, who went to the Maritimes after the American Revolution. British officials in New York described her as a "stout wench." Source: Book of Negroes.

985. SALLY (slave? c. 1784) – Sally was possibly enslaved to Lieutenant Joel Hudson, who, along with other southern Loyalists (consisting of various regiments such as the Royal North Carolina Regiment and the King's Carolina Rangers), settled at Country Harbour, Nova Scotia. The majority of these settlers and their slaves were from North Carolina, South Carolina, and Georgia. They had settled briefly in East Florida before moving to Nova Scotia. In a letter to Colonel Edward Winslow discussing these southern settlers, William Shaw expressed surprise that some of the Blacks with these southern settlers were not slaves; but his wording, as historian Carole WattersonTroxler notes, meant that some were "indeed slaves." In fact, as she points out, Blacks at Country Harbour were denied any land grants and those who were not slaves were "quasi-free." In an article, abolitionist Thomas Clarkson described what some white Loyalists did to supposedly free Black Loyalists: "It was not long till these loyalists, many of whom had been educated with all the ideas of the justice of slavery, the inferiority of negroes, and the superiority of white men, that are universal in the southern provinces of America, began to harass and oppress the industrious black settlers, and even wantonly to deprive them of the fruits of their labour, expelling them from the lands they had cleared." Clarkson continued by noting that whites reduced "again to slavery those negroes who had so honourably obtained their freedom. They hired them as servants, and, at the end of the stipulated time, refused payment of their wages, insisting that they were slaves: in some instances they destroyed their tickets of freedom, and then enslaved the negroes for want of them; in several instances, the unfortunate Africans were taken onboard vessels, carried to the West Indies, and there sold for the benefit of their plunderers." In the case of Black people at Country Harbour, they were listed on the musters as the "Servants" of a white Loyalist, which meant it was very easy for them to be re-enslaved if they were not already enslaved. Sources: Troxler, "John Legett at Country Harbour," 310; Clarkson, "Some Account of the New Colony at Sierra Leone," 229–30; Settlers at Country Harbour, Chipman Papers, Muster Master General's Office, Loyalist Musters, 1776–1785, MG 23, D1, ser. I, vol. 24, LAC. Note: Ellen Wilson believed that the information Clarkson used came from Thomas Peters' petition; see Wilson, *Loyal Blacks*, 181.

986. SAM (c. 1783, age 40) – Enslaved to Johannes (or John) Ackerman, who migrated to the Maritimes after the American Revolution with two other slaves, Sam was probably from New Jersey. British officials at New York described him as an "ordinary fellow." Source: Book of Negroes.

987. SAM (c. 1783, age 35) – Enslaved to Johannes (or John) Ackerman, who migrated to the Maritimes after the American Revolution with two other slaves, Sam was probably from New Jersey. British officials at New York described him as an "ordinary fellow." Source: Book of Negroes.

988. SAM (c. 1783, age 35) – Enslaved to Bartholomew Crannell, who migrated to the Maritimes after the American Revolution with several other slaves, Sam was probably from New York. Source: Book of Negroes.

989. SAM (c. 1783, age 26) – Enslaved to Joseph Holmes, who migrated to the Maritimes from New York along with another male slave, Sam was probably from New Jersey. British officials in New York described him as a "stout B [Black] fellow." Source: Book of Negroes.

990. SAM (c. 1783, age 22) – Enslaved to Valentine Nutter, who migrated to the Maritimes after the American Revolution with a female slave, Sam was from New York. British officials at New York described him as a "stout fellow, tall." Source: Book of Negroes.

991. SAM (c. 1783, age 22) – Enslaved to Mr. Van Horn (possibly Lawrence Van Horn?), who migrated to the Maritimes after the American Revolution with another slave, Sam was probably from New Jersey. British officials at New York described him as an "ordinary fellow." Source: Book of Negroes.

992. SAM (c. 1783, age 15) – Enslaved to Benjamin Lester, who migrated to the Maritimes with four other slaves, Sam was probably from New York. British officials in New York described him as a "stout lad." Source: Book of Negroes.

993. SAM (c. 1783, age 13) – Enslaved to John Norris, who migrated to the Maritimes after the American Revolution with a few other slaves, British officials described Sam as a "stout boy." Source: Book of Negroes.

994. SAM (c. 1784, age 32/33) – Sam was enslaved to John Grant. Originally from Scotland, after serving the British army near Ticonderoga during the Seven Years War, Grant settled in Queens County, Long Island. After the American Revolution, he settled in Nova Scotia with a large family and nine slaves. These enslaved people might have been a family unit. Sources: Cottreau-Robins, "Landscape of Slavery in Loyalist Era Nova Scotia," 131–2; also Smith, "Slave in Canada," 93–4.

995. SAM (c. 1787, age 17–18) – In 1787 Sam ran away with his sister (see entry for Beller) and another man (see entry for Tony Smith). In a runaway slave advertisement, his owner Thomas Lester commented that Sam and Beller had been "raised in the family." Lester described Sam as "between a black and dark Mulatto 17 or 18 years old, middling tall and slim; quick spoken, attempts to play the VIOLIN, has a London brown coloured coat, ticking trousers and other clothes." Source: *Royal Gazette* (New Brunswick), July 10, 1787.

996. SAM (c. 1794, age 28) – Sam was enslaved to James DeLancey, who sold him to Francis Ryerson for £50 in Nova Scotia. Source: Hanger, "Life of Loyalist Colonel James DeLancey," 49.

997. SAM (c. 1802) – In 1802 Sam ended up in the Prince Edward Island Supreme Court due to the filing of habeas corpus on his behalf. Thomas Wright, the owner, went to the court and produced a bill of sale and the court returned Sam to his owner. The court stated: "It is ordered by the court that the said Negro return to service of his said Master [whose] Title to him appears perfect and compleat." It is also clear from the document that Sam had been previously owned by John Strickland. Source: Supreme Court, Prince Edward Island, RG 6.1, ser. I, sub-ser. I, vol. 10, p. 49, PAROPEI.

998. SAMBO (c. ?) – Archibald Allardice sold Sambo to Dr. John Harris in Nova Scotia. Source: Smith, "Slave in Canada," 54.

999. SAMPSON [BUSH] (c. 1783, age 40) – Enslaved to Richard Birmingham, Sampson went from New York to the Maritimes. British officials described him as an "ordinary man." Source: Book of Negroes.

1000. SAMPSON (c. 1804, age 12) – Sampson was enslaved to Reverend James Scovil. In his will, Scovil promised his slaves Robert (see entry) and Sampson their freedom when they turned 26. The will does not mention the parents of either child. Source: Will of James Scovil, Kings County, PANB.

1001. SAMUEL (c. 1784) – Samuel was possibly an enslaved man who settled at Sheet Harbour. He is listed in the Sheet Harbour muster roll under the heading "Negroes." Source: Muster Roll of Royal Garrison Battalion Settled at Sheet Harbour, Chipman Papers, Muster Master General's Office, Loyalist Musters, 1776–1785, MG 23, D1, ser. I, vol. 24, LAC.

1002. SAMUEL (slave? c. 1784) – Samuel was possibly an enslaved man who settled at Sheet Harbour; there were two Samuels at Sheet Harbor. He is listed in the Sheet Harbour muster roll under the heading "Negroes." Source: Muster Roll of Royal Garrison Battalion Settled at Sheet Harbour, Chipman Papers, Muster Master General's Office, Loyalist Musters, 1776–1785, MG 23, D1, ser. I, vol. 24, LAC.

1003. SAMUEL (c. 1798) – Samuel was enslaved to the Rector of Shelburne, who owned a total of three slaves at the time of his death. He valued the unnamed girl at £25, Samuel at £35, and William at £30. Source: Smith, "Slave in Canada," 59.

1004. SAMUEL (c. 1801) – Enslaved to Nova Scotia politician and merchant Benjamin Belcher in Cornwallis, Nova Scotia, who noted "I give my Negro man named Jack and my Negro boy Samuel and Negro boy James and Negro Girl called Chloe to my son Benjamin and his Heirs." The relationship between Jack, Samuel, James, and Chloe is unclear. Jack might have been the father or another relative or simply fictive kin. In his will, Belcher left strict directions for his heirs about the slaves, noting that he was "for ever charging them my children unto whom I have entrusted these Negro people with never to sell barter or exchange them or any of them under any pretension except it is for whose bad [?] Offences as will render them not safe to be kept in the Family and that to be adjudged of by three Justices of the Peace in said Township and in such case as their order they may be sold and disposed of. And I further request as soon as these young Negroes shall be capable to be taught to read, they shall be learnt the word of God." Belcher had Samuel baptized in 1793. Source: Will of Benjamin Belcher, NSA.

1005. SARAH (c. 1783, age 30) – Enslaved to Jasper Buckel, who migrated to the Maritimes after the American Revolution, Sarah was probably from New York. She also had one unnamed infant child. The British official at New York noted that she had belonged to John Tabor Kempe (a well-known Loyalist) and described her as a "short wench." Source: Book of Negroes.

1006. UNNAMED INFANT CHILD OF SARAH (c. 1783) – This unnamed infant child of Sarah was enslaved to Jasper Buckel and went to the Maritimes with his or her mother. Source: Book of Negroes.

1007. SARAH (c. 1783, age 23) – Enslaved to Lewis O'Brien, who migrated to the Maritimes after the American Revolution with a few other slaves, Sarah was described by British officials as a "stout wench." Source: Book of Negroes.

1008. SARAH (c. 1783, age 22) – Sarah was enslaved to Francis Ryerson, who migrated to the Maritimes after the American Revolution. She was likely from New York. British officials at New York described her as a "stout wench." Source: Book of Negroes.

1009. SARAH (c. 1783, age 20) – Enslaved to James Bogart, who migrated to the Maritimes after the American Revolution with an infant as well, Sarah was probably from New York. British officials at New York described her as a "likely wench." Source: Book of Negroes.

1010. SUSANNAH (c. 1783, age 6 months) – Susannah was the child of Sarah and enslaved to James Bogart. Source: Book of Negroes.

1011. SARAH (c. 1783, age 17) – Enslaved to Mrs. Johnson, who migrated to the Maritimes after the American Revolution with a male slave, Sarah was described by British officials at New York as a "stout wench." Source: Book of Negroes.

1012. SARAH (slave? c. 1784) – Sarah was possibly enslaved to Robert Jackson shortly after arriving in Nova Scotia along with other Loyalists. Jackson planned to settle nearby Halifax. Source: Loyalists and Disbanded Troops at Cole Harbour, Chipman Papers, Muster Master General's Office, Loyalist Musters, 1776–1785, MG 23, D1, ser. I, vol. 24, LAC.

1013. SARAH (c. 1784) – Sarah was enslaved to Loyalist James Lysle (probably Lyle) in Nova Scotia along with her daughter and an adult male slave named Liberty. Source: Loyalists from Saint Augustine bound to Chedabucto, July 1784, Chipman Papers, Muster Master General's Office, Loyalist Musters, 1776–1785, MG 23, D1, ser. I, vol. 24, LAC; Hart, History of the County of Guysborough, 250–2.

1014. PEGG (c. 1784) – Pegg was the daughter of Sarah. Source: Loyalists from Saint Augustine bound to Chedabucto, July 1784, Chipman Papers, Muster Master General's Office, Loyalist Musters, 1776–1785, MG 23, D1, ser. I, vol. 24, LAC; Hart, History of the County of Guysborough, 250–2.

1015. SARAH (c. 1796) – Thomas Watson bequeathed Sarah – known later as Sally Surrey – to his daughter. Source: Smith, "Slave in Canada," 18.

1016. SAUZY (c. 1732, age 7) – Pierre Morpain had his slave Georges dit Sauzy (this means he preferred the name Sauzy) baptized at the age of 7. Between 1733 and 1745, Sauzy was a domestic slave to Morpain and his family. In 1745, during the siege of Louisbourg, Sauzy saved Morpain and earned his freedom. Sauzy's actions were described by another leader of the French forces during the siege: "His negro carried him, dragged him, hid him under some leaves and saved him. In recognition of his services, he gave him his liberty." Source: Donovan, "Slaves and Their Owners in Île Royale," 25–6.

1017. SAVAGE, HARRY (c. 1784) – Harry was enslaved to the Departments of the Army and Navy, which had settled at Chedabucto, Nova Scotia. Source: Muster Roll of Settlers at Chedabucto (including Departments of the Army and Navy), Chipman Papers, Muster Master General's Office, Loyalist Musters, 1776–1785, MG 23, D1, ser. I, vol. 24, LAC.

1018. SCOTT'S CASE (c. 1791) – According to John Clarkson, this person was re-enslaved in Nova Scotia. After telling the story of Lydia Jackson (who was re-enslaved and almost sold to the West Indies), Clarkson commented: "I do not know what induced me to mention the above case as I have many others of a similar nature; for example, Scott's case, Mr. Lee, Senr. Case, Smith's child, Motley Roads child, Mr. Farish's negro servant, &c." Source: Fergusson, Clarkson's Mission to America, 90.

1019. SENTRY (c. 1783, age 28) – Enslaved to Mary Rinn, Sentry went to the Maritimes from New York with seven other slaves. She had been previously owned by Marianna Jones, who had given her to Mary Rinn. British officials described Sentry as a "stout wench." Source: Book of Negroes.

1020. UNNAMED CHILD OF SENTRY (c. 1783) – This unnamed child of Sentry was enslaved to Mary Rinn. Source: Book of Negroes.

1021. SHARPER [MOFFET or COLE] (c. 1783, age 20) – Born to Anthony Moffet and Anna Cole in Rhode Island, Sharper left Rhode Island during the American Revolution and eventually settled in Parrsboro, Nova Scotia, with his owner Edward Cole. Source: Book of Negroes; Parrsboro Township Book, ECWA.

1022. SHEAFFE, CATO (c. 1760) – Enslaved to Edward Sheaffe, the commissary of Colonel Edward Bagley's Essex Regiment at Louisbourg, Cato was from New England. Source: Donovan, "Nominal List of Slaves and Their Owners," 160.

1023. SHEPPERD, DAVID (c. 1780s) – Enslaved to PEI Lieutenant Governor Edmund Fanning, David was probably from North Carolina. Source: Whitfield and Cahill, "Slave Life and Slave Law," 36.

1024. SIBBE (c. 1783, age 11) – Enslaved to Moses Ward, who migrated to the Maritimes after the American Revolution, British officials at New York described Sibbe as a "likely girl." Source: Book of Negroes.

1025. SILVEY (slave? c. 1784) – Silvey was possibly enslaved to Captain Daniel McNeil (also spelled MacNeill), who, along with other southern Loyalists (consisting of various regiments such as the Royal North Carolina Regiment and the King's Carolina Rangers), settled at Country Harbour, Nova Scotia. The majority of these settlers and their slaves were from North Carolina, South Carolina, and Georgia. They had settled briefly in East Florida before moving to Nova Scotia. In a letter to Colonel Edward Winslow discussing these southern settlers, William Shaw expressed surprise that some of the Blacks with these southern settlers were not slaves; but his wording, as historian Carole Watterson Troxler notes, meant that some were "indeed slaves." In fact, as she points out, Blacks at Country Harbour were denied any land grants and those who were not slaves were "quasi-free." In an article, abolitionist Thomas Clarkson described what some white Loyalists did to supposedly free Black Loyalists: "It was not long till these loyalists, many of whom had been educated with all the ideas of the justice of slavery, the inferiority of negroes, and the superiority of white men, that are universal in the southern provinces of America, began to harass and oppress the industrious black settlers, and even wantonly to deprive them of the fruits of their labour, expelling them from the lands they had cleared." Clarkson continued by noting that whites reduced "again to slavery those negroes who had so honourably obtained their freedom. They hired them as servants, and, at the end of the stipulated time, refused payment of their wages, insisting that they were slaves: in some instances they destroyed their tickets of freedom, and then enslaved the negroes for want of them; in several instances, the unfortunate Africans were taken onboard vessels, carried to the West Indies, and there sold for the benefit of their plunderers." In the case of Black people at Country Harbour, they were listed on the musters as the "Servants" of a white Loyalist, which meant it was very easy for them to be re-enslaved if they were not already enslaved. Sources: Troxler, "John Legett at Country Harbour," 310; Clarkson, "Some Account of the New Colony at Sierra Leone," 229–30; Settlers at Country Harbour, Chipman Papers, Muster Master General's Office, Loyalist Musters, 1776–1785, MG 23, D1, ser. I, vol. 24, LAC. Note: Ellen

Wilson believed that the information Clarkson used came from Thomas Peters' petition; see Wilson, *Loyal Blacks*, 181.

1026. SILVIA (c. 1782) – Silvia was probably enslaved to local politician and Lieutenant Colonel John Creighton who had immigrated to Nova Scotia with Edward Cornwallis. During the American Revolution, privateers attacked the town of Lunenburg where Creighton lived. During the raid, Silvia distinguished herself for hiding some of her owner's belongings. According to J. Murray Beck, "His house and its effects were burned, although his black servant Silvia, who protected his son with her body, saved some valuable coins and plate by lowering them into the well." Source: J. Murray Beck, "CREIGHTON, JOHN," *Dictionary of Canadian Biography*, vol, 5, http://www.biographi.ca/en/bio/creighton_john_1721_1807_5E.html.

1027. SILVIA (c. 1783, age 30) – Silvia was enslaved to Colonel Edward Cole. Born in Rhode Island to Anna Cole and Frederick Molbon, she spent the first several decades of her life in Rhode Island before being evacuated with her owner to New York. She gave birth to Abraham while the family lived in New York during the war. She eventually settled in Parrsboro with her owner. Source: Book of Negroes; Parrsboro Township Book, ECWA.

1028. ABRAHAM (c. 1783, age 3) – The son of Silvia, Abraham was enslaved to Rhode Island Loyalist Colonel Edward Cole. Born in New York, Abraham settled in Parrsboro, Nova Scotia, with his family and his owner. Source: Book of Negroes; Parrsboro Township Book, ECWA.

1029. SILVIA (c. 1783, age 30) – Enslaved to James Collins, who migrated to the Maritimes after the American Revolution, Silvia was probably from New Jersey. British officials at New York described her as a "stout wench." Source: Book of Negroes.

1030. SILVIA (c. 1783, age 30) – Enslaved to Valentine Nutter, who migrated to the Maritimes after the American Revolution with another slave, Silvia was from New York. British officials at New York described her as a "stout wench." Source: Book of Negroes.

1031. SILVIA (c. 1783, age 16) – Enslaved to James Ethridge, who migrated to the Maritimes after the American Revolution with another teenaged slave, Silvia was probably from New York. British officials at New York described her as a "likely girl." Source: Book of Negroes.

1032. SILVIA (c. 1788) – Silvia was enslaved to New York Loyalist Joseph Totten, whose will lists five slaves. He bequeathed three Black children to his daughters, but not the other slaves, which means that a slave family was probably broken up. Totten stated: "To my Daughter Mary Totten I Give and bequeath my Negro Girl Slave named Silvia." Source: Will of Joseph Totten, 1788, Annapolis County, RG 48, NSA.

1033. SILVIA (c. 1790, age 1) – A local church in Granville baptized Silvia in 1790. She was listed as "the property of James Etheridge." Source: Register of Baptisms and Marriages for the Three Districts of the Township of Granville, Granville Township Book, NSA.

1034. SILVIE (c. 1813) – Euphimia Harris bequeathed 50 acres of land to her "servant black woman" Silvie. The wording of the will does not clearly define Silvie's past status in the family, but she was likely enslaved, eventually freed, and subsequently lived with the Harris family. Source: Will of Euphimia Harris, Charlotte County, 1813, PANB.

1035. SIMMONS, DINAH (c. 1783, age 40) – Dinah was enslaved to Peter Fitzsimmons, who migrated to the Maritimes after the American Revolution. British officials in New York noted Fitzsimmons had purchased Dinah from another person. These same officials described her as a "stout wench." Source: Book of Negroes.

1036. SIMMONS, JOHN (c. 1791, age 5) – In this court case, a sympathetic local citizen told the court that Timothy Mahan "detains, a Negro Boy, who he hath attempted to sell, and Dispose of, without having property therein." The court ordered Mahan to appear before it along with the 5-year-old John Simmons. Mahan claimed that Simmons's parents had given him the boy three years earlier. The court found that Mahan had treated the child "kindly, and humanely," but ruled that Simmons's parents had no right to give him away and Mahan had no "property in the said Boy." What is unclear is whether Mahan originally stole the child from his parents, as saying they gave the child to him was certainly a convenient answer. Nevertheless, the boy escaped sale to another owner. The case of John Simmons underlines the tenuous nature of the line between slavery and freedom that Black people faced in the Maritimes, even – perhaps especially – if they were small children. Source: General Sessions at Shelburne, Nova Scotia, November 3, 1791; Shelburne Records, MG 4, vol. 141, NSA.

1037. SIMON (c. 1783, age 12) – Enslaved to John Jakeways, Simon went to the Maritimes from New York with his owner. British officials in New York described him as a "fine boy." Source: Book of Negroes.

1038. SIMON (c. 1802, age 3) – In 1802, Prince Edward Island slaveholder Thomas Haszard (or Hassard), originally from Rhode Island, sold two mixed-race children (he described them as "molatta") to his relatives. The bill of sale says nothing about either of the children's parents. But it seems that the two children were being sold away from them or at least separated from certain members of their family. Source: Declaration by Thomas [Haszard] re. selling mulatto children, Nov. 1802, acc. 2702, Smith Alley Collection, ser. 22, no. 878, PAROPEI.

1039. SIMON, BLAISE (c. 1732, age 15) – Enslaved to Michel Daccarette, Blaise was born in Africa. He lived with another slave who was 11 years old. Daccarette was a cruel master. In one instance, he came home late at night (4 a.m.) and found Blaise asleep in the kitchen. Daccarette proceeded to hit Blaise with his cane. Source: Donovan, "Slaves and Their Owners in Île Royale," 22.

1040. SINCLAIR, MOLLY (c. 1786) – Molly Sinclair had been born in Charleston and lived with her master, James Sinclair, for most of her life. During the Revolution, she "was taken, with the other Plantation Negros" to Charleston. She migrated to St. Augustine before settling in Country Harbour with Colonel Hamilton. Her fellow servant, Phebe Martin, was the slave of Rebel William Martin. During the war, she ran away to Ninety-Six, South Carolina, and gained her freedom. After a short time in St. Augustine, she removed to Nova Scotia and also "lived with [Colonel?] Hamilton." Although these Black Loyalists were free subjects of His Majesty, they found that freedom in the Maritime colonies could be fleeting at best. Moses Reed and Jameson Davis were "two years in the Service of Colonel Hamilton" and "received no wages." Phebe Martin claimed that she "was never [Hamilton's] slave, or ever received any Wages from him." After two years of being re-enslaved, these captive labourers resorted to escaping from their would-be master by travelling to distant Halifax where they hoped to be safe. At this point Hamilton, along with Captain Daniel McNeil, organized what can only be termed a slave patrol, which attempted to recapture the escaped labourers. The slave catchers found the four runaways, put them in irons, and locked them in a ship's hold, but not before they beat Jameson Davis with a "Cudgell." Molly Sinclair recalled "she was Chained to Moses Reed when put on the vessell." The re-enslaved men and women were taken to Shelburne, but before they could be shipped away local officials got word of their condition and ordered McNeil to bring them ashore for an enquiry and court investigation. McNeil claimed that he had been told to take the re-enslaved Black Loyalists to Shelburne and give them to a Mr. Dean, who "was to give him a Receipt for them, and, as he understood, was to carry them to the Bahamas." After hearing the testimony of the four men and women along with McNeil's statement, the Shelburne court considered whether the Blacks were the rightful property of Hamilton (there was no evidence such as a bill of sale) or should go free. The majority of the court, five in favour of freeing them and two against, decided that "the aforesaid Negros" would be allowed to "go where they pleased." Sources: Special Sessions at Shelburne, August 5, 1786, Shelburne Records, MG 4, vol. 141, NSA; Troxler, "Hidden from History." See also Troxler, "Southern Loyalists' Claim on East Florida," 582–90; Troxler, "Loyalist Refugees and the British Evacuation of East Florida," 1–28; and Troxler, "Migration of Carolina and Georgia Loyalists to Nova Scotia and New Brunswick." There were two Hamiltons – one a captain and the other a colonel.

1041. SIPPEO (c. 1797) – Sippeo was enslaved to George Harding, who later sold him to his son. Source: *Daily Sun* (New Brunswick), August 29, 1890.

1042. SKINNER, JOSEPH (c. 1783, age 35) – Enslaved to Peter Lynch, Joseph went to the Maritimes from New York with a woman and child who might have been his wife and daughter (see entries for Tinnia Lynch and Sally Lynch). Joseph was probably from New Jersey as his first owner, Thomas Skinner, was from Amboy. British officials described him as a "stout fellow." Source: Book of Negroes.

1043. SMALLWOOD, ELIZABETH (c. 1780s–1790s) – Enslaved to Joseph Smallwood, Elizabeth later married a man named Sancho on Prince Edward Island. Source: Hornby, *Black Islanders*, 9.

1044. SMITH'S CHILD (c. 1791) – According to John Clarkson, this child was re-enslaved in Nova Scotia. After telling the story of Lydia Jackson (who was re-enslaved and almost sold to the West Indies), Clarkson commented, "I do not know what induced me to mention the above case as I have many others of a similar nature; for example, Scott's case, Mr. Lee, Senr. Case, Smith's child, Motley Roads child, Mr. Farish's negro servant, &c." Source: Fergusson, *Clarkson's Mission to America*, 90.

1045. SMITH, CATO (c. 1800–1838, age 81) – Cato was enslaved to J.F.W. DesBarres, a one-time governor of Nova Scotia. Cato remained with the Des-Barres family until his death. The *Acadian Recorder* noted "He will be long remembered for his good qualities, and his death much regretted." Source: States, "Presence and Perseverance: Blacks in Hants County," 40; *Acadian Recorder*, April 7, 1838. Thanks to Shirley Tillotson for sharing Smith's obituary.

1046. SMITH, SAMUEL (c. 1784) – Samuel was enslaved to the Departments of the Army and Navy, which settled at Chedabucto, Nova Scotia. Source: Muster Roll of Settlers at Chedabucto (including Departments of the Army and Navy), Chipman Papers, Muster Master General's Office, Loyalist Musters, 1776–1785, MG 23, D1, ser. I, vol. 24, LAC.

1047. SMITH, TONY (c. 1787) – A labourer for Thomas Lester in New Brunswick, in 1787 Tony seemingly helped Lester's slaves Sam and Beller escape. According to Lester, Tony worked as "a free fellow, but hired for a time; he is tall and slim, between a black and mulatto, speaks broken, wears blue or brown coat, ticking trousers, and has other clothes with him." The fact that he ran away with Beller and Sam indicates that he saw his condition as similar to the two slaves even though Tony was free. Source: *Royal Gazette*, July 10, 1787.

1048. SOLOMON (c. 1760s) – Solomon was enslaved to Reverend Seccombe in Chester, Nova Scotia. A well-known Baptist preacher, Seccombe came from Massachusetts and brought a few slaves with him. Source: Montgomery, "Unsettled Plantation," 44.

1049. SOLOMON (c. 1783, age 12) – Enslaved to Charles Morris, who purchased him from Jeremiah Savage, Solomon went to the Maritimes from New York with one other slave; it is unclear if they were related. Solomon was from South Carolina and British officials described him as a "fine boy." Source: Book of Negroes.

1050. SPENCE (c. 1790) – Spence was enslaved to Henry Burbidge, who planned to manumit him after he served another seven years. Source: Eaton, *History of Kings County*, 234.

1051. SPRUCE (c. 1780) – Spruce was enslaved to Colonel Henry Denson, whose estate sold him for £75. Source: Smith, "Slave in Canada," 15.

1052. SQUASH, HARRY (c. 1783, age 22) – Enslaved to Mr. Lynch, who purchased him from Captain Huddleston of the Royal Artillery, Harry went to the Maritimes from New York. British officials in New York described him as "stout middle sized." Source: Book of Negroes.

1053. SQUIRE (c. 1787) – Squire was enslaved to New York Loyalist Christopher Benson, who settled at Granville, Nova Scotia, after the war. In 1787, he sold an adult male named Squire and a boy named Dave. It is unclear if these two slaves were related, but it is possible they were father and son. Source: Harris, "Negro Population of the County of Annapolis," 17.

1054. ST. JEAN (c. 1749) – St. Jean was enslaved to merchant, businessman, and large-scale slaveholder Jean Pierre Roma. Roma, who owned 12 slaves, planned to set up a settlement with slaves on Prince Edward Island, but instead went to Louisbourg in 1732. Source: Donovan, "Nominal List of Slaves and Their Owners," 153.

1055. STACH (c. 1783, age 17) – Enslaved to Gabriel Fowler, who migrated to the Maritimes after the American Revolution, Stach was accompanied by her infant son named Joe. British officials in New York described her as a "stout wench." Source: Book of Negroes.

1056. JOE (c. 1783, 9 months) – Enslaved to Gabriel Fowler, Joe accompanied his mother, Stach, to the Maritimes. British officials described him as a "likely child." Source: Book of Negroes.

1057. STAFFORD (slave? c. 1784) – Possibly enslaved to F.H. Flieger, who planned to settle near Halifax, Stafford lived with one other slave. Source: Loyalists and Disbanded Troops at Cole Harbour, Chipman Papers, Muster Master General's Office, Loyalist Musters, 1776–1785, MG 23, D1, ser. I, vol. 24, LAC.

1058. STOGDON, PETER (c. 1783, age 19) – Enslaved to Widow Stogdon, who migrated to the Maritimes after the American Revolution, Peter was described by British officials in New York as a "stout lad." Source: Book of Negroes.

1059. SUCKLES, DIMBO (c. 1780s) – Enslaved to William Creed, Suckles was born in Africa. He said his father was a chief with numerous cattle. As a young boy, slave hunters captured him and brought him to New World. He served his owner in Prince Edward Island and eventually became free. Source: Whitfield and Cahill, "Slave Life and Slave Law," 35–6.

1060. SUE (c. 1783, age 25) – Enslaved to James Alexander, who migrated to the Maritimes after the American Revolution with one other slave, Sue was probably from South Carolina or Georgia. British officials in New York described her as a "stout wench." Source: Book of Negroes.

1061. SUE (c. 1783, age 21) – Enslaved to Gabriel Purdy, who migrated to the Maritimes after the American Revolution with several other slaves, Sue was probably from New York. British officials in New York described her as a "stout wench." Source: Book of Negroes.

1062. SUE (slave? c. 1784) – Sue was possibly enslaved to Captain Marshall, who, along with other southern Loyalists (consisting of various regiments such as the Royal North Carolina Regiment and the King's Carolina Rangers), settled at Country Harbour, Nova Scotia. The majority of these settlers and their slaves were from North Carolina, South Carolina, and Georgia. They had settled briefly in East Florida before moving to Nova Scotia. In a letter to Colonel Edward Winslow discussing these southern settlers, William Shaw expressed surprise that some of the Blacks with these southern settlers were not slaves;

but his wording, as historian Carole Watterson Troxler notes, meant that some were "indeed slaves." In fact, as she points out, Blacks at Country Harbour were denied any land grants and those who were not slaves were "quasi-free." In an article, abolitionist Thomas Clarkson described what some white Loyalists did to supposedly free Black Loyalists: "It was not long till these loyalists, many of whom had been educated with all the ideas of the justice of slavery, the inferiority of negroes, and the superiority of white men, that are universal in the southern provinces of America, began to harass and oppress the industrious black settlers, and even wantonly to deprive them of the fruits of their labour, expelling them from the lands they had cleared." Clarkson continued by noting that whites reduced "again to slavery those negroes who had so honourably obtained their freedom. They hired them as servants, and, at the end of the stipulated time, refused payment of their wages, insisting that they were slaves: in some instances they destroyed their tickets of freedom, and then enslaved the negroes for want of them; in several instances, the unfortunate Africans were taken onboard vessels, carried to the West Indies, and there sold for the benefit of their plunderers." In the case of Black people at Country Harbour, they were listed on the musters as the "Servants" of a white Loyalist, which meant it was very easy for them to be re-enslaved if they were not already enslaved. Sources: Troxler, "John Legett at Country Harbour," 310; Clarkson, "Some Account of the New Colony at Sierra Leone," 229–30; Settlers at Country Harbour, Chipman Papers, Muster Master General's Office, Loyalist Musters, 1776–1785, MG 23, D1, ser. I, vol. 24, LAC. Note: Ellen Wilson believed that the information Clarkson used came from Thomas Peters' petition; see Wilson, *Loyal Blacks*, 181.

1063. SUKEY (c. 1783, age 9) – Enslaved to Thomas Wood, who migrated to the Maritimes after the American Revolution, British officials in New York noted that Sukey "says she is his own [Wood's] property having purchased her in Savannah." These same officials described her as a "fine girl." Source: Book of Negroes.

1064. SUKEY (c. 1783, age 4) – Enslaved to Nathaniel Dickenson, who migrated to the Maritimes after the American Revolution along with two other slaves, Sukey was possibly from Massachusetts. However, it seems unlikely that either of these other slaves were her parents as Dickinson purchased them from different owners who were from New Jersey and New York, respectively. Thus, the reverend must have taken Sukey away from her parents unless she had already been separated from her parents. British officials in New York noted she was a "present from the Rev. Mr. Badger." These same officials described her as a "fine girl." Source: Book of Negroes.

1065. SUKY (c. 1785) – David Randall of Wilmot bequeathed his "Negro Wench Suky" to his wife but instructed his daughter and granddaughter to sell her upon the mistress's death. There is not the slightest hint in the will that the illiterate yeoman Randall saw Suky as anything other than a mindless piece of property. She represented an economic investment, not a person. Source: Will of David Randall, 1785, Annapolis County, NSA.

1066. SUSANNA (c. 1804) – Susanna was enslaved to Mr. Budd and had a daughter named Jane. Source: List of Baptisms, September 30, 1804, Records of the Anglican Church, Digby Township Book, NSA.

1067. JANE (c. 1804) – Jane was Susanna's daughter, who was baptized in Digby in 1804. Source: List of Baptisms, September 30, 1804, Records of the Anglican Church, Digby Township Book, NSA.

1068. SUSANNAH (c. 1783, age 35) – Enslaved to Captain McPherson, who migrated to the Maritimes after the American Revolution, Susannah was described by British officials in New York as an "ordinary wench." Source: Book of Negroes.

1069. SUSANNAH (c. 1784) – Susannah was enslaved to Georgia Loyalist John Todd in Chedabucto along with several other slaves. These slaves were probably from Georgia, South Carolina, East Florida, or another southern state. Source: Loyalists from Saint Augustine bound to Chedabucto, July 1784, Chipman Papers, Muster Master General's Office, Loyalist Musters, 1776–1785, MG 23, D1, ser. I, vol. 24, LAC.

1070. SUSANNAH (c. 1784) – In 1784, John Wentworth sent 19 slaves to Suriname from Halifax. He kept two slaves with him: Matthew and Susannah. Source: John Wentworth to Paul Wentworth or his attorney, February 24, 1784.

1071. SUSANNAH (c. 1819) – Susannah was enslaved to New York Loyalist William Schurman (or Schurmann), who left the United States in 1783 with his family and two slaves to settle in Prince Edward Island. Schurman worked as farmer and businessman and thereby earned a comfortable living. He also served in the colonial legislature. Like most island slaveholders, he came from the elite of society and remained widely respected throughout his life. His will is fascinating because of the way he refers to Susannah as a member of the family. This wording was common, especially in New England and the Maritimes, where slaves lived in close contact with their enslavers. Clearly, Schurman felt some affection for Susannah in offering her lifetime support or £50 if she wished to strike out on her own. Finally, readers should recognize the term "servant" that William used to describe Susannah. In all likelihood she had been a slave for many years, but eventually William freed her and she continued on with the family as a domestic servant. In 1819, slavery remained legal in PEI and would not be outlawed for another six years. Schurman noted that "my Negro servant Susannah Schurman shall be provided for in the family as long as she wishes to remain in the family with meat drink and clothing as long as she lives, but if it be her choice to leave the family my will is to give her fifty pounds lawful money of this Island to be raised out of my Estate." Source: Will of William Schurman, 1819, RG 62, ser. I, lib. I, fol. 130, PAROPEI. His last name is spelled Schurmann and Schurman.

1072. SWINNEY, CHARLES (c. 1784) – Charles was enslaved to the Departments of the Army and Navy, which settled in Chedabucto, Nova Scotia. Source: Muster Roll of Settlers at Chedabucto (including Departments of the Army and Navy), Chipman Papers, Muster Master General's Office, Loyalist Musters, 1776–1785, MG 23, D1, ser. I, vol. 24, LAC.

1073. SWINNEY, MARY (c. 1784) – Mary was enslaved to the Departments of the Army and Navy, which settled in Chedabucto, Nova Scotia. Source: Muster Roll of Settlers at Chedabucto (including Departments of the Army and Navy), Chipman Papers, Muster Master General's Office, Loyalist Musters, 1776–1785, MG 23, D1, ser. I, vol. 24, LAC.

1074. SYLLA (c. 1776) – Nova Scotia farmer Joseph Wilson bequeathed Byna and Sylla to his family. Source: Smith, "Slave in Canada," 15.

1075. SYLVEY (c. ?) – Enslaved to Colonel Henry Purdy of Fort Lawrence, Nova Scotia, Sylvey married Samuel Gay's slave whose name is unknown. Source: Smith, "Slave in Canada," 88.

1076. SYLVIA (slave? c. 1784) – Sylvia was possibly enslaved at Belle Vue in Beaver Harbour. Although these people might have been nominally free, they were regularly subjected to re-enslavement. Source: Roll of Loyalists Settled at Belle Vue in Beaver Harbour, Chipman Papers, Muster Master General's Office, Loyalist Musters, 1776–1785, MG 23, D1, ser. I, vol. 24, LAC.

1077. TALLOW, NEWPORT (c. 1780s) – Newport was enslaved to Joshua F. de St. Croix, who was a native of New York and had "sailed for Nova Scotia in one of his own vessels, with his family and slaves." This source indicates that there were at least two or more slaves on his ship. He also owned a slave named Bess. Several well-known members of the Black community in Nova Scotia descend from the Tallow family. Sources: Ruggles Coward, *Bridgetown Nova Scotia*, 33; Karolyn Smardz Frost, "King's College, Nova Scotia," 3. This author is thankful to Karolyn for sharing her research.

1078. TAMAR (c. 1783, age 13) – Enslaved to Gilbert Pugsley, who migrated to the Maritimes after the American Revolution, Tamar was probably from New

York. British officials at New York described her as an "ordinary wench." Source: Book of Negroes.

1079. TAYLOR, MICHAEL (c. 1787) – Enslaved to John Young of Amherst, Nova Scotia, it is possible that Michael is the "Unnamed Boy" that Young owned in 1771, but this is unclear. Sources: Fairfax, "Blacks in Cumberland County"; Will of John Young, January 1787, Abstract of Cumberland County Wills and Probate, MG 4, #20, NSA.

1080. TEGGEN, BECCA (c. 1783, age 14) – Enslaved to John King, Becca went from New York to the Maritimes. British officials in New York described her as "stout." Source: Book of Negroes.

1081. TEMPE (c. 1783, age 9) – Enslaved to Captain Williams, who migrated to the Maritimes after the American Revolution, British officials at New York described Tempe as a "likely wench." Source: Book of Negroes.

1082. TERHUNE, DINAH (c. 1783, age 16) – Enslaved to Paul Speed, Dinah went from New York to the Maritimes without any other family members. British officials in New York described her as a "thin girl." She seems to have been the slave of a New York resident named Edward Bruce before being sold to Paul Speed. Source: Book of Negroes.

1083. TERHUNE, THOMAS (slave? c. 1783, age 19) – Thomas was possibly enslaved to Paul Speed. British officials noted that he was formerly enslaved to Samuel Terhune of New Jersey, but left him in 1780 or 1781. The entry for Dinah Terhune strangely notes that "both the property of Paul Speed," which indicates that the officials were probably referring to Dinah and Thomas. The entry is very confusing. Source: Book of Negroes.

1084. THIERSSY (c. 1758) – Thierssy was enslaved at Île Royale. Source: Donovan, "Nominal List of Slaves and Their Owners," 160.

1085. THOMAS (c. 1779) – Robert Baird manumitted Thomas in 1779. Source: Smith, "Slave in Canada," 61.

1086. THOMAS, JEAN (c. 1758, age 11) – Jean was enslaved to wealthy Île Royale merchant Jean Laborde, who owned other slaves. Source: Donovan, "Nominal List of Slaves and Their Owners," 159.

1087. THOMAS, JOHN (c. 1783, age 15) – Enslaved to Patrick Wall, who migrated to the Maritimes after the American Revolution with two other slaves,

John was from Massachusetts. British officials in New York described him as a "stout lad." Source: Book of Negroes.

1088. THOMSON, PETER (c. 1793) – Peter purchased his freedom from Charles McPherson in Saint John, New Brunswick. According to the manumission document, Peter intended to make two payments of £10. Source: Manumission of Peter Thomson, 1793, Oversize F 40-1, (possibly PANB or NSA, but there is not an archival stamp on the document).

1089. THOUSAIN MARIE LOUISE (c. 1758) – Thousain Marie Louise was an enslaved woman who lived in Île Royale. Source: Donovan, "Nominal List of Slaves and Their Owners," 160.

1090. THURSDAY (c. 1772) – Enslaved to John Rock, Thursday attempted to escape from him in 1772. He recaptured her and directed that she be sold in his 1776 will. Rock valued her at £25, but Rock's executors sold her for £20 to a John Bishop. Source: *Nova Scotia Gazette and Weekly Chronicle*, September 1, 1772; Smith, "Slave in Canada," 12–13.

1091. TIM (c. 1783, age 22) – Enslaved to Captain French, who migrated to the Maritimes after the American Revolution, British officials in New York noted that Tim had been purchased from a man in Charleston, South Carolina. These same officials described him as a "stout fellow." Source: Book of Negroes.

1092. TIMOTHY (c. 1783, age 33) – Enslaved to Charles Thorne, who migrated to the Maritimes after the American Revolution, British officials in New York described Timothy as an "ordinary fellow." Source: Book of Negroes.

1093. TITUS (c. 1783, age 28) – Enslaved to Stephen Sneadon, who migrated to the Maritimes after the American Revolution with one other slave, Titus was described by British officials in New York as a "stout fellow." Source: Book of Negroes.

1094. TOBE, SIMON (c. 1745) – Simon was enslaved to the Connecticut Regiment during the siege of Louisbourg. Source: Donovan, "Nominal List of Slaves and Their Owners," 156.

1095. TOBY (slave? c. 1784) – Toby was possibly enslaved to Lieutenant Joel Hudson, who, along with other southern Loyalists (consisting of various regiments such as the Royal North Carolina Regiment and the King's Carolina Rangers), settled at Country Harbour, Nova Scotia. The majority of these settlers and their slaves were from North Carolina, South Carolina, and Georgia. They had settled briefly in East Florida before moving to Nova Scotia. In a letter to Colonel Edward Winslow discussing these southern settlers, William Shaw expressed surprise that some of the Blacks with these southern settlers were not slaves; but his wording, as historian Carole Watterson Troxler notes, meant that some were "indeed slaves." In fact, as she points out, Blacks at Country Harbour were denied any land grants and those who were not slaves were "quasi-free." In an article, abolitionist Thomas Clarkson described what some white Loyalists did to supposedly free Black Loyalists: "It was not long till these loyalists, many of whom had been educated with all the ideas of the justice of slavery, the inferiority of negroes, and the superiority of white men, that are universal in the southern provinces of America, began to harass and oppress the industrious black settlers, and even wantonly to deprive them of the fruits of their labour, expelling them from the lands they had cleared." Clarkson continued by noting that whites reduced "again to slavery those negroes who had so honourably obtained their freedom. They hired them as servants, and, at the end of the stipulated time, refused payment of their wages, insisting that they were slaves: in some instances they destroyed their tickets of freedom, and then enslaved the negroes for want of them; in several instances, the unfortunate Africans were taken onboard vessels, carried to the West Indies, and there sold for the benefit of their plunderers." In the case of Black people at Country Harbour, they were listed on the musters as the "Servants" of a white Loyalist, which meant it was very easy for them to be re-enslaved if they were not already enslaved. Sources: Troxler, "John Legett at Country Harbour," 310; Clarkson, "Some Account of the New Colony at Sierra Leone," 229–30; Settlers at Country Harbour, Chipman Papers, Muster Master General's Office, Loyalist Musters, 1776–1785, MG 23, D1, ser. I, vol. 24, LAC. Note: Ellen Wilson believed that the information Clarkson used came from Thomas Peters' petition; see Wilson, *Loyal Blacks*, 181.

1096. TOM (c. 1783, age 26) – Enslaved to John Ryerson, who migrated to the Maritimes after the American Revolution with two other slaves, Tom was probably from New Jersey. British officials at New York described him as a "stout fellow." Source: Book of Negroes.

1097. TOM (c. 1783, age 22) – Enslaved to Joseph Allen, who migrated to the Maritimes after the American Revolution, Tom was probably from New Jersey. British officials at New York described him as a "stout fellow." Source: Book of Negroes.

1098. TOM (c. 1783, age 12) – Enslaved to Robert Letson, who migrated to the Maritimes after the American Revolution, Tom was probably from New

York. British officials at New York described him as a "likely boy." Source: Book of Negroes.

1099. TOM (c. 1784, age 11) – Tom was enslaved to John Grant. Originally from Scotland, after serving the British army near Ticonderoga during the Seven Years War, Grant settled in Queens County, Long Island. After the American Revolution, he migrated to Nova Scotia with a large family and nine slaves. These enslaved people might have been a family unit. Source: Cottreau-Robins, "Landscape of Slavery in Loyalist Era Nova Scotia," 131–2; also Smith, "Slave in Canada," 93–4.

1100. TOM (c. 1785) – New York Loyalist Benjamin Seaman (he served in the New York assembly before the Revolution) mentioned two slaves in his 1785 will: Tom and Will. He referred to each slave as "my Negro boy." Source: Will of Benjamin Seaman, Saint John County, 1785, PANB.

1101. TOM (c. 1786) – Tom and Pero were re-enslaved in 1786. Joseph Robins claimed that he had purchased both men for a total of £29 sterling. Patrick Licet said he had observed Joseph Robins purchase Pero for a horse and eight guineas. The second witness claimed he had hired Pero from Robins and "always understood the said Negro to be the Property of Joseph Robins." This same witness, James Stone, claimed that he had heard Pero admit to being the slave of Robins. During his examination, Pero stated that he had gone to St. Augustine with James Stone, instead of returning to his rebel master, but he denied being the property of Stone. Tom commented that he had belonged to Philip Caine in "Carolina" and had run away to Charleston where he worked in the wood yard. Tom accompanied Joseph Robins to St. Augustine. Afterwards, he recalled being sold for a horse but firmly denied being owned by Robins. The court ordered Joseph Robins to "take Possession" of Tom and Pero but required that he not sell them out of the province for 12 months. The continued enslavement or re-enslavement of these Blacks is instructive for several reasons. Tom and Pero both realized that they could assert their freedom in court. Although they lost, they either told the truth or were smart enough to construct a narrative that aligned with the history of most free Blacks in the region – that is, running away from a rebel owner and performing loyal services to His Majesty before migrating to St. Augustine and finally Nova Scotia. These slaves realized that the legalities of slavery and freedom were shifting and unclear. They attempted to use the confusion to gain their freedom. Source: General Sessions at Shelburne, Nova Scotia, April 10, 1786, Shelburne Records, MG 4, vol. 141, NSA.

1102. TOM (c. 1786, age 25) – Tom was enslaved to Captain McDonald. In a runaway advertisement, Captain McDonald, who had taken Dick Hill (see entry) to the West Indies, described Tom as stout, yellow complexioned, clever, and a sailor. Source: *Nova Scotia Packet and General Advertiser*, July 6, 1786.

1103. TOM (c. 1806, age 14) – Isaac Bonnell owned three young male slaves who he wanted to free once they reached the age of 24. In this will, Bonnell clearly expressed some sentimental attachment to his young slaves. He not only intended to free them, but also to provide them with some basic necessities such as clothing. He also wanted them to have a rudimentary understanding of the Bible, because that would help them in early nineteenth-century society. These slaves would not gain their freedom until their mid-20s, which meant that Bonnell's family would continue to benefit from their labour for many years. There is no mention of these slaves' biological parents, which means that they could have died or been sold. We simply do not have enough information to know. In discussing his slaves, Bonnell noted "My Desire is that My Black Boys George, Tom, & Bob –be Taught to Read [?] in the Bible & to write Legible hand & that they be Sett at Liberty as they [?] Arrive to the Age of Twenty four years. Each to be allow'd [?] of good new Cloathes of Every Description Beside their Common wearing apparel. George Was Born in November 1790. Tom Was born in May 1792. And Bob Was Born in February 1794." Source: Will of Isaac Bonnell, Annapolis County, 1806, RG 48, NSA.

1104. TONEY (c. 1786) – Toney was enslaved to Annapolis County resident Richard Betts (a Loyalist from New York). The 1786 inventory of Richard Betts listed four slaves and their values. According to the document, Toney, Prince (or Primus), and Jane were listed as worth £35, while Harry commanded the price of £40. The relationship of each slave to the other slaves is unclear – if they were a family or totally unrelated. The total value of Betts's inventory was about £1,053, while the combined value of the slaves was £145. Thus, slaves accounted for 13.77 per cent of the total wealth of his estate. Source: Will of Richard Betts, 1786, Annapolis County, RG 48, NSA.

1105. TONEY (c. 1787) – Enslaved to Abraham Treadell, who sold Toney to John Ward in Saint John, New Brunswick for £25. Source: Smith, "Slave in Canada," 53.

1106. TONY (slave? c. 1784) – Tony was possibly enslaved to Captain Martin, who, along with other southern Loyalists (consisting of various regiments such as the Royal North Carolina Regiment and the King's Carolina Rangers), settled at Country Harbour, Nova Scotia. The majority of these settlers and their slaves were from North Carolina, South Carolina, and Georgia. They had settled briefly in East Florida before moving to Nova Scotia. In a letter to Colonel Edward Winslow discussing these southern settlers, William Shaw expressed surprise that some of the Blacks with these southern settlers were not slaves; but his wording, as historian Carole Watterson Troxler notes, meant that some were "indeed slaves." In fact, as she points out, Blacks at Country Harbour were denied any land grants and those who were not slaves were "quasi-free." In an article, abolitionist Thomas Clarkson described what some white Loyalists did to supposedly free Black Loyalists: "It was not long till these loyalists, many of whom had been educated with all the ideas of the justice of slavery, the inferiority of negroes, and the superiority of white men, that are universal in the southern provinces of America, began to harass and oppress the industrious black settlers, and even wantonly to deprive them of the fruits of their labour, expelling them from the lands they had cleared." Clarkson continued by noting that whites reduced "again to slavery those negroes who had so honourably obtained their freedom. They hired them as servants, and, at the end of the stipulated time, refused payment of their wages, insisting that they were slaves: in some instances they destroyed their tickets of freedom, and then enslaved the negroes for want of them; in several instances, the unfortunate Africans were taken onboard vessels, carried to the West Indies, and there sold for the benefit of their plunderers." In the case of Black people at Country Harbour, they were listed on the musters as the "Servants" of a white Loyalist, which meant it was very easy for them to be re-enslaved if they were not already enslaved. Sources: Troxler, "John Legett at Country Harbour," 310; Clarkson, "Some Account of the New Colony at Sierra Leone," 229–30; Settlers at Country Harbour, Chipman Papers, Muster Master General's Office, Loyalist Musters, 1776–1785, MG 23, D1, ser. I, vol. 24, LAC. Note: Ellen Wilson believed that the information Clarkson used came from Thomas Peters' petition; see Wilson, *Loyal Blacks*, 181.

1107. TONY (slave? c. 1784) – Tony was possibly enslaved to Captain George Dawkins, who, along with other southern Loyalists (consisting of various regiments such as the Royal North Carolina Regiment and the King's Carolina Rangers), settled at Country Harbour, Nova Scotia. The majority of these settlers and their slaves were from North Carolina, South Carolina, and Georgia. They had settled briefly in East Florida before moving to Nova Scotia. In a letter to Colonel Edward Winslow discussing these southern settlers, William Shaw expressed surprise that some of the blacks with these southern settlers were not slaves; but his wording, as historian Carole Watterson Troxler notes, meant that some were "indeed slaves." In fact, as she points out, Blacks at Country Harbour were denied any land grants and those who were not slaves were "quasi-free." In an article, abolitionist Thomas Clarkson described what some white Loyalists did to supposedly free Black Loyalists: "It was not long till these loyalists, many of whom had been educated with all the ideas of the justice of slavery, the inferiority of negroes, and the superiority of white men, that are universal in the southern provinces of America, began to harass and oppress the industrious black settlers, and even wantonly to deprive them of the fruits of their labour, expelling them from the lands they had cleared." Clarkson continued by noting that whites reduced "again to slavery those negroes who had so honourably obtained their freedom. They hired them as servants, and, at the end of the stipulated time, refused payment of their wages, insisting that they were slaves: in some instances they destroyed their tickets of freedom, and then enslaved the negroes for want of them; in several instances, the unfortunate Africans were taken onboard vessels, carried to the West Indies, and there sold for the benefit of their plunderers." In the case of Black people at Country Harbour, they were listed on the musters as the "Servants" of a white Loyalist, which meant it was very easy for them to be re-enslaved if they were not already enslaved. Sources: Troxler, "John Legett at Country Harbour," 310; Clarkson, "Some Account of the New Colony at Sierra Leone," 229–30; Settlers at Country Harbour, Chipman Papers, Muster Master General's Office, Loyalist Musters, 1776–1785, MG 23, D1, ser. I, vol. 24, LAC. Note: Ellen Wilson believed that the information Clarkson used came from Thomas Peters' petition; see Wilson, *Loyal Blacks*, 181.

1108. TORRIANO, SUSANNAH (c. 1770) – Susannah was the mixed-race mistress of Prince Edward Island Governor Walter Patterson in 1770. Source: Hornby, *Black Islanders*, 2.

1109. TOTO, JACOB (c. 1745) – Enslaved to Nathan Whiting, Jacob was from New England. Source: Donovan, "Nominal List of Slaves and Their Owners," 156.

1110. TOTTEN, HARRY (c. 1783, age 12) – Enslaved to Joseph Totten [listed as James, but it is Joseph], Harry went to the Maritimes from New York with one other enslaved man and his owner. The other man, Peter Totten, might have been a relative, but it is unclear. British officials described him as a "fine boy." Source: Book of Negroes.

1111. TOTTEN, PETER (c. 1783, age 28) – Enslaved to Joseph Totten, Peter went to the Maritimes from New York with his owner and an enslaved boy. The boy, Harry Totten, might have been a relative, but it is unclear. British officials described Peter as a "stout lad." Source: Book of Negroes.

1112. TOUSSAINT (c. 1753) – Toussaint is one of the few slaves for whom we have extensive documentation. Before arriving in Louisbourg, Toussaint was an enslaved baker in St. Pierre, Martinique. Despite this special skill, Toussaint's challenging personality resulted in his exasperated owner attempting to sell him – even if the price was below market value: "I have put aboard the Ste Rose a Negro by the name of Toussaint, to ask you to get rid of him for me at any price. He belongs to one of my friends who wants to get [him] out of these islands because of the excessively strong habits he has here. Please do me the pleasure of rendering him the service of having him remain in Louisbourg, and of selling him to someone who never bring him back here. He is a baker by trade. As for the price of the sale, you can use it for whatever you think best, whether cod or something else." Toussaint's obstreperous behaviour is part of the struggle between slaveowners and strong-willed slaves, and it was a victory for Toussaint. Obviously, he refused to do what his owner wanted and the slaveholder had to get rid of him because of "the excessively strong habits he has here." While it is doubtful that Louisbourg was Toussaint's most desired place of settlement, he did have some agency in the making of his own destiny. Once in Louisbourg, in 1753, Milly Daccarette purchased Toussaint at a public auction. In terms of the art of biography, we can never know all of the complicated aspects of Toussaint's life. But we know he was an Atlantic world traveller, slave, baker, and possibly son or father. His intriguing story came to us only because a letter survived. In most cases, the personalities and lives of Black slaves in the Atlantic world are silenced and we can only fill those silences in with an occasional letter, runaway slave advertisement, or court record. In this case, historian Ken Donovan helps scholars investigate this enslaved traveller of the French Atlantic world. Source: Donovan, "Slaves and Their Owners," 22.

1113. TRIM (c. 1802) – Trim attempted to escape from his owner with another slave named Jimmey. The name of the owner is unclear from the advertisement. The advertisement provided a brief description of both men: "ABSCONDED the middle of December last, two able young Negro men belonging to the Subscriber – one named *Trim* and the other *Jimmey*, supposed a Nayo, marked A.R. on the left shoulder, and had a sore on one of his feet near the ancle; both rather of a yellow complexion, and middle sized." Source: *Royal Gazette*, December 15, 1802.

1114. TRITTON [or **TRITTEN**], **LOIS** (c. 1799) – Lois was an enslaved woman born in Halifax, who was taken to Connecticut and sold in 1824. Source: Smith, "Slave in Canada," 118.

1115. TROST, BENJAMIN (c. ?) – According to Marion Robertson, Benjamin lived with Mr. Gough but was "carried away and sold in Jamaica by a Mr. Miller." Source: Robertson, *King's Bounty*, 94.

1116. TYNG, BILL (c. 1783, age 16) – Enslaved to Colonel Tyng, Bill went to the Maritimes from New York along with four other slaves. British officials in New York described him as a "stout black" who had been "received from Mrs. Ross." Source: Book of Negroes.

1117. TYNG, DINAH (c. 1783, age 20) – Enslaved to Colonel Tyng, Dinah went to the Maritimes from New York along with four other slaves. British officials in New York described her as a "low wench" who had been "bred in [Tyng's] service." Source: Book of Negroes.

1118. TYNG, JOHN (c. 1783, age 19) – Enslaved to Colonel Tyng, John went to the Maritimes from New York along with four other slaves. British officials in New York described him as a "stout black" who had been "bred in [Tyng's] service." Source: Book of Negroes.

1119. TYNG, JULIET (c. 1783, age 5) – Enslaved to Colonel Tyng, Juliet was mulatto – Tyng might have fathered her. She went to the Maritimes from New York along with four other slaves. British officials in New York described her as being "bred in [Tyng's] service." Source: Book of Negroes.

1120. TYNG, UNNAMED (c. 1783) – Enslaved to Colonel Tyng, this slave is unnamed. Source: Book of Negroes.

1121. UNIQUE, JEAN (c. 1749) – Jean was enslaved to Philippe Beaubassin. Source: Donovan, "Nominal List of Slaves and Their Owners," 157.

1122. UNNAMED (slave? c. 1780s) – This unnamed person was possibly enslaved to Jonathan Odell. Odell might have owned enslaved people and possessed a house with slave quarters. Although some historians assert he owned slaves, it is not clearly documented and one would need to slowly go through the Jonathan Odell Papers at the University of New Brunswick. Source: "Jonathan Odell House," My New Brunswick, https://mynewbrunswick.ca/jonathan-odell-house. Thanks to Leah Grandy from the University of New Brunswick libraries for her assistance; Leah Grandy to Harvey Amani Whitfield, private email correspondence, February 3, 2020.

1123. UNNAMED (c. 1780s) – This unnamed person was enslaved to Joshua F. de St. Croix, a native of New York, who "sailed for Nova Scotia in one of his own vessels, with his family and slaves." This source indicates that there were at least two or more slaves on his ship. He also owned a slave named Bess. Source: Ruggles Coward, *Bridgetown Nova Scotia*, 33.

1124. UNNAMED (c. 1780s) – This unnamed person was enslaved to Joshua F. de St. Croix, a native of New York, who "sailed for Nova Scotia in one of his own vessels, with his family and slaves." This source indicates that there were at least two or more slaves on his ship. He also owned a slave named Bess. Source: Ruggles Coward, *Bridgetown Nova Scotia*, 33.

1125. UNNAMED (slave? c. 1784) – This unnamed person was possibly enslaved to Beverly Robinson in New Brunswick. Source: Smith, "Slave in Canada," 24.

1126. UNNAMED (slave? c. 1784) – This unnamed person was possibly enslaved to Beverly Robinson in New Brunswick. Source: Smith, "Slave in Canada," 24.

1127. UNNAMED (slave? c. 1784) – This unnamed person was possibly enslaved to Beverly Robinson in New Brunswick. Source: Smith, "Slave in Canada," 24.

1128. UNNAMED (slave? c. 1784) – This unnamed person was possibly enslaved to Beverly Robinson in New Brunswick. Source: Smith, "Slave in Canada," 24.

1129. UNNAMED (slave? c. 1784) – This unnamed person was possibly enslaved to Beverly Robinson in New Brunswick. Source: Smith, "Slave in Canada," 24.

1130. UNNAMED (slave? c. 1784) – This unnamed person was possibly enslaved to Beverly Robinson in New Brunswick. Source: Smith, "Slave in Canada," 24.

1131. UNNAMED (slave? c. 1784) – This unnamed person was possibly enslaved to Beverly Robinson in New Brunswick. Source: Smith, "Slave in Canada," 24.

1132. UNNAMED (slave? c. 1784) – This unnamed person was possibly enslaved to Beverly Robinson in New Brunswick. Source: Smith, "Slave in Canada," 24.

1133. UNNAMED (slave? c. 1784) – This unnamed person was possibly enslaved to Beverly Robinson in New Brunswick. Source: Smith, "Slave in Canada," 24.

1134. UNNAMED (slave? c. 1784) – This unnamed person was possibly enslaved to Beverly Robinson in New Brunswick. Source: Smith, "Slave in Canada," 24.

1135. UNNAMED (c. 1797, age 18) – This unnamed person was enslaved to an unknown owner who offered a young Black boy for sale. The owner described him as having had smallpox and having an ability to take care of horses and drive carriages while also being an excellent domestic servant. Source: *Royal Gazette*, March 7, 1797. Thanks to my former graduate student Sarah Chute for finding this advertisement.

1136. UNNAMED (c. 1820s) – This unnamed person was enslaved to Josiah Webbe Maynard in Nevis, who took some of his slaves to Nova Scotia to help harvest and load his vessels with timber to take back to the West Indies. It seems that there were at least two or more slaves. Source: Catherine Cottreau-Robins, "A Loyalist Plantation in Nova Scotia, 1784–1800" (PhD diss., Dalhousie University, Halifax, Nova Scotia, 2012), 10.

1137. UNNAMED (c. 1820s) – This unnamed person was enslaved to Josiah Webbe Maynard in Nevis, who took some of his slaves to Nova Scotia to help harvest and load his vessels with timber to take back to the West Indies. It seems that there were at least two or more slaves. Source: Cottreau-Robins, "Loyalist Plantation in Nova Scotia," 10.

1138. UNNAMED (c. 1820s) – This unnamed person was enslaved to Josiah Webbe Maynard in Nevis, who took some of his slaves to Nova Scotia to help harvest and load his vessels with timber to take back to the West Indies. It seems that there were at least two or more slaves. Source: Cottreau-Robins, "Loyalist Plantation in Nova Scotia," 10.

1139. UNNAMED BOY (c. 1724) – This unnamed child died in a shipwreck off Sable Island, Nova Scotia. The owner of the vessel, Michel Daccarette, had sent the vessel to France with cod fish, but the entire crew died on the return voyage. Source: Donovan, "Nominal List of Slaves and Their Owners," 152.

1140. UNNAMED BOY (c. 1733, age 10) – Originally from Martinique, this un-named boy was enslaved to Andre Moisel. The fact that historians do not know this boy's name illuminates the ways in which the archive silences the experiences of such young slaves. Source: Donovan, "Nominal List of Slaves and Their Owners," 153.

1141. UNNAMED BOY (c. 1752, age 13) – This unnamed boy was part of Joshua Mauger's slave sale in 1752. The information on this young boy is lim-ited. He was described as likely and healthy. Source: *Halifax Gazette*, May 30, 1752.

1142. UNNAMED BOY (c. 1752, age 12) – This unnamed boy was part of Joshua Mauger's slave sale in 1752. The information on this young boy is lim-ited. He was described as likely and healthy. Source: *Halifax Gazette*, May 30, 1752.

1143. UNNAMED BOY (c. 1757, age 11) – This unnamed boy was enslaved to Fp. M. Pincu's wife. Source: Donovan, "Nominal List of Slaves and Their Owners," 157.

1144. UNNAMED BOY (c. 1760, age 11) – This unnamed boy was enslaved to John Rider and was to be sold at a public auction along with another slave. Source: Smith, "Slave in Canada," 10.

1145. UNNAMED BOY (c. 1769) – This unnamed boy was enslaved to John Margerum, who had recently died. The executors of his will sold this enslaved child to someone in Carolina for about £29. Source: Smith, "Slave in Canada," 13.

1146. UNNAMED BOY (c. 1769) – This unnamed boy was enslaved to an un-named Halifax businessman, who sold the boy to someone in Carolina. Source: Smith, "Slave in Canada," 119.

1147. UNNAMED BOY (c. 1771) – This unnamed boy was enslaved to Reverend James Lyon. Although the 1771 census did not have a separate column for slaves, it did list Blacks separately and there were very few free Blacks in Nova Scotia before 1776. Source: Smith, "Slave in Canada," 16.

1148. UNNAMED BOY (c. 1771) – This unnamed boy was enslaved to John Young in Amherst, Nova Scotia. Although the 1771 census did not have a separate column for slaves, it did list Blacks separately and there were very few free Blacks in Nova Scotia before 1776. Source: Smith, "Slave in Canada," 18.

1149. UNNAMED BOY (c. 1775, age 16) – This unnamed teenager was offered for sale in a Nova Scotia newspaper. It described him as a "likely, well-made Negro boy, about sixteen years old." Source: Smith, "Slave in Canada," 11; *Nova Scotia Gazette and Weekly Chronicle*, March 28, 1775.

1150. UNNAMED BOY (c. 1778) – This unnamed boy was enslaved to Reverend Joseph Bennett, a missionary who established the first Anglican congregation at Fort Edward in Windsor, Nova Scotia. Apparently, Bennett's slave and other goods were taken from his schooner by an American privateer. Source: States, "Presence and Perseverance: Blacks in Hants County," 40.

1151. UNNAMED BOY (c. 1784) – Shelburne resident William Townsend's will briefly mentioned a "Negroe Boy," saying that he should become "the property of Thomas Cooper Son to my Sister Comfort." Source: Will of William Townsend, 1784, Estate Papers and Wills, Shelburne County, 1784–1790, NSA.

1152. UNNAMED BOY (c. 1784, age 15) – In this slave for sale notice, the owner described this unnamed boy as smart and familiar with housework. Source: *Saint John Gazette*, July 15, 1784.

1153. UNNAMED BOY (c. 1786, age 14) – James Hayt offered this young unnamed teenager for sale, noting that he was "in full vigor of health, very active, has a pleasing countenance and every ability to render himself useful and agreeable in a family." Source: *Royal Gazette*, September 12, 1786.

1154. UNNAMED BOY (c. 1786, age 14) – The *Royal American Gazette* in Shelburne advertised this young unnamed teenager for sale. The notice described the boy in glowing terms, noting that he "has been brought up in a Gentleman's Family, is very handy at Farming, House-Work, or attending Table, is strictly honest, and has an exceeding good Temper." Source: *Royal American Gazette*, June 19, 1786.

1155. UNNAMED BOY (c. 1786) – This unnamed boy was enslaved to New Brunswick innkeeper Charles McPherson and sold at public auction. Source: Royal Gazette, July 4, 1786.

1156. UNNAMED BOY (c. 1788) – Joseph Totten's will list five enslaved people of African descent. He gave the three Black children away to his daughters, but not the other slaves, which means that a slave family was probably broken up. This unnamed "Boy" might have been an adult because Joseph Totten valued him at £50 New York money in his will as opposed to the children who he valued at £5 each. Source: Will of Joseph Totten, 1788, Annapolis County, RG 48, NSA.

1157. UNNAMED BOY (c. 1790) – This unnamed slave was included in Richard Hewlett's New Brunswick inventory. It lists the boy's value, which was £25. Source: Will of Richard Hewlett, Queens County, 1790 Inventory, PANB.

1158. UNNAMED BOY (c. 1791) – A young Black boy had been indentured to a "vile" butcher until the age of 21. The butcher planned to leave Nova Scotia and "sell the boy for a slave." Clarkson intervened and reunited him with his family, so they could migrate to Sierra Leone. Source: Fergusson, *Clarkson's Mission to America*, 59.

1159. UNNAMED BOY [possibly named **PETER**] (c. 1794) – In this case, a white Nova Scotian sold an unnamed boy into slavery to the West Indies. The document does not list the boy's name or his parents. The court document clearly states the sad contours of this case: "We have this day receiv'd information that a Negro Boy formerly bound to John Stuart, & by him transferr'd, to some person in Liverpool, has lately been Carried off to the West Indies. & left Bound (as it is said) to some person there." The Nova Scotia Archives website argues that the boy's name was Peter and he was sold to a man in Liverpool who sent him to Antigua: "The grand jury complains to the magistrates in Queens County about the case of Peter, a young black indentured servant from Shelburne." Peter's services were sold to Zebulon Perkins of Liverpool, who illegally carried him off to the West Indies, claiming that he was "notoriously bad." Perkins then sold the remainder of Peter's time to a shopkeeper in Antigua. The grand jury was concerned that allowing Black indentured servants to be treated as if they were slaves could prevent free Blacks from "binding out their children in future." The matter was referred to Lieutenant Governor Wentworth, who advised that Perkins be ordered to return Peter to Nova Scotia. Source: Black Boy Carried Off, April 22, 1794, Shelburne County Court of General Sessions of the Peace, RG 34-321, J 145, NSA, https://novascotia.ca/archives/africanns/archives.asp?ID=52.

1160. UNNAMED BOY (c. 1800) – This unnamed boy was enslaved to Robert Robinson of Annapolis. In an agreement to support Douwe Ditmars regaining his slaves, there is a small notation next to the signature of Robinson stating that "his black boy is returned to him." Source: Agreement with D. Ditmars to bear an equal proportion of the expense attending him about the slaves, May 1800, MG 15, vol. 20, #86, NSA.

1161. UNNAMED BOY (c. ?) – John Cunningham allegedly killed a young, unnamed slave boy with a hammer in Windsor, Nova Scotia. Source: Smith, "Slave in Canada," 77.

1162. UNNAMED GIRL (c. 1760, age 11) – Enslaved to John Rider, this unnamed girl was to be sold at a public auction along with another slave. Source: Smith, "Slave in Canada," 10.

1163. UNNAMED GIRL (c. 1769, age 14) – This unnamed young girl was offered for sale at a public auction in 1769 along with another girl. They were described as "two well-grown negro girls." Source: Smith, "Slave in Canada," 10.

1164. UNNAMED GIRL (c. 1769, age 12) – This unnamed young girl was offered for sale at a public auction in 1769 along with another girl. They were described as "two well-grown negro girls." Source: Smith, "Slave in Canada," 10.

1165. UNNAMED GIRL (c. 1770) – This unnamed girl was enslaved to Henry Evans. Source: Smith, "Slave in Canada," 15.

1166. UNNAMED GIRL (slave? c. 1771) – According to the 1771 census, Magdalen Winniett owned three slaves: a man, woman, and child. Perhaps they were part of the same family. Although the 1771 census did not have a separate column for slaves, it did list Blacks separately and there were very few free Blacks in Nova Scotia before 1776. So, the Blacks listed in this household were probably slaves. Source: Smith, "Slave in Canada," 15.

1167. UNNAMED GIRL (c. 1779, age 14) – This unnamed young girl was offered for sale in a Halifax newspaper along with an enslaved woman. Source: Smith, "Slave in Canada," 11.

1168. UNNAMED GIRL (c. 1785, age 9) – This enslaved child was offered for sale in a newspaper. In 1785, the *Nova Scotia Gazette and Weekly Chronicle* offered for sale a "stout Negro Girl about Nine Years old." The advertisement said nothing about the child's parents. Source: *Nova Scotia Gazette and Weekly Chronicle*, February 22, 1785.

1169. UNNAMED GIRL (c. 1786, age 10–11) – This young girl was offered for sale in a local Nova Scotia newspaper. Her owner described the girl as a "likely

Negro Wench, between Ten and Eleven years of Age." Source: *Nova Scotia Gazette*, August 1, 1786.

1170. UNNAMED GIRL (c. 1798) – This unnamed girl was enslaved to Reverend John Rowland of Shelburne, who owned a total of three slaves at the time of his death. The executors of his will valued the unnamed girl at £25, Samuel at £35, and William at £30. Source: Reverend John Rowland, Estate Papers A #104, May 9, 1798, Shelburne County Archives and Genealogical Society, Shelburne, Nova Scotia; Smith, "Slave in Canada," 59.

1171. UNNAMED GIRL (c. 1802) – This unnamed girl was enslaved to Virginia Loyalist Jacob Ellegood, who mentioned her in his will. Ellegood owned several slaves, including members of the same slave family. Ellegood served in the New Brunswick legislative assembly and also owned a large farm. He was the brother-in law of John Saunders, who served as chief justice of the New Brunswick Supreme Court (and was also from Virginia). Source: Will of Jacob Ellegood, 1802, PANB.

1172. UNNAMED GIRL (c. ?) – This unnamed Black girl was enslaved to the Barclay family in Nova Scotia. What we know about this girl comes from an oral tradition about Susan Barclay, the wife of Thomas Barclay (she was James DeLancey's sister). One of Mrs. Barclay's slaves allegedly stole a pie and after eating most of it threw the leftovers to the hogs. After discovering that the pie was missing, Barclay whipped her slave and forced the "slave girl" into the pen and made her consume the leftovers she had attempted to give to the hogs. Sources: Charlotte I. Perkins, *The Oldest Houses Along St. George Street Annapolis Royal, N.S.* (Saint John, NB: Barnes & Co., 1925), 31; Smith, "Slave in Canada," 77.

1173. UNNAMED MAN (c. 1696) – This unnamed male was captured by the French during a raid and returned to his native Massachusetts. He might have been the first person of African descent in New Brunswick. Source: W.A. Spray, *The Blacks in New Brunswick* (Fredericton: Brunswick Press, 1972), 13.

1174. UNNAMED MAN (c. 1733) – This unnamed Black male was enslaved to M. Levasseur. Source: Donovan, "Nominal List of Slaves and Their Owners," 153.

1175. UNNAMED MAN (c. 1737) – This unnamed male was one of two male slaves that Boston merchant Peter Faneuil sent to Louisbourg. Source: Donovan, "Nominal List of Slaves and Their Owners," 154.

1176. UNNAMED MAN (c. 1737) – This unnamed male was one of two male slaves that Boston merchant Peter Faneuil sent to Louisbourg. Source: Donovan, "Nominal List of Slaves and Their Owners," 154.

1177. UNNAMED MAN (c. 1739) – This unnamed male was enslaved to Widow Desmarest, who purchased shoes for him on multiple occasions. Source: Donovan, "Slaves and Their Owners in Île Royale," 14–15.

1178. UNNAMED MAN (c. 1739) – This unnamed male was enslaved to Governor Isaac-Louis De Forant in Île Royale. Source: Donovan, "Nominal List of Slaves and Their Owners," 155.

1179. UNNAMED MAN (c. 1740) – This unnamed male was a slave who worked on the ship *L'Aigle.* Source: Donovan, "Nominal List of Slaves and Their Owners," 155.

1180. UNNAMED MAN (c. 1740) – This unnamed male was a slave who worked on the ship *St. Michael.* He was from the West Indies. Source: Donovan, "Nominal List of Slaves and Their Owners," 155.

1181. UNNAMED MAN (c. 1745) – All we know about this unnamed male is that he was on the French side during the siege of Louisbourg. Source: Donovan, "Nominal List of Slaves and Their Owners," 156.

1182. UNNAMED MAN (c. 1750s) – This unnamed male was enslaved to Jean Laborde, an exceedingly wealthy merchant who owned several slaves. He purchased this slave for 805 livres at a public auction in Île Royale. Source: Donovan, "Slaves in Île Royale," 32.

1183. UNNAMED MAN (c. 1751) – In 1751, 10 slaves were offered for sale in Boston after arriving from Halifax. The advertisement read: "JUST arriv'd from Hallifax, and to be sold, Ten hearty Strong Negro Men, mostly Tradesmen, such as Caulkers, Carpenters, Sailmakers, Ropemakers: Any Person inclining to purchase may enquire of Benjamin Hallowell of Boston." The man who imported the slaves seems to have known Captain Bloss, who had brought 16 slaves to Nova Scotia in 1750. Historian Karolyn Smardz Frost notes that Thomas Bloss placed an advertisement in the *Boston Post Boy* showing he and Hallowell knew each other: "RAN-away from Capt. Thomas Bloss, last Night, Two Negro Men, one named Phillip, and the other Ned, both sailmakers. Phillip is a tall spare Fellow, and walks a little lame. Ned is a spry young Fellow of about 19 Years of Age: They both talk broken English … Whoever shall take up said Negroes and bring them to their Master on board the Schooner *Success* lying at Col. Wendell's Wharf, or Mr. Benjamin Hallowell in Boston, shall have [a reward]." Bloss died on a trip to England in 1750, and his estate was left to his father. No one knows what became of the enslaved shipwrights and sailors he owned but it seems remarkably coincidental that Hallowell was advertising 10 enslaved men expert in shipbuilding who had "just arrived from Halifax" a few months after Thomas Bloss's untimely death. Sources: *Boston Post Boy*, August 8, 1750; *Boston Post Boy*, September 23, 1751.

1184. UNNAMED MAN (c. 1751) – In 1751, 10 slaves were offered for sale in Boston after arriving from Halifax. The advertisement read: "JUST arriv'd from Hallifax, and to be sold, Ten hearty Strong Negro Men, mostly Tradesmen, such as Caulkers, Carpenters, Sailmakers, Ropemakers: Any Person inclining to purchase may enquire of Benjamin Hallowell of Boston." Sources: *Boston Post Boy*, August 8, 1750; *Boston Post Boy*, September 23, 1751.

1185. UNNAMED MAN (c. 1751) – In 1751, 10 slaves were offered for sale in Boston after arriving from Halifax. The advertisement read: "JUST arriv'd from Hallifax, and to be sold, Ten hearty Strong Negro Men, mostly Tradesmen, such as Caulkers, Carpenters, Sailmakers, Ropemakers: Any Person inclining to purchase may enquire of Benjamin Hallowell of Boston." Sources: *Boston Post Boy*, August 8, 1750; *Boston Post Boy*, September 23, 1751.

1186. UNNAMED MAN (c. 1751) – In 1751, 10 slaves were offered for sale in Boston after arriving from Halifax. The advertisement read: "JUST arriv'd from Hallifax, and to be sold, Ten hearty Strong Negro Men, mostly Tradesmen, such as Caulkers, Carpenters, Sailmakers, Ropemakers: Any Person inclining to purchase may enquire of Benjamin Hallowell of Boston." Sources: *Boston Post Boy*, August 8, 1750; *Boston Post Boy*, September 23, 1751.

1187. UNNAMED MAN (c. 1751) – In 1751, 10 slaves were offered for sale in Boston after arriving from Halifax. The advertisement read: "JUST arriv'd from Hallifax, and to be sold, Ten hearty Strong Negro Men, mostly Tradesmen, such as Caulkers, Carpenters, Sailmakers, Ropemakers: Any Person inclining to purchase may enquire of Benjamin Hallowell of Boston." Sources: *Boston Post Boy*, August 8, 1750; *Boston Post Boy*, September 23, 1751.

1188. UNNAMED MAN (c. 1751) – In 1751, 10 slaves were offered for sale in Boston after arriving from Halifax. The advertisement read: "JUST arriv'd from Hallifax, and to be sold, Ten hearty Strong Negro Men, mostly Tradesmen, such as Caulkers, Carpenters, Sailmakers, Ropemakers: Any Person inclining to purchase may enquire of Benjamin Hallowell of Boston." Sources: *Boston Post Boy*, August 8, 1750; *Boston Post Boy*, September 23, 1751.

1189. UNNAMED MAN (c. 1751) – In 1751, 10 slaves were offered for sale in Boston after arriving from Halifax. The advertisement read: "JUST arriv'd from Hallifax, and to be sold, Ten hearty Strong Negro Men, mostly Tradesmen, such as Caulkers, Carpenters, Sailmakers, Ropemakers: Any Person inclining to purchase may enquire of Benjamin Hallowell of Boston." Sources: *Boston Post Boy*, August 8, 1750; *Boston Post Boy*, September 23, 1751.

1190. UNNAMED MAN (c. 1751) – In 1751, 10 slaves were offered for sale in Boston after arriving from Halifax. The advertisement read: "JUST arriv'd from Hallifax, and to be sold, Ten hearty Strong Negro Men, mostly Tradesmen, such as Caulkers, Carpenters, Sailmakers, Ropemakers: Any Person inclining to purchase may enquire of Benjamin Hallowell of Boston." Sources: *Boston Post Boy*, August 8, 1750; *Boston Post Boy*, September 23, 1751.

1191. UNNAMED MAN (c. 1751) – In 1751, 10 slaves were offered for sale in Boston after arriving from Halifax. The advertisement read: "JUST arriv'd from Hallifax, and to be sold, Ten hearty Strong Negro Men, mostly Tradesmen, such as Caulkers, Carpenters, Sailmakers, Ropemakers: Any Person inclining to purchase may enquire of Benjamin Hallowell of Boston." Sources: *Boston Post Boy*, August 8, 1750; *Boston Post Boy*, September 23, 1751.

1192. UNNAMED MAN (c. 1751) – In 1751, 10 slaves were offered for sale in Boston after arriving from Halifax. The advertisement read: "JUST arriv'd from Hallifax, and to be sold, Ten hearty Strong Negro Men, mostly Tradesmen, such as Caulkers, Carpenters, Sailmakers, Ropemakers: Any Person inclining to purchase may enquire of Benjamin Hallowell of Boston." Sources: *Boston Post Boy*, August 8, 1750; *Boston Post Boy*, September 23, 1751.

1193. UNNAMED MAN (c. 1752, age 30) – This unnamed male was part of Joshua Mauger's slave sale in Nova Scotia in 1752. Mauger noted that this man was "healthy." Source: *Halifax Gazette*, May 30, 1752.

1194. UNNAMED MAN (c. 1752) – This unnamed male was enslaved to S. Maurin. Source: Donovan, "Nominal List of Slaves and Their Owners," 158.

1195. UNNAMED MAN (c. 1755) – This unnamed male was enslaved to M. Desages. Ken Donovan identified this slave because the secretary (Thomas Pichon) complained to Île Royale Governor Comte de Raymond: "M. Desages … a Malouin merchant captain, has 2 Negroes, one of whom he wishes to sell, but the price is much too high." Source: Donovan, "Slaves and Their Owners in Île Royale," 14.

1196. UNNAMED MAN (c. 1755) – This unnamed male was enslaved to M. Desages. Ken Donovan identified this slave because the secretary (Thomas Pichon) complained to Île Royale Governor Comte de Raymond: "M. Desages

… a Malouin merchant captain, has 2 Negroes, one of whom he wishes to sell, but the price is much too high." Source: Donovan, "Slaves and Their Owners in Île Royale," 14.

1197. UNNAMED MAN (c. 1759) – This unnamed male was enslaved to Francois Solignac. Source: Donovan, "Nominal List of Slaves and Their Owners," 160.

1198. UNNAMED MAN (c. 1760) – Enslaved to Captain Parker, this unnamed male came from New England. Source: Donovan, "Nominal List of Slaves and Their Owners," 160.

1199. UNNAMED MAN (slave? c. 1771) – This unnamed male was possibly enslaved to Ebenezer Messenger. According to the 1771 census, Messenger owned one slave. Although the 1771 census did not have a separate column for slaves, it did list Blacks separately and there were very few free Blacks in Nova Scotia before 1776. So, the Blacks listed in this household were probably slaves. Source: Smith, "Slave in Canada," 15.

1200. UNNAMED MAN (slave? c. 1771) – This unnamed male was possibly enslaved to Ann Williams. According to the 1771 census, Ann Williams owned one slave. Although the 1771 census did not have a separate column for slaves, it did list Blacks separately and there were very few free Blacks in Nova Scotia before 1776. So, the Blacks listed in this household were probably slaves. Source: Smith, "Slave in Canada," 15.

1201. UNNAMED MAN (slave? c. 1771) – According to the 1771 census, Magdalen Winniett possessed three Black people: a man, a woman, and a child. Perhaps they were part of the same family. Although the 1771 census did not have a separate column for slaves, it did list Blacks separately and there were very few free Blacks in Nova Scotia before 1776. So, the Blacks listed in this household were probably slaves. Source: Smith, "Slave in Canada," 15.

1202. UNNAMED MAN (c. 1780) – This unnamed male and one other slave escaped from the commanding engineer at Halifax during the American Revolution. Source: Smith, "Slave in Canada," 12.

1203. UNNAMED MAN (c. 1780) – This unnamed male and one other slave escaped from the commanding engineer at Halifax during the American Revolution. Source: Smith, "Slave in Canada," 12.

1204. UNNAMED MAN (c. 1784) – This unnamed male was listed in John Porter's inventory, which valued him at £80. Source: Smith, "Slave in Canada," 17.

1205. UNNAMED MAN (c. 1786) – This unnamed male was enslaved to Captain Stewart in New Brunswick, who hoped to sell his land on the Saint John River of which "ninety acres of it are interval, thirty of which is fit for cultivation." The farm also had three cows and "seventy grafted fruit trees." Stewart's improvements on the land were probably due to his "Negro man and woman, slaves," whom he hoped to sell as part of the estate. Source: *Royal Gazette* (New Brunswick), March 7, 1786.

1206. UNNAMED MAN (c. 1789) – This unnamed man was enslaved to James Moody, but he died from amputation of one of his legs. Source: Death records, May 11, 1789, Records of the Anglican Church, Digby Township Book, NSA.

1207. UNNAMED MAN (c. 1790) – In a letter to the British government, Black Loyalist Thomas Peters described some of the difficulties that people of African descent faced in the Maritimes. Peters mentioned the cases of two separate men who were re-enslaved and then were either killed or viciously maimed. Specifically, Peters noted that "several of them [through] this notorious Partiality or 'Respect of Persons' (which is absolutely forbid and even deemed odious in the Laws of England) have already been reduced to Slavery without being able to obtain any Redress from the King's Courts, And that one of them thus reduced to slavery did actually lose his Life by the Beating and Ill Treatment of his Master." Source: Thomas Peters to Lord Grenville, "The Humble Petition of Thomas Peters, A Negro," 1790, FO 4/1, C 308757, TNA.

1208. UNNAMED MAN (c. 1790) – In a letter to the British government, Black Loyalist Thomas Peters described some of the difficulties that people of African descent faced in the Maritimes. Peters mentioned the cases of two separate men who were re-enslaved and then were either killed or viciously maimed. Source: Thomas Peters to Lord Grenville, "The Humble Petition of Thomas Peters, A Negro," 1790, FO 4/1, C 308757, TNA.

1209. UNNAMED MAN (c. 1790) – William Willet offered an unnamed slave for sale at an auction house in Halifax in 1790. Source: Harris, "Negro Population of the County of Annapolis," 19.

1210. UNNAMED MAN (c. 1790s?) – This unnamed male was enslaved to Elijah Miles, a politician and magistrate in New Brunswick. Apparently this slave served as the first sexton of the Anglican Church in Maugerville. Source: D.M. Young, "Miles, Elijah," *Dictionary of Canadian Biography*, vol. 6, http://www.biographi.ca /en/bio/miles_elijah_6F.html.

1211. UNNAMED MAN (c. 1791) – This unnamed male was enslaved and killed by a member of the Masonic Lodge in Sydney, Cape Breton. The man was charged and had to defend himself at the Supreme Court. He got off by pleading self-defence. The point is that a white man could be brought before the court for killing a Black slave. Source: Smith, "Slave in Canada," 34, 75.

1212. UNNAMED MAN (c. 1791) – While recruiting Blacks for the voyage to Sierra Leone, John Clarkson related the "most affecting" scene of a "Black *slave* ... with tears streaming down his cheeks" who "resign[ed]" his free wife and family to go to Sierra Leone. Clarkson, moved by this man's grief, attempted (unsuccessfully) to purchase his freedom so he could join his family on the voyage. Although the man said that "the separation would be as death to himself," he would "cheer himself" with the knowledge that his family might be in a "more comfortable and happy" situation because of their departure. Source: Fergusson, *Clarkson's Mission to America*, 56–7.

1213. UNNAMED MAN (c. 1799, age 20) – This unnamed male was enslaved to newspaper publisher John Ryan, who later offered him for sale while noting the slave's multi-occupational skills (including housework and farming) in the for sale notice: "TO BE SOLD, A NEGRO MAN, about 20 years of age – is short, but well made, and very active – can do all sorts of Farming work and is a handy House Servant. – For terms &c. enquire of Mr. Ryan." Source: *Royal Gazette*, June 11, 1799.

1214. UNNAMED MAN (c. 1801) – Enslaved to Stephen Reed in Amherst, Nova Scotia, this unnamed male probably worked as a farmer and domestic servant. Along with another slave, he helped produce wheat, potatoes, and hay. In his will, Reed told his sons to "comfortably take care" of his slaves "during their natural lives." Source: Will of Stephen Reed, 1801, Cumberland County, NSA.

1215. UNNAMED MAN (slave? c. 1806) – This man was one of "two likely negro servants" indentured to Lieutenant Hodgson of Country Harbour, Nova Scotia. This unfree person possibly joined Hodgson on his business trip to South Carolina or he may have remained in the Maritimes. It is unknown whether he and the other man once bound to Hodgson had ever been enslaved, but as unfree Black labourers they probably were not treated much differently than slaves. Source: Letter from James Morris to Michael Wallace, July 26, 1806, RG 31, ser. 120, vol. 2, no. 160, NSA.

1216. UNNAMED MAN (slave? c. 1806) – Bound to Michael Wallace, this Black "servant" laboured on Sable Island, Nova Scotia. He was "very stout for his age & active." Documentation about this man presents challenges to interpreting his unfree status throughout his history of indentured servitude or possible enslavement. Upon being "called on business to South Carolina,"

Lieutenant Hodgson of Country Harbour, Nova Scotia, offered one of his "two likely negro servants" for sale around July 1806. James Morris, superintendent of the life-saving station on Sable Island, purchased this man and his remaining "seven years to serve" for £10. The station was founded to rescue castaways, so it seems likely that this unfree man would have assisted with saving shipwrecked crewmembers and trade goods. Morris wrote a letter to Michael Wallace, a slaveholder and one of the commissioners for the Sable Island settlement, to explain his purpose of taking this indentured person "to the Island in order to discharge two of the lads from it." Morris expressed his faith that Wallace would "allow [the man] reasonable wages." In October, Morris received £10 from Wallace "in full payment of this order." It is unknown whether this unfree man and the other bound to Hodgson had ever been enslaved, but as unfree Black labourers they probably were not treated much differently than slaves. Sources: Letter from James Morris to Michael Wallace, July 26, 1806, RG 31, ser. 120, vol. 2, no. 160, NSA; Lyall Campbell, "Morris, James Rainstorpe," *Dictionary of Canadian Biography*, vol. 5, http://www .biographi.ca/en/bio/morris_james_rainstorpe_5E.html.

1217. UNNAMED MAN (c. 1820) – In 1820, an advertisement in a Halifax paper offered, "To be Sold: – Two years and a half time of a black servant man; is a good plain cook, understands family work and the care of horses." This man was likely enslaved at some point before 1820. Source: Smith, "Slave in Canada," 116.

1218. UNNAMED MAN (c. ?) – This unnamed male was enslaved to Samuel Gay. He married Sylvey (see entry). Source: Smith, "Slave in Canada," 88.

1219. UNNAMED PERSON (c. 1724) – This unnamed Black person was en-slaved to Madame Pithou in Île Royale and was from St. Domingue. Source: Donovan, "Nominal List of Slaves and Their Owners," 152.

1220. UNNAMED PERSON (c. 1724) – This unnamed Black person was en-slaved to Madame Pithou in Île Royale and was from St. Domingue. Source: Donovan, "Nominal List of Slaves and Their Owners," 152.

1221. UNNAMED PERSON (c. 1732) – This unnamed Black person was enslaved to merchant, businessman, and large-scale slaveholder Jean Pierre Roma. Roma had planned to set up a settlement with slaves in Prince Edward Island, but he went to Louisbourg in 1732. Roma owned 12 slaves. In 1732, he imported four slaves worth 3,000 livres. Roma noted that he had "2 negroes prime slaves and 2 negresses prime slaves, of the aradan nation [from the coast of Ouidah in Benin]." Please note that there are three named slaves listed in this dictionary of Roma aside from the nine unnamed slaves listed here. Source: Donovan, "Slaves and Their Owners in Île Royale," 10.

1222. UNNAMED PERSON (c. 1732) – This unnamed Black person was enslaved to merchant, businessman, and large-scale slaveholder Jean Pierre Roma. Source: Donovan, "Slaves and Their Owners in Île Royale," 10.

1223. UNNAMED PERSON (c. 1732) – This unnamed Black person was enslaved to merchant, businessman, and large-scale slaveholder Jean Pierre Roma. Source: Donovan, "Slaves and Their Owners in Île Royale," 10.

1224. UNNAMED PERSON (c. 1732) – This unnamed Black person was enslaved to merchant, businessman, and large-scale slaveholder Jean Pierre Roma. Source: Donovan, "Slaves and Their Owners in Île Royale," 10.

1225. UNNAMED PERSON (c. 1732) – This unnamed Black person was enslaved to merchant, businessman, and large-scale slaveholder Jean Pierre Roma. Source: Donovan, "Slaves and Their Owners in Île Royale," 10.

1226. UNNAMED PERSON (c. 1732) – This unnamed Black person was enslaved to merchant, businessman, and large-scale slaveholder Jean Pierre Roma. Source: Donovan, "Slaves and Their Owners in Île Royale," 10.

1227. UNNAMED PERSON (c. 1732) – This unnamed Black person was enslaved to merchant, businessman, and large-scale slaveholder Jean Pierre Roma. Source: Donovan, "Slaves and Their Owners in Île Royale," 10.

1228. UNNAMED PERSON (c. 1732) – This unnamed Black person was enslaved to merchant, businessman, and large-scale slaveholder Jean Pierre Roma. Source: Donovan, "Slaves and Their Owners in Île Royale," 10.

1229. UNNAMED PERSON (c. 1732) – This unnamed Black person was enslaved to merchant, businessman, and large-scale slaveholder Jean Pierre Roma. Source: Donovan, "Slaves and Their Owners in Île Royale," 10.

1230. UNNAMED PERSON (c. 1737) – This unnamed Black person was an enslaved person from the West Indies. Source: Donovan, "Nominal List of Slaves and Their Owners," 154.

1231. UNNAMED PERSON (c. 1737) – This unnamed Black person was an enslaved person from the West Indies. Source: Donovan, "Nominal List of Slaves and Their Owners," 154.

1232. UNNAMED PERSON (c. 1737) – This unnamed Black person was an enslaved person from the West Indies. Source: Donovan, "Nominal List of Slaves and Their Owners," 154.

1233. UNNAMED PERSON (c. 1745) – One of New York's most prominent slaveholders, Peter Warren, brought this unnamed slave to Louisbourg. Apparently the slave was an outstanding musician who, according to a local diary, "played upon the [trumpet] Elevatingly." Source: Donovan, "Slaves and Their Owners in Île Royale," 24.

1234. UNNAMED PERSON (c. 1745) – This unnamed Black person was a slave captured by New England invaders during the Siege of Louisburg in 1745. Source: Donovan, "Slaves and Their Owners in Île Royale," 156.

1235. UNNAMED PERSON (c. 1749) – This unnamed person was possibly enslaved to Militia officer John Creighton, who accompanied Edward Cornwallis to Halifax. Source: Beck, "Creighton, John," *Dictionary of Canadian Biography*, vol. 5, http://www.biographi.ca/en/bio/creighton_john_1721_1807_5E.html.

1236. UNNAMED PERSON (c. 1750) – In 1750, Captain Bloss brought 16 Black slaves to Nova Scotia. As Governor Cornwallis stated, "Captain Bloss a half pay Captain of Man of War is come here has brought with him sixteen negroes, has built a very good house at his own expense, is a sensible worthy man, he is going to pass some accounts that is necessary being abroad many years." Historians do not know much about these slaves and what happened to them. Some scholars believe that the slaves sold to Boston from Halifax in 1751 included some of these people; see entries on unnamed male slaves from Halifax sold to Benjamin Hallowell in Boston in 1751 (who knew Captain Bloss through previous slave deals). Source: Letter from Governor Cornwallis about Captain Bloss, 1750, RG 1, vol. 35, doc. 25, NSA. Ken Donovan notes that a schooner brought nine slave men, the property of Captain Bloss, to Nova Scotia from Antigua; see Donovan, "Slaves in Île Royale," 32.

1237. UNNAMED PERSON (c. 1750) – In 1750, Captain Bloss brought 16 Black slaves to Nova Scotia. As Governor Cornwallis stated, "Captain Bloss a half pay Captain of Man of War is come here has brought with him sixteen negroes, has built a very good house at his own expense, is a sensible worthy man, he is going to pass some accounts that is necessary being abroad many years." Source: Letter from Governor Cornwallis about Captain Bloss, 1750, RG 1, vol. 35, doc. 25, NSA. Ken Donovan notes that a schooner brought nine slave men, the property of Captain Bloss, to Nova Scotia from Antigua; see Donovan, "Slaves in Île Royale," 32.

1238. UNNAMED PERSON (c. 1750) – In 1750, Captain Bloss brought 16 Black slaves to Nova Scotia. As Governor Cornwallis stated, "Captain Bloss a half pay Captain of Man of War is come here has brought with him sixteen negroes, has built a very good house at his own expense, is a sensible worthy man, he is going to pass some accounts that is necessary being abroad many years."

Source: Letter from Governor Cornwallis about Captain Bloss, 1750, RG 1, vol. 35, doc. 25, NSA. Ken Donovan notes that a schooner brought nine slave men, the property of Captain Bloss, to Nova Scotia from Antigua; see Donovan, "Slaves in Île Royale," 32.

1239. UNNAMED PERSON (c. 1750) – In 1750, Captain Bloss brought 16 Black slaves to Nova Scotia. As Governor Cornwallis stated, "Captain Bloss a half pay Captain of Man of War is come here has brought with him sixteen negroes, has built a very good house at his own expense, is a sensible worthy man, he is going to pass some accounts that is necessary being abroad many years." Source: Letter from Governor Cornwallis about Captain Bloss, 1750, RG 1, vol. 35, doc. 25, NSA. Ken Donovan notes that a schooner brought nine slave men, the property of Captain Bloss, to Nova Scotia from Antigua; see Donovan, "Slaves in Île Royale," 32.

1240. UNNAMED PERSON (c. 1750) – In 1750, Captain Bloss brought 16 Black slaves to Nova Scotia. As Governor Cornwallis stated, "Captain Bloss a half pay Captain of Man of War is come here has brought with him sixteen negroes, has built a very good house at his own expense, is a sensible worthy man, he is going to pass some accounts that is necessary being abroad many years." Source: Letter from Governor Cornwallis about Captain Bloss, 1750, RG 1, vol. 35, doc. 25, NSA. Ken Donovan notes that a schooner brought nine slave men, the property of Captain Bloss, to Nova Scotia from Antigua; see Donovan, "Slaves in Île Royale," 32.

1241. UNNAMED PERSON (c. 1750) – In 1750, Captain Bloss brought 16 Black slaves to Nova Scotia. As Governor Cornwallis stated, "Captain Bloss a half pay Captain of Man of War is come here has brought with him sixteen negroes, has built a very good house at his own expense, is a sensible worthy man, he is going to pass some accounts that is necessary being abroad many years." Source: Letter from Governor Cornwallis about Captain Bloss, 1750, RG 1, vol. 35, doc. 25, NSA. Ken Donovan notes that a schooner brought nine slave men, the property of Captain Bloss, to Nova Scotia from Antigua; see Donovan, "Slaves in Île Royale," 32.

1242. UNNAMED PERSON (c. 1750) – In 1750, Captain Bloss brought 16 Black slaves to Nova Scotia. As Governor Cornwallis stated, "Captain Bloss a half pay Captain of Man of War is come here has brought with him sixteen negroes, has built a very good house at his own expense, is a sensible worthy man, he is going to pass some accounts that is necessary being abroad many years." Source: Letter from Governor Cornwallis about Captain Bloss, 1750, RG 1, vol. 35, doc. 25, NSA. Ken Donovan notes that a schooner brought nine slave men, the property of Captain Bloss, to Nova Scotia from Antigua; see Donovan, "Slaves in Île Royale," 32.

1243. UNNAMED PERSON (c. 1750) – In 1750, Captain Bloss brought 16 Black slaves to Nova Scotia. As Governor Cornwallis stated, "Captain Bloss a half pay Captain of Man of War is come here has brought with him sixteen negroes, has built a very good house at his own expense, is a sensible worthy man, he is going to pass some accounts that is necessary being abroad many years." Source: Letter from Governor Cornwallis about Captain Bloss, 1750, RG 1, vol. 35, doc. 25, NSA. Ken Donovan notes that a schooner brought nine slave men, the property of Captain Bloss, to Nova Scotia from Antigua; see Donovan, "Slaves in Île Royale," 32.

1244. UNNAMED PERSON (c. 1750) – In 1750, Captain Bloss brought 16 Black slaves to Nova Scotia. As Governor Cornwallis stated, "Captain Bloss a half pay Captain of Man of War is come here has brought with him sixteen negroes, has built a very good house at his own expense, is a sensible worthy man, he is going to pass some accounts that is necessary being abroad many years." Source: Letter from Governor Cornwallis about Captain Bloss, 1750, RG 1, vol. 35, doc. 25, NSA. Ken Donovan notes that a schooner brought nine slave men, the property of Captain Bloss, to Nova Scotia from Antigua; see Donovan, "Slaves in Île Royale," 32.

1245. UNNAMED PERSON (c. 1750) – In 1750, Captain Bloss brought 16 Black slaves to Nova Scotia. As Governor Cornwallis stated, "Captain Bloss a half pay Captain of Man of War is come here has brought with him sixteen negroes, has built a very good house at his own expense, is a sensible worthy man, he is going to pass some accounts that is necessary being abroad many years." Source: Letter from Governor Cornwallis about Captain Bloss, 1750, RG 1, vol. 35, doc. 25, NSA. Ken Donovan notes that a schooner brought nine slave men, the property of Captain Bloss, to Nova Scotia from Antigua; see Donovan, "Slaves in Île Royale," 32.

1246. UNNAMED PERSON (c. 1750) – In 1750, Captain Bloss brought 16 Black slaves to Nova Scotia. As Governor Cornwallis stated, "Captain Bloss a half pay Captain of Man of War is come here has brought with him sixteen negroes, has built a very good house at his own expense, is a sensible worthy man, he is going to pass some accounts that is necessary being abroad many years." Source: Letter from Governor Cornwallis about Captain Bloss, 1750, RG 1, vol. 35, doc. 25, NSA. Ken Donovan notes that a schooner brought nine slave men, the property of Captain Bloss, to Nova Scotia from Antigua; see Donovan, "Slaves in Île Royale," 32.

1247. UNNAMED PERSON (c. 1750) – In 1750, Captain Bloss brought 16 Black slaves to Nova Scotia. As Governor Cornwallis stated, "Captain Bloss a half pay Captain of Man of War is come here has brought with him sixteen negroes, has built a very good house at his own expense, is a sensible worthy man, he is going to pass some accounts that is necessary being abroad many years." Source: Letter from Governor Cornwallis about Captain Bloss, 1750, RG 1, vol. 35, doc. 25, NSA. Ken Donovan notes that a schooner brought nine slave men, the property of Captain Bloss, to Nova Scotia from Antigua; see Donovan, "Slaves in Île Royale," 32.

1248. UNNAMED PERSON (c. 1750) – In 1750, Captain Bloss brought 16 Black slaves to Nova Scotia. As Governor Cornwallis stated, "Captain Bloss a half pay Captain of Man of War is come here has brought with him sixteen negroes, has built a very good house at his own expense, is a sensible worthy man, he is going to pass some accounts that is necessary being abroad many years." Source: Letter from Governor Cornwallis about Captain Bloss, 1750, RG 1, vol. 35, doc. 25, NSA. Ken Donovan notes that a schooner brought nine slave men, the property of Captain Bloss, to Nova Scotia from Antigua; see Donovan, "Slaves in Île Royale," 32.

1249. UNNAMED PERSON (c. 1750) – In 1750, Captain Bloss brought 16 Black slaves to Nova Scotia. As Governor Cornwallis stated, "Captain Bloss a half pay Captain of Man of War is come here has brought with him sixteen negroes, has built a very good house at his own expense, is a sensible worthy man, he is going to pass some accounts that is necessary being abroad many years." Source: Letter from Governor Cornwallis about Captain Bloss, 1750, RG 1, vol. 35, doc. 25, NSA. Ken Donovan notes that a schooner brought nine slave men, the property of Captain Bloss, to Nova Scotia from Antigua; see Donovan, "Slaves in Île Royale," 32.

1250. UNNAMED PERSON (c. 1750) – In 1750, Captain Bloss brought 16 Black slaves to Nova Scotia. As Governor Cornwallis stated, "Captain Bloss a half pay Captain of Man of War is come here has brought with him sixteen negroes, has built a very good house at his own expense, is a sensible worthy man, he is going to pass some accounts that is necessary being abroad many years." Source: Letter from Governor Cornwallis about Captain Bloss, 1750, RG 1, vol. 35, doc. 25, NSA. Ken Donovan notes that a schooner brought nine slave men, the property of Captain Bloss, to Nova Scotia from Antigua; see Donovan, "Slaves in Île Royale," 32.

1251. UNNAMED PERSON (c. 1750) – In 1750, Captain Bloss brought 16 Black slaves to Nova Scotia. As Governor Cornwallis stated, "Captain Bloss a half pay Captain of Man of War is come here has brought with him sixteen negroes, has built a very good house at his own expense, is a sensible worthy man, he is going to pass some accounts that is necessary being abroad many years." Source: Letter from Governor Cornwallis about Captain Bloss, 1750, RG 1, vol. 35, doc. 25, NSA. Ken Donovan notes that a schooner brought nine slave men, the property of Captain Bloss, to Nova Scotia from Antigua; see Donovan, "Slaves in Île Royale," 32.

1252. UNNAMED PERSON (c. 1751) – This unnamed Black person was enslaved to Jean Jacques Brunet. Source: Donovan, "Nominal List of Slaves and Their Owners," 159.

1253. UNNAMED PERSON (c. 1751) – This enslaved person laboured to build a brig for John Gorham in Halifax. According to historian Frederick William Wallace, "It is recorded that in 1751 John Gorham built a brig with slave labour at Halifax." Source: Frederick William Wallace, *Wooden Ships and Iron Men: The Story of the*

Square-Rigged Merchant Marine of British North America, the Ships, Their Builders and Owners, and the Men Who Sailed Them (London: Hodder & Stoughton, 1924), 12.

1254. UNNAMED PERSON (ca 1752, age 18) – This unnamed Black person was part of Joshua Mauger's slave sale in 1752. Mauger noted, "2 healthy Negro slaves of about 18 Years of Age, of agreable tempers, and fit for any kind of business." Source: *Halifax Gazette*, May 30, 1752.

1255. UNNAMED PERSON (ca 1752, age 18) – This unnamed Black person was part of Joshua Mauger's slave sale in 1752. Mauger noted, "2 healthy Negro slaves of about 18 Years of Age, of agreable tempers, and fit for any kind of business." Source: *Halifax Gazette*, May 30, 1752.

1256. UNNAMED PERSON (c. 1754) – This unnamed enslaved person died in a shipwreck off the coast of Portsmouth, New Hampshire. Source: Donovan, "Nominal List of Slaves and Their Owners," 160.

1257. UNNAMED PERSON (c. 1754) – This unnamed enslaved person died in a shipwreck off the coast of Portsmouth, New Hampshire. Source: Donovan, "Nominal List of Slaves and Their Owners," 160.

1258. UNNAMED PERSON (c. 1754) – This unnamed enslaved person died in a shipwreck off the coast of Portsmouth, New Hampshire. Source: Donovan, "Nominal List of Slaves and Their Owners," 160.

1259. UNNAMED PERSON (c. 1754) – This unnamed enslaved person died in a shipwreck off the coast of Portsmouth, New Hampshire. Source: Donovan, "Nominal List of Slaves and Their Owners," 160.

1260. UNNAMED PERSON (c. 1754, age 14) – This unnamed Black person was enslaved to Philippe Beaubassin. Source: Donovan, "Slaves and Their Owners in Île Royale," 158.

1261. UNNAMED PERSON (c. 1756) – This unnamed Black person was enslaved to Julien Fisel. Source: Donovan, "Nominal List of Slaves and Their Owners," 159.

1262. UNNAMED PERSON (c. 1758) – This unnamed Black person was one of two people enslaved to Nathaniel Meserve and was from New Hampshire. Source: Donovan, "Nominal List of Slaves and Their Owners," 160.

1263. UNNAMED PERSON (c. 1758) – This unnamed Black person was one of two people enslaved to Nathaniel Meserve and was from New Hampshire. Source: Donovan, "Nominal List of Slaves and Their Owners," 160.

1264. UNNAMED PERSON (c. 1760s) – This unnamed Black person was enslaved to Ranald MacKinnon, who migrated from Scotland to the Maritimes. Eventually, MacKinnon settled at Argyle on the south shore of Nova Scotia during the mid-1760s. He obtained a large farm and "owned slaves who laboured on his farm on MacKinnon's Hill." MacKinnon owned enough acreage and slaves that he "set off land which the slaves tilled for their own living." According to Jason Ricker, MacKinnon's slaves resided in small cabins a short distance away from their owner's house, and the remains from a wall they had built were visible in the twentieth century. We do not know the exact number of slaves, but it was certainly more than one and could have been three or more. This author's best estimate is two slaves, which is an exceedingly conservative estimate. In a separate piece of work, Sharon Robart-Jackson references a 1990 interview of the contemporary property owner, who stated that "John MacKinnon" had imported 200 slaves for this project, portions of which still stand today. The number of 200 slaves seems excessive. We have not seen any documentation to support this suggestion. The people MacKinnon enslaved had access to an allocation of his land on which they farmed for themselves. Sources: Jason Ricker, *Historical Sketches of Glenwood and the Argyles, Yarmouth County, Nova Scotia* (1941; repr., Yarmouth: Sentinel Printing, 1994), 125; Robart-Johnson, *Africa's Children*, 38–9.

1265. UNNAMED PERSON (c. 1760s) – This unnamed Black person was enslaved to Ranald MacKinnon, who migrated from Scotland to the Maritimes. Eventually, MacKinnon settled at Argyle on the south shore of Nova Scotia during the mid-1760s. He obtained a large farm and "owned slaves who laboured on his farm on MacKinnon's Hill." MacKinnon owned enough acreage and slaves that he "set off land which the slaves tilled for their own living." His slaves resided in small cabins a short distance away from their owner's house, and the remains from a wall they had built were visible in the twentieth century. Source: Ricker, *Historical Sketches of Glenwood and the Argyles, Yarmouth County*, 125.

1266. UNNAMED PERSON (c. 1763) – This unnamed Black person was enslaved to Colonel Alexander McCulloch of Hants County, Nova Scotia. In 1763, McCulloch threatened two different men and promised to use his Black slaves to help him in a fight. Source: States, "Presence and Perseverance: Blacks in Hants County," 36.

1267. UNNAMED PERSON (c. 1763) – This unnamed Black person was enslaved to Colonel Alexander McCulloch of Hants County, Nova Scotia. In 1763, McCulloch threatened two different men and promised to use his Black slaves to help him in a fight. Source: States, "Presence and Perseverance: Blacks in Hants County," 36.

1268. UNNAMED PERSON (c. 1765) – This person arrived in Yarmouth from Beverly, Massachusetts, with enslaver Andrew Lovitt and his family. Apparently

Lovitt granted his slaves freedom upon their arrival to Nova Scotia, but they continued to stay with him. Lovitt enslaved at least two people. Source: Robart-Johnson, *Africa's Children*, 27.

1269. UNNAMED PERSON (c. 1765) – This person arrived in Yarmouth from Beverly, Massachusetts, with enslaver Andrew Lovitt and his family. Apparently Lovitt granted his slaves freedom upon their arrival, but they continued to stay with him. Lovitt enslaved at least two people. Source: Robart-Johnson, *Africa's Children*, 27.

1270. UNNAMED PERSON (c. 1777) – New England Planter and Liverpool resident Simeon Perkins wrote that "2 negroes [ran] away from Dav. [David] Prince, and one from Mr. Sutherland, supposed to be on board the letter of marque." Source: Innis, *Diary of Simeon Perkins, 1766–1780*, 166.

1271. UNNAMED PERSON (c. 1777) – New England Planter and Liverpool resident Simeon Perkins wrote that "2 negroes [ran] away from Dav. [David] Prince supposed to be on board the letter of marque." Source: Innis, *Diary of Simeon Perkins, 1766–1780*, 166.

1272. UNNAMED PERSON (c. 1780s) – This unnamed Black person was enslaved to Peter Anderson on PEI. Source: Hornby, *Black Islanders*, 9.

1273. UNNAMED PERSON (c. 1780s) – This unnamed Black person was enslaved to Peter Anderson on PEI. Source: Hornby, *Black Islanders*, 9.

1274. UNNAMED PERSON (c. 1780s) – This unnamed Black person was enslaved to the Bayer family, who came from Florida to Musquodoboit. There could have been more than one slave, but it is unclear. Source: Smith, "Slave in Canada," 25.

1275. UNNAMED PERSON (c. 1780s) – This unnamed Black person was enslaved to Joseph Beers on PEI. Source: Hornby, *Black Islanders*, 9.

1276. UNNAMED PERSON (c. 1780s) – This unnamed Black person was enslaved to Joseph Beers on PEI. Source: Hornby, *Black Islanders*, 9.

1277. UNNAMED PERSON (c. 1780s) – This unnamed Black person was enslaved to the Bovyer family on PEI. Source: Hornby, *Black Islanders*, 9.

1278. UNNAMED PERSON (c. 1780s) – This unnamed Black person was enslaved to the Bovyer family on PEI. Source: Hornby, *Black Islanders*, 9.

1279. UNNAMED PERSON (c. 1780s) – This unnamed person was enslaved to the Brown family, who were from Massachusetts and migrated to Horton, Nova Scotia, as a result of the American Revolution. Historian Arthur Eaton noted that the Brown family possessed "several slaves." I have taken this to mean at least three. Source: Eaton, *History of Kings County*, 587.

1280. UNNAMED PERSON (c. 1780s) – This unnamed person was enslaved to the Brown family, who were from Massachusetts and migrated to Horton, Nova Scotia, as a result of the American Revolution. Historian Arthur Eaton noted that the Brown family possessed "several slaves." I have taken this to mean at least three. Source: Eaton, *History of Kings County*, 587.

1281. UNNAMED PERSON (c. 1780s) – This unnamed person was enslaved to the Brown family, who were from Massachusetts and migrated to Horton, Nova Scotia, as a result of the American Revolution. Historian Arthur Eaton noted that the Brown family possessed "several slaves." I have taken this to mean at least three. Source: Eaton, *History of Kings County*, 587.

1282. UNNAMED PERSON (c. 1780s) – This unnamed Black person was enslaved to Colonel Compton on PEI. Source: Hornby, *Black Islanders*, 10.

1283. UNNAMED PERSON (c. 1780s) – This unnamed Black person was enslaved to Colonel Compton on PEI. Source: Hornby, *Black Islanders*, 10.

1284. UNNAMED PERSON (c. 1780s) – This unnamed Black person was enslaved to Samuel Hayden on PEI. Source: Hornby, *Black Islanders*, 9.

1285. UNNAMED PERSON (c. 1780s) – This unnamed Black person was enslaved to Samuel Hayden on PEI. Source: Hornby, *Black Islanders*, 9.

1286. UNNAMED PERSON (c. 1780s) – This unnamed Black person was enslaved to David Higgins on PEI. Source: Hornby, *Black Islanders*, 10.

1287. UNNAMED PERSON (c. 1780s) – This unnamed Black person was enslaved to David Higgins on PEI. Source: Hornby, *Black Islanders*, 10.

1288. UNNAMED PERSON (c. 1780s) – This unnamed Black person was enslaved to Mr. Hurd on PEI. Source: Hornby, *Black Islanders*, 10.

1289. UNNAMED PERSON (c. 1780s) – This unnamed Black person was enslaved to Mr. Hurd on PEI. Source: Hornby, *Black Islanders*, 10.

1290. UNNAMED PERSON (c. 1780s) – This unnamed Black person was enslaved to the McInnes family, who came from Florida to Musquodoboit. There could have been more than one slave, but it is unclear. Source: Smith, "Slave in Canada," 25.

1291. UNNAMED PERSON (c. 1780s) – This unnamed Black person was enslaved to Alexander Smith on PEI. Source: Hornby, *Black Islanders*, 9.

1292. UNNAMED PERSON (c. 1780s) – This unnamed Black person was enslaved to Alexander Smith on PEI. Source: Hornby, *Black Islanders*, 9.

1293. UNNAMED PERSON (c. 1780s) – This unnamed Black person was enslaved to John Strickland on PEI. Source: Hornby, *Black Islanders*, 9.

1294. UNNAMED PERSON (c. 1780s) – This unnamed Black person was enslaved to John Strickland on PEI. Source: Hornby, *Black Islanders*, 9.

1295. UNNAMED PERSON (c. 1780s) – This unnamed Black person was enslaved to John Throckmorton on PEI. Source: Hornby, *Black Islanders*, 9.

1296. UNNAMED PERSON (c. 1780s) – This unnamed Black person was enslaved to John Throckmorton on PEI. Source: Hornby, *Black Islanders*, 9.

1297. UNNAMED PERSON (slave? c. 1783) – This unnamed person was possibly enslaved to Andrew Barclay in Shelburne, Nova Scotia. The Port Roseway Minute Book lists Barclay as having five servants, while another document from Nova Scotia in 1783 indicates he had seven servants. It is not clear if all of the servants were enslaved Black people. Barclay did possess some servants, but they might have been re-enslaved (see this book's introduction for comments about Black people in the possession of a white person in the Book of Negroes). Source: Minute Book of Port Roseway Associates, vol. 1, 1782, MG 9, B 9-14, LAC; "Provisional Return for the Numbers of Men, Women, and Children belonging to Captain Andrew Barclay's Company of associated Loyalists," July 1783, MG 100, vol. 220, doc. 1, NSA; Karolyn Smardz Frost, "King's College," 22–6. This author is thankful to Karolyn for sharing her research.

1298. UNNAMED PERSON (slave? c. 1783) – This unnamed person was possibly enslaved to Andrew Barclay in Shelburne, Nova Scotia. The Port Roseway Minute Book lists Barclay as having five servants, while another document from Nova Scotia in 1783 indicates he had seven servants. It is not clear if all of the servants were enslaved Black people. Barclay did possess some servants, but they might have been re-enslaved (see this book's introduction for comments about Black people in the possession of a white person in the Book of Negroes). Source: Minute Book of Port Roseway Associates, vol. 1, 1782, MG 9, B 9-14, LAC; "Provisional Return for the Numbers of Men, Women, and Children belonging to Captain Andrew Barclay's Company of associated Loyalists," July 1783, MG 100, vol. 220, doc. 1, NSA; Karolyn Smardz Frost, "King's College," 22–6. This author is thankful to Karolyn for sharing her research.

1299. UNNAMED PERSON (slave? c. 1783) – This unnamed person was possibly enslaved to Andrew Barclay in Shelburne, Nova Scotia. The Port Roseway Minute Book lists Barclay as having five servants, while another document from Nova Scotia in 1783 indicates he had seven servants. It is not clear if all of the servants were enslaved Black people. Barclay did possess some servants, but they might have been re-enslaved (see this book's introduction for comments about Black people in the possession of a white person in the Book of Negroes). Source: Minute Book of Port Roseway Associates, vol. 1, 1782, MG 9, B 9-14, LAC; "Provisional Return for the Numbers of Men, Women, and Children belonging to Captain Andrew Barclay's Company of associated Loyalists," July 1783, MG 100, vol. 220, doc. 1, NSA; Karolyn Smardz Frost, "King's College," 22–6. This author is thankful to Karolyn for sharing her research.

1300. UNNAMED PERSON (slave? c. 1783) – This unnamed person was possibly enslaved to Andrew Barclay in Shelburne, Nova Scotia. The Port Roseway Minute Book lists Barclay as having five servants, while another document from Nova Scotia in 1783 indicates he had seven servants. It is not clear if all of the servants were enslaved Black people. Barclay did possess some servants, but they might have been re-enslaved (see this book's introduction for comments about Black people in the possession of a white person in the Book of Negroes). Source: Minute Book of Port Roseway Associates, vol. 1, 1782, MG 9, B 9-14, LAC; "Provisional Return for the Numbers of Men, Women, and Children belonging to Captain Andrew Barclay's Company of associated Loyalists," July 1783, MG 100, vol. 220, doc. 1, NSA; Karolyn Smardz Frost, "King's College," 22–6. This author is thankful to Karolyn for sharing her research.

1301. UNNAMED PERSON (slave? c. 1783) – This unnamed person was possibly enslaved to Andrew Barclay in Shelburne, Nova Scotia. The Port Roseway Minute Book lists Barclay as having five servants, while another document from Nova Scotia in 1783 indicates he had seven servants. It is not clear if all of the servants were enslaved Black people. Barclay did possess some servants, but they might have been re-enslaved (see this book's introduction for comments about Black people in the possession of a white person in the Book of Negroes). Source: Minute Book of Port Roseway Associates, vol. 1, 1782, MG 9, B 9-14, LAC; "Provisional Return for the Numbers of Men, Women, and Children belonging to Captain Andrew Barclay's Company of associated Loyalists," July 1783, MG 100, vol. 220, doc. 1, NSA; Karolyn Smardz Frost, "King's College," 22–6. This author is thankful to Karolyn for sharing her research.

1302. UNNAMED PERSON (slave? c. 1783) – This unnamed person was possibly enslaved to Andrew Barclay in Shelburne, Nova Scotia. The Port Roseway Minute Book lists Barclay as having five servants, while another document from Nova Scotia in 1783 indicates he had seven servants. It is not clear if all of the servants were enslaved Black people. Barclay did possess some servants, but they might have been re-enslaved (see this book's introduction for comments about Black people in the possession of a white person in the Book of Negroes). Source: Minute Book of Port Roseway Associates, vol. 1, 1782, MG 9, B 9-14, LAC; "Provisional Return for the Numbers of Men, Women, and Children belonging to Captain Andrew Barclay's Company of associated Loyalists," July 1783, MG 100, vol. 220, doc. 1, NSA; Karolyn Smardz Frost, "King's College," 22–6. This author is thankful to Karolyn for sharing her research.

1303. UNNAMED PERSON (slave? c. 1783) – This unnamed person was possibly enslaved to Andrew Barclay in Shelburne, Nova Scotia. The Port Roseway Minute Book lists Barclay as having five servants, while another document from Nova Scotia in 1783 indicates he had seven servants. It is not clear if all of the servants were enslaved Black people. Barclay did possess some servants, but they might have been re-enslaved (see this book's introduction for comments about Black people in the possession of a white person in the Book of Negroes). Source: Minute Book of Port Roseway Associates, vol. 1, 1782, MG 9, B 9-14, LAC; "Provisional Return for the Numbers of Men, Women, and Children belonging to Captain Andrew Barclay's Company of associated Loyalists," July 1783, MG 100, vol. 220, doc. 1, NSA; Karolyn Smardz Frost, "King's College," 22–6. This author is thankful to Karolyn for sharing her research.

1304. UNNAMED PERSON (c. 1783) – New England Planter and Liverpool resident Simeon Perkins wrote "Two Small Schooners from Halifax with people for Roseway [Port Roseway eventually became Shelburne] came in here in the Night. A Colonel Campbell is in one of them. He is said to be a man of Property, has Several Black Slaves with him." Perkins did not specify the number of slaves much less their names, ages, or anything else. I take the word "several" to mean at least three, but it could have been more. Source: Harvey, *Diary of Simeon Perkins, 1780–1789*, 186.

1305. UNNAMED PERSON (c. 1783) – New England Planter and Liverpool resident Simeon Perkins wrote "Two Small Schooners from Halifax with people for Roseway [Port Roseway eventually became Shelburne] came in here in the Night. A Colonel Campbell is in one of them. He is said to be a man of Property, has Several Black Slaves with him." Source: Harvey, *Diary of Simeon Perkins, 1780–1789*, 186.

1306. UNNAMED PERSON (c. 1783) – New England Planter and Liverpool resident Simeon Perkins wrote "Two Small Schooners from Halifax with people for Roseway [Port Roseway eventually became Shelburne] came in here in the Night. A Colonel Campbell is in one of them. He is said to be a man of Property, has Several Black Slaves with him." Source: Harvey, *Diary of Simeon Perkins, 1780–1789,* 186.

1307. UNNAMED PERSON (c. 1784) – This unnamed Black person was enslaved to John Grant, who was originally from Scotland and who, after serving the British army near Ticonderoga during the Seven Years War, settled in Queens County, Long Island. After the American Revolution, he migrated to Nova Scotia with a large family and nine slaves. These enslaved people might have been a family unit. Sources: Cottreau-Robins, "Landscape of Slavery in Loyalist Era Nova Scotia," 131–2; see also Smith, "Slave in Canada," 93–4.

1308. UNNAMED PERSON (c. 1784) – This unnamed Black person was enslaved to James Green. The local enumerator for the township of Chester wrote that Green had "built a large House, [and] made great improvements on his Land." He noted that Green's "three Servants are Slaves," and had helped their owner develop his property. Source: Muster Roll of the New Settlers at Chester, Chipman Papers, Muster Master General's Office, Loyalist Musters, 1776–1785, MG 23, D1, ser. I, vol. 24, LAC.

1309. UNNAMED PERSON (c. 1784) – This unnamed Black person was enslaved to James Green. Source: Muster Roll of the New Settlers at Chester, Chipman Papers, Muster Master General's Office, Loyalist Musters, 1776–1785, MG 23, D1, ser. I, vol. 24, LAC.

1310. UNNAMED PERSON (c. 1784) – This unnamed Black person was enslaved to James Green. Source: Muster Roll of the New Settlers at Chester, Chipman Papers, Muster Master General's Office, Loyalist Musters, 1776–1785, MG 23, D1, ser. I, vol. 24, LAC.

1311. UNNAMED PERSON (slave? c. 1784) – This person was probably enslaved to John Legett, a Loyalist from North Carolina who settled in Country Harbour. According to Troxler, Legett had seven "servants," who were probably enslaved. This unfree person and probably four others were in Halifax in June 1784, while a muster roll shows two others remained in Country Harbour (see entries for Michael and Phillis). Source: Troxler, "North Carolina's John Legett at Country Harbour," 285–314, esp. 296n18, 310.

1312. UNNAMED PERSON (slave? c. 1784) – This person was probably enslaved to John Legett, a Loyalist from North Carolina who settled in Country Harbour. According to Troxler, Legett had seven "servants," who were probably enslaved. This unfree person and probably four others were in Halifax in June 1784, while a muster roll shows two others remained in Country Harbour (see entries for Michael and Phillis). Source: Troxler, "North Carolina's John Legett at Country Harbour," 296n18, 310.

1313. UNNAMED PERSON (slave? c. 1784) – This person was probably enslaved to John Legett, a Loyalist from North Carolina who settled in Country Harbour. According to Troxler, Legett had seven "servants," who were probably enslaved. This unfree person and probably four others were in Halifax in June 1784, while a muster roll shows two others remained in Country Harbour (see entries for Michael and Phillis). Source: Troxler, "North Carolina's John Legett at Country Harbour," 296n18, 310.

1314. UNNAMED PERSON (slave? c. 1784) – This person was probably enslaved to John Legett, a Loyalist from North Carolina who settled in Country Harbour. According to Troxler, Legett had seven "servants," who were probably enslaved. This unfree person and probably four others were in Halifax in June 1784, while a muster roll shows two others remained in Country Harbour (see entries for Michael and Phillis). Source: Troxler, "North Carolina's John Legett at Country Harbour," 296n18, 310.

1315. UNNAMED PERSON (slave? c. 1784) – This person was probably enslaved to John Legett, a Loyalist from North Carolina who settled in Country Harbour. According to Troxler, Legett had seven "servants," who were probably enslaved. This unfree person and probably four others were in Halifax in June 1784, while a muster roll shows two others remained in Country Harbour (see entries for Michael and Phillis). Source: Troxler, "North Carolina's John Legett at Country Harbour," 296n18, 310.

1316. UNNAMED PERSON [cannot read name] (slave? c. 1784) – This person was possibly enslaved to George Westphal, who planned to settle nearby Halifax. Westphal had six Black people living in his household, and it seems likely that they were enslaved. Source: Loyalists and Disbanded Troops at Cole Harbour, Chipman Papers, Muster Master General's Office, Loyalist Musters, 1776–1785, MG 23, D1, ser. I, vol. 24, LAC.

1317. UNNAMED PERSON [cannot read name] (slave? c. 1784) – This person was possibly enslaved to George Westphal, who planned to settle nearby Halifax. Westphal had six Black people living in his household. It seems likely that they were enslaved. Source: Loyalists and Disbanded Troops at Cole Harbour, Chipman Papers, Muster Master General's Office, Loyalist Musters, 1776–1785, MG 23, D1, ser. I, vol. 24, LAC.

1318. UNNAMED PERSON (c. 1786) – This unnamed Black person was probably enslaved to Samuel Starr, who traded slaves in the West Indies. Starr resided in Nova Scotia and probably had a few slaves that resided for various amounts of time with him, but who he eventually traded to the West Indies. Source: Karolyn Smardz Frost, "Planting Slavery in Nova Scotia's Promised Land, 1759–1775," in *Unsettling the Great White North: African Canadian History*, eds. Michele A. Johnson and Funké Aladejebi (Toronto: University of Toronto Press, forthcoming), n40.

1319. UNNAMED PERSON (c. 1787?) – This unnamed person was enslaved to Prince Edward Island Lieutenant Governor Edmund Fanning. Source: Whitfield and Cahill, "Slave Life and Slave Law," 35.

1320. UNNAMED PERSON (c. 1787?) – This unnamed person was enslaved to Prince Edward Island Lieutenant Governor Edmund Fanning. Source: Whitfield and Cahill, "Slave Life and Slave Law," 35.

1321. UNNAMED PERSON (c. 1791) – This unnamed person was enslaved to Mr. Lee, and who John Clarkson thought should have been freed so he could go to Sierra Leone. Source: Fergusson, *Clarkson's Mission to America*, 77.

1322. UNNAMED PERSON (c. 1792) – This unnamed Black person was re-enslaved in the West Indies. John Wentworth wrote C.F. Greville, a governor in the West Indies, asking for "the release of a certain Negro young man" who had been "insidiously and unjustly sold as a slave in your island." Source: Smith, "Slave in Canada," 120.

1323. UNNAMED PERSON (c. 1792) – This unnamed person was enslaved to Nova Scotia Lieutenant Governor John Wentworth. The source only mentions "negro slaves" without giving an exact number. I have taken the plural to mean at least two, but it could have been more. It should also be noted that these slaves could have included Matthew and Susannah, the two enslaved children that Wentworth did not send with the 19 Black people he forced to go to Suriname. The diary entry reads: "Sir John Wentworth sworn into Office and at night the Town was brightly illuminated to celebrate and there was more drunkenness than usual in the streets which is a poor welcome to my way of thinking. Attended a ball in the evening & He and his Lady made a handsome pair on a raised dais with negro slaves fanning them with large fans of red, white and blue ostrich feathers and the silver cloth around the base." Source: Untitled Diary Entry on Smallpox Inoculation, https://emmr.lib.unb.ca/recipes/372.

1324. UNNAMED PERSON (c. 1792) – This unnamed person was enslaved to Nova Scotia Lieutenant Governor John Wentworth. The source only mentions "negro slaves" without giving an exact number. I have taken the plural to mean at least two, but it could have been more. It should also be noted that these slaves could have included Matthew and Susannah, the two enslaved children that Wentworth did not send with the 19 Black people he forced to go to Suriname. The diary entry reads: "Sir John Wentworth sworn into Office and at night the Town was brightly illuminated to celebrate and there was more drunkenness than usual in the streets which is a poor welcome to my way of thinking. Attended a ball in the evening & He and his Lady made a handsome pair on a raised dais with negro slaves fanning them with large fans of red, white and blue ostrich feathers and the silver cloth around the base." Source: Untitled Diary Entry on Smallpox Inoculation, https://emmr.lib.unb.ca/recipes/372.

1325. UNNAMED PERSON (c. 1795) – This person was probably enslaved to Mr. Jonathan Snelling, the son of a well-known Boston merchant who traded with the West Indies. The poll tax report described him as "Mr. Snelling's Negro Man." Source: Poll Tax, Rawdon, Hants County – 1795 Commissioner of Public Records Nova Scotia Archives RG 1 vol. 444½ no. 81, NSA, https://novascotia.ca/archives/census/returnsTax .asp?ID=19955.

1326. UNNAMED PERSON (c. 1799) – This unnamed person was enslaved to George Cornwall. It is not clear from his will how many slaves he owned or their names, but the wording indicates more than one: "I give to Charity my beloved wife all my negro slaves requesting her to manumit and set them free by her will after her decease, but in case they do not behave as honest and orderly servants[;] I wish she would sell them, as undeserving of her or my intended bounty towards them." Source: Will of George Cornwall, Annapolis County, 1799, RG 48, Probate Records, NSA.

1327. UNNAMED PERSON (c. 1799) – This unnamed person was enslaved to George Cornwall. It is not clear from his will how many slaves he owned or their names, but the wording indicates more than one. Source: Will of George Cornwall, Annapolis County, 1799, RG 48, Probate Records, NSA.

1328. UNNAMED PERSON (c. 1803) – This unnamed Black person was one of the 31 slaves listed in the 1803 census of Saint George, New Brunswick. We do not know their names or who owned them. These slaves performed a variety of agricultural pursuits. They made up about 3.4 per cent of the total population (31 out of 903). Although the enumerator of the return doubted the effectiveness of "Africans" in the parish because of the climate, they did work to help produce several products. He also noted that there "are large Tracts of Interval Lands of the first quality, producing Wheat, Barley, Rye, Indian Corn … potatoes and Oats with [a] large Quantity of Hay." Source: Parish of Saint Mary's, August 8,

1803, Winslow Papers, vol. 12, no. 36, Loyalist Collection, Harriet Irving Library (HIL), University of New Brunswick, Fredericton, New Brunswick.

1329. UNNAMED PERSON (c. 1803) – This unnamed person was one of the 31 slaves listed in the 1803 census of Saint George, New Brunswick. Source: Parish of Saint Mary's, August 8, 1803, Winslow Papers, vol. 12, no. 36, Loyalist Collection, HIL.

1330. UNNAMED PERSON (c. 1803) – This unnamed person was one of the 31 slaves listed in the 1803 census of Saint George, New Brunswick. Source: Parish of Saint Mary's, August 8, 1803, Winslow Papers, vol. 12, no. 36, Loyalist Collection, HIL.

1331. UNNAMED PERSON (c. 1803) – This unnamed person was one of the 31 slaves listed in the 1803 census of Saint George, New Brunswick. Source: Parish of Saint Mary's, August 8, 1803, Winslow Papers, vol. 12, no. 36, Loyalist Collection, HIL.

1332. UNNAMED PERSON (c. 1803) – This unnamed person was one of the 31 slaves listed in the 1803 census of Saint George, New Brunswick. Source: Parish of Saint Mary's, August 8, 1803, Winslow Papers, vol. 12, no. 36, Loyalist Collection, HIL.

1333. UNNAMED PERSON (c. 1803) – This unnamed person was one of the 31 slaves listed in the 1803 census of Saint George, New Brunswick. Source: Parish of Saint Mary's, August 8, 1803, Winslow Papers, vol. 12, no. 36, Loyalist Collection, HIL.

1334. UNNAMED PERSON (c. 1803) – This unnamed person was one of the 31 slaves listed in the 1803 census of Saint George, New Brunswick. Source: Parish of Saint Mary's, August 8, 1803, Winslow Papers, vol. 12, no. 36, Loyalist Collection, HIL.

1335. UNNAMED PERSON (c. 1803) – This unnamed person was one of the 31 slaves listed in the 1803 census of Saint George, New Brunswick. Source: Parish of Saint Mary's, August 8, 1803, Winslow Papers, vol. 12, no. 36, Loyalist Collection, HIL.

1336. UNNAMED PERSON (c. 1803) – This unnamed person was one of the 31 slaves listed in the 1803 census of Saint George, New Brunswick. Source: Parish of Saint Mary's, August 8, 1803, Winslow Papers, vol. 12, no. 36, Loyalist Collection, HIL.

1337. UNNAMED PERSON (c. 1803) – This unnamed person was one of the 31 slaves listed in the 1803 census of Saint George, New Brunswick. Source: Parish of Saint Mary's, August 8, 1803, Winslow Papers, vol. 12, no. 36, Loyalist Collection, HIL.

1338. UNNAMED PERSON (c. 1803) – This unnamed person was one of the 31 slaves listed in the 1803 census of Saint George, New Brunswick. Source: Parish of Saint Mary's, August 8, 1803, Winslow Papers, vol. 12, no. 36, Loyalist Collection, HIL.

1339. UNNAMED PERSON (c. 1803) – This unnamed person was one of the 31 slaves listed in the 1803 census of Saint George, New Brunswick. Source: Parish of Saint Mary's, August 8, 1803, Winslow Papers, vol. 12, no. 36, Loyalist Collection, HIL.

1340. UNNAMED PERSON (c. 1803) – This unnamed person was one of the 31 slaves listed in the 1803 census of Saint George, New Brunswick. Source: Parish of Saint Mary's, August 8, 1803, Winslow Papers, vol. 12, no. 36, Loyalist Collection, HIL.

1341. UNNAMED PERSON (c. 1803) – This unnamed person was one of the 31 slaves listed in the 1803 census of Saint George, New Brunswick. Source: Parish of Saint Mary's, August 8, 1803, Winslow Papers, vol. 12, no. 36, Loyalist Collection, HIL.

1342. UNNAMED PERSON (c. 1803) – This unnamed person was one of the 31 slaves listed in the 1803 census of Saint George, New Brunswick. Source: Parish of Saint Mary's, August 8, 1803, Winslow Papers, vol. 12, no. 36, Loyalist Collection, HIL.

1343. UNNAMED PERSON (c. 1803) – This unnamed person was one of the 31 slaves listed in the 1803 census of Saint George, New Brunswick. Source: Parish of Saint Mary's, August 8, 1803, Winslow Papers, vol. 12, no. 36, Loyalist Collection, HIL.

1344. UNNAMED PERSON (c. 1803) – This unnamed person was one of the 31 slaves listed in the 1803 census of Saint George, New Brunswick. Source: Parish of Saint Mary's, August 8, 1803, Winslow Papers, vol. 12, no. 36, Loyalist Collection, HIL.

1345. UNNAMED PERSON (c. 1803) – This unnamed person was one of the 31 slaves listed in the 1803 census of Saint George, New Brunswick. Source: Parish of Saint Mary's, August 8, 1803, Winslow Papers, vol. 12, no. 36, Loyalist Collection, HIL.

1346. UNNAMED PERSON (c. 1803) – This unnamed person was one of the 31 slaves listed in the 1803 census of Saint George, New Brunswick. Source: Parish of Saint Mary's, August 8, 1803, Winslow Papers, vol. 12, no. 36, Loyalist Collection, HIL.

1347. UNNAMED PERSON (c. 1803) – This unnamed person was one of the 31 slaves listed in the 1803 census of Saint George, New Brunswick. Source: Parish of Saint Mary's, August 8, 1803, Winslow Papers, vol. 12, no. 36, Loyalist Collection, HIL

1348. UNNAMED PERSON (c. 1803) – This unnamed person was one of the 31 slaves listed in the 1803 census of Saint George, New Brunswick. Source: Parish of Saint Mary's, August 8, 1803, Winslow Papers, vol. 12, no. 36, Loyalist Collection, HIL.

1349. UNNAMED PERSON (c. 1803) – This unnamed person was one of the 31 slaves listed in the 1803 census of Saint George, New Brunswick. Source: Parish of Saint Mary's, August 8, 1803, Winslow Papers, vol. 12, no. 36, Loyalist Collection, HIL.

1350. UNNAMED PERSON (c. 1803) – This unnamed person was one of the 31 slaves listed in the 1803 census of Saint George, New Brunswick. Source: Parish of Saint Mary's, August 8, 1803, Winslow Papers, vol. 12, no. 36, Loyalist Collection, HIL.

1351. UNNAMED PERSON (c. 1803) – This unnamed person was one of the 31 slaves listed in the 1803 census of Saint George, New Brunswick. Source: Parish of Saint Mary's, August 8, 1803, Winslow Papers, vol. 12, no. 36, Loyalist Collection, HIL.

1352. UNNAMED PERSON (c. 1803) – This unnamed person was one of the 31 slaves listed in the 1803 census of Saint George, New Brunswick. Source: Parish of Saint Mary's, August 8, 1803, Winslow Papers, vol. 12, no. 36, Loyalist Collection, HIL.

1353. UNNAMED PERSON (c. 1803) – This unnamed person was one of the 31 slaves listed in the 1803 census of Saint George, New Brunswick. Source: Parish of Saint Mary's, August 8, 1803, Winslow Papers, vol. 12, no. 36, Loyalist Collection, HIL.

1354. UNNAMED PERSON (c. 1803) – This unnamed person was one of the 31 slaves listed in the 1803 census of Saint George, New Brunswick. Source: Parish of Saint Mary's, August 8, 1803, Winslow Papers, vol. 12, no. 36, Loyalist Collection, HIL.

1355. UNNAMED PERSON (c. 1803) – This unnamed person was one of the 31 slaves listed in the 1803 census of Saint George, New Brunswick. Source: Parish of Saint Mary's, August 8, 1803, Winslow Papers, vol. 12, no. 36, Loyalist Collection, HIL.

1356. UNNAMED PERSON (c. 1803) – This unnamed person was one of the 31 slaves listed in the 1803 census of Saint George, New Brunswick. Source: Parish of Saint Mary's, August 8, 1803, Winslow Papers, vol. 12, no. 36, Loyalist Collection, HIL.

1357. UNNAMED PERSON (c. 1803) – This unnamed person was one of the 31 slaves listed in the 1803 census of Saint George, New Brunswick. Source: Parish of Saint Mary's, August 8, 1803, Winslow Papers, vol. 12, no. 36, Loyalist Collection, HIL.

1358. UNNAMED PERSON (c. 1803) – This unnamed person was one of the 31 slaves listed in the 1803 census of Saint George, New Brunswick. Source: Parish of Saint Mary's, August 8, 1803, Winslow Papers, vol. 12, no. 36, Loyalist Collection, HIL.

1359. UNNAMED PERSON (c. 1807) – New York Loyalist George Harding mentioned multiple slaves in his will, but there is no inventory and we cannot say for certain how many slaves he owned in 1807; but there were at least two slaves. He simply bequeathed "all the Negro Slaves or servants" to his daughter. Source: Will of George Harding, Sunbury County, 1807, PANB.

1360. UNNAMED PERSON (c. 1807) – New York Loyalist George Harding mentioned multiple slaves in his will, but there is no inventory and we cannot say for certain how many slaves he owned in 1807; but there were at least two slaves. He simply bequeathed "all the Negro Slaves or servants" to his daughter. Source: Will of George Harding, Sunbury County, 1807, PANB.

1361. UNNAMED PERSON (c. ?) – This unnamed Black person was enslaved to Benjamin DeWolfe and sold in the West Indies. T.W. Smith notes that De-Wolfe business records in Windsor, Nova Scotia, "show sales" in the West Indies of "slaves from Hants county." He does not give the number of slaves, but it is at least two and possibly several more. Source: Smith, "Slave in Canada," 119.

1362. UNNAMED PERSON (c. ?) – This unnamed Black person was enslaved to Benjamin DeWolfe and sold in the West Indies. T.W. Smith notes that De-Wolfe business records in Windsor, Nova Scotia, "show sales" in the West Indies of "slaves from Hants county." He does not give the number of slaves, but it is at least two and possibly several more. Source: Smith, "Slave in Canada," 119.

1363. UNNAMED PERSON (c. ?) – A South Carolina slaveowner named Captain Elderkin brought at least two unnamed slaves to Port Greville in Cumberland County, Nova Scotia, to harvest maple sugar. It seems he thought he could make a profit not unlike the massive profits made from sugar in the West Indies. Source: Fairfax, "Blacks in Cumberland County."

1364. UNNAMED PERSON (c. ?) – A South Carolina slaveowner named Captain Elderkin brought at least two unnamed slaves to Port Greville in Cumberland County, Nova Scotia, to harvest maple sugar. It seems he thought he could make a profit not unlike the massive profits made from sugar in the West Indies. Source: Fairfax, "Blacks in Cumberland County."

1365. UNNAMED PERSON (slave? c. ?) – This unnamed Black person lived with the Fordice family in Parrsboro, Nova Scotia. Source: Fairfax, "Blacks in Cumberland County."

1366. UNNAMED PERSON (slave? c. ?) – This unnamed Black person lived with the Hatfield family in Parrsboro, Nova Scotia. Source: Fairfax, "Blacks in Cumberland County."

1367. UNNAMED PERSON (slave? c. ?) – This unnamed Black person lived with the Hathaway family in Parrsboro, Nova Scotia. Source: Fairfax, "Blacks in Cumberland County."

1368. UNNAMED PERSON (slave? c. ?) – This unnamed Black person lived with the Law family in Parrsboro, Nova Scotia. Source: Fairfax, "Blacks in Cumberland County."

1369. UNNAMED PERSON (slave? c. ?) – This unnamed Black person lived with the Leonard family in Parrsboro, Nova Scotia. Source: Fairfax, "Blacks in Cumberland County."

1370. UNNAMED PERSON (slave? c. ?) – This unnamed Black person lived with the Longstreet family in Parrsboro, Nova Scotia. Source: Fairfax, "Blacks in Cumberland County."

1371. UNNAMED PERSON (slave? c. ?) – This unnamed Black person lived with the Moore family in Parrsboro, Nova Scotia. Source: Fairfax, "Blacks in Cumberland County."

1372. UNNAMED PERSON (slave? c. ?) – This unnamed Black person lived with the Patten family in Parrsboro, Nova Scotia. Source: Fairfax, "Blacks in Cumberland County."

1373. UNNAMED PERSON (slave? c. ?) – This unnamed Black person lived with the Potts family in Parrsboro, Nova Scotia. Source: Fairfax, "Blacks in Cumberland County."

1374. UNNAMED PERSON (slave? c. ?) – This unnamed Black person lived with the Ratchford family on Partridge Island (off the coast of Nova Scotia). It is clear that the Spicer and the Ratchford families did business in the West Indies regularly and this is how they brought slaves to Cumberland County, Nova Scotia. Source: Fairfax, "Blacks in Cumberland County."

1375. UNNAMED PERSON (slave? c. ?) – This unnamed Black person lived with the Raymond family in Parrsboro, Nova Scotia. Source: Fairfax, "Blacks in Cumberland County."

1376. UNNAMED PERSON (slave? c. ?) – This unnamed Black person lived with the Spicer family in Parrsboro, Nova Scotia. The Spicer family might have had several slaves. These slaves came from either Barbados or Bermuda and were buried on a hill that came to be called "Nigger Hill." It is clear that the Spicer and the Ratchford families did business in the West Indies regularly and this is how they brought slaves to Cumberland County, Nova Scotia. Source: Fairfax, "Blacks in Cumberland County."

1377. UNNAMED PERSON (slave? c. ?) – This unnamed Black person lived with the Starr family in Parrsboro, Nova Scotia. Source: Fairfax, "Blacks in Cumberland County."

1378. UNNAMED PERSON – (c.?) Enslaved to John Thomas, this unnamed person came to Shelburne from South Carolina with the Thomas family. Born in Wales, John Thomas enslaved 18 people in South Carolina, but only brought one to Nova Scotia. Source: Edwin Crowell, *A History of Barrington Township and Vicinity, Shelburne County, Nova Scotia, 1604–1870, with a Biographical and Geographical Appendix* (Yarmouth: 1923), 588, https://archive.org/details/historyofbarring00crowuoft.

1379. UNNAMED PERSON (c. ?) – According to an oral tradition, well-known Loyalist Isaac Wilkins owned at least two slaves: "Isaac kept a lot of slaves. He had a great place here." Source: Clara Dennis, *Down in Nova Scotia*, 351.

1380. UNNAMED PERSON (c. ?) – According to an oral tradition, well-known Loyalist Isaac Wilkins owned at least two slaves: "Isaac kept a lot of slaves. He had a great place here." Source: Dennis, *Down in Nova Scotia*, 351.

1381. UNNAMED PERSON (c. ?) – Presented with an offer of freedom in old age from an unknown owner, this Halifax slave reportedly said, "Master, you eated me when I was meat, and now you must pick me when I'm bone." T.W. Smith recorded this oral tradition in the late 1890s. Source: Smith, "Slave in Canada," 89.

1382. UNNAMED WOMAN (c. 1733) – This unnamed Black female was enslaved to Jean Legrange. Source: Donovan, "Nominal List of Slaves and Their Owners," 153.

1383. UNNAMED WOMAN (c. 1738?) – This unnamed female was enslaved to Simone Floury. She came from New England and would have been responsible for all kinds of domestic duties (the family had 11 children) and farm work. She would have lived with one other slave – an older man named François dit Jasmin (see entry under Jasmin). Source: Donovan, "Slaves in Île Royale," 31.

1384. UNNAMED WOMAN (c. 1743) – Enslaved to Simone Millou, this unnamed female slave was from New England. Source: Donovan, "Nominal List of Slaves and Their Owners," 155.

1385. UNNAMED WOMAN (c. 1744) – This unnamed female was enslaved to Jean de Depensens. Source: Donovan, "Nominal List of Slaves and Their Owners," 158.

1386. UNNAMED WOMAN (c. 1744) – This unnamed female was enslaved to Anne Despres, who was widowed and still built up a successful business. It seems likely that this unnamed female helped Despres in her household and business. After she died, Despres's female slave was sold at a public auction for 350 livres, which Ken Donovan argues means the woman was either old or very young because of the low auction price. Source: Donovan, "Slaves and Their Owners in Île Royale," 16; Donovan, "Nominal List of Slaves and Their Owners," 156.

1387. UNNAMED WOMAN (c. 1752) – This unnamed female was enslaved to Louis Blanchard. Source: Donovan, "Nominal List of Slaves and Their Owners," 158.

1388. UNNAMED WOMAN (c. 1752, age 35) – Joshua Mauger offered this unnamed female for sale along with several other slaves in Halifax a few years after the founding of the city. Mauger described her in terms meant to appeal to local buyers: "A very likely Negro Wench, of about thirty five Years of Age, a Creole born, has been brought up in a Gentleman's family, and capable of doing all sorts of Work belonging thereto, as Needle-Work of all sorts, and in the best Manner; also Washing, Ironing, Cookery, and every other Thing that can be expected from Such a Slave." Source: *Halifax Gazette*, May 30, 1752.

1389. UNNAMED WOMAN (c. 1753) – This unnamed female was enslaved to Louis Delort. Source: Donovan, "Nominal List of Slaves and Their Owners," 157.

1390. UNNAMED WOMAN (c. 1754, age 60) – This unnamed female was enslaved to Marie Corasinan and, at age 60, was perhaps one of the oldest slaves listed in the Île Royale records. Source: Donovan, "Nominal List of Slaves and Their Owners," 159.

1391. UNNAMED WOMAN (c. 1756) – This unnamed female was enslaved to Paris M. Source: Donovan, "Nominal List of Slaves and Their Owners," 159.

1392. UNNAMED WOMAN (c. 1758) – This unnamed female was enslaved to Louis Le Neuf la Valliere. Source: Donovan, "Nominal List of Slaves and Their Owners," 160.

1393. UNNAMED WOMAN (slave? c. 1771) – According to the 1771 census, Magdalen Winniett owned three slaves: a man, woman, and child; perhaps they were part of the same family. Although the 1771 census did not have a separate column for slaves, it did list Blacks separately and there were very few free Blacks in Nova Scotia before 1776. So, the Blacks listed in this household were probably slaves. Source: Smith, "Slave in Canada," 15.

1394. UNNAMED WOMAN (slave? c. 1771) – This unnamed female was possibly enslaved to Joseph Winniett. According to the 1771 census, Winniett owned two slaves. Although the 1771 census did not have a separate column for slaves, it did list Blacks separately and there were very few free Blacks in Nova Scotia before 1776. So, the Blacks listed in this household were probably slaves. Source: Smith, "Slave in Canada," 15.

1395. UNNAMED BOY [possibly son of above woman] (c. 1771) – This unnamed boy was possibly enslaved to Joseph Winniett. According to the 1771 census, Winniett owned two slaves. Although the 1771 census did not have a separate column for slaves, it did list blacks separately and there were very few free blacks in Nova Scotia before 1776. So, the Blacks listed in this household were probably slaves. Source: Smith, "Slave in Canada," 15.

1396. UNNAMED WOMAN (c. 1779, age 22) – This unnamed young female was offered for sale in a Halifax newspaper along with an enslaved girl. Source: Smith, "Slave in Canada," 11.

1397. UNNAMED WOMAN (c. 1779, age 21) – This unnamed female was offered for sale in a local Halifax newspaper. It described her as multi-occupational and an "exceedingly good cook." Source: Smith, "Slave in Canada," 11.

1398. UNNAMED WOMAN (c. 1780s) – This unnamed female was enslaved to New Jersey Loyalist Colonel Isaac Allen, who brought her to New Brunswick after the American Revolution. Allen apparently purchased her in New York, but after the 1800 New Brunswick slave case that returned Nancy to her owner Caleb Jones, Allen freed several slaves including this woman. This author has not been able to positively identify these other slaves through bills of sale. It is an oft-told story that Allen had up to five slaves, but he is listed in the Book of Negroes as possessing four Black servants, who were allegedly free, but were formerly the slaves of Lawrence Hartshorne. Sources: Book of Negroes; Smith, "Slave in Canada," 114.

1399. UNNAMED WOMAN (c. 1783) – This unnamed female was enslaved to Samuel Willoughby in Cornwallis, Nova Scotia. She was severely beaten by a hired white servant named George Burrows. They had been involved in a relationship and the enslaved woman was expecting a child with Burrows before he assaulted her with an "Iron flesh fork" because she had allegedly stolen wine from him. The court found Burrows not guilty. Source: Court Case Regarding a Slave, January 1783, MG 15, vol. 20, #13 and #41–2, NSA.

1400. UNNAMED WOMAN (c. 1783, age 25) – The local newspaper offered this unnamed female for sale at a public auction. The advertisement noted that she was a good domestic. Source: *Nova Scotia Gazette and Weekly Chronicle*, June 24, 1783.

1401. UNNAMED WOMAN (c. 1785) – In a New Brunswick Supreme Court case, Thomas Mullen or Mullins (a Loyalist from Massachusetts) claimed that the deceased estate of High Jones owed him £35 for a "certain Negro woman Slave." The executor, Phineas Lovitt, refused to pay Mullen. Although the case mentions slavery, it says little about the enslaved woman or slavery more generally. It does seem clear, however, that the early Supreme Court of New Brunswick did not question the right of holding Black people as slaves. Source: *Mullen v. Lovitt*, 1785, RS 42 Supreme Court Original Jurisdiction Records, PANB.

1402. UNNAMED WOMAN (c. 1785, age 18) – This unnamed female was enslaved to John Hughes, who attempted to sell her at a public auction. He described her as being brought up in a genteel family and well acquainted with housework. Source: Robertson, *King's Bounty*, 94.

1403. UNNAMED WOMAN (c. 1785, described as "old") – This unnamed female was enslaved to Captain McKay in New Brunswick. A visitor to the captain's house remarked that the only person he found at the abode was "an old colored slave woman, who said her master and his man [this person's identity or status is unclear] had gone out to see if they could obtain some potatoes or meal, having in the house only half a box of biscuits." Source: Esther Clark Wright, The Loyalists of New Brunswick (1955; reprint, Moncton: Moncton Publishing Company Limited, 1972), 97.

1404. UNNAMED WOMAN (c. 1786) – In a business record of John Chipman, he noted the price for "passage of [George Halliburton's] Negro Wench at Antigua." Source: John Chipman Invoice, 1786, 1900.353-CHI/I, John Chipman Collection, ECWA.

1405. UNNAMED WOMAN (c. 1786) – This unnamed woman was enslaved to Captain Stewart in New Brunswick, who hoped to sell his land on the Saint John River of which "ninety acres of it are interval, thirty of which is fit for cultivation." The farm also had three cows and "seventy grafted fruit trees." Stewart's improvements on the land were probably due to his "Negro man and woman, slaves" whom he hoped to sell as part of the estate. Source: *Royal Gazette*, March 7, 1786.

1406. UNNAMED WOMAN (slave? c. 1787) – This unnamed female was probably enslaved to George Ross. She was blamed for setting a fire. Source: Letter from George Ross to Gideon White, January 4, 1797, Gideon White Family Papers, MG 1, vol. 950, no. 611, NSA.

1407. UNNAMED WOMAN (c. 1787) – This unnamed female was enslaved to Richard Betts, who sold her to Frederick Sinclair in Annapolis, Nova Scotia;

this could have been Sinclair's slave named Jane – see that entry. Source: *The Times*, October 27, 1880.

1408. UNNAMED WOMAN (c. 1787, age 23) – This unnamed woman was offered for sale in New Brunswick. The advertisement outlined her skills: "A WENCH about 23 years old, is well acquainted with all kinds of household business, and particular is an excellent COOK. – To be disposed of for no fault but want of employ. – Enquire as above." Source: *Royal Gazette* (New Brunswick), August 21, 1787.

1409. UNNAMED WOMAN (c. 1788) – Joseph Totten's will lists five enslaved people of African descent. He gave the three Black children away to his daughters, but not the other slaves, which means that a slave family was probably broken up. Totten's estate valued this unnamed woman at £60, which was more than any other slave in his will. Source: Will of Joseph Totten, 1788, Annapolis County, RG 48, NSA.

1410. UNNAMED WOMAN (c. 1789) – James Hayt placed an advertisement in a New Brunswick paper hoping to sell this "Active," "singularly sober," and "diligent" slave. Her previous owner – according to the for sale notice, John H. Carey – was a Loyalist from Maryland. Source: *Saint John Gazette*, January 16, 1789.

1411. UNNAMED WOMAN (c. 1789) – This unnamed female was enslaved to Reverend Rowland at Shelburne in the late 1780s. Rowland sold her to the Bahamas and, in his notes, Captain William Booth stated "Mr. Rowland [an Anglican minister] sold his Negress for 30£ of this Currency, and 'Tis said she will fetch 300 dollars at New Providence." Source: Booth, *Remarks and Rough Memorandums*, 90–1.

1412. UNNAMED WOMAN (c. 1792) – In a case before the New Brunswick Supreme Court (*Hall V. Bennison*, 1792), Peter Hall claimed that George Bennison owed him money because he had given Bennison a "Negro Wench and child the property of him the said James Proud delivered by him this deponent to the said George Bennison at the value of thirty eight pounds money aforesaid – and that he this Deponent has not received from the said George Bennison the said Twenty one pounds nine shillings so by him paid for the said George Bennison any part thereof." In other words, Bennison was expected to convey the adult female slave and her daughter to James Proud for a sum of money previously agreed to with Peter Hall, but Bennison did not do it. Source: *Peter Hall v. George Bennison*, 1792 RS 42 Supreme Court Original Jurisdiction Records, PANB.

1413. DAUGHTER OF UNNAMED WOMAN ABOVE (c. 1792) – See entry just above. Source: *Peter Hall v. George Bennison*, 1792 RS 42 Supreme Court Original Jurisdiction Records, PANB.

1414. UNNAMED WOMAN (c. 1794) – This unnamed female was listed in an account between Charles Dixon and Amos Botsford at the price of £40. Source: Amos Botsford Account, 1794, NSA[?] This business account does not have an archive stamp, but it is probably NSA.

1415. UNNAMED WOMAN (c. 1799, age 19) – This unnamed female was offered for sale, along with her child, by John Ryan in New Brunswick. Ryan noted that she was brought up in the country and also understood how to perform household chores. Source: *Saint John Gazette*, April 12, 1799.

1416. UNNAMED CHILD (c. 1799) – This unnamed child was offered for sale along with his or her mother. Source: *Saint John Gazette*, April 12, 1799.

1417. UNNAMED WOMAN (c. 1800, age 18) – The owner offered to sell this "NEGRO GIRL" for a term of years. He described her as "good natured, fond of children and accustomed to both Town and Country work." Source: *Royal Gazette* (Nova Scotia), June 24, 1800.

1418. UNNAMED WOMAN (c. 1801) – This unnamed woman was enslaved to Nova Scotia politician and merchant Benjamin Belcher, who owned several slaves in Cornwallis. In his will, Belcher left strict directions for his heirs about the slaves, noting that he was "forever charging them my children unto whom I have entrusted these Negro people with never to sell barter or exchange them or any of them under any pretension except it is for whose bad [?] Offences as will render them not safe to be kept in the Family and that to be adjudged of by three Justices of the Peace in said Township and in such case as their order they may be sold and disposed of. And I further request as soon as these young Negroes shall be capable to be taught to read, they shall be learnt the word of God." Source: Will of Benjamin Belcher, 1801, Kings County, NSA.

1419. UNNAMED WOMAN (c. 1801) – This unnamed woman was enslaved to Stephen Reed in Amherst, Nova Scotia. This person probably worked as a farmer and domestic servant. Along with another slave, she helped produce wheat, potatoes, and hay. In his will, Reed told his sons to "comfortably take care" of his slaves "during their natural lives." Source: Will of Stephen Reed, 1801, Cumberland County, NSA.

1420. UNNAMED WOMAN (c. ?) – This unnamed Black woman was enslaved to the Barclay family. Oral traditions have painted Mrs. Barclay as an exceedingly brutal slaveowner as she was rumoured to have whipped a slave to death and allegedly "sealed her up in a fireplace." Sources: Perkins, *Oldest Houses Along St. George Street Annapolis Royal*, 31; Smith, "Slave in Canada," 77.

1421. UNNAMED WOMAN (c. ?) – This unnamed female slave, according to oral testimony from the nineteenth century, was "put on board a schooner from a wharf at the lower end of [Annapolis] to be taken away, her screaming child clinging to her till torn from her by sheer force." Source: Smith, "Slave in Canada," 121.

1422. VANBURNE, S. (c. 1784) – "S." was enslaved to the Departments of the Army and Navy, which settled at Chedabucto, Nova Scotia. Source: Muster Roll of Settlers at Chedabucto (including Departments of the Army and Navy), Chipman Papers, Muster Master General's Office, Loyalist Musters, 1776–1785, MG 23, D1, ser. I, vol. 24, LAC.

1423. VAN EMBEMORE, ELIZA (c. 1800) – Eliza was enslaved to Douwe Ditmars in Nova Scotia along with her two children. The reason we know her name is that several local slaveowners signed an agreement to financially support Ditmars so he could regain his property. These slaveowners complained that "doubts have arose, as to the legality of Slavery in the Province of Nova Scotia." Source: Agreement with D. Ditmars to bear an equal proportion of the expense attending him about the slaves, May 1800, MG 15, vol. 20, #86, NSA.

1424. ANTHONY (c. 1800) – Anthony was the enslaved child of Eliza who lived in the household of Douwe Ditmars in Nova Scotia. Source: Agreement with D. Ditmars to bear an equal proportion of the expense attending him about the slaves, May 1800, MG 15, vol. 20, #86, NSA.

1425. ELIZA (c. 1800) – Eliza was the enslaved child of Eliza who lived in the household of Douwe Ditmars in Nova Scotia. Source: Agreement with D. Ditmars to bear an equal proportion of the expense attending him about the slaves, May 1800, MG 15, vol. 20, #86, NSA.

1426. VAN HORNE, NANCY (c. 1783, age 26) – Nancy was enslaved to James Driscoll. She went to the Maritimes from New York with one other slave. British officials described her as a "stout made wench." Source: Book of Negroes.

1427. VASEY, RUTH (c. 1784) – Ruth was possibly enslaved to John Mc-Donald, who settled at Chedabucto, Nova Scotia. Source: Muster Roll of Settlers at Chedabucto (including Departments of the Army and Navy), Chipman Papers, Muster Master General's Office, Loyalist Musters, 1776–1785, MG 23, D1, ser. I, vol. 24, LAC.

1428. VENUS (c. 1784) – John Wentworth sent Venus and 18 other slaves from Nova Scotia to his "relation" Paul Wentworth in Suriname. Wentworth described these slaves as "American born or well-seasoned, and are perfectly stout, healthy, sober, orderly, Industrious, & obedient." Wentworth had the slaves Christened and claimed to be concerned for their welfare. He also claimed that the female slaves "promise well to increase their numbers." Wentworth further noted, "Venus, is useful in ye Hospital, Poultry yards, Gardens." Source: John Wentworth to Paul Wentworth or his attorney, February 24, 1784.

1429. VENUS (c. 1784) – John Wentworth sent Venus and 18 other slaves from Nova Scotia to his "relation" Paul Wentworth in Suriname. Wentworth described these slaves as "American born or well-seasoned, and are perfectly stout, healthy, sober, orderly, Industrious, & obedient." Venus was listed as a child, and it is possible that the older Venus was her mother. Source: John Wentworth to Paul Wentworth or his attorney, February 24, 1784.

1430. VINIA (c. 1783, age 25) – Vinia was enslaved to Captain Wilmot (or Willmot). She went to the Maritimes from New York with her two infant children. She was probably from New York, and British officials described her as a "stout wench." Source: Book of Negroes.

1431. HARRY (c. 1783) – Harry was the infant son of Vinia and enslaved to Captain Wilmot. Source: Book of Negroes.

1432. ROBERT (c. 1783) – Robert was the infant son of Vinia and enslaved to Captain Wilmot. Source: Book of Negroes.

1433. VIOLET (c. 1783, age 11) – Enslaved to John McKown, Violet went to the Maritimes from New York but was probably from Massachusetts. British officials described her as a "fine girl." Source: Book of Negroes.

1434. VIOLET (c. ?) – Violet was enslaved to Colonel William Freeman. Allegedly, slave traders kidnapped Violet (an African princess) while she picked flowers. Source: Smith, "Slave in Canada," 19.

1435. VIRGINIA (c. 1804) – Virginia was enslaved to James DeLancey, whose estate valued her at £20. Source: Hanger, "Life of Loyalist Colonel James DeLancey," 52–3.

1436. VULEAN (c. 1783, age 18) – Vulean was enslaved to Robert Andrews, who migrated to the Maritimes after the American Revolution. Vulean was probably from Massachusetts, and British officials in New York described him as a "stout fellow." Source: Book of Negroes.

1437. WARD, ELIZA (c. 1783, age 7) – Eliza was enslaved to Ebenezer Ward, who migrated to the Maritimes after the American Revolution. Eliza was probably from New Jersey or New York, and British officials in New York described her as a "fine girl." Source: Book of Negroes.

1438. WATSON, ELIZABETH (c. 1779) – In 1779, the Nova Scotia Supreme Court sent Elizabeth Watson (alias Phillis) back into slavery, though she claimed to have been born free in Boston. The court rejected her claim of unlawful confinement – though she had a believable witness – and returned Watson to her abusive owner. Sources: *Watson alias Phillis v. Proud*, 1779, Judgment, Supreme Court of Nova Scotia – Halifax County judgment books, RG 39 J, Halifax County vol. 6 p. 103; Franco Paz, "On the Edge of Freedom: The Re-enslavement of Elizabeth Watson" (MA Thesis, University of Vermont, 2018); Franco Paz and Harvey Amani Whitfield, "On the Edge of Freedom: The Re-enslavement of Elizabeth Watson in Nova Scotia," in *In Search of Liberty: African American Internationalism in the Nineteenth-Century Atlantic World*, eds., Ronald Angelo Johnson and Ousmane K. Power Greene (Athens: University of Georgia Press, 2021), 17–39.

1439. WELLS, VIOLET (c. 1800) – Violet was enslaved to Isaac Bonnell, and her son was baptized in 1800. Source: List of Baptisms, September 7, 1800, Records of the Anglican Church, Digby Township Book, NSA.

1440. JOHN (c. 1800) – John was the son of Violet and enslaved to Isaac Bonnell. He was baptized in 1800. Source: List of Baptisms, September 7, 1800, Records of the Anglican Church, Digby Township Book, NSA.

1441. WELSH, JAMES (slave? c. 1784) – James was possibly enslaved to Captain Hamilton, who, along with other southern Loyalists (consisting of various regiments such as the Royal North Carolina Regiment and the King's Carolina Rangers), settled at Country Harbour, Nova Scotia. The majority of these settlers and their slaves were from North Carolina, South Carolina, and Georgia. They had settled briefly in East Florida before moving to Nova Scotia. In a letter to Colonel Edward Winslow discussing these southern settlers, William Shaw expressed surprise that some of the blacks with these southern settlers were not slaves; but his wording, as historian Carole Watterson Troxler notes, meant that some were "indeed slaves." In fact, as she points out, Blacks at Country Harbour were denied any land grants and those who were not slaves were "quasi-free." In an article, abolitionist Thomas Clarkson described what some white Loyalists did to supposedly free Black Loyalists: "It was not long till these loyalists, many of whom had been educated with all the ideas of the justice of slavery, the inferiority of negroes, and the superiority of white men, that are universal in the southern provinces of America, began to harass and oppress the industrious black settlers, and even wantonly to deprive them of the fruits of their labour, expelling them from the lands they had cleared." Clarkson continued by noting that whites reduced "again to slavery those negroes who had so honourably obtained their freedom. They hired them as servants, and, at the end of the stipulated time, refused payment of their wages, insisting that they were slaves: in some instances they destroyed their tickets of freedom, and then enslaved the negroes for want of them; in several instances, the unfortunate Africans were taken onboard vessels, carried to the West Indies, and there sold for the benefit of their plunderers." In the case of Black people at Country Harbour, they were listed on the musters as the "Servants" of a white Loyalist, which meant it was very easy for them to be re-enslaved if they were not already enslaved. Sources: Troxler, "John Legett at Country Harbour," 310; Clarkson, "Some Account of the New Colony at Sierra Leone," 229–30; Settlers at Country Harbour, Chipman Papers, Muster Master General's Office, Loyalist Musters, 1776–1785, MG 23, D1, ser. I, vol. 24, LAC. Note: Ellen Wilson believed that the information Clarkson used came from Thomas Peters' petition; see Wilson, *Loyal Blacks*, 181.

1442. WEST (c. 1767) – In the River St. John area (later New Brunswick), businessman James Simonds wrote to business partners about his slave West, who he called a "rascal negro." Simonds complained that West could not "be flattered or [driven] to do one-fourth of a man's work: shall give him a strong dose on Monday morning which will make him better or worse; no dependence can be put on him." Source: Smith, "Slave in Canada," 11.

1443. WILL (c. 1785) – New York Loyalist Benjamin Seaman, who served in the New York assembly before the Revolution, mentioned two slaves in his 1785 will: Tom and Will. He referred to each slave as "my Negro boy." Source: Will of Benjamin Seaman, Saint John County, 1785, PANB.

1444. WILLIAM (c. 1783, age 20) – William was enslaved to Captain Hicks, who migrated to the Maritimes after the American Revolution with several other slaves. William was probably from Pennsylvania, and British officials in New York described him as a "stout fellow." Source: Book of Negroes.

1445. WILLIAM (c. 1783, age 14) – William was enslaved to John Anderson, and went to the Maritimes from New York with his owner and an older man. British officials in New York described him as a "fine boy" who was previously owned by Hugh Dunn and another man "taken with a Guard of the Enemy by a party from the Garrison, 1779." Source: Book of Negroes.

1446. WILLIAM (c. 1783, age 6) – William was enslaved to William Chandler. He went to the Maritimes from New York with his owner and was from Massachusetts. British officials described him as a "fine boy." Source: Book of Negroes.

1447. WILLIAM (slave? c. 1784) – William was probably enslaved to Joseph Russell, who planned to settle nearby Halifax. Russell had three other Black people in his household, all of whom were likely enslaved. Source: Loyalists and Disbanded Troops at Cole Harbour, Chipman Papers, Muster Master General's Office, Loyalist Musters, 1776–1785, MG 23, D1, ser. I, vol. 24, LAC.

1448. WILLIAM (c. 1784) – John Wentworth sent William and 18 other slaves from Nova Scotia to his "relation" Paul Wentworth in Suriname. Wentworth described these slaves as "American born or well-seasoned, and are perfectly stout, healthy, sober, orderly, Industrious, & obedient." William was listed as a child. Source: John Wentworth to Paul Wentworth or his attorney, February 24, 1784, Wentworth Letters, vol. 49, NSA.

1449. WILLIAM (c. 1791) – Liverpool resident Simeon Perkins mentioned that two Black men named David and William had escaped from their owners in his diary: New York Loyalist and Nova Scotian politician Thomas Barclay and a Mr. Simmons. They attempted to recover their escaped human property. Source: Fergusson, *Diary of Simeon Perkins, 1790–1796*, 104.

1450. WILLIAM (c. 1798) – William was enslaved to Reverend John Rowland of Shelburne, who owned a total of three slaves at the time of his death and had sold another to New Providence. He valued the unnamed girl at £25, Samuel at £35, and William at £30 (see entries for the unnamed girl and Samuel). Source: Smith, "Slave in Canada," 59; Reverend John Rowland, Estate Papers A #104, May 9, 1798, Shelburne County Archives and Genealogical Society, Shelburne, Nova Scotia.

1451. WILLIAMS, SILL (c. 1783, age 15) – Sill was enslaved to Frederick Williams; it is possible she was one of the adult females included in 1807 Digby slave petition, but that is unclear. She went to the Maritimes from New York along with a 17-year-old boy (see entry for Prince). British officials in New York described her as a "stout wench." Source: Book of Negroes.

1452. WILLIAMS, THOMAS (c. 1785) – Thomas was enslaved to John Clark in Prince Edward Island. Clark sold Williams to a man named George Harding, who murdered the slave in 1787. Sources: *King v. Jupiter Wise*, 1786, PAROPEI; Holman, "Slaves and Servants on Prince Edward Island," 100–4; Hornby, *Black Islanders*, 15–19.

1453. WILLOUGHBY, ISAAC (c. 1834, age 71) – In 1834, Isaac petitioned the Nova Scotia House of Assembly for some form of financial support. Historians do not have many documents where we hear the voice of a former slave in the Maritimes. Although mediated through another person (probably white), the document provides an important insight into the troubles that Black people faced in the Maritimes after gaining their freedom. Before the House could act, the petition was withdrawn for unclear reasons, but perhaps this was because private charities intervened. The petition deserves to be quoted fully: "The Petition of Isaac Willoughby Humbly Sheweth That your Petitioner who has now arrived at the age of seventy-one years is induced by his peculiar circumstances of distress to solicit the aid of your Honorable House, convinced that such an appeal will not be unregarded. That your Petitioner was born a slave and continued as such until he was 36 years of age, when he purchased his freedom, for which he paid twenty pounds and feeling desirous of procuring the freedom of his brother (who was also a slave) he paid the sum of forty pounds for that purchase, and his brother having been shortly afterwards [put] on board of a British Man of War, your Petitioner never received any part of the sum so advanced, and has since met with many severe losses in his struggle through life. That your Petitioner's mother who was a slave also, and who is now nearly ninety years of age, was left destitute by the death of her master Jonathan Shearman Esquire of the Township of Cornwallis and your Petitioner feeling the affection of a son towards a parent undertook to support and provide for her. That your petitioner has also a wife and two children depending upon him for sustenance, and feeling that the support of his family combined with the hardships of the times, is a burthen too heavy for his advanced years, he is reduced to the necessity of appealing to your Honorable House in order that you may be [inclined/induced] to grant to him such necessary aid." Source: Petition of Isaac Willoughby, February 8, 1834, RG 5, ser. P, NSA.

1454. UNNAMED BROTHER (c. 1834) – This unnamed Black male was Isaac Willoughby's brother. In the above petition, Willoughby attempted to purchase his brother's freedom, but his sibling seems to have been impressed into the Royal Navy. Source: Petition of Isaac Willoughby, February 8, 1834, RG 5, ser. P, NSA.

1455. UNNAMED MOTHER (c. 1834) – Willoughby noted that his unnamed mother was nearly 90 years old in 1834. Apparently, she had been "left destitute" upon the death of her owner (Jonathan Shearman). Source: Petition of Isaac Willoughby, February 8, 1834, RG 5, ser. P, NSA.

1456. UNNAMED WIFE (slave? c. 1834) – The only mention of this unnamed wife is in Isaac Willoughby's petition where he commented that she depended on him for support. She was probably enslaved earlier in her life, but it is not clear. Source: Petition of Isaac Willoughby, February 8, 1834, RG 5, ser. P, NSA.

1457. UNNAMED CHILD (c. 1834) – In his petition, Isaac Willoughby mentioned this unnamed child as depending on him for sustenance. Source: Petition of Isaac Willoughby, February 8, 1834, RG 5, ser. P, NSA.

1458. UNNAMED CHILD (c. 1834) – In his petition, Isaac Willoughby mentioned this unnamed child as depending on him for sustenance. Source: Petition of Isaac Willoughby, February 8, 1834, RG 5, ser. P, NSA.

1459. WILSON, JAMES (c. 1764) – James was enslaved to Joseph Wilson. He worked as an axe man and for his extra labour the town of Falmouth granted him a small sum of money. Source: States, "Presence and Perseverance: Blacks in Hants County," 38.

1460. WILSON, MARGRET (slave? c. 1788) – Margaret was possibly an enslaved person who was baptized along with several other Black people in New Brunswick. Source: Early Parish Records, New Brunswick, September 14, 1788, possibly PANB.

1461. WISE, ADAM (c. 1798) – Adam was enslaved to Virginia Loyalist Jacob Ellegood, who had him baptized in Maugerville, New Brunswick. Source: Smith, "Slave in Canada," 85.

1462. WISE, JUPITER (servant? c. 1785) – Although the Book of Negroes listed Jupiter as free, historian Jim Hornby called him a "black slave." But it seems that he was probably an indentured servant to Captain Burns, though his actual day-to-day life might have been very similar to those of enslaved Black Islanders. The court record and secondary sources are some of the best sources we have for how Prince Edward Island slaves thought about and reacted to their lives. James Stevens, a free Black man who was a servant, gave information in court in November 1785 that accused Jupiter Wise of burglary to steal rum. In his statement, Stevens also admitted that the summer prior he and Island slaves Ben, Peter, and Mingo had planned to run away, arm themselves with a musket, and then escape to Boston in a sloop owned by Governor Walter Patterson. When they could not find the boat, the men abandoned their plans to escape. Wise shared the stolen rum with James Stevens and other servants and slaves at a party that included supper and dancing. Despite Stevens's accusation, Wise was not charged with a crime until tavern keeper and legislator John Clark submitted a memorial to the court. According to Clark, he and a white indentured servant named Sylvester Petty found Jupiter Wise and Clark's slave Thomas Williams sitting around goods that Petty claimed had been stolen from his master. That evening, Wise, Williams, and another Black man named James (probably James Stevens) attacked Clark and Petty. A brawl broke out in the street until someone illuminated the scene with a candle. After hearing Clark's statement, the court convicted Wise of felony assault, which carried the death penalty. However, Wise pleaded "Benefit of the Clergy," an English legal concept that allowed a person to receive a pardon after they were convicted of a capital crime and sentenced to death, and he was supposed to be sent to the West Indies for seven years. A record shows Wise and another convict named John O'Neil escaped from jail where they had been awaiting transportation to the Caribbean. A sheriff caught them in Pictou, Nova Scotia, and brought them back to island authorities. If he made it to the West Indies, Wise would almost certainly have faced re-enslavement or brutal work patterns on a sugar plantation that might have resulted in his death. Sources: *King v. Jupiter Wise*, 1786, PAROPEI; Holman, "Slaves and Servants on Prince Edward Island," 100–4;

Hornby, *Black Islanders*, 15–19. Thank you to Sarah Chute for sharing her forthcoming publication about Jupiter Wise with me.

1463. WISE, SALLY (c. 1798) – Sally was enslaved to Virginia Loyalist Jacob Ellegood, who had her baptized in Maugerville, New Brunswick. Source: Smith, "Slave in Canada," 85.

1464. YOUNG, GEORGE (c. 1784) – George was enslaved to the Departments of the Army and Navy, which settled at Chedabucto, Nova Scotia. Source: Muster Roll of Settlers at Chedabucto (including Departments of the Army and Navy), Chipman Papers, Muster Master General's Office, Loyalist Musters, 1776–1785, MG 23, D1, ser. I, vol. 24, LAC.

1465. YORK (c. 1784) – York (writing is unclear, possibly Jack?) was enslaved to the Departments of the Army and Navy, which settled at Chedabucto, Nova Scotia. Source: Loyalists from Saint Augustine to Chedabucto, Chipman Papers, Muster Master General's Office, Loyalist Musters, 1776–1785, MG 23, D1, ser. I, vol. 24, LAC.

STUDIES IN ATLANTIC CANADA HISTORY

Editors: John G. Reid and Peter L. Twohig

Milton Keynes UK
Ingram Content Group UK Ltd.
UKHW012351190424
441406UK00007B/573